A Dictionary of
AMERICAN
POLITICS

Edited by

Edward Conrad Smith
and
Arnold John Zurcher
New York University

New York
BARNES & NOBLE, Inc.
1944

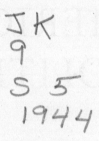

JK
9
S 5
1944

Printed in the United States of America
By De Pamphilis Press, Inc., New York, N.Y.

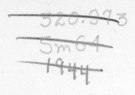

Preface

This is the third volume that has appeared under the title, *A Dictionary of American Politics*. The first, prepared by Everit Brown and Albert Strauss, was published in 1888. The second, almost completely rewritten from new materials and with a great increase in the number of entries, was prepared by Edward C. Smith and published in 1924. The present volume, a co-operative undertaking, is a thoroughgoing revision, with again a considerable addition to the number and scope of entries. It contains about 3,020 entries, not including cross references, as compared with 1,861 in the volume published in 1924.

In part the increase in the number of entries is due to the expansion of administrative services, the enactment of new laws, the development of new political issues, and the broadened concept of the role of government during the past twenty years. In greater part, perhaps, it is due to the diligent efforts of editors and contributors to include definitions of the terms in general use within the broad field of American government and politics. In addition to national, State, municipal, and local rural government and administration, this field includes: legislative methods and procedures; public administration; American political and constitutional history; judicial procedure and administration; public opinion; political parties; suffrage and elections; public law; American political theory; public finance; international law; and American foreign relations. Foreign institutions and ideas have also been introduced occasionally, particularly those which are normally encountered in discussions of comparative political institutions.

In explanation for what may seem to the specialist in government an undue proportion of entries relating to politics of past decades, it may be stated that the editors have proceeded on the assumption that the institutions of the present are in great part the product of the experience of the past. The gradual development of policies relating to many phases of our social and economic life has been outlined in many of the entries; and other entries may help the reader to identify allusions to our past political experience.

It would be impossible to include in a volume of this size all the decisions of the Supreme Court relating to constitutional questions or all the acts of Congress. The selections made here are, however, not wholly arbitrary. They include the cases which have, in the course of frequent discussion, acquired titles different from those by which they are officially cited, as well as a few whose official titles are familiar to students of our constitutional history. And the acts of Congress included are normally those which have in-augurated significant changes in governmental organization or in policies.

A considerable amount of space has been devoted to the administrative establishments of the national government, including most of those which have come into being as a result of the wartime emergency. The descriptions of these establishments will, it is hoped, include all the more important changes resulting from the large-scale reorganizations carried out since 1938; but these reorganizations occur so frequently that the reader is advised to supplement the information contained in this *Dictionary* with the latest edition of the *United States Government Manual*.

Another considerable segment of entries comprises slogans, political slang, and the nicknames of statesmen and institutions which usage has permanently incorporated into the American political lexicon. Those versed in such argot may occasionally learn from the entries why and how it came into existence; those unfamiliar with American politics may find such entries valuable in facilitating their understanding of the finer points of discussions of American public affairs in the press and elsewhere.

The editors make no apology for including the considerable number of entries relating to international law; for the Constitution of the United States incorporates international law into our law by specifically granting to Congress the power "to define and punish piracies and felonies committed on the high seas and offences against the law of nations"; and the present position of the United States in world affairs imposes an obligation, in a work of this sort, to define at least the basic concepts and describe the principal institutions in the international field.

One of the principal innovations in this edition is the inclusion of illustrations supplementing and making more vivid the definitions in the text. In particular, the attention of the reader is invited to the 24 black-and-white maps interspersed at appropriate places in the text. Some of them show the areas within which certain governmental establishments operate; others illustrate the territorial growth of the United States, show the points at issue in boundary disputes, or indicate the focal areas involved in matters of policy.

Throughout the work the contributors have kept the idea in mind that this is a dictionary, and have sought in writing every entry to answer the question, What is the meaning of this particular word or phrase?

In common with everyone else who has written in the field of political science, the editors and contributors have been troubled by certain confusions in nomenclature. The word "state," for instance, means both an independent sovereign entity and a nonsovereign component of a federal union. The editors have sought to indicate the distinction between the two meanings by arbitrarily capitalizing the word "State" when it refers to one of the States of the American Union, and by having it printed without capitals when it refers to a sovereign entity. In some entries where the word "state" might be confusing, it has been omitted altogether and some other less exact term, like "country," has been substituted for it. The word "federal" has presented another difficulty. In its strict sense it refers, of course, to a governmental system composed of both a central government and of numerous States bound together under the terms of a constitutional document; but in popular American usage it is loosely applied to institutions which belong wholly to the central government. To avoid confusion, and to reserve the word "federal" for use in its more exact scientific sense the word "national" has in most cases been used in referring to institutions of the central government of the United States.

To conserve space, cross references have been employed for a number of entries of a subsidiary nature directing the reader to a more important term, the definition of which includes a brief discussion of, or makes a distinction among, various adjectival qualifications. Sometimes the Latin abbreviation *q.v.* has been used to refer the reader from one entry to another; but a conscious effort has been made to avoid cluttering the text by restricting the use of *q.v.* only to the occasion when the entry referred to adds something to the definition already given.

The editors take this opportunity to thank their colleagues whose names appear among the list of contributors on a subsequent page. Acknowledgments are also due to numerous other individuals and organizations whose aid has been considerable. The editors are especially indebted to the following: Mr. Dwight H. Brown, Secretary of State of Missouri; Mr. S. Howard Cohen, President of the Board of Elections in the City of New York; Mr. Edward J. Hummel, Secretary of State of Ohio; Mr. Frank Marsh, Secretary of State, and Mr. J. C. Coupland, Jr., Deputy Secretary of State of Nebraska — all of whom furnished sample ballots from which reproductions have been made; the Automatic Voting Machine Corporation of Jamestown, N. Y., which provided illustrations of the voting machine; the Bureau of Public Relations of the Department of War; and the Office of Public Relations of the Department of the Navy.

Key to Contributors

JTC — JESSE T. CARPENTER,* Ph.D., Associate Professor of Political Science, New York University

GHD — GEORGE HOMER DURHAM, Ph.D., Associate Professor of Political Science, Utah State Agricultural College

ME — MARTIN ESTEY, Research Associate, The American Federation of Labor

JWF — JOHN W. FOLLOWS, Ph.D., Hearing Officer, National War Labor Board; formerly Instructor in Political Science and History, New York University

JMcC — JOHN W. MCCONNELL, Ph.D., Associate Professor of Sociology, New York University

JAP — JAMES A. PADGETT, Ph.D., at present with the War Production Board

JRP — J. ROLAND PENNOCK, Ph.D., Associate Professor of Political Science and Chairman of the Department of Political Science, Swarthmore College

JJR — JAMES J. ROBBINS, Ph.D., Dean, Graduate Division, School of Social Sciences and Public Affairs, The American University

CHS — C. HART SCHAAF,* Ph.D., Associate Professor of Government and Public Administration, Richmond Professional Institute of the College of William and Mary

CS-H — CATHERYN SECKLER-HUDSON, Ph.D., Professor of Political Science and Public Administration and Chairman of the Department of Public Administration, The American University

EES — ELMER E. SMEAD, Ph.D., Assistant Professor of Political Science, Dartmouth College

S — EDWARD C. SMITH, Ph.D., Professor of Political Science and Administrative Chairman of the Department of Political Science, New York University

AJW,Jr. — ARTHUR J. WATERMAN, JR.,* Ph.D., formerly Instructor in Political Science, New York University, and Associate Economic Statistician, War Production Board

Z — ARNOLD J. ZURCHER, Ph.D., Professor of Political Science and Director of the Institute on Postwar Reconstruction, New York University

* At present with the armed forces or in government service abroad.

A

A.A.A. *See* Agricultural Adjustment Administration.

abatement. Abolishment, as of a nuisance; reduction, as of an assessment or the amount of a tax. s.

A.B.C. Mediation. The mediation of Argentina, Brazil, and Chile after the United States had occupied Vera Cruz in reprisal for an attack on American sailors at Tampico. It resulted in the Niagara Falls Conference in August, 1914, at which it was agreed that American troops would be withdrawn as soon as a Mexican government, popularly elected, had restored order. s.

abdication. Renunciation of the privileges and prerogatives of an office. The act of abdication is usually personal and does not affect the existing rules of succession to the office unless so stipulated. z.

ability theory. A theory that taxes should be levied upon persons in accordance with their ability to pay them, measured either by the amount of property owned or by income received; opposed to the benefit theory. s.

abolitionist. An extreme opponent of Negro slavery who sought to do away with the institution — by propaganda based on moral principles, as William Lloyd Garrison; by force, as John Brown; or by the organization of parties, appeals to Congress, and other political means. s.

Abominations, Tariff of. The tariff law of 1828 dissatisfaction with which led to South Carolina's ordinance of nullification. The tariff was generally unpopular and was modified by the act of 1832 and the Compromise Tariff of 1833. z

abrogation. Annulment by competent authority. s.

absentee voting. Participation in elections by qualified voters who, because of illness or absence from home for business or other reasons, are unable to appear at the polls in person on election day. Under the laws of nearly every State, they are permitted to mail their ballots to the proper election officials. s.

absolute contraband. Arms and munitions of war. *See* Contraband. s.

absolute majority. More than half of the number of persons entitled to vote on a given question, regardless of the number in attendance or voting. JRP.

absolutism. A government in which unlimited and arbitrary

1

power over persons and property is committed to a monarch or dictator; the exercise of unlimited and absolute power.   z.

acceptance speech. *See* Speech of acceptance.

accession. 1. The act of taking office or coming to power. 2. The act of entering a confederation or of accepting the terms of a multilateral treaty or convention.   s.

accident, industrial. An injury arising out of, or in the course of, employment which causes temporary or permanent disability or death. Laws in nearly every State require safety devices, the screening of dangerous machinery, fire escapes, and adequate lighting; and detailed rules for conducting operations involving extraordinary hazards. Women and children may be excluded from such operations. For many occupations, some States require the passing of tests for general health, vision, and technical competence as a condition of employment. Industrial accidents constitute about one-fifth of all accidents in the United States, but the ratio is declining steadily. *See* Workmen's compensation.   JMcC.

accident insurance. A system of insurance which indemnifies its beneficiaries for disability resulting from personal injury. Laws in all States require employers to insure against such accidents through State compensation insurance funds or accredited private insurance companies, or to prove financial ability to pay compensation.   JMcC.

acclamation. Overwhelming approval expressed by cheering, shouts, or handclapping in a party convention or similar body. It is practically the only method of voting used in the parliaments of contemporary authoritarian governments.   z.

accord. A diplomatic entente or international understanding usually of a verbal character. The term is also applied to agreements or compromises reached by erstwhile conflicting groups within a country; *e.g.,* labor and capital.   z.

accounts, committee on. A standing legislative committee charged with the duty of determining whether or not funds appropriated have been expended honestly and for the public interest. Unlike the British counterpart, American committees on accounts perform a more or less nominal function.   s.

accretion. Addition to territory through a gradual rise of the land surface at the coast line or through the deposit of silt.   s.

acquisition. The securing of title to a territory either by such legal means as discovery, occupation, purchase, treaty, or peaceful annexation, or by forcible annexation.   z.

acquittal. A court decision declaring an accused person not guilty of criminal charges formally brought against him and absolving him from further prosecution for the same offense.   JWF.

action. A legal proceeding (strictly speaking, at common law) to enforce one's rights against another.   z.

act of Congress. In American parliamentary usage, this term embraces only statutes of Congress which originated as bills introduced by the clause, "Be it enacted, etc." It is not used to describe statutes of Congress couched in the form of joint resolutions; nor does it ordinarily refer to any other action of Congress. Acts of Congress are published after every session in the *Statutes at Large of the United States* and those in force may be found in the *Code of Laws of the United States* as revised and supplemented.   z.

Adams and Clay Republicans. The faction of the Democratic-Republican party which after 1825 supported John Quincy Adams and Henry Clay.   s.

Adamson Act. An act of Congress Sept. 3, 1916, which gave legal recognition to the eight-hour day for employees on interstate railroads and established a procedure for the solution of pending railroad labor controversies.   z.

adjournment. The closing of business for a day, for several days, or indefinitely (sine die). Neither house of Congress may adjourn for more than three days without the consent of the other. If the two houses disagree as to the time of adjournment, the President may adjourn them; but he has never had occasion to exercise the power. An adjournment closes the legislative day; a recess does not.   s.

adjudication. The process of trying causes or settling controversies in courts of law.   JWF.

adjusted compensation. A bonus paid in 1924 to veterans of World War I in the form of paid-up life insurance, later (1936) converted to bonds or cash, the amount being based on length of service, with a premium for foreign service.   s.

adjutant general. The chief staff officer of a military organization. The Adjutant General's Department communicates all orders and instructions from the War Department to the army, supervises recruiting, issues publications, and keeps the nation's military archives.   z.

administration. 1. In general, the management of public affairs, the enforcement of law, and the fulfillment of public policy. It is usually differentiated from the executive and legislative function in its lack of power to determine and declare public policy; and from the judicial function in its ability to arrive at decisions with relative freedom from the formality of procedural rules. Because of the growing complexity of government in a technological civilization and the increased social responsibility of the state, these distinctions, always somewhat vague, have become more so. Concrete evidence that they are disappearing may be found in the creation of numerous independent commissions in the United States with quasi-legislative and quasi-judicial powers and in the tendency of Congress and the State legislatures to delegate power to administrative "experts." The growing importance of public administration is reflected in contemporary emphasis upon the proper articulation of governmental agencies, improvement in the techniques of management, the substitution of trained for amateur personnel, and the increasing attractiveness and prestige of public service. 2. The whole body of executive officials.   3. The tenure of a President or a governor.   AJW,Jr.

administrative. Pertaining to management generally, or to the art or function of managing public affairs, or to the agencies or branches of government which perform the task of administration.   JRP.

administrative court.   On the Continent of Europe, a court organized outside the regular system of judicial courts which applies administrative law, including the right to declare administrative orders invalid for want of proper legal authority. It has also important advisory functions. In America such legislative courts as the Court of Claims and the Court of Customs and Patent Appeals are often improperly called administrative courts.   S.

administrative law.   1. That part of public law which regulates the conduct of public officials and determines the rights of individuals in their dealings with these officials, including the legal remedies available to individuals for the protection of these rights. 2. The body of law created by administrative agencies in the form of rules and regulations, administrative orders, and administrative decisions.   JRP.

administrative lie.   A statute passed in response to public demand for moral reform which is purposely made so stringent as to be unenforceable. The term originated with W. T. Jerome, former district attorney of New York County.   S.

administrative order.   A regulation issued by an administrative officer amplifying and making more specific the provisions of a statute. In the United States the power to issue such an order is normally expressly granted by a statute; and when properly issued, the order has the force of law. Increasing use of administrative orders is one of the striking governmental phenomena of recent years.   CHS.

administrative reorganization.   The effort in the United States to promote governmental economy, efficiency, and more effective control by reconstructing and simplifying the administrative apparatus of government. Some 27 States have reformed their administrative systems since 1917 by means of constitutional amendment or statute. The reforms have usually embraced: (1) the consolidation of numerous administrative agencies into relatively few single-headed, integrated departments under the direct supervision of the governor; (2) the appointment and removal of principal officials or department heads by the governor with, or without, the advice and consent of the State senate, and the abolition of popular election of such officials; (3) investiture in the governor of the preparation of the budget, fiscal controls, and staff services. A similar trend in the national government has been apparent in the adoption of the Budget and Accounting Act of 1921 and in various administrative reorganization measures which have given the President important staff services and considerable discretion in reallocating and consolidating administrative agencies. In municipalities the reorganization movement has been strongly influenced by such reforms as the strong-mayor, the commission, and the council-manager types of government.   GHD.

admiral. The highest grade among naval officers. In the American navy it is a temporary rank for permanently commissioned rear admirals while they are acting as chiefs of naval operations or as commanders-in-chief of the fleet, or of the battle fleet, or of the Asiatic fleet.   JWF.

admiralty jurisdiction. Authority to determine cases involving maritime contracts, collisions, and torts on the part of American vessels on the high seas or on navigable lakes and rivers; and also on the part of foreign vessels which later enter American ports. Admiralty cases are first heard in district courts and follow the usual course on appeal.   S.

admissions tax. An excise tax levied upon patrons of places of amusement or recreation usually in the form of a fixed percentage of the price of admission.   Z.

admission to the Union. An act of Congress which has the irrevocable effect of creating a new State equal in every respect to States already in the Union. With the exceptions of Vermont, Kentucky, Texas, California, and West Virginia, all new States have been elevated from a territorial status. The procedure usually followed is a petition of the territory for statehood, the passing by Congress of an enabling act which authorizes the inhabitants to draft a constitution, and the passing of an act of admission following the acceptance of the constitution. Although Congress may make certain conditions in the act of admission, only such conditions are valid as regulate national governmental or proprietary rights. Congress may not admit new States formed out of the territory of an existing State or combine two existing States without the consent of the legislatures of the States affected.   Z.

admonition. A reprimand or warning carrying an implied penalty or sanction.   GHD.

adulteration. The addition of a foreign substance to an article of commerce such as food or drugs, thereby reducing the quality below the accepted legal or published standards and deceiving prospective purchasers as to its true value.   JMCC.

ad valorem. According to value, as determined by assessment, invoice, or appraisal. Such duties are fixed as a percentage of the value of goods abroad (foreign valuation) or of their value in the American market (domestic valuation). s.

advisory ballot. A poll, the results of which are not binding but which are designed to exhibit the voters' preferences and possibly instruct their representatives. z.

advisory commission. A permanently organized or *ad hoc* body authorized to make recommendations to a principal and to consult with him. z.

advisory opinion. An opinion rendered by a court as to the constitutional or legal effect of a bill or a statute when no actual case is before it. From the beginning the Supreme Court of the United States has refused to render such opinions on the ground that it would be engaging in nonjudicial activity. When rendered in the States, advisory opinions have no binding force except in Colorado. *See* Declaratory judgment. s.

advisory recall. The extension of the principle of the recall in North Dakota and Arizona to Congressmen and local federal judges. The recall decision under such circumstances, however it may be formulated at the polls, can be interpreted merely as an invitation to the officeholder to resign, since his tenure is controlled by national, and not by State, law. z.

A.E.F. *See* American Expeditionary Force.

aerial domain. The air space beginning some miles from the terrestrial surface and continuing outward into the stratosphere. Private proprietary rights do not extend to it; its use and regulation are entirely under public control. Though the States still exercise considerable regulatory power over their respective aerial domains, pre-eminent authority rests with the national government because of its power over interstate and foreign commerce and national defense. z.

affidavit. A written statement by an individual under oath or by affirmation attesting to certain beliefs on his part or to the truth of statements which he has made. JWF.

affirmation. A solemn declaration, made under circumstances normally requiring an oath and legally equivalent thereto, by a person whose moral or religious scruples prevent his taking an oath. z.

agenda. Items of business in the program of a public meeting, council, or deliberative assembly. z.

agent provocateur. An unofficial police agent who incites suspected persons to commit overt acts indicative of guilt; also loosely applied to an agent hired by one nation to encourage disaffected elements of another state's citizenry to commit acts of sabotage, sedition, or treason. z.

aggravation. 1. Any action or circumstance which increases the magnitude of a crime or its penalties. **2.** Any action or circumstance which intensifies the seriousness of a dispute and makes its solution more difficult. z.

aggression. An attempt by one state to impair another's political sovereignty or territorial integrity by forcible means devoid of moral or legal justification. z.

agitation. Efforts to stir up popular enthusiasm and support for some political nostrum or cause; colloquially, such efforts as are considered subversive. z.

agrarian. Pertaining to landed property or to agriculture; also to political action designed to promote the interests of the farming classes. JWF.

agreement. A mutual arrangement or understanding among two or more parties which, if legally enforceable, is equivalent to a contract. *See* Executive agreement. z.

Agricultural Adjustment Administration. A division of the United States Department of Agriculture whose principal purposes are to maintain a continuous and adequate supply of basic agricultural commodities at prices fair to consumer and producer and to conserve soil resources. Operating through local farm representatives and with the co-operation of farmers, it establishes national acreage goals and market quotas for selected commodities, supplies payments for the observance of conservation practices, and provides loans on surplus crops which permit the farmer to hold them in reserve. The Administration is under the direction of the Agricultural Adjustment and Conservation Administrator. z.

agricultural and mechanical college. A college established and operated by a State for instruction in agricultural, engineering, military, and other subjects, and endowed with funds from the sale of public land provided by the Morrill Act (*q.v.*) z.

agricultural bloc. *See* Farm bloc.

agricultural credit. Financial credit extended to farmers and co-operative associations for the purchase and improvement of land; for feed, seeds, fertilizers, etc.; and for assistance in marketing crops under the terms of various acts of Congress beginning with the act of July 17, 1916, which established the federal land banks. The Farm Credit Administration (*q.v.*) administers the laws. z.

agricultural experiment station. A local establishment usually maintained in connection with some educational or scientific institution, for testing, research, and the publication and dissemination of scientific information, under the direction of the Department of Agriculture. z.

Agricultural Extension Service. A branch of the Department of Agriculture established in 1924 which, through land-grant colleges and county agricultural and home demonstration agents, brings the results of scientific research in agriculture and home economics to farms and rural homes.   z.

Agricultural Marketing Service. An agency of the Department of Commerce under the immediate direction of the Agricultural Marketing Administrator which provides farmers with statistical data concerning national and world-wide crop conditions, yields, prices, and general market conditions.   z.

Agricultural Wheel. A farmers' association founded in Arkansas in 1882 and active in politics in the Southwest.   s.

Agriculture, Department of. 1. The eighth of the departments of the national government, which was created Feb. 9, 1889, succeeding an office of the same name, dating from 1862, which was administered by a commissioner. At first confining its activities to experimentation, research, and the dissemination of information concerning agriculture and rural problems, it has recently been charged with the enforcement of more than fifty regulatory laws to protect the farmer and the general public. It maintains an inspection service for meats and other products, eradicates plant and animal diseases, promotes soil conservation and rural electrification, supervises the extension of credit for the purchase of farms and the raising of crops, and insures wheat and cotton farmers against loss of crops through natural hazards.   2. The title of an administrative unit in many States which independently, or in co-operation with the national Department of Agriculture, engages in research and the dissemination of information, promotes the welfare of farmers, and enforces many laws enacted under the State police power to compel the observance of sanitary regulations, to eradicate plant and animal diseases, and to maintain marketing standards. s.

aid and comfort to the enemy. An overt attempt by a person owing allegiance to a belligerent state to render material assistance to the government or combatants of an enemy belligerent. If proved in court, such action may be punished as treason in the United States.   z.

air, jurisdiction over. The exclusive sovereignty of every state over the air space above its territory. The Paris Convention for the Regulation of Aerial Navigation, 1919, provides for innocent passage of aircraft of one state over the territory of another, subject to nondiscriminatory municipal regulations. *See* Aerial domain.   jwf.

air-mail service. Regular transportation of mail by airplane. begun by the United States Post Office Department in 1919 and since extended to almost every part of the world.   jwf.

air-raid protection. A service rendered through the Office of Civilian Defense which provides for equipment and personnel to prevent loss of life and property in air raids.   jmcc.

Alabama. The 22nd State, admitted Dec. 14, 1819, from terri-

tory ceded by Georgia, plus a part of West Florida. It adopted an ordinance of secession Jan. 11, 1861, and was readmitted June 25, 1868. Capital, Montgomery; area, 51,078 sq. mi.; population (1940), 2,832,961; presidential electors, 11. Under the present constitution, adopted in 1901, the governor and members of both houses of the legislature are elected for four-year terms, and suffrage is limited by strict property or literacy, and poll-tax requirements.
s.

Alabama **claims.** Claims by the United States against Great Britain for damages to American commerce by the *Alabama* and other Confederate war vessels and privateers which were built in England in violation of international law and British statutes. By the Treaty of Washington, May 8, 1871, the United States and Great Britain agreed that the claims should be submitted to arbitrators, who later met at Geneva, Switzerland, and awarded the United States $15,500,000.
s.

alarmist. One who attempts to excite popular fears of the consequences of some governmental policy.
s.

Alaska. An incorporated and fully organized territory of the United States, purchased from Russia by treaty signed Mar. 30, 1867, for $7,200,000, and valuable for its fisheries, mineral wealth, and strategic position in the Pacific. Area, 586,400 sq. mi.; population (1940), 73,023; seat of government, Juneau. It was made a "district" in 1884, and a territory in 1912, with an appointive governor and judiciary and a popularly elective legislature of two houses. It is a fully incorporated territory.
s.

Alaskan Boundary Dispute. A controversy between the United States and Great Britain arising from the indefinite terms of an

Alaskan Boundary Dispute

Anglo-Russian treaty of 1825. It had fixed the boundary between Alaska and Canada along the crest of a range of mountains which was supposed to parallel the coast; but if the crest was not ascertainable, the line was to be drawn not more than ten marine leagues from the coast, following its sinuosities. There was no continuous range of mountains in the position indicated. The United States claimed that the distance of ten marine leagues should be measured from the heads of fiords which deeply indent the coast; Great Britain, that it should be measured from the headlands, thereby including most of the ports. In 1903 a joint com-

mission of three persons from each country fixed a compromise
boundary line.   s.

Albany Plan of Union. A scheme of colonial union proposed
by Benjamin Franklin at the Albany convention, 1754, which provided for a president-general appointed by the Crown and delegates
from colonial assemblies meeting annually with power to regulate
Indian affairs, levy taxes, and raise armies.   s.

Albany regency. A group of Democratic politicians in New
York, among whom were Silas Wright and William L. Marcy,
who controlled their party from 1821, when Martin Van Buren
went to Washington, until about 1850.   s.

alderman. Formerly a member of a municipal council of
higher rank than common councilor; later a member of the upper
house of a council and often the title of a councilman.   s.

Aldrich-Vreeland Act. An act passed, 1908, after the financial
crisis of 1907 which permitted associations of national banks to
issue emergency bank notes secured by commercial paper and the
securities of States and their subdivisions. A few million dollars
of this currency were placed in circulation prior to the inauguration
of the Federal Reserve System.   z.

Algeciras Conference. A diplomatic conference at Algeciras,
Spain, 1906, called to adjust conflicting interests of Germany,
France, and other powers in Morocco. The attendance of American representatives is historically significant as evidence of the
growing concern of the United States in world diplomacy.   z.

alien. A person domiciled in a state of which he is not a citizen. Aliens enjoy most of the civil rights and the same measure of
protection for those rights that citizens enjoy, especially in the
United States, where the national and State bills of rights expressly
extend their guarantees to "persons," whether citizens or aliens.
Aliens, however, are often denied the right to own or inherit property, particularly real property, to engage in the exploitation of
natural resources, to compete with citizens for certain types of private employment, or to engage in the practice of certain professions.
They are excluded from the enjoyment of political rights, such as
voting, officeholding, and public employment. Sometimes they are
allowed to volunteer in the armed forces of the state of their domicile although such action usually requires as a preliminary some
modified declaration of allegiance or a declaration of intention to
become a citizen. In most states aliens are required to register,
giving information as to their origin, their place of domicile, and
other pertinent personal data. For moral turpitude or activities
detrimental to the integrity of the political institutions of the state
granting them hospitality, aliens may be deported.   z.

Alien and Sedition laws. Several acts passed by Congress in
1798 which increased the period of residence required before nat-

uralization to 14 years, authorized the President to deport aliens dangerous to the peace of the country, and punished the writing, printing, or publication of any false, scandalous, or malicious writing against Congress or the President. s.

alienation. The transfer of property owned by a city to an individual or to another unit of government. s.

Alien Property Custodian. A federal official appointed to act as a trustee to hold, use, administer, or sell property belonging to alien enemies. s.

Alien Registration Act. An act of Congress June 29, 1940, which required all aliens domiciled in the United States to file a detailed personal and occupational record and a statement of their political beliefs. JWF.

allegation. A statement by a party to a legal controversy the truth of which he proposes to prove in court. JWF.

allegiance. The duty of fidelity and obligation of service owed by a citizen to his state or by a subject to his king. Aliens owe a local allegiance to the state in which they reside in contrast to the natural allegiance of the native-born, or the express allegiance of naturalized citizens or subjects. z.

allegiance, oath of. A solemn affirmation or declaration of fidelity to a state on the part of a person who is, or is about to become, a citizen of that state. z.

alliance. A formal agreement, secret or public, between two or more states in which they mutually pledge military and diplomatic support for the furtherance of a common policy towards another state or states. The publicly avowed purpose of an alliance is usually the defense of the territorial and political integrity of the allied states. z.

allotment plan. A fiscal practice in Nebraska and Illinois by which annual lump-sum appropriations for a department become available to it only when, at intervals of three months, the governor approves the anticipated expenditures and allocates sufficient funds therefor. AJW,Jr.

almshouse. A public welfare institution in the United States, usually known as the county farm, which provides shelter for the aged poor and sometimes for orphans, mental defectives, and other persons incapable of self-support. JWF.

alphabetical agency. A popular designation for one of many administrative commissions, boards, and other agencies of the national government which are often identified by the initial letters of the words of their official names. JWF.

alternate. A person chosen to attend a party convention and act in place of a delegate who is absent at any time. s.

ambassador. A diplomatic envoy of the highest rank, usually entitled ambassador extraordinary and minister plenipotentiary, who is sent by the head of a state to serve as his personal representative at a foreign government or court. The United States began to accredit ambassadors in 1893.   z.

Amen Corner. A room in the Fifth Avenue Hotel in New York City where Senator Thomas C. Platt conferred, in his "Sunday school," about 1900, with State officials and politicians.   s.

amendment. **1.** A change made or proposed on the floor of a legislative body or in committee by adding to, striking out, or altering the wording of, any part of a bill or resolution. Legislative rules usually require that the amendment be germane to the subject matter, but violations are not uncommon. **2.** An addition to, or a change of, a constitution or an organic act which is appended to the document rather than intercalated in the text. The Constitution of the United States provides for two methods of proposing amendments: (1) by a convention called by Congress on the application of two thirds of the States; or (2) by a two-thirds vote of both houses of Congress. Amendments so proposed may be ratified either by the legislatures or conventions of three fourths of the States. A State legislature which has rejected an amendment may afterward accept it; but, conversely, if it has once accepted an amendment it cannot recall its action. The Supreme Court has held that a legislature must act, and not the voters in a referendum, though an advisory referendum has sometimes been employed. In proposing amendments Congress may set a time limit, seven years, within which they must be ratified or considered to be rejected. The first ten amendments, constituting the Bill of Rights, were adopted in 1791. Two others, adopted in 1798 and 1804, remedied defects in the original Constitution. The 13th, 14th, and 15th Amendments, adopted between 1865 and 1870, freed the slaves and guaranteed their civil and political rights. Since 1913 six other amendments have been adopted dealing with the income tax, the prohibition question, the suffrage, and presidential and congressional terms.   EES.

amendment limitation. Any restriction upon the process of amending a State constitution. It may affect the subject matter of the proposed amendment, or the number of proposals which may be offered within a given period, or the methods of submission or ratification.   z.

America for Americans. A slogan of the Know-Nothing, or American, party.   s.

American Cato. A nickname of Samuel Adams.   s.

American Colonization Society. A society formed Jan. 1, 1817, for the purpose of transporting free Negroes from the United States. It settled Monrovia, Liberia, in 1821.   s.

American Expeditionary Force. The American army sent to

France during World War I and forces sent to the United Kingdom, Australia, Africa, and elsewhere in World War II.   z.

American Farm Bureau Federation. *See* Farm bureau.

American Federation of Labor. A federation of more than 100 national and international trade-unions with approximately five million members. It was founded in 1886 as a reaction against the revolutionary and industrial unionist policies of the Knights of Labor (*q.v.*) The federation promotes the cause of labor by means of publicity and political pressures upon legislative and executive officers. It also encourages the growth of unionization and lends its support to the activities of its constituent unions, which, however, remain largely autonomous in managing their own affairs and supply the funds for the federation's activities. Since 1936 the federation's virtual monopoly of the national labor movement has been challenged by the Congress of Industrial Organizations (*q.v.*)   JMCC.

American Knights. A Copperhead society founded in 1862.   s.

American Labor party. A minor political party in New York founded in April, 1936, which has generally nominated the same candidates as the Democratic party in national and State elections, but has opposed Tammany Hall in New York City.   s.

American Legion. A servicemen's organization established in 1919 to protect and defend the interests of veterans of World War I and to promote preparedness, patriotism, and Americanism. Its present membership is more than a million, and it has both a woman's and a son's auxiliary.   z.

American Liberty League. A conservative organization formed in 1934 and dissolved in 1940 which opposed the New Deal.   s.

American National party. A minor party founded in 1874 mainly to oppose secret societies, though it also advocated prohibition of liquors, resumption of specie payments, restriction of monopolies, and direct presidential elections. It had presidential candidates in 1876 and 1880.   s.

American National Red Cross. A quasi-official agency of the national government chartered by act of Congress Jan. 5, 1905, to perform all duties with which each national society is charged by the Geneva Convention (*q.v.*); to furnish voluntary aid to the sick and wounded in time of war; and to provide a system of national and international relief for suffering caused by famine, pestilence, flood, fire, earthquakes, and other great calamities. It makes inquiries concerning people in war-affected countries, affords relief to prisoners of war, and assists in distributing supplies in war-torn countries.   s.

American party. 1. The official title adopted by the Know-Nothings. In 1856 they nominated Millard Fillmore for President, who received 874,538 popular, and eight electoral, votes.

2. A minor party organized in 1887 which advocated 14 years' residence as a prerequisite for naturalization and the exclusion of socialists and anarchists.   s.

American Political Science Association. An organization of political scientists, public officials, and others interested in the art and science of government, founded in 1903. It publishes the *American Political Science Review* (bimonthly).   z.

American Protective Association. A secret anti-Catholic and antiforeign organization founded in Iowa in 1887.   s.

American Samoa. Tutuila and five lesser islands in the Pacific some 4,100 miles west of San Francisco, over which the United States assumed control under an agreement with Great Britain and Germany in 1899. The islands were ceded to the United States by the natives in 1900, and Congress ratified the cession in 1929. They are governed by an American commandant-governor under the Navy Department and are particularly valuable as a naval and air station.   z.

American system. The policy of developing American industry by protective tariffs and a national system of internal improvements, formulated about 1824 and later advocated by the Whig party.   s.

amicus curiae. A person not identified with either party to a controversy, who is heard by leave of the court in order to assist it on matters of law.   jjr.

amnesty. A general oblivion of punishment or legal disabilities incurred usually as a result of political offenses. It may be granted by act of Congress or by the President as a corollary of his pardoning power. Both Lincoln and Johnson issued proclamations of amnesty for the benefit of persons who had participated in rebellion against the United States.   s.

Ananias club. A supposititious society to which President Theodore Roosevelt nominated several persons whose truthfulness he impugned.   s.

anarchism. The belief that all government is evil and unnecessary, generally combined with opposition to the institution of private property. Anarchists vary from the individualism of Godwin and Proudhon to the communism of Kropotkin; and although their philosophy exhibits a high degree of diversity, they generally base their conclusions upon faith in the natural goodness, sociability, and reasonableness of man. Since Bakunin, an increasingly common characteristic of anarchistic doctrine has been belief in individual or mass violence against established order. As a practical movement anarchism has been chiefly represented abroad by syndicalist parties and in the United States by the Industrial Workers of the World.   jrp.

anarchy. 1. A society in which government is completely lacking. 2. The condition which prevails in the absence of government. The word also generally connotes absence of law and order, although this is not the objective of those who strive for anarchy on principle. JRP.

angary. The legal right of a belligerent, under pressure of urgent necessity, to destroy or requisition for his own use ships and other property belonging to neutral states or their nationals. The neutral owner must be indemnified. JWF.

angel. A man of wealth who finances the pre-primary or election campaign of a candidate for office. S.

Anglomania. Unreasoning attachment for England or things English. Z.

Anglophobia. Unreasoning hostility to England or things English. Z.

Annapolis Convention. A convention called by Congress to meet at Annapolis, Md., in 1786 to consider means for regulating interstate commerce. Twelve delegates from five States attended. These, at Alexander Hamilton's insistence, recommended to Congress and the States the calling of the convention which met at Philadelphia in 1787 and drafted the Constitution of the United States. Z.

annexation. A unilateral act by which sovereignty is formally extended over territory acquired by discovery, occupation, or absorption of the territory of another state. By joint resolution of Congress the republics of Texas and Hawaii were annexed in 1845 and 1898 respectively. S.

annexationist. One who, after 1830, advocated expansion of the United States by annexing Texas and other territory. S.

annuity. Income from a pension or old-age retirement fund, payable in annual instalments beginning at the age of retirement from active employment or from the public service, and provided for through the payment of premiums to the fund during the years of gainful employment. The national Social Security Act has made limited provision for paying annuities to beneficiaries upon reaching retirement age. GHD.

Anschluss. Annexation of the territory of one state by another; *e.g.,* Hitler's merging of Austria and Germany in 1938. JWF.

Anthony rule. A rule of the United States Senate limiting speeches to five minutes on all measures not objected to during the calling of the Calendar of Bills and Resolutions. S.

anticipatory borrowing. Short-term borrowing for current expenses in anticipation of taxes not yet due, through the sale of tax-anticipation notes. The device is frequently used by American municipalities. GHD.

Antifederalist. One who, because of particularistic tendencies, fear of centralized power, or other motives, opposed ratification of the Constitution of the United States. In North Carolina the Antifederalists delayed ratification until Nov. 21, 1789, and in Rhode Island, until May 29, 1790. They were also very numerous in New Hampshire, Massachusetts, New York, Pennsylvania, and Virginia. After the inauguration of the new government, the main body of Antifederalists became supporters of Jefferson and the Republican party which he led. z.

Antigua. A British possession in the Leeward Island group situated in the Caribbean southeast of Puerto Rico. In 1940 a site near Partain harbor, the principal port, was leased by the United States for a naval and air base. z.

anti-Lecompton Democrat. A Northern Democrat who opposed the admission of Kansas under the proslavery constitution drafted at Lecompton in 1857. s.

antilynching bill. A measure of doubtful constitutionality introduced in Congress which would impose penalties upon local government areas or their officials when lynchings occur. JMCC.

Antimasonic party. A third party which sprang into existence during the intense popular excitement which followed the disappearance of William Morgan and his alleged murder by members of the Masonic order. It held the first national convention in 1831 and nominated William Wirt for President. He received the electoral votes of Vermont and many popular votes, particularly in Pennsylvania and western New York. s.

Antimonopoly party. A minor party which nominated Benjamin F. Butler for President in 1884 and advocated a federal interstate commerce act, direct election of senators, a federal income tax, and industrial arbitration. s.

anti-Nebraska men. Northern Democrats opposed to the Kansas-Nebraska Act, 1854. Many of them helped to form the Republican party. s.

antirenters. A group in New York who, between 1839 and 1846, violently agitated for the abolition of semifeudal tenures which had continued from the period of the Dutch colony. s.

Anti-Saloon League of America. An organization founded in 1895 which by propaganda and pressures on candidates and officeholders was influential in the prohibition movement which culminated in the 18th Amendment and the national and State laws to enforce it. s.

anti-Semitism. Hatred for and legal and social discrimination against Jews, practiced by many peoples throughout history, and, in modern times, by German National Socialists and their imitators. JWF.

Antisnapper. A New York Democrat who supported Cleveland and denounced the snap convention called by D. B. Hill early in 1892. s.

antitrust. Pertaining to the regulation of cartels, trusts, pools, monopolies, interlocking directorates, and other devices to restrain trade. *See* Sherman **Antitrust** Act; Rule of reason; Clayton Act; Federal Trade Commission; Webb-Pomerene Act; National Industrial Recovery Act. s.

A.P.A. *See* American Protective Association.

appeal. The transfer of a case from an inferior to a higher tribunal for review with the possibility of reversing or modifying the decision below. JJR.

appeasement. A foreign policy of pacification or yielding to the demands of a potential enemy rather than opposing him by force. JWF.

appellate. Pertaining to the authority to hear and decide cases or controversies on appeal. AJW,Jr.

appellate court. A judicial tribunal which reviews interpretations of law in cases originally tried and decided by inferior tribunals. The United States Supreme Court is primarily a court of appellate jurisdiction and the United States Circuit Courts of Appeals are wholly appellate in their activity. Similar tribunals exist in various States. AJW,Jr.

appellate jurisdiction. The authority of a court or similar tribunal to review either the law or facts, or both, in cases or controversies decided by a tribunal of inferior jurisdiction. AJW,Jr.

appointment. The process, which may include both nomination and confirmation, by which a superior exercises discretion in designating a person to hold an office. In some jurisdictions the issuance of a commission is necessary to complete an appointment. Ambassadors, other public ministers, consuls, and judges of the Supreme Court, together with several thousand others who have been designated by law as "officers," must be confirmed by the Senate. When it is not in session the President may fill vacancies by temporary appointments which expire at the end of the next session of the Senate. Appointments of inferior officers may be made under the laws of Congress by the President alone, by the courts, or by the heads of departments, independent agencies, and government-owned corporations. Most of them are chosen under civil service rules. In the States gubernatorial appointments generally require confirmation, and those made by heads of departments do not. s.

apportionment. Determination by law of the number of representatives which a State, county, or other subdivisions may send to a legislative body; or by a competent party authority of the number of delegates to a party convention. The Constitution provides for a census every ten years, on the basis of which Congress apportions representatives according to population; but each State must have one representative. No reapportionment was made following the census of 1920. In June, 1929, Congress passed a law providing that the President, after every decennial census, should submit tables showing the number of representatives each State would be entitled to in a House of 435 members. If Congress failed to act, the presidential apportionment should be effective. s.

appraisal. Any estimate of value, specifically the valuation of imported goods for the purpose of determining the amount of customs duties.   AJW,Jr.

appropriation. A sum of money set aside to be expended for a public purpose and in a manner determined by law; also the act of appropriating. An itemized appropriation goes into great detail as to the purpose for which often small amounts may be spent. A lump-sum appropriation allows the executive considerable discretion. By custom, because revenue bills must originate in the House of Representatives, appropriation bills originate there also. The Committee on Ways and Means prepared appropriation bills until 1865, when a committee on appropriations was created. Later eight other committees were authorized to introduce appropriation bills. Since the passage of the Budget and Accounting Act of 1921 the expenditures recommended in the President's budget message have been referred to the Committee on Appropriations which, through its subcommittees, prepares all appropriation bills. In the Senate, which has power to amend by increasing, decreasing, or eliminating items, the Committee on Appropriations is enlarged by the addition of two or three members of other committees when items falling within their legislative province are under consideration. *See* Budget; Pork barrel.   s.

approval of bills. The addition of the signature of the chief executive to measures formally passed by the legislature, which is the final step required to make such bills law, except in North Carolina. It is now established that the President may sign a bill after Congress has adjourned. Several States allow the governor an extended period after the legislature has adjourned in which to approve bills. *See* Veto.   JWF.

arbitration. 1. The submission of an international dispute to an umpire or tribunal chosen by the states who are parties to the controversy, judgment being rendered subject to such limitations and on the basis of such rules and principles as may be set forth in the *compromis,* or agreement to arbitrate. The judgment is usually called an award. A permanent panel of judges or umpires, available to states wishing to arbitrate disputes, was provided when the Permanent Court of Arbitration was established at The Hague in 1899. 2. In municipal law, the hearing, investigation, and determination of a controversy by an arbitrator or arbitration tribunal to whom the cause has been submitted by consent of the parties and by whose decision they agree to be bound. The award is enforceable by an action at law. Arbitration is to be distinguished from conciliation and mediation (*qq.v.*)   JJR.

Architect of the Capitol. An official, acting as agent of Congress, who has charge of the structural and mechanical care of the Capitol, the Library of Congress, court buildings in the District of Columbia, etc.   JWF.

archives. A collection of public records. *See* National Archives.   S.

area of the United States. The continental area of the United States, excluding Alaska, is 3,022,387 sq. mi., of which 2,977,128 sq. mi. is land area and 45,259 sq. mi. is inland water area. Including territories and possessions (but excluding the Philippine Commonwealth, area, 114,400 sq. mi.), the area is 3,619,593 sq. mi.   z.

aristocracy. 1. A state in which political power is possessed by a relatively small and especially qualified class. In the original and purest sense of the word, a state which is ruled by its best citizens. 2. The ruling class in an aristocratic state.   JRP.

Arizona. The 48th State, admitted to the Union Feb. 14, 1912, from territory included in the Mexican cession of 1848 and the Gadsden Purchase. Capital, Phoenix; area, 113,956 sq. mi.; population (1940), 499,261; electoral votes, 4. The original constitution, which is still in effect, provides for the constitutional and statutory initiative, the referendum, the recall, and a literacy test for voters.   S.

Arkansas. The 25th State, admitted June 15, 1836, from territory included in the Louisiana Purchase. It adopted an ordinance of secession May 6, 1861, and was readmitted June 22, 1868. Capital, Little Rock; area, 53,335 sq. mi.; population (1940), 1,949,-387; presidential electors, 9. The present constitution was adopted in 1874 and, as amended, provides for the constitutional and statutory initiative, the referendum, and a poll-tax requirement for the suffrage.   S.

Armageddon. The site of the last decisive battle at the Day of Judgment (Revelation 16:16); hence any great conflict against alleged forces of evil, as the Progressive campaign of 1912, or World War I.   S.

armament. A state's military equipment, including warships and planes, weapons, armed forces, potential man power, control of strategic raw materials, weapon-producing capacity, and peacetime plant and equipment and other resources convertible to war needs.   JWF.

armed neutrality. The position assumed by a neutral when it serves notice on belligerents that it is prepared to protect its neutral rights by force. The Armed Neutrality of 1780 was the concerted action of Denmark, Sweden, and Russia, later joined by other states.   EES.

Arm-in-Arm convention. A convention of Republicans supporting President Johnson, held at Philadelphia in 1868, at which the delegates from Massachusetts and South Carolina entered arm-in-arm.   S.

armistice. An agreement between belligerents or military commanders for the cessation of hostilities.   EES.

armory. A public building used primarily for the storage of military weapons and for training the National Guard.   EES.

arms, right to bear. The right of citizens, protected against abridgment by Congress, to use military weapons in order to preserve a well-regulated militia. It does not include other weapons, such as the sawed-off shotguns regulated by the National Firearms Act of 1934.   JJR.

army. The entire military force of a state as distinguished from its naval force and sometimes also from its air forces; also an organized military force in the field commanded by a general officer.   Z.

Army War College. The highest institution in the military educational system, located at Washington, D. C., where selected officers are trained for duties in the general staff and for high command.   Z.

Aroostook War. A disturbance along the disputed northern boundary of Maine in 1838, caused by the governor's sending troops to expel Canadian lumbermen.   S.

arraignment. A proceeding in which a prisoner is called to the bar of the court to be identified, to hear the charges against him, and to plead guilty or not guilty.   JJR.

arrest. The legal detainment of a person to answer for criminal charges or (infrequently at present) civil demands upon him. Constitutional limitations prevent detention under false or assumed authority and harassment of persons without warrants properly issued.   JJR.

arsenal. A state-owned establishment for the manufacture and storage of munitions of war and military and naval equipment. Z.

arsenal of democracy. A phrase in a speech delivered by President F. D. Roosevelt, Dec. 29, 1940, descriptive of the significant role of the United States as supplier of munitions to those nations opposing the Axis powers in World War II.   Z.

arson. The crime of setting fire to buildings or property with malicious intent or with intent to defraud fire-insurance companies.   JWF.

Articles of Confederation. The framework of a "perpetual union" drafted by a committee which was appointed by the Continental Congress, June 11, 1776; approved by Congress, Nov. 15, 1777; and effective after the ratification of all the States, Mar. 1,

1781. Many provisions of the Articles, especially those relating to the obligations of States and the powers of Congress, were later incorporated into the Constitution of the United States. Congress was made the repository of all legislative and executive authority, but it had no power to raise revenue by taxation, and no means to compel the States, which were declared to be sovereign, to pay the amounts apportioned among them for the expenses of the Confederation. Efforts to correct these defects by amendment proved to be abortive because of the provision requiring ratification by every State. The Confederation Congress ceased to exist on Mar. 2, 1789.　　　　　　　　　　　　　　　　　　　　　　　　s.

articles of war. Regulations made by Congress defining the duties of officers and enlisted men, providing for the maintenance of discipline, and establishing the organization and procedure for courts-martial which try all cases of infraction of the articles.　s.

Article X. Part of the Covenant of the League of Nations which provides that members "undertake to respect and preserve as against external aggression the territorial integrity and existing political independence of all Members of the League."　　　s.

assassination. The commission of a homicide by treacherous means or through the agency of a hireling, often employed by anarchists.　　　　　　　　　　　　　　　　　　　　　　jwf.

assault. To menace another's safety by uttering threats of immediate bodily harm or by attempting to commit violence upon his person.　　　　　　　　　　　　　　　　　　　　　　　jwf.

assay. Analysis of ores to determine the amount and quality of ingredients; especially analysis of the content of gold and silver taken in at a government mint to be used for coinage or currency reserve.　　　　　　　　　　　　　　　　　　　　　　　jmcc.

assembled examination. The standard written or printed examination for a particular grade or classification in the civil service administered at a particular time and place to qualified applicants on a competitive basis; to be distinguished from nonassembled examinations in which an applicant's qualifications for civil service are determined by his experience, professional attainments, publications, and other factors.　　　　　　　　　　　　　　　　ghd.

assembly. 1. A legislature.　2. The more numerous house of a legislature, as in New York.　3. In the League of Nations, a body composed of representatives of all the member states.　　　z.

assembly, right of. The right of the people under free or popular governments to assemble for the discussion of public or other questions and to petition the public authorities. The right is affirmed by the national and State constitutions in the United States and by basic public documents in British constitutional history. An assembly of three or more persons is unlawful if its express purpose is to commit an illegal act, and it becomes unlawful if its action involves a breach of the peace or results in riot or forcible resistance to public authority.   z.

assemblyman. The title of a member of the lower house of certain State legislatures; *e.g.,* New York.   JWF.

assessment. 1. The determination of the amount of a tax to be paid. 2. The valuation of property by public authority for the purpose of taxation, the market value or a percentage thereof being used to compute the official valuation.   JMCC.

assessment, political. A levy, usually in proportion to salary and collected every pay day, which is imposed by a political organization on holders of appointive positions under the implied threat of dismissal. Such levies are forbidden by civil service laws.   s.

assessor. A public official, often elective in America, who determines the value of land, buildings, and other property for purposes of taxation.   AJW,Jr.

assimilation. The process of absorbing immigrants of an alien culture by accustoming them to the political ideology and ways of the American community.   JWF.

assistance clause. A provision in the laws of many States by which an illiterate or physically handicapped voter may receive help from an election official or, in some cases, any qualified voter whom he may select, in marking his ballot.   s.

association, right of. The right of persons to act together for some common purpose, without public grant or charter, whether transiently, as in peaceable assembly; or permanently, as by formal organization. It is protected against legislative encroachment by constitutional provisions, but is limited by the power of the government to preserve the public peace, health, morals, and safety. It is partly protected against private encroachments by statutory and common-law rules and by the conceded power of associations themselves to exclude and expel members.   JJR.

Association, The. Articles drawn up by the Continental Congress of 1774 under which it was agreed that Americans would not import any goods from Great Britain.   s.

association of states. A league or confederation of sovereign states.   z.

assumption of risk. A common-law defense in workmen's compensation cases that persons entering upon an employment know the hazards involved and assume them. The statutes of most States have outlawed this defense.   s.

assumption of State debts. The fiscal policy proposed by Hamilton as Secretary of the Treasury in 1789 and subsequently approved by Congress of having the national government assume responsibility for all unpaid debts contracted by the States for the prosecution of the Revolutionary War. Certain Southern States, notably Virginia, bitterly opposed assumption because they had paid off their debts, but were won over as a result of Hamilton's success in winning Northern approval for the location of the national capital on the Potomac. z.

asylum, right of. 1. The freedom from arrest of an individual who takes refuge in a foreign ministry, embassy, or visiting warship, subject to the will of the diplomatic or naval officers therein. 2. The sanctuary enjoyed by belligerent troops or naval vessels in neutral territory or territorial waters. They may be interned or allowed freedom depending upon circumstances. jwf.

asylum of the oppressed of every nation. The United States according to the Democratic platform of 1856. s.

Atlantic Charter. A program of postwar reconstruction announced by President F. D. Roosevelt and Prime Minister Churchill of Great Britain after their conference on a British battleship in the Atlantic, Aug. 14, 1941. The program consisted of eight "points" or declarations pledging the United States and Great Britain jointly to take measures to prevent national aggrandizement, to encourage international trade, and to secure to individuals everywhere "freedom from fear and want." z.

at large. A term applied to congressional representatives chosen by the entire electorate of a State. jwf.

attaché. A diplomatic official of minor grade attached to the staff of an embassy. His special province may be military, naval, diplomatic, or commercial. z.

attachment. The taking of a defendant's property into legal custody as security for settlement, pending judgment in a civil action. jjr.

attainder. The annihilation of all civil rights and privileges which in early English law followed a condemnation for treason or felony. The person attainted forfeited all property and lost all capacity to inherit or transmit property to his descendants; nor could he appear in court or claim the protection of law. In the United States "no attainder of treason shall work corruption of blood or forfeiture except during the life of the person attainted." A bill of attainder, which is prohibited by the Constitution, is a legislative condemnation without the formality of a judicial trial. s.

attestation. The act of verifying or affirming, orally or in writing, the genuineness or validity of some legal document, such as a will or an affidavit. z.

attitude, social. The state of mind of an individual or his tendency to act in response to specific social situations resulting from his innate biological and psychological characteristics or from the environmental factors which condition his existence. jmcc.

Attorney General. 1. The head of the Department of Justice and a member of the President's cabinet. He gives legal advice to the President and heads of departments, supervises district attorneys and United States marshals, oversees criminal investigations, and has charge of cases in which the government is involved. He may appear in court, but rarely does so. **2.** The chief legal officer of a State who advises State and local officers and may appear in cases in which the State is sued by another State. He usually lacks the power to supervise locally elected prosecutors.   s.

Auburn system. A penal system originated at Auburn, N. Y., about 1825 and now generally used in America. Prisoners are allowed to associate together during the day in prison workshops; and are confined at night to single-person cells arranged back-to-back in tiers of a cell block.   JMCC.

auditor. An elective or appointive official who periodically examines governmental expenditures to determine whether or not they conform with the law, and who occasionally makes investigations of the fiscal practices of public agencies.   JWF.

Austinian theory. The doctrine of the Analytical School of Jurisprudence, of which the English utilitarian jurist John Austin (1790-1859) is regarded as the founder, that legal sovereignty resides in a determinate human superior and that law, as distinguished from custom and morality, consists of those rules tacitly or expressly sanctioned by the legal sovereign.   z.

Australian ballot. A secret ballot printed at state expense and containing the names of all candidates who have been nominated according to law, with usually a space for voters to write in other names. It is distributed within the polling place by election officials to qualified voters who are required to mark it before leaving. As originally used in Australia it listed the names of candidates without party designations, but since its adoption in the United States, beginning in 1888, it has appeared generally as the Indiana, or party-column, ballot; or the Massachusetts, or office-block, ballot (*qq.v.*)   s.

autarchy. The condition of a state which is self-sufficient. The totalitarian states have striven for autarchy by limiting imports and encouraging domestic production of goods previously imported, or the use of substitutes.   JRP.

authoritarian. Quality of a political system which concentrates supreme authority without legal responsibility in the hands of a "leader" or a few oligarchs; opposed to "democratic," "liberal," and "constitutional"; emphasizing obedience rather than individual rights.   JRP.

authority. **1.** The legal power vested in a public agency to enable its officials to execute its functions. **2.** A type of public administrative agency with quasi-governmental powers; *e.g.,* Tennessee Valley Authority.   JWF.

autocracy. A state in which one person possesses unlimited political power which is considered as not flowing from any external source. JRP.

autonomy. The degree of legal self-determination enjoyed by a minority group or a territorial division in its relations with the political community of which it is a part. Group autonomy may be conceded in matters affecting religion, language, education, culture, or economic institutions. The maximum degree of territorial autonomy is exhibited by the position of the dominions in the British Commonwealth of Nations. Members of a federal union have a lesser degree of autonomy, and local-government units under home rule have still less. The status of autonomous groups and areas suggests a condition of social pluralism incompatible with the contemporary doctrine of state sovereignty; in juristic theory, however, autonomy and sovereignty are generally considered reconcilable. AJW,Jr.

award. The judgment of an arbitrator or board of arbitration in a dispute between nations or between capital and labor. JWF.

Axis. The military alliance of Germany and Italy created in 1939, and expanded in 1941 to include Japan, for warfare against the United Nations. Certain Hitlerian puppet governments, such as Croatia, Slovakia, and Rumania, are nominally members of the Axis. JWF.

B

Bacon's Rebellion. An insurrection in Virginia in 1676 led by Nathaniel Bacon in opposition to Governor Sir William Berkeley's policies concerning taxation and Indian trade. s.

Badger State. A nickname of Wisconsin. s.

Bahama Islands. A chain of islands in the Atlantic between southern Florida and Hispaniola which constitute a British crown colony. In 1940 the United States leased an area for a naval base on one of the islands, Great Exuma. JWF.

bail. The persons giving surety, also the surety given, that an accused person will appear in court at the proper time. When bailed out he is released into the custody of his sureties. Bail is refused to persons accused of capital crimes. When allowed, it must not be excessive in proportion either to the gravity of the crime or to the resources of the accused. s.

bailiff. A sheriff's assistant who executes writs. z.

Baker Island. A small mid-Pacific island occupied by the United States in 1936 as a meteorological station. z.

balance of power. The policy, especially favored by European diplomatists, which seeks to prevent any state on the Continent from acquiring a hegemony or from achieving such a position of power and influence as to become a potential menace to the integrity of the remaining states. z.

balance of trade. A quantitative comparison between a country's exports and imports. The balance is "favorable" if exports exceed imports; "unfavorable" if the reverse is true.   JWF.

Ballinger-Pinchot controversy. A dispute which began in August, 1909, when Chief of Forestry Gifford Pinchot publicly criticized his superior, Secretary of the Interior R. A. Ballinger, for having reopened for sale certain public lands previously closed. An investigation was ordered, but before it ended Pinchot wrote a letter condemning Ballinger, and was dismissed by President Taft. Theodore Roosevelt's friends sided with Pinchot.   s.

ballot. A method of secret voting, at first by putting colored balls, beans, or grains of Indian corn into an urn, and later by depositing written or printed voting papers in an appropriate receptacle. The ballot superseded *viva voce* voting in four of the American colonies, and in all but three of the States by 1850; but it was not required in English elections until 1872. Before the adoption of the Australian ballot (*q.v.*), ballots were generally printed at party expense and contained the names of candidates of only one party.   EES.

ballot box stuffing. The clandestine insertion of illegal ballots into a ballot box, either by the use of tissue ballots (as formerly) or when made possible by the carelessness or connivance of election officials.   s.

band wagon, climbing aboard the. Throwing one's support to the candidate or proposal that appears to be winning.   s.

banishment. The expulsion and enforced exclusion of a person from the country or region where he normally resides, as a result of the sentence of a court or the decree of public authorities. *See* Deportation.   z.

bank. A financial institution which receives deposits, makes loans, and functions in the circulation of credit. The power to charter a bank, though not expressly granted to Congress, was implied from the borrowing and currency powers and other powers involving the collection of revenue and the transfer of funds from one part of the country to another. State banks have been in continuous operation from Revolutionary days, though their issuance of bank notes, formerly the chief currency of the country, ceased with the imposition of a tax of 10 per cent on such notes by act of Congress, July 13, 1866. Both State and national banks are closely supervised, and their books are subject to periodical inspection by examiners. Recently State banks have come under limited national regulation in such matters as membership in the Federal Reserve System, reorganization, and the insurance of deposits up to $5,000. *See* Bank of the United States; National banks; Federal Reserve System.   s.

bank deposits guarantee. Insurance of bank deposits up to $5,000 against bank failure made available to banks at reasonable rates through the semi-public Federal Deposit Insurance Corporation. All federal reserve member banks are required to carry deposit insurance.   JMCC.

bank examiner. An official charged with making periodic unannounced inspections of banks and fiduciary institutions to determine whether or not their practices are in accord with legal requirements and sound banking policies, and whether or not they are solvent.   Z.

Bank for International Settlements. An institution at Basle, Switzerland, created under the Young plan (*q.v.*), 1930, for administering German reparation payments. It provides machinery for major international financial operations.   JWF.

Bankhead-Jones Farm Tenant Act. A law of Congress, 1934, authorizing the Farm Security Administration to make long-term, low-interest loans to competent tenant farmers, sharecroppers, and farm laborers to enable them to purchase farms, livestock, farm equipment, and supplies.   JMCC.

bank holiday. The period from Mar. 4 to Mar. 14, 1933, when all banks in the United States were closed by presidential proclamation; probably so called after any of six legal holidays in Great Britain.   JWF.

bank note. A promissory note or bill of credit issued by a bank, with such security as the law requires, payable to bearer on demand, which serves as currency. The privilege of issuing such notes is now virtually confined to the federal reserve banks, national bank notes having been largely retired.   Z.

Bank of the United States. A quasi-public bank with branches in various parts of the country. The first bank was chartered by Congress for the period, 1791-1811. The second bank was chartered for 20 years in 1816. In 1829 President Jackson expressed the opinion that it should not be rechartered, and the issue was fought out in the election of 1832. The next year President Jackson ordered the removal of all federal deposits. The bank ceased to exist in 1836.   S.

bankruptcy. The condition of a person when a court has determined that his property is to be administered for the benefit of his creditors. Under its power to pass uniform laws on the subject Congress enacted statutes which were in effect 1800-1803; 1841-1843; 1867-1878; and since 1898. When there is no national law on the subject, the States may legislate providing they do not impair the obligation of a contract. At present a person may file a voluntary petition of bankruptcy, listing his assets and liabilities; or he may be forced into bankruptcy on petition of his creditors. In either case his assets are disposed of by an officer appointed by the court, his creditors are paid *pro rata,* and he is discharged from further obligation. In 1933 special provision was made by law to facilitate the reorganization of railroads and other corporations. S.

banner State. The State which gives the greatest plurality to a party.   s.

bar. Collectively, all the lawyers who are competent to practice in a court.   s.

Barbary pirates. Tripoli, Tunis, Algiers, and Morocco, which were engaged in official piracy, and to which the United States and other nations were accustomed to pay tribute to avoid depredations on their commerce. Wars with Tripoli, 1801-1805, and with Algiers in 1815 broke up the practice.   s.

bargain and corruption. A campaign slogan of Jackson's followers after Clay's influence in the House of Representatives had proved decisive in electing J. Q. Adams President, and Adams had appointed Clay Secretary of State in 1825.   s.

Barnburners. A faction of the Democratic party in New York, 1847-1852, which opposed slavery. Their opponents declared that they resembled the Dutch farmer who burned his barn in order to rid it of rats.   s.

bar of the Senate. The well before the desk of the presiding officer to which are brought impeached officers for trial, and persons who have been formally summoned for inquiry or contempt proceedings.   JJR.

base. A fortified location, usually possessing natural defensive advantages, from which hostile operations of a nation's military, naval, or air forces may begin and which serves as a supply and communications center for such forces.   z.

Battling Bob. A nickname of the elder R. M. LaFollette.   s.

Baumes Law. An act of the New York legislature, 1926, which made mandatory the imposition of a sentence of life imprisonment upon habitual criminals, that is, upon persons convicted of four felonies. It has been imitated in many other States.   JWF.

Bayou State. A nickname of Mississippi.   s.

Bear Flag Battalion. A group of American residents of California who, on the outbreak of the Mexican War, expelled Mexican authorities and set up a provisional government.   s.

belligerency. The international status, and its consequent rights and duties, assumed by a state which wages war against another state. The status is also enjoyed by an organized rebellion which is diplomatically recognized by other states.   z.

bench. A collective term for the judiciary.   s.

benefit payment. A payment made by government for compliance with a program of regulation, particularly a payment made to farmers under the Agricultural Adjustment Act of 1933 for limiting production of certain commodities.   AJW,Jr.

benefit theory. A theory that taxes should be imposed in proportion to the benefit which taxpayers derive from the government.

Though outmoded in general, it is still used as a justification for automobile, gasoline, business, poll, and ad valorem property taxes. s.

benevolent assimilation. The motive assigned by President McKinley for taking over the Philippines and other Spanish possessions in 1898. s.

Bering Sea Arbitration. The settlement of a dispute which arose from the conviction of Canadian seal hunters for violating

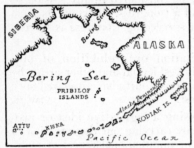
Bering Sea Arbitration

American regulations forbidding the killing of seals in the open sea near the Pribilof Islands in the Aleutians. The arbitrators in 1893 denied American claims to property in the seals or to jurisdiction over the Bering Sea. A later agreement with Russia, Japan, and Great Britain provided a means to safeguard the seal herds from destruction. s.

Berlin Decree. The announcement of a paper blockade of Great Britain and all her possessions in Europe by Napoleon at Berlin, Prussia, Nov. 21, 1806; partly responsible for the passage of the Embargo Act. s.

Bermuda. A representative colony of Great Britain comprising a group of coral islands some 600 miles off the coast of North Carolina. Sites on the islands were leased by the United States in 1940 for naval air bases. z.

betterment tax. A tax or special assessment levied upon property to pay for a public improvement adjacent to or near the property taxed which is calculated to enhance its capital value. z.

B.E.W. *See* Board of Economic Warfare.

bicameral. Having two houses in a legislature. s.

biennial session. A meeting once in two years, the common practice among all but a few State legislatures. EES.

biennium. A two-year period, especially the period for which appropriations are made in 43 State legislatures. JWF.

big fix. An arrangement between political machines and the underworld for the nonenforcement or partial enforcement of laws relating to bootlegging, racketeering, and other forms of organized crime and vice. s.

big stick. Forceful methods in dealing with foreign — and, by extension, domestic — problems. When recommending increased appropriations for the navy, President Theodore Roosevelt used the expression, "Speak softly and carry a big stick." s.

bill. The draft of a proposed law from the time of its introduction in a legislative house through all the various stages in both houses, including reference to committee, consideration and amendment in committee, committee report, debate and amendment on the floor of the chamber or in committee of the whole, passage on three readings, conference, engrossment, enrollment, and approval by the executive or passage over his veto. Bills for raising revenue for the national government must originate in the House of Representatives, and by usage appropriation bills must also originate there. Once introduced, a bill may be considered in any session of a Congress, but it dies at the end of a Congress. Its contents must be reintroduced as a new bill if a succeeding Congress is to consider it.   s.

billboard regulation. The limitation or prohibition of billboards as an advertising medium in residential and other areas, by statute or municipal zoning ordinances. Courts have declared such regulation to be in the public interest.   AJW,Jr.

bill drafting. The art of expressing a legislative idea or proposal in concise legal terms faithfully carrying out the intention of the sponsors, avoiding duplication or unintentional repeal of existing legislation, and, as far as possible, assuring the measure against judicial annulment. Congress has had the services of a bill-drafting agency, known as the Office of Legislative Counsel, since 1918; and State legislatures are making increased use of experts in bill drafting.   z.

billeting. Quartering soldiers in private dwellings.   JWF.

Billion Dollar Congress. The 51st Congress (1889-91) which was the first peacetime Congress to make appropriations in excess of a billion dollars.   s.

bill of attainder. *See* Attainder.

bill of rights. A brief summation of certain fundamental rights and privileges which are guaranteed to the people against infringement by any part of the government. A bill of rights is nearly always the first article of an American State constitution. The first ten amendments to the Constitution of the United States are popularly called the bill of rights. The English bill of rights from which most of the provisions of American bills of rights have been drawn is a statute of Parliament passed in 1689.   s.

bimetallism. The use of both gold and silver, more or less freely coined in some legally fixed ratio of value, as the standard of value. The United States was on a bimetallic basis before 1900. s.

Biological Survey. *See* Fish and Wildlife Service.

bipartisan deal. An understanding among opposing party leaders, usually secret and prejudicial to the public interest, as to the disposition of patronage or other perquisites, or as to the course to be followed with respect to pending public issues.   z.

biparty system. *See* Two-party system.

birth registration. Legal certification of the birth of an infant which the laws or administrative regulations of most States now require the attending physician or midwife to file with local and State registrars of vital statistics. JMCC.

Bituminous Coal Division. A division of the Department of the Interior charged with the stabilization of the soft-coal industry. It promotes conservation of coal resources and attempts to establish fair trade and employment practices in the industry. Z.

Black and Tans. A faction of the Republican party in the Solid South which believes in the participation of both white and colored voters in all party affairs; opposed to Lily-whites (*q.v.*) S.

black belt. 1. A strip of territory extending south and southwest from eastern Virginia to the Texas border in which the colored population exceeds the white. 2. A strip of deep, black alluvial soil 40 to 100 miles wide extending across southern Alabama and Mississippi. S.

blackbirding. Illegal importation of slaves. S.

Black Code. Laws passed in Southern States prior to the adoption of the 14th Amendment which placed rigid restrictions upon Negroes and imposed penalties upon them more severe than those imposed by law upon other persons. S.

Black Hawk War. An Indian war with the Sacs and Foxes under the chieftain Black Hawk, which was fought in northern Illinois and southern Wisconsin in 1831 and 1832. S.

black horse cavalry. Members of a legislature who conspire to extort money or favors from corporations by threatening to pass "regulator" or strike bills; specifically a group in the New York legislature about 1905. S.

Black Jack. A nickname of Senator John A. Logan of Illinois; also of General John J. Pershing. S.

blacklist. A list of persons or organizations who, because of alleged unfriendly, illegal, or unethical activity, have been singled out for discriminatory action. It is used especially by employers against prospective employees who have been active in labor unions and by labor unions against workmen who have incurred the unions' displeasure. Z.

blackmail, political. The corrupt exploitation of political influence or official position by a member of a legislature, public officer, or political boss in order to extort money or other favors from private citizens or corporations. Z.

black market. An establishment which sells goods in violation of rationing and price-fixing regulations. S.

black Republican. A derisive nickname of the Republican party shortly after its founding, apparently bestowed because it espoused the cause of the Negro. S.

Bland-Allison Act. A law of Congress Feb. 28, 1878, which made the silver dollar of 412½ grains legal tender and provided that the Secretary of the Treasury should purchase from two to four million dollars worth of silver monthly.   s.

blanket ballot. A printed ballot which lists many names of candidates for elective offices and legislative proposals; hence prevents intelligent and discriminating choice by the voter.   z.

blanket code. A popular name for the President's Re-employment Agreement which was signed in July, 1933, by many businessmen engaged in industries for which no codes had been formulated under the provisions of the National Industrial Recovery Act (*q.v.*)   JJR.

bloc. 1. A temporary combination of parties in French legislative assemblies who agree upon a common parliamentary policy or to support or oppose a ministry. Blocs were frequent in the parliamentary history of the French Third Republic. Some of them, notably the Bloc of the Left formed after the Dreyfus affair and the National Bloc formed in 1919, held together for considerable periods. The term may be applied to similar arrangements in other legislative assemblies. 2. In America, a group of Congressmen whose devotion to some common economic interest, *e.g.*, agriculture, often transcends their formal party allegiance. *See* Farm bloc.   z.

blockade. The effort of a belligerent to cut off neutral commerce or communication with an enemy's ports. It is incumbent upon the blockading belligerent to give notice of the blockade and to provide more than mere token enforcement; otherwise neutral shipping is not legally expected to observe the blockade. A "pacific" blockade is sometimes used in peacetime to compel a state to pursue, or refrain from, some course of action; such a blockade, however, is not recognized in international law.   JAP.

blockade runner. A vessel employed in carrying persons and goods to and from ports under blockade.   s.

blocked credit. Governmental restrictions upon the time and manner in which a debtor may pay obligations to a creditor in a foreign country.   JWF.

blocked currency. A currency subject to legislative or administrative restrictions when used to acquire foreign exchange.   JWF.

blocked national. A firm or individual, in a neutral country, with whom American citizens are forbidden to trade except under license because of supposed sympathies or previous co-operation with the Axis powers.   s.

Bloody Bill. The Force Bill (*q.v.*) of 1833.

bloody shirt, waving the. Accusing the Democratic party of having caused the Civil War — a characteristic campaign device of the Republican party, 1868-1896.   s.

Blue Eagle. The symbol of the National Recovery Administration, first used in 1933 as an award of merit to be displayed by employers who had signed a code of fair competition or the President's Re-employment Agreement. JJR.

Bluegrass State. A nickname of Kentucky. z.

Blue Hen State. A nickname of Delaware. s.

blue laws. 1. A rigorous code of the New Haven Colony. 2. Any laws prohibiting athletic contests or the opening of stores and theaters on Sunday, race-track betting, or any other activities usually regulated by individual conscience. EES.

Blue Lights. An opprobrious name for the Federalist party dating from 1814, when attempts of an American fleet to put to sea from the harbor of New London, Conn., were reported to have been thwarted by blue signal lights displayed at the mouth of the harbor to warn a British blockading squadron. s.

blue-sky laws. State laws designed to protect investors from buying securities of companies which have "capitalized the blue sky." Common provisions are that distributors must register securities with the appropriate State official, giving detailed information concerning the capitalization and assets of the issuing company, and obtain a certificate before offering them for sale. EES.

board. A plural body consisting of three or more persons which is charged with some specific public function, such as parole, elections, education or health or welfare administration. Its functions are generally supervisory where it is charged with specific administrative duties, such duties being delegated to experts under its jurisdiction. Where its formal functions are political or quasi-judicial in nature, the board itself performs them. GHD.

board of control. An ex officio board, common in State governments, and consisting of the governor, attorney general, and other members, whose consent is required in apportioning funds and settling accounts and claims against the State; now often superseded by a director of finance or controller. GHD.

Board of Economic Warfare. A board, consisting of the principal executive officers of the United States with the Vice President as chairman which was created July 30, 1941, to regulate the export of important defense materials or articles. Its functions were transferred to the Foreign Economic Administration Sept. 25, 1943. z.

Board of Estimate. A branch of the municipal government of New York City, consisting of the mayor, president of the council, the controller, and the five borough presidents, which must approve budgets and certain other matters before they may be voted upon by the council. JWF.

Board of Governors of the Federal Reserve System. A board of seven members which stipulates what reserves shall be maintained by federal reserve member banks against their deposits; controls the issuance and retirement of federal reserve notes by the 12 federal reserve banks; determines the federal reserve bank rediscount rate; examines the condition of reserve banks and member banks; and generally supervises the federal reserve banking system. The members of the board are appointed for 14-year terms. Each member also serves on the Open Market Committee (*q.v.*), which regulates the purchase and sale of United States Government and other obligations on the open market.   z.

Bolshevism. Lenin's program, accepted in 1903 by the left wing of the Russian Social Democratic party (later the Russian Communist party), which opposed as ineffective the use of established parliamentary methods, and advocated instead the inevitability of class war, the violent overthrow of capitalist political institutions, and the establishment of a dictatorship identified with the toiling masses.   JJR.

bolter. One who deserts his party and supports opposition candidates or proposals. Supposedly derived from the sudden running away of a horse, the word has been used in a political sense since about 1812.   s.

Bonanza State. A nickname of Montana.   s.

bond. 1. A pledge of money or assets of value offered as bail by an accused person or his surety to secure the former's temporary release from custody. Bond is forfeited if the conditions of bail are not fulfilled. 2. An evidence of indebtedness, of limited negotiability, issued to long-term creditors by governments or corporations. 3. A binding legal claim or covenant.   z.

bondage. 1. Indentured service or slavery. 2. Any form of political or civil servitude.   z.

bondsman. One who provides bond or surety for another to guarantee the subjection of the latter's person or property to a specific future judicial or administrative order.   JWF.

bonus. Any payment over and above regular compensation for services; a payment to war veterans in addition to that to which they were entitled during their period of service.   z.

boodle. Graft; money paid for the use of political influence or as a bribe. The term originated in New York City about 1886. s.

boom. A decided advance in public favor; extensive propaganda in favor of a candidate.   s.

boondoggling. A term of opprobrium used to describe some of the less useful or patently useless works projects upon which the national government sought to provide employment during the depression period of the 1930's; hence the expenditure of public funds on useless public works.   z.

bootlegging. Illicit traffic in liquors or in any proscribed or heavily taxed commodity, especially in retail distribution.   s.

border ruffian. A resident of Missouri who crossed into Kansas after the passage of the Kansas-Nebraska Bill in 1854 for the purpose of intimidating free-soil settlers and participating illegally in elections. s.

Border States. 1. The northern tier of slave States : Delaware, Maryland, Virginia, Kentucky, and Missouri, which were more inclined to compromise, and less disposed to insist on Southern rights than the States farther south. Of them, only Virginia seceded ; but the western part of the State, now West Virginia, remained loyal to the Union. 2. In recent political parlance, the same States, omitting Virginia, but including also West Virginia, Tennessee, and Oklahoma, which have sometimes given their electoral votes to Republican candidates. s.

Border War. The armed conflict in Kansas between proslavery and antislavery men following the opening of Kansas to settlement under the Kansas-Nebraska Act (*q.v.*), 1854. s.

boring from within. Opposition tactics carried out by hostile persons who have become formally allied with a group for the purpose of weakening its organization and program. JJR.

borough. 1. In England and in certain States of the United States, an incorporated self-governing town or village. 2. One of the five subdivisions of the municipal government of New York City since 1898. JWF.

borrowing power. The authority of a government to borrow money or to sell or compel the purchase of its long- or short-term securities based upon the public credit. In the United States this power resides in Congress without limitation and in State legislatures subject to such limitations as the State constitutions impose. The borrowing power is normally employed to finance capital outlays or emergency expenditures such as those incurred during a war. AJW,Jr.

boss. The autocratic and usually irresponsible leader of a political machine in a State, county, or city whose power rests upon devious or corrupt methods of controlling the electorate and the processes of nomination and election. Because the officers of all branches of the government owe their positions to him he can dictate appointments by executive officers, votes in the passage of legislation, judicial decisions from the bench, and a great variety of acts and determinations on the part of administrative and law-enforcement agencies. s.

Boston Massacre. A street encounter in Boston, Mass., Mar. 5, 1775, in which, under serious provocation, British soldiers killed five citizens and wounded six others. The troops were afterward removed to a fort in the harbor. s.

Boston Police Strike. A strike of the Boston police in September, 1919, as part of a union organization campaign. Governor

Calvin Coolidge's statement, "There is no right to strike against the government any time, anywhere, any place," made him a presidential prospect.   JMCC.

Boston Tea Party. The dumping of 342 chests of tea into Boston harbor, Dec. 16, 1773, by a crowd of citizens disguised as Mohawk Indians, who were determined to prevent the breaking of a colonial nonimportation agreement.   S.

boundary. The territorial limit of a state or of its political subdivisions. It may be fixed artificially in terms of latitude or longitude or consist of some natural barrier such as a mountain, river, or sea, the latter type being favored for purposes of national defense. Existing political boundaries often violate economic, cultural, or ethnic considerations.   Z.

bounty. A premium offered by public authority for the performance of some service useful to the community, such as the production of certain articles, or, formerly, enlistment in the armed forces.   S.

bounty jumper. A soldier who deserted after accepting a bounty for enlisting.   S.

Bourbon. A reactionary Democrat, corresponding to a stand-pat Republican; so called because of his supposed resemblance to the later members of a European royal family who could "learn nothing and forget nothing."   S.

bourgeoisie. Originally the merchants and artisans or town dwellers of mediaeval Europe who, as a social class, fell between the gentry and the peasantry. Marxian literature identifies the bourgeoisie as the owning or profit-making class and distinguishes them from the wage-earners or proletariat. Median social groups are now usually identified by terms more descriptive of their economic function.   JMCC.

Boxer Indemnity. A compensation paid by China to several foreign powers for loss of life, damage to property, and the cost of armed intervention during an uprising of Boxers, an antiforeign, anti-Christian secret society who, in the summer of 1900 seized the city of Peking, besieged the foreign legations, and killed many foreigners. The American share of the indemnity was $24,000,000. The United States later returned $13,000,000 to China, which devoted the refund to fellowships for Chinese students in American colleges.   S.

boycott. A concerted agreement to refuse to have any dealings with a nation, corporation, or employer with the object of bringing pressure to bear. If third parties are coerced into joining, the boycott is usually considered illegal.   S.

Boy Orator. A nickname of William Jennings Bryan, who was nominated for the presidency at the age of 36.   S.

brain trust. A name first used by a New York reporter to describe the small group of professors and other experts who assisted Franklin D. Roosevelt in the campaign of 1932 and who were reported to have had much influence on his early policies as President; since used, often in a derogatory sense, to identify any body of experts in the public service. z.

brave. A member of Tammany Hall. s.

breach of privilege. The use of force against, or of words reflecting upon the integrity of, a legislative body or any of its members. z.

breach of the peace. Disturbance of public order and tranquillity by an act of violence, or by an act inciting to violence. JJR.

break. The point in the proceedings of a nominating convention when, after a deadlock, the switching of a block of votes causes a pronounced trend in favor of the candidate who is eventually nominated. s.

bribe. The attempt to gain some illegal advantage by corrupting or attempting to corrupt a voter or official with an offer or bestowal of money or favors. AJW,Jr.

Broad Seal War. A dispute over the election of six congressmen at large from New Jersey, 1838-39. The Democratic candidates had pluralities on the face of the returns, but the State board of canvassers issued certificates of election under the broad seal of the State to Whigs. After some delay in organizing an almost equally divided House of Representatives, the Democratic contestants were seated. s.

Brother Jonathan. A jocular name for the United States derived supposedly from Washington's habit of saying, "We must consult Brother Jonathan" (Governor Jonathan Trumbull of Connecticut), when he needed supplies for the Revolutionary army. s.

brown derby. A personal symbol of Alfred E. Smith, Democratic candidate for President in 1928. s.

Buckeye State. A nickname of Ohio. s.

Bucklin plan. A scheme of preferential voting invented by James W. Bucklin and first used at Grand Junction, Colo., in 1909, by which a voter expresses first, second, and third choices among candidates. A candidate with a majority of first choices is declared elected. If no one has a majority, the first and second choices are added together, and so on. s.

Buckshot War. A riot in Harrisburg, Pa., in 1838 caused by an attempt by the Antimasonic party led by Thaddeus Stevens to organize the legislature without admitting Democratic members from Philadelphia. The governor ordered the militia to load with buckshot, and the Democratic members were seated. s.

Bucktails. A faction of the Democratic party in New York, 1816-26, opposed to the Clintonians; so called because a buck's tail worn on the hat was an emblem of the Tammany Society. s.

budget. A balanced estimate of expenditures and receipts for the coming fiscal year or other period made for the purpose of planning and effectuating an orderly financial policy. (An "unbalanced budget" is an estimate in which during peacetime the ordinary expenditures far exceed estimated revenues, thus necessitating recourse to heavy borrowing for current expenses.) Under the Budget and Accounting Act of 1921 the Director of the Budget gathers from the departments and other spending agencies itemized estimates of their needs which he must assemble and correlate, and may revise, reduce, or increase. This material, together with statements of the condition of the treasury, the amount of the national debt, and the expected revenue is given to the President, who may make further alterations before presenting it to Congress in his annual budget message. If estimated expenditures exceed estimated revenues the President must recommend new or increased taxes or loans. Congress may reduce, revise, or increase items at its discretion (*see* Appropriation). In the States budgets are variously prepared under the direction of the governor, a board of administrative officers, or a commission including leaders of the legislature. A few States forbid the increase or addition of items by the legislature unless accompanied by specific proposals to raise the necessary revenue. The British budget is prepared by the Chancellor of the Exchequer. Parliament by its own rules may only reduce or eliminate items.   s.

buffer state. Any small state occupying a territory which neighboring great powers may covet for strategic or other reasons, but which none dares to annex because of mutual rivalry or distrust; also any small state which separates great powers whose boundaries would otherwise be contiguous, and which thereby reduces the possibility of diplomatic friction between the great powers and provides a potential military barrier.   z.

building code. The regulations governing the construction of all buildings within a given municipality.   JWF.

building line. The margin upon a piece of private property beyond which municipal building regulations or the terms of a deed or contract prohibit the owner from building.   JWF.

building permit. Permission granted by a municipal government to build a structure of approved design upon a specified site within the city limits.   JWF.

bulldoze. To coerce by threats or violence. In a political sense the word is said to have originated in Louisiana about 1875 to describe the process by which colored voters were excluded from the polls.   s.

bullionist. An advocate of a metallic currency.   z.

Bull Moose. An emblem of the Progressive party in 1912. It is said to have been derived from a statement by Theodore Roosevelt that he felt "like a bull moose."   s.

buncombe. Speechmaking for the purpose of winning the approval of a constituency. The word originated from the statement of Felix Walker, representing the North Carolina district which included Buncombe County, that he wished "to make a speech for Buncombe" during the later stages of the debate on the Missouri Compromise, 1820, when other members of the House of Representatives were impatiently calling for the question.   s.

Bund. The German word for confederation or federation, used in America to designate a disloyal group of German Nazi aliens and sympathizers during World War II.   z.

Burchard incident. A statement that the Democrats were the party of "rum, Romanism, and rebellion," which was made by the Rev. S. D. Burchard at a New York political meeting in 1884 and which Blaine, who was present, did not deny. By alienating Catholic voters, the remark is supposed to have cost Blaine the election. s.

bureau. The basic unit of the hierarchical administrative structure of the French state; part of the title of a functional unit of subordinate grade in the American national administrative system.   z.

bureaucracy. The highly centralized, autonomous, and quasi-military type of administrative system developed in France after the First Napoleon, the principal units of which were called bureaus; hence a government dominated by permanent administrative agencies and inclined to be unresponsive to the political authorities of the government and to public opinion. Bureaucracies tend to reduce administration to the application of a set of rigid rules and formulas and to insist on a slavish devotion to routine, with the effect of exasperating the people and delaying public business. They are inclined to be satisfied with existing methods and are not disposed to experiment with new ones.   s.

Bureau of Aeronautics. A bureau of the Department of the Navy charged with the design and construction of naval aircraft and the upkeep of aeronautic shore installations.   z.

Bureau of Agricultural Economics. A bureau of the Department of Agriculture created in 1922 to co-ordinate the department's research and planning activities in relation to land use and the production and distribution of farm products.   z.

Bureau of Foreign and Domestic Commerce. One of the principal divisions of the Department of Commerce which, through its publications and its field service, supplies current information on conditions affecting domestic production and markets and on the conditions which control the export and sale of American products abroad.   z.

Bureau of Labor Statistics. One of the older units of the Department of Labor responsible for the collection and publication of statistics relating to wages, hours of employment, and other conditions affecting labor as a class.   z.

Bureau of Marine Inspection and Navigation. A bureau of the Department of Commerce charged with the administration of laws relating to the construction, equipment, inspection, and registration of merchant vessels. It licenses ship personnel, promotes maritime safety measures, collects tonnage and similar dues, and regulates the employment of crews.   z.

Bureau of Mines. A unit of the Department of the Interior whose chief activities are to eliminate health hazards and promote safety in mines and provide statistical information on domestic and foreign mineral production and consumption.   z.

Bureau of Pensions. Formerly a unit of the Department of the Interior in charge of pensions for veterans — merged since 1930 with the Veterans Administration (*q.v.*)   z.

Bureau of the Budget. An agency placed nominally in the Department of the Treasury when it was created in 1921, but since 1939 a part of the Executive Office of the President. The Director of the Budget prepares the budget (*q.v.*) under the immediate supervision of the President.   z.

Burlingame Treaty. A treaty negotiated by Anson Burlingame, an American citizen acting as minister plenipotentiary for China, and concluded at Washington, July 28, 1868. The United States and China reciprocally guaranteed to citizens of each other liberty of conscience and worship and rights of residence and travel, as accorded to the most favored nation.   s.

Burr Conspiracy. A scheme to detach Louisiana from the Union, or to seize and colonize Texas, hatched by Aaron Burr, former Vice President of the United States, and communicated to many persons in the course of his Western travels in 1806. Burr was indicted for treason but acquitted for want of proof.   s.

business affected with a public interest. A virtually abandoned concept of American constitutional law in accordance with which the government may fix the prices charged by certain businesses for commodities or services and subject them to regulations which if imposed upon ordinary business would be deemed inconsistent with due process of law. The businesses thus set apart have never been fully defined; but they are supposed to be monopolistic in character or traditionally regulated callings like that of innkeeper. Public utilities constitute the bulk of the class.   JRP.

butternut. A backwoodsman who wore clothing dyed with butternut bark; later a Confederate soldier, or a resident of the Middle West who sympathized with the Confederacy.   s.

by-election. A special election held in Great Britain to fill a vacancy in the House of Commons occurring within the life of a Parliament. The term is also used occasionally in the United States and elsewhere to denote a special election of a representative to fill an unexpired term.   z.

by-law. A regulation adopted by a corporation for the government of its own internal affairs. It must be in accord with the terms, strictly interpreted, of the national and State constitutions and statutes, and of the corporation's charter. JWF.

C

C.A.A. *See* Civil Aeronautics Administration.

C.A.B. *See* Civil Aeronautics Board.

cabinet. An executive council, particularly one which has grown up without specific constitutional or legal authorization. President Washington summoned the heads of the three departments, the Vice President, and the Attorney General to meet with him, and the cabinet has since existed. By custom it is composed of the heads of the ten executive departments, who are often named as such because the President wants their advice in the cabinet, or because they represent important geographical sections or economic groups; but the President may invite others. Cabinet meetings are held once a week or oftener. The sessions are secret and informal. No minutes are kept, and only rarely is a vote taken; for a vote could not bind a President, who must take personal responsibility for every decision. The English cabinet, a much older body, consists of the heads of the principal administrative departments, with perhaps a few ministers without portfolio, which under the leadership of a prime minister, directs the administration and exercises political leadership in legislation. s.

Cable Act. A law of Congress Sept. 22, 1922, which, as amended, provides that an alien woman shall no longer automatically acquire American citizenship by marriage with an American citizen, but may acquire it within a minimum period of one year through naturalization. Conversely it provides that an American woman marrying an alien retains her citizenship unless she formally renounces it. JWF.

calamity howler. One who predicts that certain governmental policies will lead to disaster; a Populist. s.

calendar. 1. A list of cases pending in a court of justice. 2. A list of bills, resolutions, or other items, in the order of their presentation for action by a legislative house as a whole, which usually serves as a convenient order of business. The Union and House calendars of the House of Representatives, however, are merely records of the order in which financial and other public measures are reported from committee, and give no clue as to the order in which they will be considered. s.

Calendar of Bills and Resolutions. A calendar of the Senate called at the end of morning business on each day. It contains such items as unfinished business, special orders, notices of motions, reported bills and joint resolutions, subjects on the table, and resolutions carried over.   s.

Calendar Wednesday. Wednesday of each week in the House of Representatives when committees, as they are called in turn, may bring up unprivileged bills from the House or Union calendars; but no committee may ordinarily occupy more than one Wednesday until all have been called. The rule was adopted to obtain a hearing for public nonfinancial bills which could not be passed under unanimous consent, suspension of the rules, or special orders. Calendar Wednesday may be suspended only by a two-thirds vote, or during the last two weeks of a session.   s.

California. The 31st State, admitted to the Union Sept. 9, 1850, without having passed through the territorial stage, from part of the Mexican cession of 1848. Capital, Sacramento; area, 158,693 sq. mi; population (1940), 6,907,387; presidential electors, 25. The present constitution was adopted in 1879 and, as amended, provides for the constitutional and statutory initiative, the referendum, the recall, a literacy test for the suffrage, and a legislative split session.   s.

call. A document issued by a national party committee in December or January preceding a presidential election which fixes the date and place of the convention, the number of delegates to which each State is entitled, the method of choice, and the procedure in case of contesting delegations.   s.

call of the House. A roll call of members of the House of Representatives in alphabetical order.   s.

call of the States. A roll call of the States in alphabetical order in a national nominating convention for the purpose of making nominations or voting.   s.

Calvo Doctrine. The principle advanced in 1887 by Carlos Calvo, Argentinian publicist, that a state should never resort to armed or diplomatic intervention to enforce pecuniary claims of its citizens sustained as a result of mob violence, insurrection, or civil war, in another state. *Compare with* Drago Doctrine.   z.

camp. An area with suitable accommodations for sheltering and training troops.   z.

campaign. The contest of rival nominees for a particular office and of their respective political organizations to win the support of voters at the polls. The methods used are limited only by the law and the ingenuity and financial resources of the contestants and their supporters; but much reliance is placed upon platform and radio speeches, printed appeals for support sent through the mails, the distribution of posters, placards, buttons, and similar materials, parades and other spectacles, and personal solicitation from door to door.   z.

campaign fund. The total monetary resources at the disposal of a candidate or party committee to be used to win a nomination or an election. National party funds, despite strenuous efforts to obtain many small contributions from the rank and file, have mostly been made up of large contributions. For State and municipal elections much money is raised by assessments upon officeholders and candidates. Funds are used to maintain headquarters and to pay for radio broadcasting time, newspaper advertising, billboard space, posters, handbills, lithographs, pamphlets, special trains, rental of halls, and expenses of precinct workers. Expenditures of national committees tend to be concentrated in a few large doubtful States. Attempts have been made to regulate the amounts, sources of income, and objects of expenditure of campaign funds by corrupt practices acts (*q.v.*) passed by Congress and the States.   s.

campaign textbook. A pocket-sized volume issued by each party in a presidential campaign for the use of party speakers, editors, and workers. It contains the party platform, biographies of candidates, and other pertinent information.   s.

Canal ring. A corrupt collusion of politicians and contractors for repairs of the Erie Canal which was exposed by Governor Samuel J. Tilden of New York in 1875.   s.

Canal Zone. A tract of land extending five miles on either side of the Panama Canal over which the United States acquired jurisdiction by the Hay-Bunau-Varilla Treaty with the Republic of Panama signed Nov. 18, 1903. The government of the Zone is under the control of the President through a governor and other officials appointed by him.   s.

Canal Zone

candidate. A person who seeks public office through the established procedures of nomination and election.   EES.

Cannonism. Undue control over the process of legislation by the Speaker of the House of Representatives, especially by Joseph G. Cannon, who was Speaker 1903-11.   s.

canon law. The law of the Roman Catholic Church. It is made up in part of rulings and interpretations of ecclesiastical jurists and courts but consists chiefly of legislation of popes and church councils.   JRP.

Canton Island. One of the Phoenix group in the mid-Pacific, jointly administered by the United States and Great Britain since

April, 1939. It is valuable as an air transit and communications post.										z.

canvass.	1. Solicitation for votes and political support.	2. Re-examination of election returns.						s.

canvassing boards.	State, county, or municipal boards, often ex officio, which review the work of precinct election officials, determine the validity of the votes cast, and certify the official returns.										s.

capital.	1. Wealth saved from income which is being, or may be, utilized in the production of goods and services.	2. The city in which the seat of government is located.			JWF.

capital gains tax.	A national tax levied upon gains from the sale or exchange of capital assets not ordinarily involved in the owner's business or profession. It is normally administered as part of the general income tax.						z.

capitalism.	An economic system in which the ownership and management of productive wealth is vested in private enterprisers who hire labor and compete with one another in providing goods and services for profit.						s.

Capitol.	The building occupied by the United States Congress or by the offices of an American State government.			z.

capitulation.	1. Surrender by a belligerent force or nation, or the agreement containing the terms of such surrender.	2. A convention or treaty in which nations of the Near East have in the past granted rights of a sovereign character to Occidental powers.	z.

captive.	A prisoner or prize of war.					z.

captive mine.	A mine which produces for consumption by the producer, or by a subsidiary or affiliate thereof.		ME.

career service.	Government employment which provides opportunity for a career. The minimum requirements for such a service are: employment based on tested fitness; promotion according to merit; the possibility of advancing to the highest ranks in the service; and tenure secure against dismissal for reasons unrelated to performance.						JRP.

Carey Act.	An act of Congress Aug. 18, 1894, granting desert land to States for irrigation and sale to farmers.		s.

Caroline, The.	An American steamer fitted out to aid Canadian insurgents in 1837 which was destroyed in American territory by Canadian authorities, with the result that war was threatened between the United States and Great Britain.			s.

carpetbagger.	1. A speculative or "wildcat" banker in the West before the Civil War whose worldly possessions were supposed to be carried in a carpetbag.	2. A Northern adventurer who migrated to the South after the Civil War to obtain office or employment by morally questionable and often corrupt methods. JAP.

cartel. 1. A relatively loose association of businessmen in similar industries in the same or different countries who agree to control the amount and method of production and sale of their product or services. Found chiefly in Europe, it is becoming Americanized in the form of a trade association. 2. An agreement between belligerents for such purposes as the exchange of prisoners, the treatment of the wounded, the use of flags of truce, and methods of communication. JMCC.

case. Any suit, action, or other proceeding in law or equity contested before a court of justice. JJR.

cash and carry. A policy of the United States, 1939-41, which required foreign belligerents when purchasing supplies within the United States to pay cash for them on delivery and transport them abroad in non-American bottoms. JWF.

casting vote. The vote of a presiding officer to break a tie or, if there is a difference of only one vote on a motion, to create a tie and thus cause the motion to be lost. The Vice President and lieutenant governors may vote only in case of equal division. The Speaker of the House, whose name appears last on the roll, is required to give a casting vote when the number of yeas and nays is equal or differs by only one. S.

casus belli. An incident or series of incidents provocative of war or used by one state as an excuse to make war on another. JWF.

caucus. 1. A secret meeting of party leaders to agree upon candidates or to arrange compromises. 2. Another name for the primary or mass convention of voters in townships or wards, used especially in Western States. 3. A closed meeting of all the members of one or both legislative houses who belong to the same political party for the purpose of making nominations to offices and committee posts, choosing party leaders, and agreeing on concerted action on pending legislation. The decision of the Democratic house caucus, if made by a two-thirds vote, is binding on all members of the party unless they are excused because of previous pledges, instructions of constituents, or conscientious scruples concerning an interpretation of the Constitution. The congressional caucus, composed of party members from both houses, nominated candidates for President and Vice President from 1800 to 1824, when the practice broke down because of objections from most of the candidates and popular fear of congressional domination of the executive. S.

caveat. Literally, "Let him beware." A notice directed to a public officer requiring him to delay a contemplated action until the party filing the notice has had an opportunity to express formal opposition to the action. Z.

C.C.C. *See* Civilian Conservation Corps, or Commodity Credit Corporation.

cease-and-desist order. An order issued by an administrative agency to an individual, firm, or corporation requiring that a particular fiscal or business practice be discontinued. It is commonly used by agencies charged with the regulation of business; *e.g.,* the Federal Trade Commission or a State public service, or railway, commission.   JRP.

censors, council of. A board provided for in the first constitutions of Pennsylvania and Vermont to report on the conduct of government and propose constitutional amendments.   S.

censorship. Examination by a public authority of any printed matter, telephonic or telegraphic dispatch, wireless dispatch or broadcast, or dramatic or similar spectacle, prior to publication or transmission, with a view to making such deletions or revisions as the preservation of military secrets, public morality, the interests of religion, or some other consideration may require. Except in time of war or national emergency, authorities in English-speaking states rarely exert a censorship over printed matter or over instrumentalities for transmitting intelligence. In this respect they differ sharply from the authorities of most modern states and particularly from contemporary authoritarian governments under which censorship is constant and universal. Liberals have always regarded the absence of public censorship as a basic condition for the exercise of the twin rights of freedom of speech and the press.   z.

censure. A formal resolution of a legislative body expressing dissatisfaction with a public official, or disapproval of one or more of his actions.   JWF.

census. An official count of the population instituted primarily to establish a basis for the periodical apportionment of representatives and direct taxes among the States, and within the States to reapportion the representatives in the legislature. The national census, which has been taken decennially since 1790, has increasingly listed a great variety of social and economic data; and several special censuses are taken at intervals ranging from two to ten years. The census office, formerly set up *ad hoc* and then disbanded, has developed into a bureau of the Department of Commerce engaged continuously in collecting and compiling statistical information.   S.

Centennial State. A nickname of Colorado, which was admitted in 1876.   S.

center. The position usually assigned in the seating arrangements of Continental European legislative bodies to deputies belonging to moderate parties.   S.

center of population. That point in any geographical area through which a straight line drawn in any direction from boundary to boundary would leave approximately equal numbers of people on each side. The center of population of the United States

in its westward movement during the past 150 years has followed
closely the 39th parallel.   JMCC.

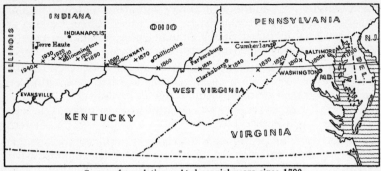

Center of population— At decennial years since 1790

centralization. The shifting of political authority from local
governmental bodies to or toward the central government; also the
transfer of authority from the legislature to the executive.   JRP.

centralized purchasing. Procurement of supplies, material,
and equipment by a central purchasing agency, an increasingly
common procedure in State and municipal governments. It is designed to eliminate waste and duplication, to secure the advantages
of large-scale purchasing, and to provide more effective control
over the spending departments of the government.   GHD.

certificate. 1. A document which formally establishes the existence of a fact or set of facts. 2. A record of proceedings filed
by one court with another.   Z.

certificate of election. An official certificate issued by a governor, a board of elections, or other competent authority that the
person or persons named therein have been duly elected.   Z.

certificate of public convenience and necessity. A license issued by the public service commission of a state permitting an individual or corporation to engage in a particular kind of business.
Statutes withholding the right to do business without such a certificate first applied to common carriers, but now apply to many
businesses. The purpose of such certificates is to prevent duplication of plants and services, when such duplication is not in the
public interest.   JJR.

certification of eligibles. The act by which a civil service
commission or equivalent agency supplies names of qualified applicants for a position to the appointing authority which has final
power to make a choice. Three names are usually certified for each
vacancy.   GHD.

certiorari. A writ issued at the discretion of a higher court
calling upon a lower court or an administrative agency to hand over
the record of a stated case for review.   JRP.

cession. The act of transferring territory from the sovereignty of one state to that of another; also the territory thus transferred. z.

chain banking. A number of banks operating under the same management, but in different geographical areas. Chain banking is prohibited in the United States although branch banking may be permissible when confined to metropolitan areas. JMCC.

chain-store tax. A steeply graduated tax levied by 28 States upon stores in excess of a specified number when operated under single management or under some common agreement. When the original tax on gross receipts was declared unconstitutional the tax was exacted as a license fee. JMCC.

chairman. 1. The presiding officer and recognized spokesman of a group such as a legislative committee or an administrative commission. 2. The presiding officer of a party convention. EES.

challenge. 1. An allegation that a vote or decision is invalid or that a voter at the polls is not legally qualified to cast his ballot. 2. An objection entered against the service of a prospective juror. z.

chamber. A division of a legislative assembly; frequently in Romance states, part of the title of the first or lower house of the national parliament. z.

chancellor. In a few States, a judge who presides over courts of equity. JWF.

chancery, court of. A court having jurisdiction in equity cases. s.

Charcoals. A Unionist faction in Missouri, 1863-65, who wished to abolish slavery in the State; opposed by the Claybanks (*q.v.*) s.

charge. A statement of the law governing a case and other instructions given by a judge to the jury at the conclusion of a trial. z.

chargé d'affaires. The head of a diplomatic mission, inferior in rank to an ambassador or minister, and usually accredited to the department for foreign affairs rather than to the head of a state; sometimes placed temporarily in charge of an embassy or legation. z.

charter. A formal document issued by authority of a government granting rights and privileges to act in a corporate capacity and imposing conditions and obligations. The charter of a corporation, whether public or private, is to be strictly construed; that is, no privileges may be assumed to exist without specific grant of power. The charter is the basic law of a municipal corporation which describes its governmental apparatus and defines its powers and responsibilities. z.

charter colony. A colony governed under the terms of a charter granted by the Crown and usually exempt from all but incidental control by royal officials. s.

Charter-of-Democracy Speech. An address by Theodore Roosevelt at Columbus, Ohio, Feb. 11, 1912, in which he stated his personal platform for the coming presidential campaign.   s.

Chartism. A mid-nineteenth century English laboring-class political movement. The name is derived from the movement's manifesto, "The People's Charter" (1838), which demanded manhood suffrage, annual parliaments, vote by ballot, abolition of property qualifications for membership in the House of Commons, payment of members of the House, and equal electoral districts.   JRP.

chauvinism. Uncritical admiration of the First Napoleon and his exploits; hence excessive and bellicose patriotism.   z.

checkoff. The collection of union dues through the employer, who deducts them from wages due to members of the union.   JMCC.

checks and balances. A system of "so contriving the interior structure of the government as that its several constituent parts may, by their mutual relations, be the means of keeping each other in their proper places" (*The Federalist,* No. 51). While recognizing the principle of separation of powers (*q.v.*) among the legislative, executive, and judicial departments, this system seeks to protect each of them against the others, and the people against all, by requiring the approval by one department of certain acts of another. The term is also used to describe certain aspects of the relations between the States and the national government, and the requirement of concurrent action by both houses of a legislature.   s.

cheeseparing. Niggardliness in making appropriations.   s.

chemical warfare. The application of the products of chemical science to combat tactics in warfare, particularly the military use of toxic or lethal gases and incendiary materials.   z.

Cherokee cases. Two cases which arose over efforts of the State

Boundaries of the Cherokee Nation in 1831

of Georgia to gain jurisdiction over lands held by the Cherokee Indians under treaties with the United States. In *Cherokee Nation* v. *Georgia,* 5 Pet. 1 (1831), the Supreme Court held that it had no jurisdiction to hear a case brought against a State by an Indian tribe because it was a "domestic dependent nation." In *Worcester* v. *Georgia,* 6 Pet. 515 (1832), it was held that the Cherokee nation was a distinct community over which Georgia could not exercise jurisdiction except with the assent of the tribe or under the terms of a treaty between the United States and the tribe.   s.

Cherokee Outlet. A rectangular tract of land, 50 by 25 miles, in the southeastern corner of Kansas which was purchased by the United States from the Cherokee Indians in 1866; also a large tract in northern Oklahoma purchased from the same tribe in 1893. *See* map, page 161.   s.

Cherokee Strip. A narrow belt within the southern Kansas border ceded by the Cherokees to the United States in 1872. *See* map, page 161.   s.

Chicago Sanitary District. An administrative area comprising part of Chicago and its environs, established by Illinois in 1890 to dispose of sewage without contaminating the city's Lake Michigan water supply. All sewage within the area is dumped into the South Branch of the Chicago River, the flow of which is diverted through canals into the Mississippi watershed by way of the Desplaines River.   JWF.

chief justice. The official head of a collegially organized court of justice. The Chief Justice of the Supreme Court of the United States presides over the hearing of cases and over meetings of justices for the purpose of reaching decisions; assigns the writing of opinions to different justices, himself taking his turn; appoints members of the court to consider revisions of the rules of procedure; and performs other administrative duties. He presides over the Senate when the President or Vice President is impeached. His salary is now $20,500, only $500 more than the salary of an associate justice. The following named jurists have held the office: John Jay, 1789-95; John Rutledge, 1795-96; Oliver Ellsworth, 1796-1800; John Marshall, 1801-35; Roger B. Taney, 1835-64; Salmon P. Chase, 1864-73; Morrison R. Waite, 1874-88; Melville W. Fuller, 1888-1910; Edward D. White, 1910-21; William Howard Taft, 1921-30; Charles E. Hughes, 1930-41; and Harlan F. Stone, since 1941.   s.

child labor. The employment of children below a legal or traditional age for wages by persons other than their parents. The legal working age in the United States, as determined by the national government for interstate commerce, is 16 years, or 18 in hazardous occupations.   JMCC.

Child Labor Amendment. An amendment to the Constitution which Congress referred to the State legislatures in 1924. It authorized Congress to limit, regulate, or prohibit the labor of persons under 18 years of age. Though not yet ratified by the necessary three fourths of the States, the Supreme Court in 1939 held that the proposed amendment was still before the States. However, the need for it, except in certain types of intrastate industries, has largely disappeared because of the passage of the Fair Labor Standards Act, 1938.   JMCC.

Children's Bureau. A unit of the Department of Labor which investigates child life and welfare and has charge of the enforcement of national legislation relating to child and maternal welfare and child labor. z.

Chinese exclusion. Denial of permission to all but a few excepted classes of Chinese nationals, such as merchants, students, and travellers, to enter the United States, which first began with the Act of Congress of May 6, 1882, annulling provisions of the Burlingame Treaty (*q.v.*) s.

chosen freeholder. A member of a county board in New Jersey. s.

Cincinnati, Society of the. An association of officers of the American Revolutionary army, formed at the close of the war and intended to be hereditary, which exerted a great influence in securing the adoption of the Constitution. s.

Cincinnatus of the West. A nickname of William Henry Harrison. s.

circuit court. 1. A State court whose jurisdiction may extend over several counties, in each of which sessions are regularly held. It is usually the lowest court of record. 2. A federal court created in 1789 with original jurisdiction over cases involving diversity of citizenship and a limited appellate jurisdiction. The latter was transferred to the Circuit Court of Appeals (*q.v.*) in 1891, and in 1911 the Circuit Court was abolished. JJR.

Circuit Court of Appeals. An appellate court created in 1891 and sitting in each of ten circuits and the District of Columbia. Each court consists of from two to six judges, two of whom con-

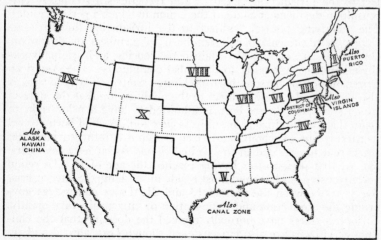

Circuit Court of Appeals — Circuits

stitute a quorum. Its jurisdiction is confined to cases appealed from the district courts and to the review and enforcement of the deter-

minations of the Interstate Commerce Commission, the Federal
Trade Commission, and some other administrative bodies. Its decisions are final in diversity of citizenship cases and in those arising
under the revenue, criminal, patent, copyright, bankruptcy, and admiralty laws (except prize cases) where the amount involved does
not exceed $1,000. But any case may be appealed from its decision
whenever it declares a State law invalid because in conflict with the
national Constitution, laws, or treaties; and the Supreme Court, on
petition of either party, may at any time order a case transferred
to its own docket.   s.

citizen.   A member in full standing of a political community.
As a citizen, a person owes the state allegiance, that is, the obligation of fidelity, the duty of compulsory military service, and the
faithful performance of such other duties as the state imposes upon
its members. Within his own state a citizen normally secures no
greater protection from the laws than is accorded to noncitizens;
but the citizen alone usually enjoys whatever privileges of popular
participation in government may be accorded by the constitution
and laws of the state, and laws extending economic privileges and
regulating professional status may discriminate in his favor. Under
international law the state is regarded as responsible for safeguarding the rights of such of its citizens as may travel or reside abroad.
In the United States national citizenship was regarded as incidental
to citizenship in one of the States until the adoption of the 14th
Amendment. This Amendment confers national citizenship directly
upon all persons born or naturalized in the United States and "subject to the jurisdiction thereof"; and recognizes a secondary citizenship in the member State of the Union in which a person resides.
The qualifying phrase, "subject to the jurisdiction thereof," ex-
cludes from citizenship children born to members of diplomatic
entourages and natives of certain dependencies, and originally excluded Indians belonging to the tribal community. The American
citizenship of all persons born of United States citizens abroad is
also recognized by law, subject to the qualification that the state in
which such persons are born is admitted to have a prior right to
claim them as its citizens or subjects *jure soli.* A child born abroad
to parents one of whom is a citizen is also a citizen provided that
the parent has resided in the United States for at least ten years,
half of that period after having reached the age of 16. To retain
his citizenship, such a child must reside in the United States at least
five years between the ages of 13 and 21. Laws and usages governing the acquisition and renunciation of citizenship vary greatly.
European states have normally applied the doctrine that the children of citizens are also citizens even though born abroad and remaining outside the immediate jurisdiction of the state which thus
claimed them, and they have until recently been loath to recognize
any personal right of expatriation. *See* Naturalization.   z.

citizens' military training camps. Voluntary organizations for military training established in the United States during World War I and continued subsequently. Supported in part by private funds and in part by the States and the national government, the camps provide rudimentary training for reservists and volunteers under the supervision of national guard and army reserve officers.   EES.

citizens' tickets. Independent nonpartisan nominations, generally for local or municipal offices.   S.

Citizens' Union. A good-government association founded as a political party in New York City in 1897, but which since 1905 has made recommendations to voters concerning the records of candidates nominated by political parties.   Z.

city. A densely populated urban center; in some States the highest grade of municipal corporation.   Z.

city court. A court which tries persons accused of violating municipal ordinances and has jurisdiction over minor civil or criminal cases, or both.   Z.

city manager. An official employed, usually for an indefinite term, by a commission or by a mayor and council to be in charge of the enforcement of ordinances and the construction, maintenance, and administration of all municipal works and services. *See* Commission-manager plan.   S.

city planning. The policy of providing for the orderly future development of a city, of which early examples are afforded by the original plans for Philadelphia and Washington, D.C., but which was not generally applied in America until 1900. City planning at first emphasized the physical aspects of urban development but in recent years has given increasing recognition to the interrelationship of economic, social, political, and physical factors. In only a few cities, such as New York, has the planning agency been assimilated into the actual structure of urban government; and the difficult problem of correlating planning and administration has still to be solved. The growing importance of metropolitan regions has greatly widened the scope of municipal planning.   AJW,Jr.

civic center. An area within a city or town in which all of the principal public buildings are located.   JWF.

Civil Aeronautics Administration. A division of the Department of Commerce which may designate airways, encourage the creation or improvement of airways, airfields, and aids to air navigation or itself establish such facilities, inspect and register aircraft, examine airmen, recommend air safety regulations, and supervise civilian pilot training. Its chief officer is the Administrator of Civilian Aeronautics.   Z.

Civil Aeronautics Board. A board in the Department of Commerce consisting of five members appointed for six years. Under the Civil Aeronautics Act of 1938 it prescribes safety standards for air commerce, regulates rates for air transportation, and issues certificates of convenience and necessity to domestic air carriers and permits to foreign air carriers. z.

civil case. A judicial proceeding to enforce a private right or to obtain compensation for its violation. It is to be distinguished from a criminal case. JJR.

civil code. A Roman-law code; also a systematic compilation of the laws of a State, including statutes and court decisions, in force at the time it is re-enacted. In some States the "civil code" is distinguished from the "political" and "criminal" codes. JJR.

civil disobedience. The collective application against the government of the techniques of passive resistance and non-co-operation. Civil disobedience has had its most extensive development in India under the leadership of Gandhi. Picketing, boycotting, refusal to pay taxes, and peaceable demonstrations are typical of the means used. JRP.

civilian. One who is not a member of the armed services. JWF.

Civilian Conservation Corps. A national agency created by Congress in 1937 and disbanded in 1942. It provided a work program for youths between 18 and 25 (later 17 and 23) years of age to restore and conserve the nation's natural resources. JMcC.

civil law. 1. The law of Rome, or law derived therefrom. 2. The law applicable to civil disputes. z.

civil liberty. 1. Liberty as defined by law; personal security and the peaceful enjoyment of property and other lawful rights which result from the existence of organized government, in contradistinction to the supposed liberty of a state of nature. 2. Personal and property rights guaranteed by constitutions and laws against infraction by governments or individuals. *See* Civil rights. JJR.

civil list. 1. A register of officeholders in the civil service. 2. In Great Britain and other monarchies, the public appropriations annually made, at an amount normally fixed at the beginning of a reign, for the personal and household expenses of the royal family. GHD.

civil office. An elective or appointive office in any branch of the government except the armed services. JWF.

civil rights. Those liberties possessed by the individual as a member of the state; more particularly, those liberties guaranteed to the individual in the state against encroachment by his government. In this latter sense, civil rights are found enumerated in the bills of rights of State and national constitutions and include both substantive rights, such as freedom of speech, press, assembly, or religion; and procedural rights, such as protection against unreasonable searches and seizures or against punishment without a fair trial. The most important of these rights is embodied in the clause which prohibits the government from depriving anyone of life, liberty, or property without due process of law. Twice found in the Constitution, this clause imposes a limitation upon the States as well as Congress. By its interpretation of the "due process" clauses, the Supreme Court of the United States largely determines the scope of civil rights in America. Recently interest in civil rights has been directed toward positive legislation by the government guaranteeing certain liberties to the individual against encroachment by other individuals or groups. Examples of this tendency are State civil rights acts in which individuals or groups are forbidden to discriminate against other individuals or groups because of their race, color, religion, or membership in labor unions. JTC.

Civil Rights cases. Five cases in which the Supreme Court in 1883 held void the Civil Rights Act of 1875 insofar as it forbade proprietors of public conveyances, hotels, restaurants, and places of amusement to refuse accommodations to a person on account of his race, color, or previous condition of servitude. The prohibitions of racial discrimination in the equal protection and due process clauses (*qq.v.*) of the 14th Amendment were thus confined to State action and were not extended to invasions of private rights by individuals. JJR.

civil service. Collectively the whole body of appointed officers and employees of the government not members of the military or naval services, who rank below the principal administrative and judicial officers; sometimes the term is restricted to those who acquire their positions by merit rather than by appointment for political reasons. The foundations of a modern civil service were laid in Prussia by 1700 and in several other European countries at the beginning of the 19th century. In America effective civil service reform began with the Pendleton Act, 1883, which established a bipartisan Civil Service Commission of three members and provided for a rudimentary system of selecting civil servants by examination. Subsequent legislation and executive orders have extended the merit system of selection to an ever-increasing number of the nation's public servants, improved recruitment facilities, broadened the scope and type of examinations, established salary and service classifications, instituted efficiency ratings for promotion, and provided retirement allowances. Progress in this direction in some of the States has been equally rapid; in others it has been disappointingly slow. No country concedes the right of public servants to strike against the government; but all permit professional associations, and in the United States such associations may affiliate with labor unions. Numerous laws, of which the latest are the Hatch acts (*q.v.*), protect civil servants against political exploitation and define the degree of political neutrality which they must observe. AJW,Jr.

civil war. An armed conflict within a state arising from two or more factions fighting for control of the government, or from a community within a state seeking by force of arms to gain its independence. As distinguished from insurgency or mere banditry, civil war demands that the competing forces possess the qualifications of belligerents; that is, that they maintain some form of government over the territory they control, and support organized armies in the field capable of holding out prospects of ultimate success.   JTC.

Civil War, American. The armed conflict, otherwise known as the War of the Rebellion and as the War for Southern Independence, between eleven seceded Southern States, calling themselves the Confederate States, and the remainder of the American Union. It began at Fort Sumter, S. C., Apr. 12, 1861, and ended with the surrender of Kirby Smith, May 26, 1865. Extensive operations were conducted on several land fronts and on the high seas; and more than 2,000 separate engagements were fought. The victory of the Union forces resolved the long-standing controversy between advocates of State sovereignty and of national supremacy in favor of the latter principle, and effectively ended Negro slavery.   JAP.

Civil Works Administration. A national agency created in November, 1933, and disbanded in March, 1934, which provided employment on public projects in co-operation with the States without reference to the relief status of the employees.   JMCC.

claim. To assert possession, as of territory; to assert a privilege, as under the patent, pension, or homestead laws; to demand as due. Contractual claims against the national government are decided by the Court of Claims (*q.v.*); some others in limited amounts may be settled by departments; but in many cases claimants must appeal to Congress to pass private bills in their behalf.   s.

class. Any division of society based upon individuals possessing common characteristics or having the same status, as determined by wealth, income, franchise, education, religion, culture, etc. CS-H.

classification. The establishment of categories of municipalities, taxpayers, or property to which certain legislation applies, unequally from category to category. The courts tend to uphold the classification as long as it is reasonable and the law applies equally to all persons or things within a category.   GHD.

classification of cities. The practice pursued by many State legislatures of grouping cities into three or more classes according to their populations, and providing general legislation or charters for each class.   Z.

classified service. That portion of the civil service to which entrance is gained by some form of examination, and which affords promotional opportunities and tenure free from ordinary political influence with removal only for cause. The Classification Act of 1923, as amended, organizes the service into five great classes — professional; subprofessional; clerical, administrative, and fiscal;

custodial; and clerical-mechanical (P, S-P, CAF, CU, CM) — and establishes grades and salaries within each class.   GHD.

classified tax. A system of taxation used in various States under which different rates are levied upon various types of property, and certain property is classified as exempt from taxation. It is occasionally used for other than property taxes.   z.

class struggle. The alleged hostility mutually displayed towards each other by economic groups in modern society and the efforts on the part of each group to aggrandize itself at the expense of another. The theory plays an important role in Marxian and allied doctrines in which modern capitalistic society is divided roughly into owners and proletariat, the militancy of workers against owners being regarded as a prime factor in hastening the world towards the Marxian millenium.   z.

Claybanks. A Unionist faction in Missouri, 1863-65, which placed the preservation of the Union above the slavery issue; opposed to the Charcoals (*q.v.*)   s.

Clayton Act. A law of Congress Oct. 14, 1914, which clarified and strengthened the Sherman Antitrust Act (*q.v.*) It forbade rebates, tying contracts, price discriminations, price cutting to restrain trade, the ownership of stock in competing companies, and interlocking directorates in banks and large businesses. Officers of corporations were made personally responsible. Competitors when injured were allowed to use the injunction and to utilize evidence unearthed by the government. Labor and agricultural organizations not conducted for profit were exempted from the provisions of the Act.   s.

Clayton-Bulwer Treaty. A treaty between the United States and Great Britain signed Apr. 14, 1850, which provided that neither nation should control a proposed interoceanic canal in Central America by fortification or the occupation of adjacent territory, but that such a canal should be neutralized and open on equal terms to all nations.   s.

clean sweep. The removal of all or nearly all subordinate administrative servants belonging to a faction or party opposed to that of a newly elected executive head of a government: an integral factor of the spoils system.   z.

clearance. Permission to vessels or aircraft to discharge passengers or cargo or to leave port or landing field. The Bureau of Customs in the Treasury Department is charged with the supervision of such activity.   z.

clearance, political. *See* Political clearance.

clear-and-present-danger rule. A rule of constitutional interpretation formulated by Justice Holmes in *Schenck* v. *U.S.*, 249 U.S. 47 (1919), that in all prosecutions for allegedly seditious utterances in which statutory encroachment on freedom of speech is pleaded in defense, the question is "whether the words used are used in such circumstances and are of such a nature as to create a clear and present danger that they will bring about the substantive evils that Congress has a right to prevent." JJR.

clerk. An official of the House of Representatives who has the care and custody of the records and papers of the House and the keeping and printing of the *Journal;* who attests the passage of bills and joint resolutions, makes contracts, keeps accounts, and performs other duties of a clerical nature. A similar official exists in State legislatures. z.

clerk of bills. A subordinate of the clerk of a legislative chamber who keeps track of the progress of all bills and resolutions introduced. z.

clerk of court. A popularly elected county official who records the proceedings and issues the processes of courts of record sitting in the county. His office is sometimes combined with that of the county clerk (*q.v.*) z.

Clintonians. A faction of the Republican party in New York, 1812-20, with strong support upstate, but opposed by Tammany Hall. s.

closed primary. A primary election in which participation is limited to members of a particular party, as determined by enrollment, challenge, or declarations by voters of their past affiliation with the party or of their intentions to vote for its candidates. s.

closed sea. A gulf, bay, or other arm of the ocean, the shores of which are exclusively owned by one state. s.

closed shop. An industrial establishment in which only union members may be employed; it is often distinguished from the union shop, in which nonunion men may be employed, but must join the union within a limited time and continuously maintain their membership in it. JJR.

closure. The stoppage of debate and amendment and the bringing of a question to a vote. In the House of Representatives and in most State legislatures it is accomplished by a mere majority vote on a motion for the previous question; in the Senate, by the written request of 16 Senators followed by a two-thirds vote, after which individual speeches are limited to one hour. s.

club, political. A local organization which engages in various social, educational, and charitable activities for the purpose of winning votes. It is usually controlled by the recognized local party leader. s.

coalition. A temporary alliance or union of parties for the purpose of promoting a common legislative policy or electing candidates. s.

Coast and Geodetic Survey. One of the oldest services of the United States government, known by its present title since 1878 and now a part of the Department of Commerce. It surveys and charts coasts and coastal waters to facilitate navigation and compiles and distributes topographical, gravitational, seismological, and astronomical observations of great value to mariners, aviators, and surveyors.   z.

Coast Guard. *See* United States Coast Guard.

coasting trade. Sea-borne commerce between different ports of the same state. It is usually restricted by law to ships of the state's registry.   JWF.

code. 1. In Roman-law countries, the systematic body of the law upon which judicial decisions must be based. 2. In America, a private or official compilation of all the permanent laws in force consolidated and classified according to subject matter. Such compilations of national laws are the *Revised Statutes of the United States,* first enacted in 1874, and *A Code of the Laws of the United States* (1926) and later supplements. Many States have published official codes of all laws in force, including common law and judicial decisions, carefully prepared by code commissions and enacted by the legislatures. American codes lack the authority and permanence of European codes because they are immediately subject to legislative addition and amendment and to development by judicial decisions.   s.

code authority. Representatives of a particular industry who, 1933-35, formulated codes of fair competition, subject to governmental approval, and assisted in their administration under the National Industrial Recovery Act (*q.v.*)   JJR.

Code Napoleon. The codification of French private substantive law prepared at the instance of Napoleon Bonaparte. It became widely accepted as a model among Latin peoples.   JRP.

coercion. Application of sanctions by government or the use of force to compel observance of law or public policy.   z.

coinage. The minting or stamping of metal into pieces which bear marks showing their value for purposes of exchange. The States are forbidden to coin money. Congress in 1792 established a mint at Philadelphia which began to issue gold, silver, and copper coins of an intrinsic worth approximately equal to the face value. Changes in metal prices led to the disappearance of many gold coins from circulation, the suspension over long periods of the coinage of silver dollars, and a drastic reduction in 1853 of the weight of coins of less than one dollar. The coinage of gold ceased in 1933.   s.

Coin's Financial School. The title of newspaper articles and pamphlets written by W. H. ("Coin") Harvey and effectively used in the campaign of 1896 to win votes for Bryan.   s.

collective bargaining. Negotiation between an employer and organized employees as distinguished from individuals, for the purpose of determining by joint agreement the conditions of employment. The right of workers in interstate commerce to bargain with the employer collectively through representatives of their own choosing is protected by federal statute by a series of acts beginning with the Railway Labor Act of 1926. Similar legislation for intrastate employees has been enacted in Massachusetts, Michigan, Minnesota, New York, Pennsylvania, Puerto Rico, Utah, Wisconsin, Vermont, and Rhode Island.   JJR.

collective representation. The theory that a member of a legislative assembly represents the interests not merely of his immediate constituency but of the state as a whole.   z.

collective security. Formal agreement among the states of the world or a substantial portion thereof to maintain international peace through the instrumentality of a league or confederation of states endowed with power to compose international differences and to use force against potential aggressors.   JWF.

collectivism. Any social movement in which independent individual control of property is systematically subordinated to collective or group action, the instrumentality being either the state or some private organization having power over the property of its members.   JJR.

collector of internal revenue. One of some 65 officials of the Bureau of Internal Revenue who, in various areas of the country, immediately superintend the collection of federal taxes and excises other than customs duties.   z.

collector of taxes. A county or other local official, often elective, charged with the collection of certain taxes, particularly property taxes.   z.

collector of the customs. One of 51 officials of the Bureau of Customs of the Department of the Treasury engaged in the collection of import duties upon goods entering the United States.   z.

collusive bidding. The submission of prearranged bids by ostensibly competing firms.   JMCC.

colonial agent. The emissary of a colony, chosen to represent its special interests at the seat of government of the mother country.   z.

colonial system. The maintenance by a great power of colonies, spheres of influence, or other politically subject areas, primarily because of the economic advantages derived from them.   z.

colonization. 1. The occupation and permanent settlement of undeveloped or newly acquired territory by the nationals of a state under the political control of that state; sometimes loosely used to denote the extension of sovereignty by an imperialist power over the peoples and lands of weaker or semicivilized nations. 2. The illegal introduction of nonresident voters into a doubtful electoral area for the purpose of carrying an election.   z.

colony. A politically subject area usually inhabited by persons who have migrated from the country exercising sovereignty and by their descendants; also such an area inhabited by an economically backward people.   z.

Colorado. The 38th State, admitted to the Union Aug. 1, 1876, from territory acquired by the Louisiana Purchase (1803) and the Mexican cession of 1848. Capital, Denver; area, 103,948 sq. mi.; population (1940), 1,123,296; presidential electors, 6. The original constitution is still in effect. As amended, it provides for the constitutional and statutory initiative, the referendum, and the recall. s.

Colorado River Compact. An interstate compact, 1922, to which Wyoming, Utah, Nevada, New Mexico, Colorado, Arizona, and California were parties. It provided for their respective interests in the contemplated exploitation of the waters of the Colorado River and its tributaries and was an essential preliminary to the construction of the Boulder Dam and other works in the basin.   z.

Colossus of Debate. A nickname of John Adams.   s.

Columbia River Compact. An interstate compact, 1925, to which Washington, Idaho, Oregon, and Montana were parties. It provided for their respective rights in the contemplated exploitation of the Columbia River and its tributaries and led subsequently to the construction of the Grand Coulee and Bonneville dams.   z.

Colorado and Columbia River Compacts — Drainage areas and dams constructed

Columbus Day. A legal holiday in several States commemorating the first landfall of Columbus in the New World at Watlings Island in the Bahamas, Oct. 12, 1492.   JWF.

combat area. The zone of hostile operations of belligerents or the area so defined by proclamation of one belligerent.   z.

combination in restraint of trade. An agreement or understanding between two or more persons, in the form of a contract, trust, pool, holding company, or other form of association, for the purpose of unduly restricting competition, monopolizing trade and commerce in a certain commodity, controlling its production, distribution, and price, or otherwise interfering with freedom of trade without statutory authority. Such combinations within a State were prohibited by State constitutions and statutes after 1870; and in interstate commerce by the Sherman Antitrust Act, 1890, and later statutes.   JJR.

comity. The recognition which one nation allows within its territory to the legislative, executive, or judicial acts of another; the neighborly spirit which impels nations to render up fugitives from justice or do other favors not required by treaty stipulations. The statement in the Constitution that "the citizens of each State shall be entitled to all privileges and immunities of citizens in the several States" is sometimes called the comity clause.   s.

commander-in-chief. The title of a general in supreme command of military forces engaged in operations against the enemy; also the position of the head of a state who has the supreme administrative control, in time of peace and war, of all the combat forces of the state.   z.

commerce. The exchange of commodities and commercial intercourse and traffic, including navigation, the transportation of goods and persons, and the transmission of messages. The meaning of the term is not confined to the instrumentalities in existence at the time of the adoption of the Constitution, but extends immediately to every new invention to facilitate transportation and communication. The regulatory powers of Congress, which extend over foreign and interstate commerce and commerce with the Indian tribes, is considered not to include bills of exchange, the issuance of insurance policies, or manufacturing; though since 1937 the Supreme Court has upheld several congressional statutes regulating manufacturing and related industries under the commerce power. Commerce begins when goods are delivered to the depot or warehouse of a common carrier and ends when goods are delivered to the consignee and are broken up into convenient lots for sale. Almost every aspect of water-borne commerce is under the control of Congress because of its specific constitutional powers over navigation. The States retain the power to regulate intrastate commerce; but their regulations are not enforceable if they adversely affect the free flow of interstate commerce, and State commissions often find themselves obliged to play a subsidiary role to the regulatory activities of national commissions. On the other hand, the States may make certain regulations which may affect the instrumentalities of foreign or interstate commerce if such regulations have a reasonable relation to the protection of public health, safety, morals, or convenience.   s.

Commerce, Department of. A department of the national administration which was established as the Department of Commerce and Labor, Feb. 14, 1903, and received its present title in 1913. Besides subjects and agencies more immediately identified with commerce, its authority extends over patents, the census, the Bureau of Standards, the Weather Bureau, the Coast and Geodetic Survey, and temporarily, at least, the Reconstruction Finance Corporation. s.

Commerce Court. A federal court created in 1910 and abolished in 1913 which had power to review and enforce determinations of the Interstate Commerce Commission. s.

commercial treaty. An international agreement regulating trade in specified products, establishing reciprocal tariff reductions or trading privileges, or providing for the settlement of commercial claims. *See* Treaty. JWF.

commissary. A branch of the military establishment concerned with the procurement of supplies for troops. In the United States this service is known as the Quartermaster Corps. z.

commission. 1. A warrant usually issued by the chief executive which confers the powers and privileges of an office upon a person newly appointed thereto. 2. A body of three or more officials who collectively discharge the duties of some administrative agency. z.

commissioned officer. A military officer of the rank of second lieutenant or above, or a naval officer of the rank of ensign or above. z.

commissioner. 1. A member of the principal county board or of the governing body of a city under the commission form of government. 2. Part of the title widely used for heads of national bureaus and State and municipal departments. GHD.

commission-manager plan. A system of municipal government which originated in Staunton, Va., in 1908 but received its first important application in Dayton, O., in 1913. Ordinance-making powers and the determination of general policy repose in a small council the members of which are sometimes elected by proportional representation. Responsibility for the entire administration of the municipality is given to a city manager who is appointed by the council and serves at its pleasure. The plan contemplates that the manager shall be an expert administrator and that he shall be chosen for his demonstrated abilities and without reference to political affiliation or place of residence. Cincinnati, O., is now the largest city operating under a commission-manager plan, but about 600 smaller communities have also adopted it in preference to the mayor-council or commission plans. A few American counties also use a similar plan. GHD.

commission plan. A form of municipal government, first adopted at Galveston, Tex., in 1901, in which all executive and legislative powers are combined in a commission of, usually, five or six members each of whom administers a department of municipal government subject to the control of the whole body. It was widely adopted elsewhere, but is now being rapidly superseded by the commission-manager plan (*q.v.*) s,

commission of inquiry. A board composed of members of the legislature, administrative officials, nonofficial members, or a combination of two or more of these groups, appointed to investigate and report on a particular problem.   s.

commitment. 1. An order to imprison a person. 2. Reference of a bill to a legislative committee.   jwf.

committee. A portion of the members of a legislative assembly organized to give special and detailed consideration to pending legislative business. A *standing committee,* essentially a permanent body, is organized to consider all bills, resolutions, and other items of legislative business falling within the category of matters over which it has been given jurisdiction. A *special committee* is appointed to investigate and report on a specific matter and expires when that service has been rendered. *Joint committees* are occasionally appointed by the two houses. Membership and rank on standing committees are largely controlled by the seniority rule, the chairman usually being the member of longest continuous service on the committee who belongs to the majority party. The formal choice of members is a function of each house of Congress, but the actual choice is made by a committee of the party caucus. Majority and minority parties secure membership on a committee roughly in proportion to their strength in a house. Minority members have the right to make a formal minority report. The power and influence wielded by standing committees in Congress and State legislatures is probably greater than that wielded by comparable bodies in any other legislative assembly. They may hold open or secret sessions, invite outside testimony, and compel the attendance of witnesses. They may organize subcommittees for special phases of their activities. They have considerable power to initiate legislation. All bills and resolutions introduced in one or the other house are referred to them. Such as are reported back may be amended or emasculated beyond recognition. In the British House of Commons the legislative leadership of the cabinet has prevented the standing committees from assuming positions of importance. They number five at present, are composed of a numerous personnel, and have little power to emasculate, sift, or initiate legislation. Special committees are created to improve the details of bills after the general principle has been decided in the Commons acting as a plenary body or as a committee of the whole. *See also* Committee of the whole; Party committee.   z.

committee of correspondence. Originally a committee of a colonial legislature appointed to correspond with the agent of the colony in London and with other legislatures. In 1773 a hierarchy of such committees was created extending into counties and towns to exchange information and promote the patriot cause.   s.

Committee of Forty-Eight. A liberal Socialist group formed in 1919, and representative of each of the States, which helped to found the Farmer-Labor party in 1920.   s.

committee of the whole. The entire membership of a legislative house sitting under modified rules to consider a specific measure or class of measures. It has its own chairman. Its quorum in the House of Representatives is 100. It takes no record votes. Its sessions are divided into general debate and the consideration of amendments under the five-minute rule. All revenue and appropriation bills must be, and other bills may be, considered in committee of the whole. To become effective its conclusions must be approved by the House in formal session. The committee of the whole is little used in the Senate.   s.

committee on committees. A committee of the party caucus which determines the assignment of members to committee posts in the House of Representatives. Because of the seniority rule its discretion is normally limited to filling vacancies. The Democratic committee consists of the Democratic members of the Ways and Means Committee; the Republican committee consists of one member from each State having Republican representation, and he has as many votes as his State has Republican representatives.   s.

Committee on Rules. *See* Rules, Committee on.

Commodity Credit Corporation. An agency in the Department of Agriculture, chartered in Delaware in 1933, which is authorized to make loans on agricultural produce and to purchase such produce with a view to stabilizing the agricultural market. Loans may be made directly or through approved banks or loan associations. The Corporation has a capital of $100,000,000 and may issue bonds and similar obligations up to $2,650,000,000. z.

common carrier. A proprietor, as of a railroad, ship, airplane, pipe line, bus, or taxicab, who undertakes to carry any goods or persons of a general class for hire. His business is affected with a public interest because of public dependence upon his service, and may be regulated extensively through legislation.   JJR.

common council. The name of the ordinance-making branch of some municipalities.   JWF.

common law. The basic law of Anglo-Saxon countries which originated from decisions of judges based on customary law in different parts of England and later became common to the realm through regular conferences of judges and the writings of commentators. It rests on judicial precedent, "the fruit of reason ripened by experience." As unusual cases arose the law was gradually broadened in scope. During the colonial period the doctrine associated with Lord Chief Justice Coke that the common law was fundamental and afforded protection against oppressive acts of government found ready acceptance in America. After the Revolution practically all the common law was inherited by the States, since Congress has only delegated powers; but the federal courts adopted common-law procedure. Under the decisions of different courts common law has tended to vary somewhat from State to State. Common law may be repealed or modified by statute. Much of it has been converted into statute law by legislative revisions or codifications of laws; on the other hand, common law continues to be developed by decisions. s.

common pleas. The title of a court of civil jurisdiction in some American States. z.

Common Sense. The title of a pamphlet written by Thomas Paine in 1776 which helped to crystallize popular sentiment in favor of independence. s.

commonweal army. May-day demonstrators before the National Capitol in 1894 led by "General" Jacob S. Coxey. s.

commonwealth. 1. A politically organized people; hence a state. 2. Part of the formal name of certain American States; *e.g.,* the Commonwealth of Pennsylvania. z.

communication. The transmission of intelligence and the various facilities employed therefor. Such inventions as the locomotive, the internal combustion engine, the telegraph, telephone, radio, and airplane have exerted an incalculable influence in the rapid expansion of federal powers and in creating a strong sense of national union among the American people. In Europe modern communication has demonstrated the anachronistic character of many political institutions, especially those based on the principle of national sovereignty. AJW,Jr.

communism. The political and social theory of Soviet Russia nominally derived from the same Marxian sources as contemporary socialism. Until recently, at least, the theory included advocacy of violent revolutionary transition to social ownership of capital, and a soviet form of government nominally expressing the will of enfranchised masses but actually controlled by a closely knit, oligarchically controlled, class-conscious party. z.

Communist Manifesto. A proclamation of the principles of Marxian Socialism drawn up and published in London in 1848 by Karl Marx and Friedrich Engels. z.

Communist Party of the U.S.A. A minor party in the United States allied, or having aims in sympathy, with the Third International (Moscow, 1919). It was organized in 1919 from the Communist and Communist Labor parties. Its largest vote in a presidential election, 102,991, was cast in 1932. After the Voorhis Act, 1940, it severed its formal affiliation with the Third International. JJR.

commutation. The alteration of a punishment to one which is less severe. It may be granted only by the person or body which may legally exercise the pardoning power. s.

compact. 1. A contract or covenant; a fancied or actual agreement among a large number of persons by which political society is brought into being; *e.g.,* Mayflower Compact. **2.** An agreement among two or more States regulating matters of common concern normally requiring the ratification of Congress in order to be valid. z.

companion bills. Identical bills introduced in both houses of a legislative body. s.

company union. An employee organization limited in membership to the employees of one plant or employer. Recent federal and State labor relations acts, while not outlawing such unions, seek to prevent their creation, domination, control, or maintenance by the employer. JJR.

compensating duty. A duty levied upon an imported commodity in order to compensate for an internal tax levied on the commodity when grown or produced within the importing country. z.

compensation. **1.** The pecuniary award made by a tribunal to the owner of property condemned under the power of eminent domain. **2.** Money paid to an employee or his beneficiaries from a state insurance fund because of injury or death sustained in the course of employment. JWF.

competition. Rivalry among producers or distributors under a regime of free enterprise to capture a larger share of the available market by underselling rivals, lowering costs of production, or improving the quality or increasing the desirability of goods or services. JWF.

competitive system. The recruitment of civil service employees through examinations open to all persons having minimum qualifications in competition with one another. s.

complimentary vote. Scattered votes cast by delegates at a political convention for a person whom they wish to honor but who is not an avowed candidate and who is not seriously considered for a nomination. z.

compound duties. Both specific and ad valorem duties levied on the same article. s.

compromis. A written statement, agreed to by states in controversy, as to the rules and principles to be followed and the limitations to be observed when a question is submitted to arbitrators for an award. z.

compromise. The adjustment of differences among disputants through mutual concession by the parties involved; hence any agreement secured through mutual concession. Compromises are a normal part of the action of arbitral tribunals and of deliberative political assemblies. z.

Compromise of 1850. A compromise arranged by Henry Clay and enacted in five separate bills which provided for the admission of California as a free State, the organization of Utah and New

Mexico territories without reference to slavery, the assumption of the debt of the former Republic of Texas and a settlement of its boundaries, abolition of the slave trade (but not slavery) in the District of Columbia, and a more effectual law for the return of fugitive slaves.   s.

compromises of the Constitution. Adjustments of many conflicting interests and points of view in the Convention of 1787. The most important were the Connecticut and three-fifths compromises (*qq.v.*) and the one which gave Congress power to regulate foreign and interstate commerce, but prohibited it from stopping the importation of slaves before 1808.   s.

Compromise Tariff. The tariff law of 1833 which provided for the gradual reduction of duties over the next ten years.   s.

comptroller. The title or part of the title given an official charged with the examination and auditing of public accounts; also known as the controller.   z.

Comptroller General. An officer provided for by the Budget and Accounting Act of 1921. He is appointed by the President and the Senate and can be removed only through the process of impeachment or by joint resolution of Congress. His office audits the accounts of all government agencies; effectually prevents the disbursement of public funds for matters which it considers unauthorized by law; and has power to standardize the methods of keeping government accounts.   z.

Comptroller of the Currency. An official of the Department of the Treasury who is responsible for supervising and examining the national banks, and for the issue and redemption of federal reserve notes and federal reserve bank notes. He is ex officio a member of the Federal Deposit Insurance Corporation.   s.

compulsory arbitration. A proposed requirement that all international or industrial disputes must be submitted to an arbitral tribunal whose decision will be binding. It has been used for labor controversies with equivocal success in New Zealand. A law of Kansas requiring arbitration in specific industries was declared unconstitutional by the United States Supreme Court in 1923. *See* Arbitration.   JWF.

compulsory military service. Service in the armed forces of a state enjoined by law upon those capable of bearing arms. *See also* Draft; Selective Service System.   z.

compulsory school attendance. The policy of compelling young people between certain ages, except those attending a private school, to attend a public elementary or high school for at least part of an academic term or for a minimum number of days each year; in effect in every State since 1918.   z.

compulsory vaccination. Immunization from smallpox required by law in eleven States, usually as a prerequisite to admission to elementary schools. The power of a State legislature to determine the general necessity for it was upheld in *Jacobson* v. *Massachusetts,* 197 U.S. 11 (1905). JJR.

compulsory voting. A legal requirement that qualified voters cast ballots at every election or suffer penalties provided by law. It exists nowhere in the United States, though one or two State constitutions authorize the legislature to provide for it. Experience in a few countries abroad indicates that such laws, though increasing participation in elections, result in a tendency to vote recklessly or cast blank ballots. Z.

concentration. The tendency to centralize all power of decision in the head of an administrative establishment, thereby decreasing the discretionary authority of subordinates. Z.

concentration camp. A place for the incarceration or detainment, usually without any process of law, of persons who oppose an existing political regime or are otherwise politically suspect; particularly prevalent in authoritarian states. Z.

concert of powers. A loosely defined diplomatic agreement, particularly among the great European powers in the 19th century, to preserve peace and the international *status quo.* Z.

concession. A privilege or right, usually economic, granted by a government to another government or to individuals. Z.

concession theory. The legal doctrine in England and the United States that the power of a person or a group to act as a corporation exists only by express legislative authority. JJR.

conciliation. Counsel by a friend common to the parties to a dispute, accompanied by an attempt to reach a compromise acceptable to them. There is no submission of an agreed issue, as in arbitration (*q.v.*), nor consent by the parties to be bound by the mediator's judgment. An increasing number of labor disputes is settled every year by permanent national and State conciliators. JJR.

concordat. An agreement between the Pope, as head of the Roman Catholic Church, and the authorities of a state regulating the position of the Church and its hierarchy within that state. Concordats deal with such matters as exemption from taxation, public financial support, and control over marriage and matters affecting morality. Z.

concurrent jurisdiction. Authority shared by two or more legislative, judicial, or administrative officers or bodies, to deal with the same subject matter. When federal and State courts have concurrent jurisdiction the parties may usually decide where a case is brought. JJR.

concurrent power. The power of either Congress or the State legislatures, each acting independently of the other, to make valid regulations of the same subject matter, as in the 18th Amendment. An older use of the term referred to valid State police regulations over subjects committed to Congress, but on which Congress had not acted.   s.

concurrent resolution.   An action of Congress passed in the form of a resolution of one house, the other concurring, which expresses the sense of Congress or accomplishes some purpose of common interest to the houses, with which the President has no concern. It is not submitted to the President for his signature. Recently the use of this device has been extended in statutes delegating powers to the President, which contain the provision that the delegation may be terminated upon the passing of a concurrent resolution.   s.

concurrent voice.   The expression of political opinion by the different interests of society, each separately recorded, in order to create a "concurrent majority" basis for governmental action that will equitably protect minority groups from numerical majority rule.   jtc.

concurring opinion.   A separate opinion delivered by one or more judges which agrees with the decision of the majority of the court but offers different reasons for reaching that decision. jwf.

condemnation.   1. A judicial proceeding in which private property is taken for public use under the power of eminent domain (*q.v.*), and compensation to the owner is determined.   2. The determination of a court that a ship is unfit for service, or was properly seized and held as a prize.   3. The judgment by which property seized for violation of revenue or other laws is declared forfeited to the state.   jjr.

conditional contraband.   Merchandise capable of either a peaceful or military use. It may be seized by a belligerent if it is destined for the armed forces of the enemy. *See* Contraband.   jwf.

condominium.   The exercise of sovereign power jointly by two states over a colony or politically dependent territory; *e.g.,* the joint sovereignty of Egypt and Great Britain over the Anglo-Egyptian Sudan.   z.

Confederate States of America.   A government established provisionally at Montgomery, Ala., Feb. 4, 1861, by delegates from South Carolina, Mississippi, Florida, Alabama, Georgia, and Louisiana. Within a few months Texas, Arkansas, Virginia, North Carolina, and Tennessee were added, and the number of States became 13 when minority provisional governments were recognized in Missouri and Kentucky. Under a constitution adopted in the fall of 1861 the President was to be elected for six years, but was ineligible for re-election; cabinet members might speak but not vote on the floor of Congress; an extra-majority vote was required to pass appropriations not requested by the heads of departments, and the President was given an item veto; internal improvements and protective tariffs were practically prohibited; and any three States could compel Congress to call a constitutional convention. s.

confederation. A league or association of sovereign states usually possessing a central political or administrative organ to which is delegated power to act on matters of common concern. *See* Articles of Confederation. z.

conference. 1. A meeting of managers appointed by each of the houses of a legislature to adjust differences when a bill passed by one house is amended by the other and the first house refuses to accept the amendment. In a *simple conference* managers act under instructions; in a *free conference* they may make compromises within the limits of difference between the houses. The number of managers appointed by each house, is usually three, but it may be more. A majority in each group is necessary to reach an agreement. Though the houses must each vote on the agreement, it is customary for them to accept it. 2. An open meeting of members of a legislative body belonging to one party, in contradistinction to a secret caucus. s.

Conference for Progressive Political Action. A meeting of various labor and agrarian organizations in 1922 which paved the way for the independent candidacy of Robert M. LaFollette for President in 1924. s.

Conference of Commissioners on Uniform State Laws. A body of lawyers appointed by the several States which, since 1892, has drafted model laws and worked to secure their enactment by State legislatures. s.

confirmation. The ratification or approval of executive acts by a legislature or one house. In order to be valid, presidential appointments of all important officers of the United States require approval by a majority of the Senate, and treaties must be approved by two thirds of the Senate. Most gubernatorial appointments in the States require approval by the upper house of the legislature. Legislative confirmation of executive appointments weakens the administrative control of the executive over his appointees; it is also responsible for the practice which allows members of the confirming body unofficially to select many of the appointees, the appointing authority being obliged to nominate such selections by the tacit threat of the confirming body to withhold approval of all executive appointments. Confirmation of treaties is a practice which is logically more defensible since treaties are political instruments and directly affect the normal sphere of activity confided to legislative bodies. z.

confiscation. Seizure of private property by the government without compensation to the owner, often a consequence of conviction for crime or participation in rebellion, or because possession of the property was contrary to law, or because it was being used for an unlawful purpose. z.

conflict of laws. 1. An inconsistency in the laws relating to

one subject. **2.** Another name for private international law (*q.v.*)
                                                                    JWF.

congress. 1. A formal assembly of heads of states, ministers, and envoys. **2.** The legislature of the national government, which consists of the Senate and the House of Representatives. With the exception of the executive power to ratify treaties and appointments which belongs to the Senate, the sole right of initiating revenue bills which is reserved to the House, and different roles in impeachments and the election of the President and Vice President, the two houses are legally co-ordinate. Congress may legislate on all subjects expressly granted by the Constitution, or reasonably implied from specific grants, or resultant from the general constitutional structure, subject to certain limitations in the Bill of Rights and elsewhere in the Constitution. The houses are reasonably free from procedural limitations. Each must have a majority present in order to do business, must keep a journal, and must take a record vote whenever one fifth of those present demand it or when reconsidering a bill after a presidential veto. A two-thirds vote is required in certain matters, such as the passing of a bill which has been vetoed, the expulsion of a member, and, in the Senate, judgment in impeachments and the ratification of treaties. Otherwise each house is free to adopt any rules it chooses. Each elects its own officers (the Vice President presides over the Senate), determines the elections and qualifications of its members, and may punish for disorderly behavior. Speeches made in either house may not be called in question outside it, and members are free from arrest except in the most extreme circumstances while attending the sessions and in traveling to and from them. They receive salaries of $10,000 per year and liberal allowances for traveling expenses and clerk hire.
                                                                    S.

congressional campaign committee. A party committee first created in 1866 to conduct the re-election campaigns of Radical Republican representatives who feared to trust the national committee. The Democratic committee began in 1880. Since that date both committees have been active in "off-year" elections and have recognized their subordination to the national committees in presidential years. Each party caucus chooses one member, nominated by the State delegation, for each State having party representation in Congress. The chairman of the Democratic caucus may appoint an outsider to the committee for each State not represented by a Democrat.
                                                                    S.

congressional caucus. *See* Caucus 3.

Congressional Directory. A volume published annually or oftener containing biographies of Congressmen, maps of congressional districts, and valuable information on the organization of Congress, courts, and executive agencies.
                                                                    S.

congressional district. A division of a State for the election of one member of Congress. A law of Congress, in effect from 1842 to 1929, required compactness and contiguity of territory and equality of population in each, district; but partisan majorities in State legislatures often violated all these principles by redrawing boundaries with an eye to party advantage (*see* Gerrymander). State legislatures now have unlimited discretion in redistricting, and they may act after a decennial census or at any other time. s.

Congressional Medal of Honor. The highest military decoration awarded by the American government, voted by Congress to a person in the armed services who distinguishes himself by gallantry and courage in action at the risk of life and beyond the call of duty. Its obverse is a bronze five-pointed star within a green-enameled laurel wreath. z.

Congressional Medal of Honor
for Valor

Congressional Record. An official publication of the debates and proceedings of Congress established in 1873 and superseding the *Congressional Globe* which was privately published after 1830. Members of Congress are allowed to edit their speeches which appear in it. They may insert material never spoken by securing from their respective houses leave to print or to extend their remarks. EES.

Congressman. A member of Congress; colloquially a member of the House of Representatives. s.

Congressman at large. A member of the House of Representatives elected by the voters of the whole State and not from a district. Such members are chosen when a State is entitled to increased representation after a census and the legislature does not care to disturb existing district boundaries; also when the legislature ignores the principle of the single-member district. s.

Congress of Industrial Organizations. A labor organization formed in 1935 by eight unions within the American Federation of Labor as a "Committee for Industrial Organization" primarily to extend unionism along industrial rather than craft lines to unorganized large-scale industries. Ten unions, suspended by the Federation in 1936, organized a rival body which held its first convention under the present name in 1938. The C.I.O. had about five million members in 1943. JJR.

Connecticut. One of the original States and the fifth to ratify the Constitution of the United States, Jan. 9, 1788. Capital, Hartford; area, 5,004 sq. mi.; population (1940), 1,709,242; presidential electors, 8. The present constitution dates from 1818. It was the first State to adopt a literacy test for the suffrage.   s.

Connecticut Compromise. An arrangement promoted by Connecticut delegates to the Convention of 1787 by which the desires of small States to be equally represented in Congress was satisfied by the creation of the Senate, and the large States were satisfied by representation in the lower house according to population.   s.

conquered territory. Territory which, by reason of invasion by the armed forces of a hostile power, has temporarily come under the immediate control and jurisdiction of the commander of such forces. Such territory may ultimately be permanently assimilated to the territory of the conquering power; but international usage normally requires a treaty or formal cession or proclamation of annexation to transform the mere fact of conquest into a right of sovereignty. In conquered territory the authority of the conqueror supersedes that of the existing government; but civilian rights normally remain *in statu quo* except that the commander of the invading forces may make such requisitions on the property of individuals as the usages of war permit. In the United States, the interim power of governing conquered territory is vested in the President as commander-in-chief. Congress may legislate for such territory only if and when it is definitely annexed to the United States.   z.

conquest. The territorial expansion of a state through war; hence all permanent territorial acquisitions resulting from a victorious war or aggression.   z.

conscience money. Occasional funds paid into the Treasury by persons who feel that they have cheated the government in tax payments or otherwise.   s.

Conscience Whigs. Antislavery Whigs who disapproved of several provisions of the Compromise of 1850, particularly the part relating to the return of fugitive slaves.   s.

conscientious objector. A person who, because of religious or humanitarian convictions, refuses to take any part in war, or in combat duty. The Selective Service Act of 1940 allowed bona fide objectors to substitute service on public conservation projects or noncombat duty for active military service.   JMcc.

conscription. The forced enrollment and induction of men for military or naval service. *See* Draft; Selective Service System. s.

conservation. The preservation, protection, and planned use of natural resources such as water power, land, forests, and minerals. Begun somewhat tardily in America, the conservation movement has recently made great strides, as in the development of forest and game preserves, the national park system, the Tennessee

Valley, Boulder Dam, and similar projects, in federal control of power sites and the output of crude oil, and in legislation to encourage crop rotation and prevent soil erosion. Conservation has been greatly aided by the activities of the National Resources Committee and the Departments of the Interior and Agriculture.   JMCC.

conservatism. **1.** General and uncritical opposition to change of any sort. **2.** A reasoned philosophy, associated with the English writer Edmund Burke, directed toward the control of the forces of change in such a way as to conserve the best elements of the past by blending them into an organic unity with new elements in an ever-evolving society.   JRP.

conservative. **1.** One who follows the philosophy of conservatism (*q.v.*) **2.** A supporter of President Johnson's administration, 1865-69, who opposed the Radical Republicans.   S.

consolidated fund. The pooled receipts of all State revenues, except those marked for a special purpose, from which withdrawals are made to defray the general expenses of government.   Z.

consolidated laws. A compilation of all the laws of a State in force, arranged according to subject matter.   Z.

consolidation. The combination of two or more administrative or territorial units of government to form a single entity; *e.g.*, the combination of several administrative agencies to form a single department or the combination of school districts, counties, or counties and cities, within a State.   GHD.

conspiracy. A combination of two or more persons to do an unlawful act or accomplish some lawful purpose by illegal means. S.

constable. The elective peace officer of a town or township. GHD.

constabulary. Originally a group of constables or the sheriff and his deputies; now the professional police force of a State or locality used for the prevention and suppression of disorders and the enforcement of law.   GHD.

constituency. The inhabitants of a legislative district; also the district itself.   S.

constituent power. **1.** The power officially to propose or ratify a new constitution or amendments. **2.** The body, or groups of persons, who are authorized to revise or amend a constitution. In the federal system of the United States, Congress may propose specific revisions or call a national convention for the purpose; to become effective revisions or amendments must be ratified by the legislatures or specially elected conventions in three fourths of the States. In the States new constitutions or extensive revisions are usually proposed by a constitutional convention, and separate amendments by the legislature or by initiative petition; ratification must be by the electorate, except in Delaware.   JJR.

constitution. The fundamental law, or the fundamental principles underlying the organization of a state, which determines the powers and duties of the principal governmental authorities and guarantees certain rights of the people against infringement. It may be simply an uncollected body of legislative acts, judicial decisions, and political precedents and customs extending over a long period, like the British constitution; or a number of separate organic laws, like the constitution of the Third French Republic; or a formal written document drafted and promulgated at a definite date by an authority of higher competence than that which makes ordinary laws, like American constitutions. It may be enforced by the courts as superior to statutes or acts which may be in conflict with it, as in the United States and a few other countries, chiefly in Latin America; or its preservation may be entrusted to the political authorities. In the latter case, which is the usual one in Continental Europe, a written constitution serves as a convenient standard of comparison by which the people may judge the conduct of the government and insist on the maintenance of their rights. Constitutions are sometimes classified as *written* or *unwritten,* according to whether or not their written material is presented in consolidated form; or as *flexible* or *rigid,* according to the relative ease or difficulty of amendment.   s.

Constitution of the United States.   The fundamental law of the American federal system drafted by the Convention of 1787 (*q.v.*), and submitted by the Confederation Congress to conventions in the States, Sept. 28, 1787. Shortly after the ratification of the ninth State (*see* Art. VII) the Congress determined that the Constitution should go into effect Mar. 4, 1789, and congressional and presidential elections were held; but the inauguration of Washington was delayed until Apr. 30. The ratifications by several State conventions were conditioned upon the adoption of a Bill of Rights; and so the first ten amendments which were speedily proposed by Congress and ratified in 1791 may be regarded as part of the original Constitution. All unrepealed amendments are in as full force and effect as if they were parts of the original Constitution. The Constitution is a grant of powers to the national government, which are definitely enumerated (most of them are in Art. I, Sec. 8), or which may reasonably be implied from express grants, or which result from the constitutional structure as a whole. Some powers, such as those over the army and navy, foreign affairs, currency, and coinage, were expressly forbidden to the States; and others were expressly forbidden to both the national government and the States. When a limitation is expressed in general terms, as in the first ten amendments, it has been held to apply only against Congress; though recent decisions of the Supreme Court under the due process and equal protection clauses have applied some of these limitations against the States. Since its adoption the Constitution has become more and more national in character through the processes of formal amendment, judicial interpretation, statutes, usages, and customs.   s.

constitution, State. A body of limitations on a State legislature, or sometimes a grant of power from the people to the government. All the States adopted constitutions during the Revolutionary period, and every territory applying for statehood has been required to submit a draft constitution to Congress. The first State constitutions were brief documents which recognized the principle of legislative supremacy, provided for the organization of the government, and guaranteed the people against legislative oppression. New constitutions adopted early in the 19th century made the governors and courts independent of the legislatures, provided for manhood suffrage and the direct popular election of nearly all State and local officials, and freed local governments from State control. After the Civil War the Southern States were required, as a prerequisite for readmission, to adopt new constitutions incorporating guarantees of equal rights; and Northern States did likewise in order to expand their governmental organizations to meet rapidly growing social and economic needs. Since 1900 complete revisions have been less frequent, but piecemeal amendment is an incident of nearly every general election in many States. Today most State constitutions are long, detailed, and prolix, with a large admixture of provisions of a statutory character which require frequent amendment. Though most State constitutions contain statements that they are made by the people or proceed from the principle of popular sovereignty, the courts rarely interpret them as grants of power, but rather as limitations on the power of the legislatures. s.

constitutional amendment. *See* Amendment 2.

constitutional convention. A unicameral body which in an earlier period of the American republic was conceived to represent the people in their sovereign capacity, with the power to promulgate new constitutions, adopt ordinances of secession, and even, as in Missouri in 1861, to depose the governor and legislature and assume authority to govern directly. A contrary view that the convention was an agent whose action must be ratified by the principal was expressed in Massachusetts where the constitution of 1780 had to be approved by the people before being proclaimed. This view gained rapid acceptance in the North and later spread throughout the country. Conventions have been held in the States on an average of about once in 30 years. Arrangements as to the date of meeting and the election and compensation of members are made by the legislature; but any attempt on its part to set limits on the convention may be ignored. The membership of a convention is about as numerous as that of the legislature. The convention appoints committees to consider separate articles or subjects and make recommendations for approval by the whole body. It may submit a new constitution to the people or it may follow the growing practice of submitting several amendments piecemeal in order

to avoid the possibility that its whole work may be negatived because of the unpopularity of one or two provisions. The Convention of 1787 has been the only national constitutional convention,
but the Constitution provides that others shall be called on demand
of three fourths of the States.   s.

constitutional courts. Courts established by Congress under
the specific power granted in Art. III of the Constitution, which
share the judicial power given in that section and can be invested
with no other power; and their judges hold office during good behavior. The Supreme Court of the United States, the Circuit
Courts of Appeals, and the district courts are constitutional
courts.   s.

constitutionalism. The doctrine that the power to govern
should be limited by definite and enforceable principles of political
organization and procedural regularity embodied in the fundamental law, so that basic constitutional rights of individuals and
groups will not be infringed.   JJR.

constitutional law. The body of legal rules and principles
which define the nature and limits of governmental power as well
as the rights and duties of individuals in relation to the state and
its governing organs. These rules and principles are usually formulated in a written constitution and are interpreted and extended
by courts of final jurisdiction exercising their power of judicial
review (*q.v.*)   JJR.

constitutional limitations. Provisions and judicial interpretations of written constitutions which restrict the powers of government, especially of the legislative branch. In most States the legislature may exercise all powers not prohibited to it or assigned to
another branch by the State or federal constitution. The Constitution of the United States contains numerous limitations on both
national and State organs, and by implication all branches of the
national government are limited to the powers delegated to them
by the Constitution.   JJR.

Constitutional Union party. One of the four parties which
contested the election of 1860. It was composed chiefly of former
Whigs and Know-Nothings in the South. Its candidates, John
Bell and Edward Everett, received the electoral votes of Virginia,
Kentucky, and Tennessee.   s.

construction. The determination of the meaning of a constitution or statute by taking into account the intention of the framers, as shown in committee reports, debates, etc., or the circumstances which brought it into being. It is to be distinguished from
interpretation which is the process of determining the meaning of
an instrument from its terms. In the early years of the Republic
heated debates were frequent as to the proper construction of the
Constitution. *Liberal,* or *loose, construction* recognizes implied and
resultant powers under the theory that the framers intended to

establish a government with adequate powers to carry out its proper functions. *Strict construction* constitutes a denial that the framers had any other intentions than were expressed in the language they used. s.

consul. A public official stationed in a foreign industrial or commercial city to foster the economic interests of his government and look after the welfare of such of his government's nationals as may be traveling or residing within his jurisdiction. United States consuls are of various grades: consuls general at large, consuls general, consuls, vice consuls, and consular agents. They form a part of the foreign service of the United States and are under the Department of State. z.

consular agent. The lowest rank of consular officers sometimes filled by appointing a foreign resident or national. s.

consular immunity. Inviolability of archives and other privileges granted by a state to foreign consular agents under the provisions of applicable treaties. JWF.

consulate. 1. The residence or official quarters of a foreign consul. 2. Historically, the office or period of incumbency of Roman or French executive officers called consuls. JWF.

consul general. A consular representative stationed in a principal commercial city who, in addition to usual consular duties, supervises other consuls within a district. JWF.

consumers' advisory board. One of five advisory boards whose purpose was to represent the interests of consumers in the formulation of codes of fair competition under the National Industrial Recovery Act (*q.v.*) of 1933. Such boards were continued in subsequent agricultural and defense programs of the national government. JMCC.

contempt. Wilful disregard or disobedience of a court, committed in its presence (direct contempt) or so near thereto as to impair its authority (constructive contempt). It is criminal when directed against the court itself, since the proceeding is between the public and the defendant, whereas mere failure to carry out the court's orders for the benefit of the other party to a civil action is civil contempt. Both are punishable after summary proceedings by fine and imprisonment. The Clayton and Norris-LaGuardia acts now require trial by jury in most criminal contempt cases arising out of labor disputes. The President may pardon those convicted for criminal, but apparently not for civil, contempt. JJR.

contested election. An election the result of which is contested by two claimants before the authority which is empowered to admit a person to an office. Legislative houses settle such contests through investigations by committees on elections whose recommendations must be approved by a majority of the house. Often the vote follows party lines. Contests for nonlegislative offices are settled by the courts. s.

contesting delegations. Groups of delegates to a nominating convention, each of which claims to be the rightful representative of the party membership.   s.

Continental Congress. The *de facto* body first organized by the delegates of the 13 American colonies at Philadelphia in 1774 to petition the British government for redress of grievances. The second Continental Congress, which met in 1775, adopted measures of resistance against the British government and became the responsible political agency for carrying on the Revolution against Great Britain. Other Continental Congresses met at intervals until the adoption of the Articles of Confederation in 1781.   z.

contingent expense. An incidental or unforeseen expenditure usually of a petty nature.   z.

contingent fund. A fund created in anticipation of incidental or unforeseen expenditures. As systematic accounting, budgetary, and expenditure controls are developed such funds tend to become formalized, and questionable manipulation is minimized.   GHD.

continuous voyage. A doctrine traditionally applied by British and American prize courts that merchandise ostensibly bound for a neutral port but intended to be transshipped either in the same carrier or another to an enemy port is in continuous voyage from the consignment point to belligerent destination, and subject to the law of contraband.   JWF.

contraband. Those commodities which neutrals may not supply to belligerents. The Declaration of London, 1909, classified neutral goods as *absolute contraband,* or goods exclusively used in war; *conditional contraband,* or goods used in both war and peace; and *free goods,* or goods of no use in war. A belligerent may exercise the right of visit and search on neutral vessels and confiscate absolute contraband as well as goods which are conditional contraband if it is apparent that the latter are destined for the enemy's military establishment.   JAP.

contract. A legally enforceable agreement between two parties under the terms of which, for valid consideration, one of the parties agrees to perform some act or refrain from performing some act.   z.

contract clause. The clause in the Constitution of the United States (Art. I, Sec. 10) which forbids a State legislature to enact any law impairing the obligation of a private contract. In the Dartmouth College case (*q.v.*) the force of this clause was extended by the Supreme Court to include charters or franchises granted by public authority to individuals or corporations.   z.

contract labor. Immigrants brought to the United States under contract to work for persons who advanced their passage money. Since 1885, such contracts have been forbidden by law. s.

contract theory. A class of theories which strives to explain the origins of, and the existing obligation to conform to, social and political institutions. Theories of a *social contract, social compact,* or *original contract* should be carefully distinguished from *governmental contract* theories. The former, as the phrases imply, deal with the origin of civil society itself. They assume that men originally lived in a "state of nature" and brought society into being by general agreement to give up some or all of the "rights" which they were supposed to enjoy in their natural state in return for certain advantages to be derived from organized society, particularly the protection provided by government. In one sense, the theories are all highly individualistic in that they assume the existence of unrelated individuals at the outset and make all social institutions the product of the deliberate contrivance of such individuals. The conclusions which may be derived from these theories, however, vary from the individualism of Locke to the absolutism of Hobbes, for whom all individual rights (except that of self-defense) ceased to exist as soon as the contract had been made. *Social contract* theories had their heyday in the 17th and 18th centuries. *Governmental contract* theories seek to explain and define the limits of governmental authority by reference to a supposed contract between subjects and a ruler. Such a theory was characteristic of the Middle Ages, but the device was most fully developed as a justification for resistance to absolute monarchy in France, the Low Countries, and the British Isles during the 16th and 17th centuries. JRP.

contractual rights. Property or other rights secured under a contract. The courts afford protection for such rights, an action for damages being available to an injured party under a contract against the other party or parties thereto who have failed to fulfill their covenanted obligations. Equity also offers remedies, such as writs of specific performance, to secure the fulfillment of contractual rights. Contracts, and rights thereunder, are protected by the contract clause (*q.v.*) of the United States Constitution as well as by the due process clauses of the Constitution against impairment by State legislatures; but contractual rights are safeguarded no more than other rights against the exercise of a State's prerogatives of eminent domain, taxation, and the police power. z.

contribution. *See* Campaign fund.

contributory negligence. An old common-law rule that any lack of care on the part of an injured employee relieves the employer of liability for damages. It has been modified by statute in most States in favor of a rule of comparative negligence by which the employer is relieved of responsibility only in proportion to the relative negligence of himself and the employee. JJR.

controller. *See* Comptroller.

convention. 1. An agreement between states relating to trade, finance, the administrative details of international intercourse, or other matters considered less important than those usually regulated by a treaty. **2.** An extraordinary assembly, conceived to possess the full powers of sovereignty, which is convoked to consider sweeping changes in the constitution, as the Convention parliaments of 1660 which recalled Charles II, or of 1689 which placed William and Mary on the throne; or the French National Convention, 1792-95. **3.** A unicameral body which meets at irregular intervals to draft constitutional revisions for the approval of the electorate. *See* Constitutional convention; Convention of 1787. **4.** A meeting of voters belonging to one party in a town, township, ward, or other minor division, or of delegates in larger areas, which nominates candidates, frames a platform, adopts rules of party organization, and appoints a committee to advance the interests of the party during the interval between its sessions. Until the advent of the primary election the convention system was based on mass meetings of voters which elected delegates to county conventions, which in turn elected delegates to the next higher convention, and so on to the national convention. At present this system survives in full force only in two States. In some others, conventions are held for the nominations of certain officers or the adoption of platforms.   z.

Convention of 1787. A convention composed of 55 delegates from all the States except Rhode Island which met in secret session from May 25 to Sept. 17, 1787, on the call of the Congress to revise the Articles of Confederation. Its discussions, which were not known in detail until the publication of Madison's *Debates* in 1840, were devoted mainly to compromising differences between the advocates of a strong central government and of a weak confederation; between large States and small States; between North and South; between commercial and agrarian points of view; between advocates of a strong and a weak executive; etc. Some provisions were altered several times before the Constitution was ready to be put into final form by a committee on style and submitted to State conventions for ratification.   s.

conversations. Exploratory conferences between diplomats of two or more states to determine whether, and in what manner, a pending issue may be adjusted.   z.

convict. A person committed to a penal institution following conviction for a crime.   JWF.

convict labor. Work performed by inmates of penal institutions either under contract with private parties or directly for the State, the products of which were divested of interstate character by an act of Congress effective in 1934.   s.

Conway Cabal. A New England plot, 1777-78, to remove Washington from the command of the Continental army and appoint General Horatio Gates in his stead.   s.

Coodies. New York Federalists who favored the vigorous

prosecution of the War of 1812. The name is derived from "Abimelech Coody," the pseudonym of Gulian C. Verplanck.   s.

cooling-off period. 1. The interval after the beginning of a dispute during which states which have ratified conciliation treaties agree not to resort to war. 2. In labor disputes, a similar period during which the parties may not resort to strikes or lockouts. JWF.

co-operatives, agricultural. Organizations of farmers to market produce and purchase supplies without the services of middlemen. The national and State governments have encouraged the formation of co-operatives through special incorporation laws, exemption from certain taxes, and cheap credit.   JMCC.

Copperhead. A Northerner who sympathized with the South during the Civil War. The name is derived from the copperhead snake, which strikes without warning. Copperheads sometimes wore as an emblem the head of Liberty cut from a copper cent. s.

copyright. An exclusive right granted by law to an author or artist to publish or reproduce his work for a term of years. Holders of copyrights may protect themselves against infringement in the courts. In the United States a copyright runs for 28 years and may be renewed for a similar period; thereafter the copyrighted work is held to be in the "public domain." An international convention to which most of the states of the world adhere prevents infringement by the nationals of one state of the copyrighted productions of nationals of another state. *See also* Library of Congress.   z.

Corncracker State. A nickname of Kentucky.   s.

Cornerstone Speech. An address of Alexander H. Stephens at Savannah, Ga., Mar. 21, 1861, in which he declared that the cornerstone of the Confederacy "rests upon the great truth, that the Negro is not equal to the white man; that slavery . . . is his natural and normal condition."   s.

Cornhusker State. A nickname of Nebraska.   s.

coroner. A local government official who is required to hold an inquest, assisted by a jury, over the body of every person who is supposed to have met a violent death. In some States the coroner has been supplanted by the medical examiner.   s.

corporal punishment. Flogging or other forms of bodily chastisement inflicted as punishment for crime or violation of discipline.   JWF.

Corporal's Guard. A nickname for President Tyler's supporters after the defection of leaders of the Whig party.   s.

corporation. An artificial body created by law under a charter or act of incorporation, with a special name, and having certain legal capacities separate and distinct from those of the natural persons composing it, such as perpetual succession, the power to make contracts, to sue and be sued as an individual under a corporate name, to have a common seal, and to make and repeal bylaws. All corporations derive their legal capacities from State or national constitutions or statutes. The charters of private corporations are contracts which States may not impair by subsequent laws. Public corporations, being created exclusively as instruments of public administration, have no such immunity. JJR.

corporation tax. A special tax levied on the grant of a charter, the admission of a corporation to the privilege of doing business in another State, the amount of capital stock, the value of a franchise and other intangibles, or corporate income, as distinguished from other forms of income taxes. S.

corporative state. The systematic organization of the whole social and economic life of a state into a limited number of "corporations" or "estates" which have extensive authority over persons and activities within their respective jurisdictions, functionally rather than territorially defined, and are in turn supervised and controlled by state organs. JJR.

correction. Activities of judicial and administrative officers for the reformation of young delinquents. S.

corruption of blood. The legal consequence, under the old common law, of conviction of treason or felony, according to which the person so convicted could neither possess nor transmit by inheritance any property, rank, or title. JRP.

corrupt practices act. A statute defining crimes against the purity of elections and prohibiting under penalties the purchase of votes, bribery, personation or the procurement of personation, treating, betting on elections, payment of naturalization fees or taxes by persons other than the voter, excessive campaign expenditures, campaign contributions from corporations, any campaign contribution above a maximum set by law, failure to report campaign expenditures, or other acts tending to bring undue influence upon the electorate. S.

cosmopolitanism. A philosophy or way of life which tolerates and attempts to understand ideals and institutions other than one's own, and which rejects intense local attachments and narrow patriotism in favor of more general, and even universal, cultural and political values. Z.

cost-plus contract. A government contract which provides for the payment not of a definite sum but of the cost of producing an article plus a fixed percentage or a fixed fee. S.

Cotton is king. A Southern slogan in 1861 based on the belief that both the English government and Northern manufacturers would prevent war because of their dependence on cotton. S.

Cotton States. The Carolinas, Tennessee, Arkansas, Georgia, and the States bordering on the Gulf of Mexico whose politics were dominated by cotton-growing interests. Z.

Cotton Whigs. Northern Whigs who supported the Mexican War, the Compromise of 1850, and "our country however bounded." They were opposed by the Conscience Whigs (*q.v.*) s.

council. 1. A municipal legislature, or its lower house. 2. An official body created for the purpose of performing or assisting in the performance of work which is essentially administrative in nature. *See* Executive council; Judicial council; Legislative council. s.

councilman. A member of a city council. GHD.

council-manager plan. A form of municipal government in which a council, or a mayor and council, pass ordinances, make appropriations, and exercise general supervision over a city manager (*q.v.*), who is employed to take charge of the administration of city affairs. The term is preferred by some authorities to *commission-manager plan* (*q.v.*), which is in general use. s.

Council of Appointment. The governor and four state senators of New York who from 1777 to 1821 appointed State and local officials. s.

Council of National Defense. A planning board consisting of the secretaries of War, the Navy, the Interior, Agriculture, Commerce, and Labor, first created by Congress, Mar. 29, 1916, to co-ordinate transportation, mobilize industry, develop merchant shipping, and speed production of essential materials. s.

Council of Revision. A body consisting of the governor, chancellor, and judges of the supreme court of New York which had the power to veto acts of the legislature, 1777-1821. s.

Council of State Governments. A joint agency, founded in 1925 as the American Legislators' Association, which is maintained by the States as a research center and permanent secretariat for associations of State officials. It publishes the monthly *State Government* and a biennial *Book of the States*. s.

counselor of embassy. The legal adviser on an ambassador's staff. JWF.

counterfeit. A spurious coin or piece of paper money in imitation of one issued by public authority. s.

counterrevolution. Organized opposition to a revolutionary political movement on the part of those who wish to preserve the *status quo;* also the reaction which follows a political revolution, reversing the revolutionary trend and producing institutions antithetical in form and spirit to those which the revolution has established. z.

countervailing duty. An additional duty or surtax levied upon an imported commodity in order to neutralize bounties and other favors granted the producer or exporter of that commodity by the country of origin. JWF.

counting board. A board of three or more members which counts the votes cast at an election precinct.   s.

counting out. The illegal rejection of some ballots by a partisan election board in order to secure the election of a fellow-partisan.   s.

county. The most important unit of local government in the United States except in New England, where it exists mainly for judicial administration, and in Louisiana, where the equivalent unit is called a *parish*. In general, the county is the unit for judicial administration and the enforcement of the criminal law of the State; the assessment and collection of State and local taxes; the selection of polling places, appointment of election officials, and the canvassing of votes; the administration of schools and libraries; the construction and repair of roads and bridges; and indoor and outdoor relief and assistance. In nearly every State counties are governed by boards, either of supervisors or county commissioners, and by numerous officials, nearly all elective, of whom the most important are the sheriff, prosecuting attorney, coroner, assessor, and recorder.   s.

county clerk. A popularly elected county official who supervises registration of voters, prepares ballots, records land titles, mortgages, liens, etc., issues licenses, and performs other miscellaneous duties.   z.

county commissioner. A member of a board of usually from three to seven members which administers the affairs of a county, determines tax rates, appropriates funds, manages property, and appoints minor officials and employees.   s.

county court. A body formerly composed of all the justices of the peace within a county which was both the chief county administrative board and a court inferior to the circuit court. At present it may have purely administrative, or purely judicial functions, or combinations of both, depending on the laws of particular States.   s.

county manager. The executive head of a few American counties which have been reorganized on the analogy of the commission-manager plan for cities. He often lacks supervisory power over the entire administration of the county.   z.

coup d'état. A sudden attempt by a faction or band of conspirators to overthrow an existing government by violence or stratagem. z.

court. A tribunal which administers justice by enforcing laws, maintaining the rights of persons against impairment by government officials and private parties, and adjudicating controversies between individuals. *See* Judiciary.   s.

courtesy of the Senate. *See* Senatorial courtesy.

court martial. A tribunal consisting of military or naval officers which tries members of the armed forces or other persons accused of violating military or naval law. A *general court martial,* consisting of five or more officers, a judge advocate, and a defense counsel, may try any offense. *Special* and *summary courts martial* with limited jurisdictions are also authorized. JWF.

Court of Claims. A legislative court consisting of a chief justice and four associates set up in 1855 with recommendatory powers only, and in 1866 granted jurisdiction to decide claims against the government arising under contracts. In most cases its decisions are final, subject to appeal to the Supreme Court. S.

court of record. A court which exists independently of the magistrate who presides over it, which keeps a permanent record, which may punish contempt by fine or imprisonment, and to which writs of error may be directed. Courts of justices of the peace, and municipal, police, and probate courts are not of record unless so designated by statute. JJR.

covenant. A solemn contract between two or more parties. S.

Covenant of the League of Nations. That part of the Treaty of Versailles, 1919, which forms the constitution of the League of Nations (*q.v.*) S.

Covenant with the People. The introductory portion of the platform of the Progressive party in 1912. S.

Cowboy President. A nickname of Theodore Roosevelt. S.

Coxey's Army. A group of unemployed persons led by "General" Jacob S. Coxey which went to Washington, D. C., to present a "petition-in-boots" to Congress on May 1, 1894. S.

Cracker State. A nickname of Georgia. S.

Cradle of Liberty. Fanueil Hall in Boston, used as a meeting place for patriots at the beginning of the Revolution. S.

craft union. A labor union with membership limited to workers in a particular trade, as distinguished from an industrial union to which all who work within an industry are eligible. JJR.

Crawford County system. An early name for the direct primary election, derived from Crawford County, Pa., where the delegate convention was first abolished by party action. S.

credentials. Documentary testimonials offered by a principal recommending his agent to others or certifying to the agent's official status. Z.

credentials committee. The committee of a party convention which examines the credentials of delegates, holds hearings when contests occur, and recommends appropriate action. S.

Crédit Mobilier. A Pennsylvania corporation which in 1867 became the instrument by which officials of the Union Pacific Railroad transferred property of the railroad to themselves. Fearing an investigation they attempted in 1872 to bribe Congress. S.

Creole **case.** An incident arising from the freeing of slaves on board the American vessel *Creole* by the authorities of the Bahama Islands, where the vessel had been run into port by mutineers while *en voyage* from Virginia to New Orleans. On protest by the United States, Great Britain paid an indemnity to the owners of the slaves.   s.

Creole State. A nickname given to Louisiana because of its original colonial French population.   s.

crime. An offense against the law of the land, whether a felony or misdemeanor. Violations of local ordinances and police offenses are normally not considered crimes.   JWF.

Crime against Kansas. The title of a speech by Charles Sumner of Massachusetts in the United States Senate, May 19 and 20, 1856, which cast reflections on the methods of Southerners in trying to secure the admission of Kansas to the Union under the Lecompton Constitution (*q.v.*) After its delivery Representative Brooks of South Carolina assaulted Sumner with a heavy cane. s.

Crime of '73. The act of Congress of Feb. 12, 1873, which discontinued the coinage of silver dollars.   s.

criminal. A person who violates a law and who suffers punishment as a consequence after trial and conviction by a court; especially a person who commits an offense punishable by death or imprisonment.   JMCC.

criminal identification. The recording of significant physical characteristics of individual criminals, especially finger prints as in the Bertillon system, for rapid and permanent identification. JMCC.

criminal law. The branch of jurisprudence which deals with offenses committed against the safety and order of the state.   s.

criminal syndicalism. The advocacy of sabotage, violence, terrorism, or other unlawful methods for revolutionary purposes. Statutes imposing severe penalties for such advocacy, directed mainly against the Industrial Workers of the World, but enforced against Communists and others, were enacted in most of the States of the Union between 1917 and 1920.   JJR.

critical material. A material essential to national defense, the procurement of which in wartime poses a less difficult problem than that of a strategic material (*q.v.*) either because it is less essential, or is obtainable in more adequate quantities from domestic sources. s.

Critical Period. The period between the close of the Revolutionary War and the adoption of the Constitution.   s.

Crittenden Compromise. A proposal of Senator John J. Crittenden of Kentucky made in the winter of 1860-61 to restore the Missouri Compromise line, allow new States to decide the question of slavery for themselves, maintain interstate commerce in slaves, and provide federal compensation to owners of slaves freed by violence.   s.

Cross-of-Gold Speech. An address by William Jennings Bryan at the Democratic national convention at Chicago, June 10, 1896, which ended with the words: "You shall not crucify mankind upon a cross of gold" [the gold standard]. s.

cruel and unusual punishment. An inhumane punishment, such as torture, lingering death, or breaking on the wheel, applied in previous centuries but now generally condemned; or any punishment which is disproportionate to the offense, or which outrages the sensibilities of a community. Death by electrocution, unusual when introduced, is not within this category. JJR.

Cuba. A republic in the West Indies whose freedom from Spain was secured with the aid of the United States by the Treaty of Paris, Dec. 10, 1898. Following a period of American occupation, Cuba was set up as an independent republic in 1902, although under the Platt Amendment (*q.v.*), which Cuba was required to attach to its constitution, the United States reserved the right to intervene in Cuban domestic affairs to maintain order. The United States relinquished this right by treaty in 1936 but retains a naval and air base at Guantanamo Bay under a nominal rental. z.

Cumberland Road. A national highway projected and partly completed between Cumberland, Md., and the Ohio River, for which Congress appropriated $6,821,246 between 1806 and 1822. s.

cumulative voting. A system of minority representation which has been used since 1870 for the election of members of the lower

---

For State Senator, 28th District,
JOSEPH W. FIFER.

For Representative, 28th District,
THOMAS F. MITCHELL, 1½ votes.

GEORGE B. OKESON, 1½ votes.

For States Attorney,
ROBERT B. PORTER.

Cumulative voting — Part of Illinois ballot of 1880 (facsimile)

house of the Illinois legislature. Each voter has three votes which he may "plump" on one candidate or distribute among two or three candidates as he chooses. s.

curative statute. A law, retrospective in effect, which is designed to remedy some legal defect in previous transactions and validate them. Contractual obligations may not be impaired by such a statute, nor may unconstitutional statutes be revived. JJR.

currency. Any medium of exchange which is received everywhere throughout a country, whether it be coin or paper; or sometimes only paper money. The present currency of the United States consists chiefly of federal reserve notes, silver certificates, United States notes, silver dollars, and subsidiary coins of silver and base metals, with small amounts of national bank notes, federal reserve bank notes, and treasury notes, which are being rapidly retired from circulation. Gold coins and gold certificates were retired from circulation in 1933. The issuance of currency is a function solely of the national government. The States are forbidden to issue bills of credit.   s.

custody. The state of being watched or guarded, especially the guarding of accused persons to prevent escape.   jwf.

customary law. Law derived from long-established usages and customs, as distinguished from written law.   s.

customhouse. A public establishment for the inspection and assessment of duties on merchandise imported from other countries.   jwf.

customs. Taxes levied on imported goods at the time they enter a country.   s.

customs and patent appeals. *See* United States Court of Customs and Patent Appeals.

Customs Court. *See* United States Customs Court.

customs union. An agreement between two or more states to abolish tariffs and other restrictions upon their interstate trade and to adopt a common commercial policy towards other states. jwf.

czar. 1. The former absolute monarch of Russia. 2. A nickname of Thomas Brackett Reed, whose rulings as Speaker of the House of Representatives, 1889-91 and 1895-99, greatly limited the powers previously enjoyed by the minority.   s.

D

damages. Compensation, usually in money, awarded in a court of law for an injury inflicted upon person or property by another's wrongful action or failure to act.   z.

Danbury Hatters' case. A case, *Loewe* v. *Lawlor,* 208 U.S. 274 (1908), in which a nation-wide boycott instituted by employees against the products of an employer was declared to be in restraint of trade under the Sherman Antitrust Act.   s.

Danite. A Democrat who opposed Douglas in the Illinois senatorial campaign of 1858.   s.

Dark and Bloody Ground. A nickname of Kentucky.   s.

dark horse. A man who is unexpectedly nominated after a long course of futile balloting has resulted in a deadlock among the leading candidates. Among presidential dark horses were Polk, Pierce, Garfield, and Harding. s.

Dartmouth College case. *Dartmouth College* v. *Woodward,* 4 Wheat. 518 (1819), in which the Supreme Court decided that an act of the New Hampshire legislature altering the charter of Dartmouth College without its consent was in violation of the clause of the Constitution of the United States forbidding a State to impair the obligation of a contract. s.

Davis-Wade Manifesto. An ill-tempered paper issued by Representative Henry Winter Davis and Senator Benjamin F. Wade impugning President Lincoln's motives in failing to sign a bill for the reconstruction of seceded States in July, 1864. s.

Dawes Act. *See* Indian.

Dawes plan. A comprehensive plan, prepared by a committee of American and European experts headed by Charles G. Dawes, which fixed the total of German reparations payments to the Allied and Associated Powers of World War I and indicated the methods by which such payments were to be made. The plan was accepted and placed in operation Sept. 1, 1924, but was later superseded by the Young plan (*q.v.*) z.

daylight saving. The advancement of clocks one hour ahead of customary "sun time" in order to utilize a greater proportion of the daylight hours for work or recreation. JMCC.

dead-letter office. The Division of Dead Letters and Dead Parcels Post and its various branches in the Post Office Department, to which are sent all undeliverable letters and valuable parcels to be disposed of according to law. z.

deadlock. The refusal of parties engaged in a controversy to make further concessions or compromises, as in a party convention or a legislature. It may arise between two houses of a legislature, between the legislature and the executive, between two administrative agencies, or between states engaged in diplomatic negotiations. z.

deal. A secret bargain or understanding among politicians for the exchange of influence, support, appointment to public office, or other advantage not in the public interest. s.

death penalty. Death by electrocution, hanging, or other means exacted by the state of a person adjudged guilty of a heinous crime. JMCC.

death sentence clause. A provision of the federal Public Utility Holding Company Bill of 1935 which would have made public utility holding companies illegal. As passed, the law made possible the dissolution by legal proceedings of all but single integrated holding companies. JMCC.

debasement. The practice, once common among certain governments, of reducing the weight of gold and silver coins of standard value or of increasing the amount of alloy in such coins. z.

debate.   The examination of any project and the resolution of attendant issues in a legislative assembly or other public deliberative body by means of argumentation and discussion. Most contemporary legislative assemblies restrict opportunity for debate and limit the time of participants although they usually apportion available time equally between opponents and proponents of a measure.   z.

debt limit.   1. The maximum amount fixed by Congress from time to time beyond which the Secretary of the Treasury may not raise the public debt by borrowing even though existing statutes may authorize him to borrow.   2. The maximum amount of indebtedness fixed by a State constitution which a legislature may authorize. It may be either an absolute figure or a certain percentage of the assessed valuation of taxable property. The borrowing power of a municipality may be limited in a similar manner either by its charter or by law.   z.

debt service.   The allocation of funds in the annual budget or appropriation bills for the payment of legally required sums into a sinking fund, for the immediate amortization of such portions of the outstanding indebtedness as policy or the law may require, and for the payment of interest on outstanding debt.   z.

decentralization.   Division or dispersion of powers previously centralized in one place or under a single authority.   s.

decision.   The determination of a legal controversy or issue upon the law and facts involved by a judicial or similar tribunal. z.

declarant alien.   An alien in the United States who has formally declared his intention to become a citizen and who has been granted the appropriate certificate, or "first papers," in a court of record.   JWF.

declaration.   1. A document formally proclaiming the principles and aims of some public body and recommending, approving, or adopting a specific program of action.   2. An inventory of personal effects, currency, and merchandise in the possession of travelers crossing frontiers, often required in the administration of customs and frontier regulations.   z.

Declaration of Independence.   A document drafted by a committee consisting of Thomas Jefferson, John Adams, Benjamin Franklin, Roger Sherman, and Robert R. Livingston in response to a resolution presented in the Second Continental Congress, June 7, 1776. The draft, which was almost wholly the work of Jefferson, was reported from committee on June 28, and was adopted July 4, 1776. It consists of an enumeration of tyrannical acts by the King and Parliament of Great Britain, a justification for resistance to these acts on the basis of theories of natural rights and governmental contract, and a declaration that the colonies "are, and of Right ought to be, Free and Independent States; that they are Absolved from all Allegiance to the British Crown, and that all political connection between them and the State of Great Britain is, and ought to be, totally dissolved." Though the Declaration forms no part of the law of the land, the sentiments expressed in it of natural liberty, inalienable rights, and self-government have continued to exert a profound influence on American political thinking. s.

Declaration of London. A code of rules on naval warfare signed in London, Feb. 26, 1909, by representatives of the chief European states, Japan, and the United States. Although no power ratified it, most of its provisions were observed by belligerents in World War I. JWF.

Declaration of Paris. An agreement concluded by European powers in 1856, and since accepted by most states, that privateering was abolished; that enemy goods on neutral ships and neutral goods on enemy ships (except contraband) were free from seizure; and that a blockade must be effective to be binding. JWF.

declaration of war. A formal announcement transmitted by one state to another that war exists between them. International usage formerly required that the announcement precede hostilities; but of late some states, seeking the advantage of surprise attack, have issued the declaration after hostilities have commenced; and occasionally, in order to avoid legal disadvantages of formal belligerency, have dispensed with a declaration altogether. In the United States Congress declares war. JWF.

declaratory judgment. A judicial declaration, in an actual controversy, of the existing rights of parties under a statute, contract, will, or other document, without executory process granting relief, but binding upon the parties. It is not necessary to show that any wrong has been done, as in action for damages; or that any is immediately threatened, as in injunction proceedings. In most States and territories, and in federal courts since 1934, this remedy has been made available by statute as a means of ascertaining the rights of parties without expensive litigation, though the courts tend to construe these statutes narrowly. JJR.

deconcentration. Division or dispersal of powers formerly under a single authority. s.

dedication. A donation of property for public use, as for a street or sidewalk, which precludes the owner from ever claiming it again as his private property. z.

de facto. Actual; in fact; pertaining to a condition of affairs actually existing, in contradistinction to a *de jure* situation which is based on law, or right, or previous recognition. z.

Defender of the Constitution. A nickname of Daniel Webster. s.

defense, national. A broadly conceived effort to prepare a nation successfully to repel actual or potential external aggression. z.

Defense Homes Corporation. A United States government

corporation chartered in October, 1940, to provide funds for the building of homes in defense manufacturing areas and areas adjacent to combat training centers.   z.

Defense Plant Corporation.   A United States government corporation created by the Reconstruction Finance Corporation in August, 1940, to deal in and acquire strategic defense materials and to acquire equipment and provide plants to produce such materials.   z.

Defense Supplies Corporation.   A United States government corporation set up by the Reconstruction Finance Corporation in August, 1940, to acquire and deal in critical and strategic materials in the interests of national defense.   z.

deficiency bills.   Appropriation bills passed late in the fiscal year to provide for carrying out authorized projects when the regular appropriations are insufficient.   s.

deficit.   The difference between income (revenue) and expenditure when expenditure is greater.   JWF.

deficit financing.   Stationary or increased appropriations in the face of a sharp decline in public revenues: a characteristic of the 1930's when certain economists urged that the government should borrow for public works to speed up general economic activity, claiming that the burden of added debt would be more than offset by the resulting rise in national income.   z.

deflation.   An economic condition characterized by a fall in prices, that is, an increase in the value of the unit of a currency in terms of the commodities it will purchase or in terms of its exchange value with units of other currencies in a free international money market.   JWF.

degressive rate.   A uniform rate of taxation applied to a tax base from which increasing exemptions are made at different levels. It is in effect a progressive tax.   s.

de jure.   By right; according to law.   z.

Delaware.   One of the original States, and the first to ratify the Constitution of the United States, Dec. 7, 1787. Capital, Dover; area, 2,370 sq. mi.; population (1940), 266,505; presidential electors, 3. The present constitution was adopted in 1897. It is unique in that it may be amended without popular ratification by a two-thirds vote of the legislature in two successive regular sessions. A literacy test for the suffrage is required.   s.

delegate.   1. One who is selected by a constituency and authorized to act for it at a party or State constitutional convention. 2. A representative of a territory who has the right to speak but not to vote in the House of Representatives.   3. A member of the lower house of the legislature in Maryland, Virginia, and West Virginia.   EES.

delegated legislation. General rules having the validity of law, formulated and put into effect by an agency which has been authorized by the legislature to act for it; *e.g.,* in making detailed regulations to fit specific circumstances.   JJR.

delegation. Collectively, all the delegates from a State to a national nominating convention or from a county to a State or other party convention. Each delegation elects its chairman who is required to poll the delegates before announcing their votes.   S.

delegation of powers. The transfer of authority by some organ or branch of government in which such authority constitutionally reposes to some other organ or branch or to administrative agencies. Relying on the principle of *delegatus non potest delegare,* the courts have consistently denied that Congress can delegate legislative power; but they have upheld increasingly numerous legislative acts in which the legislature has outlined a broad policy or fixed certain limits, leaving to administrative officers or boards a large rule-making authority.   Z.

delinquency. 1. Minor infraction of the law or neglect to perform specific obligations established by law. 2. Vicious or criminal conduct or ungovernable character on the part of a child.   JMCC.

delinquent taxes. Taxes unpaid after the stated date for collection. Penalties are imposed for short-term delinquency. In case of persistent refusal to pay taxes on property, the property may revert to the taxing authority through foreclosure proceedings in the courts.   JMCC.

demagogue. A politician who lacks moral scruple and who attempts to gain popular favor by flattery, false promises, and appeals to the prejudices or passions of the mob.   Z.

demilitarization. The proscription of military activity within a designated area, involving usually the removal of all garrisons, armament, and military equipment and the razing of existing fortifications.   Z.

demobilization. The wholesale reduction of a nation's military establishment following a war or other national emergency, effected chiefly by discharging conscripts and reservists from active service. The sudden return to civilian life of millions of discharged soldiers disturbs the national economy, already seriously dislocated by the sudden stoppage of wartime demands, and usually influences adversely the national morale.   Z.

democracy. Rule by the people. In practice this means that power to determine the major issues of public policy must reside in the bulk or majority of the community and that in the making of such decisions, the vote of each individual shall count for one and none for more than one. Hence democracy may be described as government by consent and political equality. The people may exercise power either directly, as in city-states or town meetings, or indirectly through representative institutions in which the popular role is confined to using the ballot to enforce responsibility upon those to whom authority is entrusted. Since political democracy is based on the concept of equality, the term is often extended to cover institutions necessary to the preservation of the substance of such equality. Thus in a democratic system elections must be held with reasonable frequency and regularity, the ballot must be secret, and the individual must be secure against arbitrary arrest. Likewise there must be freedom of speech, of the press, of assembly, and of petition, as well as equality before the law. Democracy in its political sense seems to have come into modern usage in connection with a broad social ideal of which democratic government formed only a part. This broadened concept is apparent in the Puritan Revolution, and in the French revolutionary slogan of "Liberty, Equality, and Fraternity." The relative stress placed on each of these terms, and especially on the first two, has varied from time to time. As long as the major threat to both liberty and equality was to be found in the autocratic state and a feudal social system, the potential conflict between the ideals of liberty and equality did not become evident. When these elements had been swept away, however, it began to appear that some of the reformers were more interested in individual liberty than in equality, and others in the reverse. The fact emerged that complete liberty of the individual permits the development of serious inequalities of wealth and power, and that complete equality of political power is likely to result in action inimical to individual liberty, while economic equality can be achieved only at the expense of the liberty of the individual in certain respects. This conflict was somewhat mitigated by the interpretation of political democracy to include the protection of certain minority rights. It is through an interpretation of the third of the basic concepts, fraternity, that a reconciliation is best achieved, since it contains within it both the notion of equality and that of liberty, and since rights are protections against invasions of liberty. "Equality of opportunity" and "equality of consideration" are other phrases used to convey the same idea. The basic notion is that each individual is an end in himself, and that as such he is entitled to a certain presumption of equality with other human beings. Logically then, if not historically, the demand for equality of political power is based upon the conviction that in practice this is essential to equality of consideration in the long run: that without such equality, the "essential dignity of man" suffers. Social democracy entails the denial of all special privileges, political or social, not based upon merit. Those who lay their major emphasis upon the equalitarian aspect of democracy frequently insist that it involves a substantial degree of economic equality, and apply the term "economic democracy" to this ideal. Sometimes this phrase also implies a measure of direct regulation of industry by the workers themselves. JRP.

Democratic party. A major party which traces its origin from the Republican party of Jefferson, but which may be said to have arisen from the personal following of Jackson in the campaign of 1824 and the Democratic-Republican party of 1828. In that period it stood for frontier democracy, equality, the abolition of special privileges, the discontinuance of centralizing and loose-construction tendencies, and the maintenance of the Union. It won all but two presidential elections before 1860. During the slavery controversy it gained strength in the South but alienated Northern support. In 1860 it split into Northern and Southern Democratic parties. During the Civil War period it lost the support of War Democrats, who were only in part replaced later by the adherence of Liberal Republicans; but it became the "white man's party" in the South where it soon disposed of colored and carpetbag opposition. It has been rather more inclined than the Republicans to favor the common man, and less disposed toward the promotion of business interests. It has opposed imperialism, a completely centralized banking system, and, until 1928, high protective tariffs. On the currency question it has swung back and forth between advocacy of cheap money to attract greenback, populist, and silver support in the West; and "sound" money to bolster its Eastern following. Its presidential candidates have generally been successful State governors. It won the elections of 1884, 1892, 1912, and 1916 by close votes; and those from 1932 to 1940 inclusive by thumping majorities. In and out of power it has been hampered by conflicts among its Southern, Northern urban, and Western agrarian supporters. s.

Democratic-Republican party. The party which supported Jackson in the election of 1828. The name had been applied earlier to the Republican party (Jeffersonian) and is still occasionally used, *e.g.,* in New York City, as the official title of the Democratic party organization. s.

democratic societies. Organizations widely established in America, 1793-94, which expressed sympathy for the French Revolution, criticized Washington's foreign policy, and agitated for a wider suffrage. s.

demonetization. The withdrawal of a metal from use as money, thus taking from it a standard value and causing it to be merely a commodity. s.

denunciation. The act of giving notice of the termination of a treaty. The right of one party to terminate a treaty is usually defined in the treaty itself though in international law such a right is sometimes asserted in the principle of *rebus sic stantibus* (*q.v.*) Congress may fail to pass legislation to enforce a treaty municipally or pass legislation in contradiction with the terms of a treaty. The treaty, however, is still binding internationally unless formally denounced; and this power, subject to the rules of international law, appears to reside constitutionally in the President alone or in the President and Senate.   z.

department. 1. One of the three great divisions, legislative, executive, and judicial, into which governmental authority is divided.   2. One of ten administrative divisions of the national government, each presided over by a cabinet officer.   3. The most important administrative subdivision of a State or municipal government.   4. In France, a territorial division presided over by a prefect.   s.

dependency. An outlying possession subject to the sovereignty of a state but not incorporated into it.   s.

deportation. Forcible removal of an alien to his country of origin, resorted to in the United States in the case of aliens who become public charges within five years of entry or who commit serious crimes or engage in subversive activities.   z.

depositary. A treasury, bank, or vault where public monies are deposited and records are stored for safekeeping.   JWF.

deposit bank. A State bank in which federal funds were deposited after having been withdrawn from the Bank of the United States on President Jackson's orders.   s.

deposition. Testimony taken on oath in writing outside the courtroom to be used as evidence. The deponent may be cross-examined by the adverse party.   JJR.

depression. One of the several phases of the business cycle marked by business stagnation, low prices, and mass unemployment.   JMCC.

deputy. 1. Any person commissioned to represent another or to act in his behalf, the scope of such representation being either comprehensive and embracing all the principal's interests, or limited to specified interests.   2. Part of the title of a person acting either as the agent or substitute for a public official; *e.g.*, deputy prime minister; deputy sheriff.   3. A member of the lower house of the legislature in some European countries.   z.

deputy sheriff. An assistant appointed by a sheriff who serves writs, aids in law enforcement, and in some States may act in place of a sheriff. He is usually paid in fees.   z.

Deseret. A provisional territory organized by Mormons in 1849 including all the Mexican cession between the Rockies and the Sierra Nevada range. A petition to Congress for recognition as a State was disregarded, and Utah Territory was created in 1850.   z.

desertion. 1. Abandonment of duty in the military or naval service without leave and without intention of returning.   2. Abandonment of one of the partners in marriage by the other without prior arrangement for the discharge of responsibilities such as financial support or the care of the home and children.   JMCC.

Des Moines plan. A commission form of city government originating in Des Moines, Iowa, in 1907 which provided for nonpartisan nominations, the initiative and referendum, and the merit system in appointments.   S.

despotism. A political system in which the power to govern is concentrated in a ruler whose authority is unlimited.   JJR.

Destroyer deal. An executive agreement in September, 1940, between President F. D. Roosevelt and the British government under the terms of which the United States exchanged 50 overage destroyers in return for 99-year leases of several sites on British island and continental territory in the western Atlantic to be developed into American naval and air bases.   Z.

Destroyer deal — Bases secured from Great Britain

detention, house of. A building maintained by local governments to house lost or abandoned children, juvenile delinquents awaiting trial, and youthful material witnesses, when in the custody of the police.   JMCC.

devaluation. Reduction in the gold or silver content of the basic monetary unit; or the repeal of an existing privilege of converting paper money into metallic currency of a standard weight and fineness or the equivalent in uncoined metal. The American dollar was devaluated, Jan. 31, 1934, from 23.22 grains to 15 and 5/21 grains nine-tenths fine, or to 59.06 per cent of its former value in gold.   Z.

devolution. Allocation or delegation of powers normally exercised by a central governmental authority to several local or regional authorities or to functional groups.   Z.

Diamond State. A nickname of Delaware.   S.

dictatorship. 1. Absolute power vested in one or two persons, as in ancient Rome, for a strictly limited period during a crisis.

2. Absolute power over a state granted to, or seized by, a leader without effective constitutional limitation.   JJR.

die-hard. An irreconcilable.   S.

Dies Committee. A congressional committee to investigate "un-American" activities headed by Representative Martin Dies of Texas, first appointed in 1938 and continued with generous appropriations subsequently. Although apparently supported by Congress and the country, it has occasionally been denounced because of alleged recklessness in bringing charges of communism against various public figures and for usurping the functions of the Federal Bureau of Investigation.   z.

differential duty. A duty, roughly equivalent to the difference between the market value of an imported article in the country of origin and its cost to an importer, which is added to the normal duty on such an article. It is designed to discourage dumping or to overcome advantages accruing to an exporter because his country has depreciated its currency.   z.

Diggers. Members of an extreme leveling movement in England, led by Winstanley and Everard, who in 1649 began raising crops on the commons.   JJR.

dilatory motion. A parliamentary motion made for the purpose of delaying action on a legislative proposal, disrupting the time schedule of the majority party, and forcing it to make concessions to the minority.   S.

Dingley Act. The high protective tariff law of July 24, 1897, named for Nelson Dingley, of Maine, chairman of the House Committee on Ways and Means.   S.

diplomacy. The art and practice of conducting negotiations between sovereign states for the attainment of mutually satisfactory political relations. The term does not embrace international relations of an administrative character. It deals with phases of such relations which lie outside the scope of law and is normally based on considerations of national interest or expediency, and directed toward the maintenance or increase of national power and prestige. Direct diplomatic negotiations between heads of states occasionally take place, but for the most part they are conducted through diplomatic agents (*q.v.*)   z.

diplomatic agent. An agent sent by one state to the seat of government of another to conduct negotiations and serve as an intermediary in international intercourse. He observes and reports political events of importance, adjusts claims, and seeks to protect the citizens and nationals of his state against wrongful acts by officers of the state to which he is sent. He is appointed by the head of his state. If his conduct is unsatisfactory he may be recalled on the demand of the state to which he is sent or in extreme cases he may be dismissed. Diplomatic agents rank as follows: (1) ambassadors, legates, and nuncios, who represent the person of the head of the state; (2) envoys, ministers, etc., accredited to the sovereign; (3) ministers resident, who are of lower rank than ministers but are accredited to the sovereign; (4) chargés d'affaires, accredited to the head of the office for foreign affairs.   s.

diplomatic corps. Collectively, the whole body of foreign diplomatic agents residing at the capital of a state.   JWF.

diplomatic immunity. The exemption under international law of a foreign diplomat, his entourage, and the premises they occupy, from taxation, civil suit, criminal process, searches and seizures, and the obligation to appear as witnesses in court in the state to which the diplomat is accredited or through which he may be traveling.   JWF.

direct action. Resort to intimidation or violence to secure political power within a state or to achieve some political objective. z.

direct initiative. *See* Initiative.

directive. An order or instruction issued by a superior to a lesser administrative official.   s.

direct legislation. Participation by the electorate in the process of lawmaking, as in the initiative and referendum (*qq.v.*), or in town meeting.   s.

direct nomination. The nomination of a candidate for public office by means of a petition circulated among voters or through the direct primary.   z.

direct primary election. *See* Primary.

direct tax. A tax the burden or incidence of which cannot readily be shifted from the person or the property upon which it has been formally levied. Under the Constitution poll taxes and taxes upon property or the income therefrom are direct taxes. z.

disability. 1. Legal incapacity, which may result from infancy, insanity, or some overt act in contravention of law. 2. Lack of legal qualifications to hold an office. Want of sufficient age or period of residence, the holding of an incompatible office, foreign citizenship, and, for the presidency, foreign birth, are disabilities. s.

disallowance. The power of the government of a metropolitan state to reject or annul acts of a colonial legislature; *e.g.,* the power of the British Crown to annul American colonial legislation, or the power of Congress to annul legislation of territories and dependencies. A similar power is wielded by the Dominion government over legislative acts of Canadian provinces.   z.

disarmament. The limitation of the size of the world's armies, navies, and air forces and the reduction of the amount and caliber of their armament and equipment. Many efforts in this direction, usually abortive, were made in the period between World War I and World War II.   z.

Disaster Loan Corporation. A United States government corporation created by Congress in 1937 to provide rehabilitation loans to persons who are victims of floods or other natural disasters. z.

disbarment. Deprivation of the privilege of an attorney to practice his profession. z.

discharge. 1. The release of an individual from custody, from legal obligations, or from the jurisdiction of some tribunal. 2. The release of a committee from further consideration of any matter which may have been submitted to it by a legislative assembly. It has the effect of bringing a matter to the floor. z.

discipline. The maintenance of order and decorum in any organized public body, or the maintenance of the authority of an administrative superior over a subordinate. z.

discovery, right of. A claim to sovereignty over territory based on its prior discovery by nationals of a state. z.

discrimination, racial. Unfair or unequal treatment accorded by custom or law to some of a community's members because of their color or other alleged racial characteristics. JWF.

discrimination, social. Denial to some members of a state or society of privileges which other members enjoy because of their allegedly superior birth or their economic status, education, or occupation. JWF.

disfranchisement. Deprivation of some right or privilege previously enjoyed, particularly the privilege of voting. It may result from raising the suffrage requirements, discriminatory acts of election officials, or intimidation. EES.

disgruntled. Disappointed; dissatisfied with nominations, party policies, or failure to obtain appointive office. S.

dishonorable discharge. Dismissal from military service for undignified, shameful, or disgraceful conduct or conduct involving moral turpitude. z.

dismissal from office. Removal from office either summarily or after a hearing. z.

disorderly conduct. An act legally interdicted as an offense against public morals, peace, or safety. z.

dispensing power. The power of the President to make political appointments to offices which by executive action had been previously placed under civil service rules. S.

disputed election. An election which both leading candidates claim to have won. It differs from a contested election (*q.v.*), in that no regular provision has been made by constitution or statute to determine the result; *e.g.,* the presidential election of 1876, which was finally decided by an electoral commission. S.

disqualification. Inability to hold public office or employment, or to continue in such office or employment, or to exercise some public privilege such as voting because of lack of positive legal requirements, or mental or physical incapacity, or the commission of a crime.   z.

dissenting opinion. A statement by one or more members of a tribunal of their reasons for disagreement with the majority in the disposition of a case. Such opinions sometimes foreshadow changing rules of the law.   JJR.

Distinguished Flying Cross. A bronze cross *pattée* with a four-blade propeller superimposed on the obverse awarded to combat flyers for extraordinary heroism or achievement in aerial flight. z.

| Distinguished | Distinguished | Distinguished |
| Flying Cross | Service Cross | Service Medal (Army) |

Distinguished Service Cross. A bronze cross with an eagle and the inscription "For Valor" on the obverse awarded to soldiers for extraordinary heroism in combat operations.   z.

Distinguished Service Medal. A medal awarded to members either of the military or naval forces for exceptionally meritorious service in the performance of duties requiring great responsibility. The army medal bears the coat of arms of the United States in bronze surrounded by a blue-enameled circle bearing the words "For Distinguished Service"; the navy medal has the figure of an American eagle within a band inscribed, "United States of America and Navy."   z.

district. A definite territorial area of a nation, State, county, city, or other unit delimited by law for judicial, electoral, or administrative purposes.   s.

district attorney. 1. A representative of the Department of Justice in each of the judicial districts into which the United States is divided who represents the United States in bringing indictments and prosecuting criminal cases for violations of national law. 2. A locally elective State official, otherwise called the prosecuting attorney or State's attorney, with similar duties in the enforcement of State law.   s.

district court. The lowest constitutional court in the federal judicial system. It has original jurisdiction over nearly all civil, criminal, and admiralty cases arising under national laws, and over cases resulting from diversity of State citizenship. There are more than 90 district courts, with about 180 district judges.   s.

district leader.   The boss or leader of a political party in an assembly district or ward.   s.

District of Columbia.   The seat of government of the United States over which Congress may exercise "exclusive legislation in all cases whatsoever." It originally embraced 100 square miles ceded by Maryland and Virginia, but in 1846 the Virginia cession was returned, leaving an area of about 62 square miles. Its population in 1940 was 663,091. Two municipal corporations, Washington and Georgetown, existed until 1871 when Congress set up a government resembling that of a territory. By a temporary law, 1874 (made permanent in 1878), Congress made the District a municipal corporation and directly assumed sole legislative authority, even to the passing of laws resembling local ordinances elsewhere. Three commissioners appointed by the President, one of whom must be an officer in the Engineer Corps of the Army, perform the usual functions of the municipal executive. Education is administered by a board appointed by the judges of the Supreme Court of the District. A board of charities is appointed by the President. The national government pays a portion — now about one seventh — of the expenses of the District. The people are guaranteed all civil rights under the Constitution, but they may not vote except in States in which they have a legal residence.   s.

divided sovereignty.   The theory, now generally regarded as obsolescent, that the national government and the States are each sovereign within the fields of authority respectively allocated to them by the Constitution.   JWF.

divine right.   The right of a monarch to his office because of (1) the divinity of his person, or (2) the divine origin and authority of his office, or (3) inheritance of the right from ancestors who were divinely appointed to rule.   JJR.

division.   **1.** A subordinate administrative unit ranking in most cases below a bureau.   **2.** A method of voting in an assembly by which members for and against a motion alternately stand and are counted by the presiding officer (United States), or pass in two files before tellers (Great Britain).   s.

division of powers.   **1.** The strict allocation of governmental authority between the States and the national government.   **2.** The principle (more accurately called separation of powers) that legislative, executive, and judicial powers should be assigned to mutually independent authorities.   s.

Division of Territories and Island Possessions.   A division in the Department of the Interior created by executive order in July, 1934. Through local officials in the territories and possessions. this division supervises various services of the national government, including those formerly administered by the Bureau of Insular Affairs. z.

Dixie. A familiar name for the States south of the Mason and Dixon line. s.

docket. A list of cases pending before a court or in which judgment has been rendered with brief minutes of all proceedings thereon. z.

doctrinaire. One who attempts to apply some logical system of thought, abstract philosophy, doctrine, or dogma, with little or no regard for practical considerations. z.

document. An official paper, deed, manuscript, or any other written or inscribed instrument which has informational or evidentiary value. z.

dole. An English nickname for public unemployment relief. The term is used in a disparaging sense in America. JMCC.

dollar. The basic monetary unit of the United States; a gold or silver coin or paper note of the legal value of 100 cents. z.

dollar-a-year man. A government official or employee who accepts the minimum salary required by law. EES.

dollar diplomacy. A nickname for the foreign policy of the United States early in the 20th century which was alleged to be for the purpose of expanding American financial and commercial interests abroad under the guise of promoting international friendship. s.

domain. Territory over which sovereignty or public authority is exerted. z.

domestic corporation. A corporation created under the laws of the State in which it does business. JJR.

domestic relations court. A judicial tribunal of inferior grade, usually part of a system of municipal courts, the jurisdiction of which extends to petty family disputes. z.

domestic violence. Extensive disorder within a State of the Union. Under the Constitution and an act of Congress of 1795 the legislature, or when it is not in session, the governor, may apply to the President for military intervention to suppress domestic violence; but the President may act without such application in order to enforce national law. JJR.

domicile. The permanent place of residence of a person or the place to which he intends to return even though he may actually reside elsewhere. The legal domicile of a person is important since it, rather than the actual residence, often controls the jurisdiction of the taxing authorities and determines where a person may exercise the privilege of voting and other legal rights and privileges. z.

domination. The exercise of sovereignty or controlling authority without constitutional or moral restraints. z.

Dominican Republic. A Spanish-speaking republic, formerly called Santo Domingo, on the island of Hispaniola in the West Indies. A treaty to annex it was negotiated by President Grant, 1869, but failed of ratification in the Senate. By executive agreement in 1905 and by treaty in 1907, the collection of customs duties and the debt service of the Dominican Republic were placed in charge of a receiver appointed by the President of the United States.   s.

dominion. 1. One of the self-governing nations in the British Commonwealth; *e.g.,* the Dominion of Canada. 2. The exercise of sovereignty or governmental supremacy over territory.   z.

donkey. A symbol for the Democratic party originated by the cartoonist Thomas Nast in 1874.   s.

doorkeeper. An employee of a legislative chamber who has charge of furniture and equipment and enforces rules governing the admission of persons to the floor or galleries.   JWF.

Dorr Rebellion. A violent, but luckily bloodless, incident in the manhood-suffrage movement in Rhode Island. In 1842 Thomas W. Dorr was elected governor under a constitution framed by an unofficial "people's convention" and ratified by an unofficial popular vote. When President Tyler supported the legitimate government, Dorr fled the State and his followers disbanded.   s.

double jeopardy. Putting a person on trial for an offense for which he has previously been properly indicted and a jury has been empaneled and sworn to try him, provided that the jury has not disagreed or been discharged because of the illness of a juror or other sufficient reason. *See* Jeopardy.   s.

double standard. The coinage of two metals at the same time both having a standard value and both being legal tender.   s.

doubtful State. Any State where the voting strength of the major parties is so evenly divided that the outcome in a presidential election is unpredictable, or where experience has demonstrated that the candidate of no one party consistently obtains a plurality. z.

doughface. One easily molded to forsake his principles, as — according to John Randolph of Roanoke — a Northern member of Congress who voted with Southern members when the Missouri Compromise was under consideration.   s.

draft. Originally the selection of men from the organized or unorganized militia for compulsory active service with the armed forces. At present the organized militia (National Guard) is drafted into the federal service. Others are chosen for duty under the Selective Service System (*q.v.*)   s.

draft riots. Riots in protest against the draft law of 1863. They were especially serious in New York City, July 13-16, where 1,000 persons were killed and property was destroyed to the value of more than $1,500,000.   s.

Drago Doctrine. A principle formulated in 1902 by Luis M. Drago, foreign minister of Argentina, that "a public debt cannot give rise to the right of intervention, and much less to the occupation of the soil of any American nation by any European power." In 1907 the Hague Conference endorsed the doctrine in the modified form that intervention should not be used in the collection of debts unless the creditor nation had proposed, and been refused, arbitration. s.

drawback. A rebate of customs duties paid when articles on which they were levied are re-exported either in their original or a manufactured form. s.

Dred Scott case. The case, *Dred Scott v. Sandford,* 19 How. 393 (1857), of a Negro slave who had resided with his master for several years in the free State of Illinois and at Fort Snelling, which was in a territory that had been made free by the Missouri Compromise. On being returned to Missouri, Scott sued his master, a citizen of New York, for his freedom. The Supreme Court held, Justices Curtis and McLean dissenting, that Scott was not a citizen and therefore had no standing in court under the diversity of citizenship clause of the Constitution; that national citizenship was determined by State citizenship; and in *obiter dicta,* that the Missouri Compromise was unconstitutional because Congress had no right to prevent citizens from carrying their slaves into a territory or to impair the protection which should be given to property while it is in a territory. s.

Droop quota. A quota devised by H. R. Droop in 1869 and normally used with the Hare system of proportional representation. To find it in any election divide the total vote cast for all candidates by the number of seats to be filled plus one, disregard fractions, and add one to the quotient. s.

dry. One who advocates prohibition of the manufacture, sale, or use of intoxicating liquors. s.

dual citizenship. 1. In the United States, possession of both State and national citizenship. 2. Simultaneous possession of citizenship in two countries resulting from diversity of nationality laws or the unwillingness of one country to permit the expatriation of a citizen or subject who has been naturalized in another. jwf.

dual federalism. A doctrine occasionally maintained by the courts that the powers of the national and State governments are separate and distinct, and that the powers delegated to the national government are limited by the powers reserved to the States under the 10th Amendment. z.

dual officeholding. The holding of two public offices simultaneously, prohibited when one office is membership in a legislative body. z.

dudes and pharisees. Republicans who were accused of over-scrupulousness and a "holier-than-thou" attitude because they refused to support Blaine for the presidency in 1884.   s.

due process. Legal restrictions confining the government "within the limits of those fundamental principles of liberty and justice which lie at the base of all our civil and political institutions" (*Hurtado* v. *California,* 110 U.S. 516, 1884). Originally derived from the common law and directed in England to restraining the executive from adopting arbitrary methods of depriving persons of life, liberty, or property, these restrictions in America have been expanded to cover all departments of government and now include both procedural limitations and limitations upon the substance of the laws themselves. *Procedural due process* was defined by Daniel Webster as a procedure "which hears before it condemns, which proceeds upon inquiry, and renders judgment only after trial." *Substantive due process* requires that the statutes under which a person is tried must be free from arbitrary and unjust provisions. What fundamental principles of liberty and justice constitute due process may be discovered in part from bills of rights whose specific provisions are usually considered to be within the scope of the general due process clauses. Otherwise, due process derives its meaning from those customs, traditions, legislative enactments, judicial precedents, and current views of right and wrong which collectively have come to be accepted as a part of the established law of the land. In this sense, the due-process clauses of American State and federal constitutions become a reservoir of implied constitutional limitations upon governmental authority whose content is largely determined by actual litigation in the courts.   JTC.

dues. Regular contributions demanded of members of an organization such as the Socialist party.   z.

Duke's Laws. The framework of government established for the Colony of New York after its conquest from the Dutch in 1664 by the Duke of York.   s.

dumping. The disposal of a surplus of a given commodity by selling it abroad at or below cost of production. Possible reasons include limitation of the home supply to maintain a price level, production at capacity to reduce unit cost, and the destruction of competitors by underselling them in their best markets.   JWF.

duty. 1. An obligation imposed by law on an officer or private person. 2. A moral obligation upon a citizen, subject, or voter. 3. A tax on imported goods.   z.

E

earned income. Income derived from wages, salaries, profits, or fees, as opposed to income derived from rents, dividends, interest, gifts, or the returns from trust funds. Roughly, the distinction is one between income derived from labor or entrepreneurship and income derived from invested capital. z.

easement. A privilege or liberty of use without right to profits, as distinguished from complete ownership or a revocable license to use, which one person enjoys in the estate of a neighbor. It may arise by deed or prescription (*q.v.*) JJR.

Easy Boss. A nickname of Senator Thomas C. Platt. s.

Eaton affair. A tempest in Washington society caused by the refusal of the wives of high officials to recognize the wife of Secretary of War John H. Eaton in defiance of President Jackson's wishes. Martin Van Buren, a widower, is sometimes supposed to have won his advancement through conspicuous gallantry toward Mrs. Eaton. s.

economic council. A body composed of representatives of economic interests and occupational groups, having advisory governmental functions or direct governing power either as an organ co-ordinate with the political parliament or as a legislative assembly the members of which represent economic groups and interests. JJR.

economic determinism. The theory that in every historical epoch, the prevailing mode of economic production and exchange determines the form of social and political organization and explains the political, intellectual, and moral history of the people. JMCC.

economic nationalism. The policy of a state in imposing protective tariffs, quotas, and other trade barriers, establishing exchange controls, monopolizing raw materials by embargoes, creating cartels to control foreign trade, or acquiring colonies and other sources of strategic raw materials, in order to assure economic self-sufficiency and protection against other states. s.

economic planning. *See* Planning.

economic warfare. The use of any means, ranging from blockade to preclusive buying of strategic or critical materials in neutral countries, blacklisting, and pressures upon neutral states, which is designed to hamper an enemy's ability to obtain munitions or cripple his domestic economy. JWF.

Edge Act. A law of Congress Dec. 24, 1919, which permitted the national chartering of corporations to engage in trade or financial operations abroad. s.

Edmunds Act. A law of Congress Mar. 22, 1882, prohibiting polygamy in the territories under severe penalties. s.

education, public. Provision for schooling at state expense and under public control. It began early in the colonial period in New England but was not in effect in some States until long after the Civil War. It is usually administered by school districts, towns, or townships, and recently in some States by county boards of education. State regulations providing minimum requirements for teachers, equipment, length of school terms, etc., and uniform courses of study, textbooks, and requirements for graduation are usual and are especially effective where State aid to local areas is conditioned upon the maintenance of certain standards. Most of the States maintain universities and teachers' colleges and other institutions of higher education. *See also* Agricultural and mechanical college; United States Office of Education.   s.

educational order. A government contract for the production of a small quantity of munitions given to a manufacturer in order that he may learn through experience how to produce efficiently a much larger quantity later.   s.

educational qualification. A requirement that a person, in order to vote, must have successfully pursued his studies through a certain grade in school or give satisfactory evidence of his ability to read and write. *See* Literacy test.   s.

Egypt. A nickname for southern Illinois.   s.

E.H.F.A. *See* Electric Home and Farm Authority.

Eighteenth Amendment. An amendment to the Constitution of the United States, proclaimed Jan. 29, 1919, which prohibited the manufacture, transportation, and sale of alcoholic beverages and granted Congress and the States concurrent powers to enforce these prohibitions. The Amendment was repealed Dec. 5, 1933, by the 21st Amendment.   EES.

eight-hour movement. The effort on the part of organized labor in the United States and elsewhere to secure recognition, in agreements with employers and in the law, of the proposition that eight hours of continuous labor constitutes a maximum working day and that time in excess of that maximum should receive extra compensation. Beginning with the Adamson Act, 1916, which legalized the eight-hour day for railway employees, labor has secured increasing legal recognition of the eight-hour day in private employment. More recently, national law has established a maximum working week which averages considerably less than eight hours for six consecutive working days. *See* Fair Labor Standards Act. z.

elastic clause. The 18th clause of Art. I, sec. 8 of the Constitution of the United States, sometimes referred to as the "necessary and proper clause," which grants Congress power to make all laws necessary and proper for carrying into execution all other legislative powers committed to it. Chief Justice Marshall in the case of *McCulloch* v. *Maryland* (*q.v.*) gave this clause a liberal interpretation, declaring that if no other motive for its inclusion in the Constitution could be suggested, a sufficient one was found "in the desire to remove all doubts respecting the right to legislate on that vast mass of incidental powers which must be involved in the constitution if that instrument be not a splendid bauble."   z.

elastic currency. A monetary system such as that inaugurated in the United States in 1933 in which the standard currency unit ceases to have a constant value in terms of a certain weight and fineness of some precious metal, administrative authority being competent to change the value ratio from time to time within legal limits; or in which the exchange value of the standard currency unit can be deliberately increased or decreased by administrative authority. z.

election. A choice, by persons qualified to vote, among candidates for a public office. (Referenda are sometimes erroneously called elections.) In the United States the administration of elections is under State authority, subject to the provision that in the election of members of Congress and presidential electors the regulations contained in national corrupt practices acts must be observed and national officers may be assigned to attend the polls and prevent fraud, intimidation and other irregularities. Legally Congress might require that elections of national officers be conducted by nationally appointed election officials. The preparation of ballots, including the determination of the validity of nominations, is usually a function of a State secretary of state. Locally appointed bipartisan boards, clerks, and other officers conduct the polling in the precincts. The counting of votes is usually done in the separate precincts, though recently in Kentucky there has been a state-wide central count, and the same principle has been applied in counties and cities in some other States. s.

election board. A bipartisan board, usually consisting of three inspectors or commissioners and two clerks appointed in each election precinct by county authorities, which determines whether individual voters are qualified, supervises the polling, and often counts the votes. s.

election certificate. *See* Certificate of election.

election district. 1. An election precinct. 2. The area from which one or more officers are chosen by popular vote. z.

election precinct. A compact area usually including from 150 to 800 voters in which there is established one polling place. s.

elector. 1. Any person who is entitled to vote. 2. A member of an electoral college (*q.v.*) s.

electoral college. Any body of electors, limited in number, meeting in one place to choose a public official. The Constitution actually provides for 48 electoral colleges, or one in each State, constituted in whatever manner the legislature of the State may provide. Today the laws of every State require that electors shall be popularly chosen. All the colleges meet at the same time in their respective State capitals and ballot separately for President and Vice President. Since 1796 the members of the colleges have with one exception (in 1820) invariably cast their ballots for the presidential and vice presidential candidates placed in nomination by the electors' respective party caucuses or conventions. z.

Electoral Commission. A body consisting of five Senators, five Representatives, and five Justices of the Supreme Court created by act of Congress Jan. 29, 1877, to resolve the deadlock between the two houses of Congress as to the proper method of counting the disputed electoral votes in that year. It decided all disputes in favor of the Republicans by a strict party vote of eight to seven, thus insuring the election of the Republican candidate, Rutherford B. Hayes.   s.

Electoral Count Act. An act of Congress Feb. 3, 1887, which provides that disputes concerning the election of presidential electors shall be settled by a judicial or other authority designated by law within each State six days before the date set for the meeting of the State's electors. If a State neglects to provide for such a body, the decision is to be made by the two houses of Congress voting separately. If they disagree the returns certified by the governor are to be accepted; otherwise the State's electoral votes are not to be counted.   s.

electoral quota (or quotient). The smallest number of votes which will suffice for election under a system of proportional representation. *See* Droop quota.   s.

electorate. Collectively, the whole body of persons who are legally qualified to vote.   s.

Electric Home and Farm Authority. A United States government corporation chartered in the District of Columbia in 1935, and now operating under the Department of Commerce. Through private utility companies it aids consumers in buying electrical appliances on the instalment plan.   z.

electric voting. A device used in a few State legislatures by which votes may be flashed to the clerk by pressing different buttons at members' desks, thus saving time in roll calls.   s.

elephant. A symbol for the Republican party originated by the cartoonist Thomas Nast in 1874.   s.

Eleventh Amendment. An amendment to the Constitution proposed after the Supreme Court had accepted jurisdiction in a suit brought by one Chisholm, a citizen of South Carolina, against the State of Georgia (2 Dall. 419, 1793); and proclaimed in force Jan. 8, 1798. It provides that the judicial power shall not be construed to extend to any suit in law or equity commenced or prosecuted against one of the United States by citizens of another State or of a foreign country.   z.

eligibility. Fulfillment of the qualifications legally required for election or appointment to some public office, for the enjoyment of some civic privilege such as voting, or for the performance of some civic duty such as jury service. Citizenship, the possession of one's mental faculties, and the absence of a criminal record are practically the only qualifications for elective office universally required of adult persons. Special minimum age and residential requirements are established for Representatives, Senators, and certain other officials. To be eligible for the office of President or Vice President, a person must be a native-born citizen, be at least 35 years of age, and have resided in the United States for at least 14 years prior to election.   z.

eligible list. A list of qualified persons drawn up by a civil service commission or equivalent agency from which are supplied candidates to fill vacancies in the civil service.   z.

Elliot's *Debates*. The standard source for the debates of State conventions ratifying the Constitution of the United States in four volumes edited by Jonathan Elliot. The first edition was published in 1827-30.   s.

emancipation. The act of freeing a slave. All the Northern States passed acts of absolute or gradual emancipation between 1774 and 1804, and there was an active emancipationist movement in all the border slave States until about 1850.   s.

Emancipation Proclamation. A proclamation issued by President Lincoln, Jan. 1, 1863, after 100 days' preliminary notice, which declared all slaves free in the States then in rebellion except Tennessee and the parts of Virginia and Louisiana occupied by Union troops. It did not affect slavery in the loyal slave States. It was justified as an act of military necessity under the President's powers as commander-in-chief.   s.

embargo. An order issued by a state detaining vessels in its ports, usually as an act of reprisal or coercion against another state. A *hostile embargo* is a seizure of foreign ships, which may become permanent if war follows. A *civil embargo,* such as the Embargo Act of 1807 (repealed in 1809), prevents the departure of vessels or goods belonging to the state which declares it. Often it is accompanied by the closing of ports to vessels of an offending state.   s.

embassy. 1. The official residence of an ambassador. 2. The mission on which an ambassador is sent. 3. The entourage of persons attached to his staff.   JWF.

embezzlement. Misappropriation of funds or illegal diversion of funds to the personal use of an employee to whom such funds have been entrusted.   JWF.

emergency measure. A law which is urgently required for the preservation of the public peace, health, or safety, and which goes into effect immediately, and is not subject to a referendum. s.

emergency powers. 1. Powers conferred upon the executive for a limited time or until withdrawn by the legislature. 2. Powers, such as the war powers, granted in the Constitution but not used in ordinary times. The Supreme Court has declared that "although an emergency may not call into life a power which has never lived, nevertheless emergency may afford a reason for the exertion of a living power already enjoyed." *Wilson* v. *New* 243 U.S. 332 (1917). The President or Congress has sometimes claimed the existence of other "emergency powers."   s.

emigrant aid societies. Organizations in the North which aided antislavery men to settle in Kansas, 1854-61.   s.

eminent domain. The paramount right of the sovereign to take over, or use, private property. It may be exercised by both national and State governments, but only for a public purpose and on payment of just compensation. "Public purpose" includes the power to confer the right upon public service companies. "Just compensation" means a monetary award which is determined by judicial proceedings, often with a jury, in which an owner has a right to be heard.   s.

emolument. The salary, fees, or perquisites of an office or of any specific employment.   z.

Empire State. A nickname of New York.   s.

employer's liability law. Any law, such as those passed by most of the States since 1910, which modifies common-law rules respecting an employer's responsibility for accidents and requires him to make compensation through an insurance fund or otherwise. It does not, except in a few States, provide compensation for farm laborers, domestic servants, or employees in very small establishments.   s.

enabling act. 1. A legislative act authorizing an executive or administrative official, organ of local government, or a corporation to exercise some unusual power. 2. An act of Congress authorizing the people of a territory to call a constitutional convention or take other steps preparatory to admission to statehood.   z.

enacting clause. An indispensable clause at the beginning of every statute which states the authority by which it is made. For an act of Congress the clause is: "Be it enacted by the Senate and House of Representatives of the United States of America, in Congress assembled"; for a joint resolution: "Resolved by, etc."; for an act in New York: "The people of the State of New York, represented in Senate and Assembly, do enact as follows."   s.

enactment. The action, usually completed by the signature of the chief executive, by which a legislature creates a statute from a bill.   z.

Enderbury Island. One of the Phoenix group in the mid-Pacific which, with Canton Island, has been jointly administered by the United States and Great Britain since April, 1939. It is valuable as a communications and air transit station.   z.

endless chain. The repeated selling of bonds by the United States Treasury in 1894-95 to replenish the gold reserve, which continued to be drawn upon by persons who feared for the stability of the currency. s.

endless chain fraud. *See* Tasmanian dodge.

enemy. In warfare the term applied to one belligerent by the other. JWF.

enemy alien. An alien domiciled or traveling within a belligerent state who is a national of an enemy state. Enemy aliens may be interned or restricted as to place of residence, freedom of travel, possession of arms and equipment for sending or receiving information, and otherwise, at the discretion of the state. For good behavior a class of such persons may be removed from the restrictions imposed under this status. s.

enforcement. An action or process to compel observance of law or the requirements of public policy. z.

Enforcement Act. A law of Congress passed in 1870 and repealed in 1894 which prohibited racial discrimination by election officials, and bribery, intimidation, and violence by private parties in national elections. s.

enfranchise. To confer the privilege of voting upon classes of persons who have not previously possessed it. s.

engrossment. The action of drafting an authoritative copy of a resolution or bill just prior to the final vote upon it in a legislative house. z.

enlistment. The action of joining voluntarily the personnel of one of the state's armed services. z.

Enoch Arden law. A New York statute granting permission to remarry without fear of legal penalty to a person whose spouse has been absent for five successive years and is presumed to be dead; or a similar law in another State. JMCC.

enrolled bill. The final copy, printed or written in permanent form, of every bill or joint resolution which has passed both houses of a legislature and is ready for signature. s.

enrollment. 1. The action of registering or recording a document, or of preparing an enrolled bill (*q.v.*) 2. The official listing of vessels engaged in fisheries or limited domestic commerce which, because they do not engage in foreign commerce, are not entitled to registry. 3. The act of registering one's affiliation with a political party in order to participate in a primary election. z.

ensign. 1. A national flag. 2. A flag or banner indicating the nationality of a ship at sea. z.

entail. The transmission of the ownership of land by inheritance in accordance with a predetermined order of succession, the one holding the land at any given time being legally forbidden to change the order of succession to ownership or to alienate the property. Entail has been abolished in the United States. z.

entangling alliance. A treaty with a foreign state which would obligate the United States to participate in some future action in circumstances over which it may have no control or real interest. The phrase, first officially used in Jefferson's first inaugural address, has been repeated by isolationists ever since.   s.

entente. A general understanding reached by two or more states to compose all outstanding differences and to pursue a policy of reciprocal aid and diplomatic solidarity in their relations with other states. An entente is broader in scope and less explicit than an alliance although it may embrace a tacit alliance.   z.

enumerated powers. The 18 powers specifically given to Congress in Article I of the Constitution; in a more general sense, the powers specifically delegated by the Constitution to some branch or authority of the national government, and which are not denied to that government or reserved to the States or to the people. JWF.

envelope ballot. A device, used now only in Delaware, by which official ballots mailed to voters before election day may be marked at their homes, taken by them to their polling places, and deposited in sealed envelopes.   s.

envoy. A diplomat of the rank of minister or ambassador sent by a state to an international conference or to the government of a foreign state to execute a special mission or to serve as a permanent diplomatic representative.   JAP.

E Pluribus Unum. A Latin motto, meaning "one from many," appearing on the obverse of the Great Seal of the United States and on many pieces of currency.   s.

equality. The principle stated in the Declaration of Independence and similar public documents which asserts the fundamentally similar worth of every human being. It is a cardinal premise of democracy and provides the logical and moral justification for such democratic institutions as universal suffrage, rule by popular majorities, equal treatment before the law, and equal educational opportunities.   z.

equalization fee. A fee collected from all the beneficiaries of a plan in order to compensate a few participants who may suffer loss from its operation; a principal feature of the McNary-Haugen Bill (*q.v.*)   z.

equalization of assessments. The action of a board or other administrative authority in revising valuations made by assessors for direct property taxation, in order to secure a more equitable distribution of the tax burden among taxpayers of a particular locality, or among counties or other taxing districts in a State.   z.

equal protection. A requirement of the 14th Amendment that classification of persons for purposes of governmental control by the States be reasonably adapted to the accomplishment of proper governmental functions, and that all persons falling within a given class be accorded like treatment. Classifications based on race, color, citizenship, occupation, wealth, sex, or residence are valid despite the provision that no State shall deprive any person of equal protection of the laws, so long as action based on differences among classes is substantially related to the promotion of the health, morals, safety, or welfare of the State. Thus special laws may discriminate between aliens and citizens in access to the professions, between men and women in opportunities for employment, between residents and nonresidents in the distribution of public relief, between chain stores and department stores in the rate of taxation, and between residential and commercial districts in zoning regulations, because of a reasonable relation to the State's police power. But class legislation may not discriminate between Catholics or Protestants, Jews or Gentiles, or union and nonunion men in access to employment, since these distinctions bear no reasonable relation to the police power. Equal protection does not mean identical treatment: Negroes may be separated from whites in schools, public conveyances, and places of public accommodation, as long as the facilities offered each race are substantially equal; and the State need not act with such "mathematical nicety" as would eliminate all traces of inequality. Equal protection against discrimination by individuals and groups is not guaranteed by the 14th Amendment. Some States have passed civil rights acts which usually require full and equal treatment for all persons regardless of race, color, or creed in public conveyances, lodging houses, amusement centers, and other places of public accommodation; though none of these laws is as yet effectively enforced.   JTC.

Equal Rights party. 1. Another name for the Locofocos (*q.v.*) 2. A minor party advocating woman suffrage and equal rights for women which cast a few votes in 1884 and 1888.   s.

equity. A branch of remedial justice which arose, perhaps by the 12th or 13th century in England, when petitions to the King for relief from the positive and rather inflexible rules of the common law were referred to the Lord Chancellor — hence the name "chancery" which is used for an equity court. At first based on abstract principles of justice which were expressed in maxims, equity gradually developed its own set of rules and precedents. Procedure in equity is relatively simple. An attempt is made to present the whole case, with all possible grounds for decision, to a court; and for that purpose all individuals having an interest may be summoned as parties even after the beginning of a case. The court has a considerable choice of remedies in "commanding what is right and prohibiting what is wrong." The most important are the requirements of specific performance, and preventive justice by means of the injunction. Separate equity courts, once the general rule, now exist in only half a dozen States. In most States both common law and equity are administered by the same judge in the same case; but in others separate proceedings must be held for law and equity cases, even though the same judge may preside over both.   s.

Era of Good Feeling. The period in American politics during the presidency of James Monroe when, because of the virtual extinction of the Federalist party, partisan differences tended to disappear. It was none the less a period in which personal rivalries and factional dissensions flourished.   z.

Erdman Act. An act of Congress June 1, 1898, which set up machinery for the mediation and arbitration of labor disputes between railroad companies and their trainmen and switchmen, and outlawed the "yellow-dog" contract and discriminatory discharge by employers.   s.

Erie Canal. A canal constructed by the State of New York between Albany and Buffalo, 1817-25. It is still in operation as a barge canal.   s.

error. *See* Writ of error.

escalator clause. A provision in the London Naval Treaty, 1930, enabling any signatory to increase replacement tonnage upon due notice if required in the interest of national security.   jwf.

Esch-Cummins Act. *See* Transportation Act 1.

escheat. The reversion of land to the state, as the original and ultimate proprietor, by reason of failure of heirs.   s.

Espionage Act. An act of Congress June 15, 1917, imposing severe penalties for uttering statements deliberately intended to impede the operations of the armed forces. It was strengthened by the Sedition Act (*q.v.*)   s.

Essex Junto. A group of able leaders in Essex County, Mass., who opposed Governor John Hancock, 1780-89, and sided with Hamilton in his opposition to President Adams, 1798-1801. The name was later applied to all Federalists.   s.

estate tax. An indirect or excise tax levied on the whole estate of a deceased person. *See* Inheritance tax.   s.

estimates. Statements of anticipated expenditures for the next fiscal year furnished by the spending agencies to the budget-making authorities.   z.

ever normal granary. A continuous and stable supply of basic farm products accumulated by the national government as collateral for loans and as premiums for crop insurance, and administered by the Agricultural Adjustment Administration (*q.v.*)   z.

Every man a king. The slogan used by the demagogic Huey P. Long in his "share the wealth" crusade during the considerable period when he was virtual dictator of Louisiana.   z.

evidence. Legally admissible information submitted to a court

or investigating body orally, in writing, or as an exhibit, in order
to determine the truth concerning any matter in issue.   z.

excess condemnation. The taking of private property by right
of eminent domain in excess of what is absolutely necessary for
immediate public use. Though urged by city planners on aesthetic
and fiscal grounds and regularly used in Europe, it is legally possible in only a few States of the Union.   JJR.

excess profits tax. A graduated tax on business profits in excess of a fixed percentage of invested capital or of average profits
over a given period.   s.

exchange stabilization fund. A fund of $2,000,000,000 from
the profits of dollar devaluation placed at the disposal of the Secretary of the Treasury by the Gold Reserve Act, 1934, for the purchase of gold, foreign exchange, and similar instruments of credit,
thereby to promote equilibrium in the value of American and foreign currency.   z.

excise. An indirect tax levied on goods produced, manufactured, sold, used, or transported within a country, or upon various
privileges. In current usage the term has been extended to include
various license fees and practically every internal revenue tax except the income tax.   s.

exclusion. The policy of denying admission into a state of the
nationals of a foreign state, or classes of such nationals. The
United States has passed various exclusion acts directed against
the immigration of Oriental peoples, and the present effect of such
acts is to debar all but a small, selected number of such nationals
from entry into the country.   z.

exclusive power. Complete power exercised by Congress or
a State legislature over some matter of legislation which may not
be regulated by the other legislative body.   z.

execution. 1. A judicial writ directing an officer to carry out
the judgment of a court of law. 2. Enforcement of the death
penalty following conviction of a capital crime and sentence by a
court of law.   JWF.

executive. 1. One of the three traditional departments or
branches of government to which is confided the responsibility for
executing the laws, supervising the civil and military administration, and managing foreign relations. The executive branch also
provides political leadership for the legislature in all parliamentary
forms of government and to a less extent in presidential forms as
well. 2. The head of the state or principal official of the government, such as a President, prime minister, or governor; or, collectively, the heads of the principal administrative establishments
who form a ministry or cabinet.   EES.

executive agent. A personal representative of the President
entrusted with special missions to foreign governments or heads of

state. He is to be distinguished from a regular diplomatic official, although he is often accorded the privileges and immunities, and even the rank, of regular diplomats.   z.

executive agreement. An agreement between heads of state or governments. The President may make such agreements without senatorial ratification by virtue of his position as commander-in-chief, his constitutional authority over foreign relations, or under specific statutory authority. An executive agreement usually deals with administrative matters or with matters of policy less portentous than those normally incorporated in the more enduring international treaties and conventions.   JWF.

executive council. An executive cabinet, or a body of advisers of a chief executive such as the governor's council of colonial America. It still survives in Maine, New Hampshire, Massachusetts, and North Carolina.   z.

executive department. 1. One of the ten principal administrative agencies of the national government, the heads of which perform supervisory duties under the direction of the President and sit in the President's cabinet. 2. A comparable administrative unit in a State or municipal government.   z.

executive discretion. The choice of means which an executive officer possesses in carrying out all except his mandatory powers. s.

Executive Office of the President. A grouping of the following offices under the direction of the President: the White House Office, the Bureau of the Budget, the Office for Emergency Management, and the Liaison Office for Personnel Management.   z.

executive session. Originally a session devoted to executive business; but because the Senate, until June 18, 1929, regularly considered such business in secret, the phrase is commonly applied to any secret session.   s.

exempt class. That class of civil servants who are appointed without examination.   JWF.

exemption. Immunity from certain legal obligations such as jury duty, military service, or the payment of taxes. The latter immunity is usually extended to charitable, religious, and educational institutions.   z.

exequatur. A document issued to a foreign consul or consular agent by the government to which he is accredited permitting him to take up his residence and perform his official duties.   z.

ex officio. By virtue of office or official position.   z.

expansion. The process of enlarging a state's territory either by annexing unoccupied territory or at the expense of other states. z.

ex parte. Pertaining to a proceeding where there is no adverse party; or where the adverse party is absent or without opportunity to be heard.   JJR.

expatriation. 1. The action of an individual in renouncing his allegiance to the state of which he has been a citizen or subject. Most contemporary states permit their citizens or subjects to expatriate themselves and become the naturalized citizens of other states. 2. Banishment of a citizen or subject by a state.   z.

experiment station. *See* Agricultural experiment station.

export. Pertaining to commodities, merchandise, money, or credit sent out of a country.   s.

Export-Import Bank of Washington. A corporation authorized by executive order of the President, Feb. 2, 1934, and chartered in the District of Columbia with a capital stock of $175,000,-000. It is authorized to engage in a general banking business in order to promote American export and import trade, and is charged with the duty of making loans for the stabilization of the economies of Western Hemisphere countries and for the promotion of trade with them.   z.

export tax. A duty levied upon merchandise shipped out of a country. Such a tax is prohibited by the Constitution of the United States, Art. I, secs. 9 and 10.   JWF.

exposition. 1. The action of clarifying or providing a detailed commentary upon some theme. 2. A fair or exhibition usually supported in whole or in part by public funds.   z.

ex post facto law. A retroactive criminal law which is unconstitutional when it declares an act a crime which was not a crime when it was done; or, with retrospective effect, increases a crime or a penalty; or alters the rules of evidence to the disadvantage of an accused person; or in other ways decreases the protection which the law previously afforded to him.   s.

Expounder of the Constitution. A nickname of Daniel Webster. s.

express powers. Powers specifically granted to the national government or one of its branches by the Constitution of the United States.   s.

expropriation. In Roman-law countries, the act by which a state acquires private property by compulsory purchase, practically equivalent to eminent domain in the United States; sometimes accompanied, as recently in Mexico, by proceedings to resume public title to land granted to private parties under defective or fraudulently obtained patents.   JWF.

expulsion. Enforced withdrawal of a person from a country or society or from some public body such as a legislative assembly. By a two-thirds vote, members may be expelled from either house of Congress.   z.

expunge. To strike out or rescind entries in a permanent record, as by writing the word "Expunged" across lines in the Senate *Journal*, or "Rescission" in the House *Journal*.   s.

extension of remarks. The printing in the *Congressional Record,* by permission of either house, of material not spoken in debate. If in continuation of remarks on the floor, such material follows the reported speech in the body of the *Record;* otherwise it is printed in the appendix.   s.

extension service. *See* Agricultural Extension Service.

external loan. A loan obtained by a government from foreign sources.   JWF.

exterritoriality. A fiction in international law, now generally discarded, that merchant ships on the high seas and the residences of sovereigns and diplomatic agents when abroad are detached portions of their own country's soil.   s.

extraconstitutional. 1. Not expressly or impliedly provided for by the constitution. 2. Unconstitutional.   JJR.

extradition. The delivery of fugitives from justice by the authorities of the state where such fugitives have sought asylum to the authorities of the state from which they fled. Extradition may be demanded in accordance with applicable provisions of international treaties, and such provisions normally do not call for the surrender of fugitives charged with political offenses. Among the States of the Union the return of fugitives is more properly called rendition (*q.v.*)   z.

extralegal. Outside or beyond the scope of law.   z.

extramural. Pertaining to activities or works of a municipal corporation, *e.g.,* water supply, which are conducted outside the corporation's boundaries.   z.

extraordinary session. A legislative session, called generally by the executive, which meets in the interval between regular sessions. In 30 States such sessions are limited to the consideration of matters specified in the governor's call.   s.

F

faction. One wing of a political party or a personal clique within such a party; generally any loosely knit group of politicians, with or without defined leadership, who seek to aggrandize themselves by pursuing opportunistic policies or by promoting dissension within the ranks of an organized political party or within the state at large.   z.

factory legislation. *See* Labor legislation.

Fair Labor Standards Act. An act of Congress June 25, 1938, which set a minimum standard wage of 40 cents an hour and a maximum work week of 40 hours in industries engaged in interstate commerce, and prohibited the labor of children under 16 years of age.   JMCC.

fait accompli. A transaction which is regarded as completed and therefore not subject to further action. s.

faith and credit. *See* Full-faith-and-credit clause.

false imprisonment. Detention under false or assumed authority; or any unlawful restraint of a person's liberty. z.

family of nations. The world community of independent sovereign states. JWF.

farm bloc. A bipartisan group of Senators and Representatives from agricultural constituencies first organized in 1921 to secure legislation favorable to the farming class by the usual methods of minorities, including dilatory tactics and refusal to support other legislation until the farmers' demands have been satisfied. s.

farm bureau. A local organization of farmers first created about 1915 for the purpose of bringing pressure to bear on county boards for the employment of county agricultural agents and for co-operative activities. They were later combined into State federations and an American Farm Bureau Federation which maintains a lobby directing the farm bloc (*q.v.*) s.

Farm Credit Administration. A division of the Department of Agriculture which supervises and co-ordinates the federal land banks, intermediate credit banks, production credit corporations, and banks for agricultural co-operatives located in each of the 12 federal farm credit districts into which the United States is divided. Its principal officer is the Governor of the Farm Credit Administration. z.

Farmer-Labor party. 1. A minor party with socialistic tendencies which in 1920 cast 265,000 votes for Arthur Christensen for President and in 1924 joined the LaFollette Progressives. 2. A third party in Minnesota which grew out of the Nonpartisan League. It succeeded in electing several of its candidates to important offices between 1922 and 1936. s.

Farmers' Alliance. 1. A secret farmers' organization founded in Texas in 1874 which, after absorbing other groups, attempted to capture the Democratic party in the South about 1890. 2. A nonsecret organization founded in the Northwest in 1880 which, after sponsoring third-party tickets in State elections, was instrumental in forming the Populist party. s.

farm loan association. A group of ten or more farmers which, under the Federal Farm Loan Act of 1916, can make long-term loans to its members with funds supplied by a federal land bank, taking in exchange the member's mortgage which it endorses and turns over to the bank.. z.

Farm Security Administration. A unit of the Department of Agriculture created by executive order Apr. 30, 1935, and originally called the Resettlement Administration. It makes loans to low-income or destitute farmers for the purchase of agricultural equipment or to finance indebtedness; and to tenant farmers, sharecroppers, and farm laborers to enable them to purchase land.   Z.

fascism. The authoritarian political system and totalitarian social regime evolved by Benito Mussolini and his followers of the Fascist party in Italy after 1922; hence any actual political system such as the regimes of the German Nazis or the Spanish Falangists inspired by the Italian model or comparable to it. Also any set of ideas which advocates the destruction of democratic parliamentarism, every kind of personal liberty, and a pluralistic social order; and which demands instead the institution of an irresponsible political dictatorship supported by a single hierarchically organized party, the regimentation of all forms of social and economic activity under a regime of totalitarian governmental control, and the liberal use of force, violence, and arbitrary power in the process of government. Fascist ideas have had no great currency in America although they have been advocated by the so-called Silver Shirts, the German-American Bund, and like organizations.   Z.

fat cat. Political slang for a man of wealth from whom a party expects liberal campaign contributions.   S.

fat frying. Bringing pressure to bear on business interests which have benefited from a party's policies to contribute to its campaign fund.   S.

Father Abraham. A nickname of President Lincoln.   S.

Father of his Country. An appellation of George Washington. S.

Father of the Constitution. A nickname of James Madison. S.

Father of the House. The oldest member in point of service in the House of Representatives.   S.

Father of the Revolution. A nickname of Samuel Adams. S.

Fathers, The. *See* Founding fathers.

favorite, the. The candidate who, before a convention or in its early stages, has the most pledged delegates or appears to have the best chance of nomination.   S.

favorite son. An aspirant for a presidential nomination who has little or no support beyond an instructed delegation from his own State.   EES.

F.B.I. *See* Federal Bureau of Investigation.

F.C.C. *See* Federal Communications Commission.

F.D.I.C. *See* Federal Deposit Insurance Corporation.

federal. Pertaining to the division of public powers in a state between one central government with authority to legislate on certain subjects and to enforce its will upon individuals, and numerous regional governments each having authority in other matters within its restricted territorial jurisdiction, the division being established and maintained by a constituent authority legally superior to both the central and the regional governmental areas.   AJW,Jr.

federal aid. Any form of national subvention or grant-in-aid to States and local governments to finance in whole or in part approved local projects or activities. *See* Grant-in-aid.   z.

Federal Board of Hospitalization. A board of seven officials, variously connected with public health or veterans' affairs, created in 1921, to advise the President upon the development and more efficient use of public hospitalization facilities.   z.

Federal Bureau of Investigation. A bureau of the Department of Justice which investigates violations of federal laws except violations of currency, customs, internal revenue, and postal laws. It has some 55 field divisions throughout the United States.   z.

Federal Communications Commission. An independent regulatory commission, consisting of seven members, established by Congress in 1934 to administer the Federal Communications Act of that year. The commission licenses radio stations and operators and regulates interstate and foreign communications by telephone, telegraph, cable, and radio. It is also engaged in the promotion of safety at sea through the use of communications facilities.   z.

Federal Crop Insurance Corporation. A corporation within the Department of Agriculture which insures growers of wheat and cotton against loss by natural hazards such as drought, flood, insects, and plant disease, and damage resulting from inability to obtain labor and other essentials.   z.

Federal Deposit Insurance Corporation. A United States government corporation created in 1933 to insure depositors against loss in banks which have closed or suspended payments. It is managed by a bipartisan board consisting of two directors appointed by the President and Senate and of the Comptroller of the Currency. Deposits are insured up to $5,000. The corporation may act as receiver of closed banks, take steps to avoid unsound banking practices, and purchase the assets of a bank which finds itself in difficulties in order to facilitate its merger with another bank, thereby reducing or avoiding potential losses to the corporation.   z.

Federal Emergency Relief Administration. An emergency agency created by Congress in 1933 to expend and administer federal funds in collaboration with the States and their political subdivisions for the relief of the unemployed. It expired June 30, 1938.   JMCC.

federal land bank. Any one of a system of twelve banking institutions created by Congress in 1916 to make loans to farmers and agricultural corporations for the purchase of land and equipment. Loans are secured by mortgages on land and appurtenances and are financed by the sale of consolidated federal farm loan bonds to the public. The twelve federal land banks are under the jurisdiction of the Farm Credit Administration.   z.

Federal Farm Loan Board. A board created to administer the Federal Farm Loan Act of 1916. Its functions have since been transferred to the Farm Credit Administration.   z.

federal home loan bank. One of twelve regional banks created under act of Congress July 22, 1932, to provide a credit reserve for building and loan, savings and loan, and homestead associations, savings and co-operative banks, and insurance companies. Every federal savings and loan association is required to become a member of its regional bank, and other thrift associations may do so. The regional banks are under the Federal Home Loan Bank Administration.   s.

Federal Home Loan Bank Administration. A grouping of the Federal Home Loan Bank System, the Federal Savings and Loan Insurance Corporation, the Home Owners' Loan Corporation, and the United States Housing Corporation.   z.

Federal Housing Administration. A national agency created in 1934 to insure loans made by private lending agencies for the repair, alteration, or improvement of small existing dwellings and to insure mortgages on newly constructed multiple dwellings.   jmcc.

federal intermediate credit bank. One of a system of twelve federal banks created in 1923 to discount obligations of agricultural credit corporations and similar institutions making short-term loans to farmers. These banks are under the Farm Credit Administration of the Department of Agriculture and are financed by the sale of short-term debentures to the public.   z.

federalism. A principle of political organization which permits erstwhile independent states to combine under a common central government while retaining some portion of their former power and identity.   z.

Federalist. 1. An advocate of a federal form of government. 2. An advocate of the adoption of the Constitution of the United States, 1787-88.   3. A supporter of the Federalist party.   z.

Federalist, The. A series of 85 essays contributed by Alexander Hamilton, James Madison, and John Jay to various New York newspapers in the fall and winter of 1787-1788 with the object of securing the ratification of the Constitution. They have been reprinted in several editions and constitute one of the best sources for the construction of the Constitution and for the study of federal government.   s.

Federalist party. The first of the national parties in the United States created after the split between Hamilton and Jefferson in Washington's cabinet, Hamilton being regarded as its principal leader until his death in 1804. The party was somewhat authoritarian in its political theory, nationalistic in its foreign policy, and liberal in its interpretation of the national government's powers under the Constitution. Its policies dominated the administrations of Washington and the elder Adams. Its later decline was caused partly by its lack of effective organization, partly by its factious opposition to measures which appealed to the judgment and patriotism of the people. It disappeared from national politics after 1816, though its organization continued in Delaware until 1828.   z.

Federal Power Commission. An independent commission of five members established by Congress in 1920 and set up in its present form by the Federal Power Act, June 30, 1930. It issues licenses for the construction of works to develop hydroelectric power and improve navigation at nationally-owned power sites and on navigable waters. It also determines rates for electric power generated and transmitted interstate and for natural gas transported and sold interstate, controls the issuance of securities by companies engaged in such activity, and generally supplements and strengthens State regulation of utilities furnishing electric power and natural gas.   z.

Federal Public Housing Authority. A division of the National Housing Agency whose principal purpose is to co-ordinate the activities of various earlier agencies having to do with relieving the shortage of housing and community facilities in areas adjacent to war plants and military reservations.   z.

Federal Register. An official daily publication begun May 14, 1936, which contains proclamations and executive orders of the President and general and special orders, rules and regulations, and notices of hearings issued by executive departments or agencies.   s.

federal reserve bank notes. Currency issued in small amounts under different laws and normally based on certain issues of United States bonds, though silver and commercial paper have each once been used as bases.   s.

Federal Reserve Board. *See* Board of Governors of the Federal Reserve System.

federal reserve notes. The principal currency of the United States issued in various denominations by the federal reserve banks and originally based on 100 per cent nonspeculative commercial paper, later reduced to 60 per cent commercial paper and 40 per cent gold. The notes are direct obligations of the United States.   z.

Federal Reserve System. Twelve mutually independent quasi-public banks located at Boston, New York, Philadelphia, Richmond, Atlanta, Dallas, Cleveland, Chicago, St. Louis, Minneapolis, Kansas City, and San Francisco, which function under the general supervision of the Board of Governors of the Federal Reserve System (*q.v.*) The stock of each bank is owned by the member banks of each district, and they elect a majority of the reserve bank's board of directors. The minority are appointed by the Board of Governors of the Federal Reserve System. The reserve banks, which are "bankers' banks," deal directly with banks and hardly at all with the general public. They rediscount commercial paper, hold reserves for member banks, assist in the transfer of funds, issue notes, act as fiscal agencies for the government, and hold gov-

Federal Reserve System — Federal Reserve districts

ernment funds on deposit. Through an Open Market Committee, they buy and sell bankers' acceptances and government securities and thereby attempt to stabilize the financial situation.   z.

Federal Savings and Loan Insurance Corporation. A national credit corporation which insures savings in private building and loan associations under the supervision of the Federal Home Loan Bank Administration.   z.

Federal Security Agency. An independent agency in charge of the Federal Security Administrator which was created in 1939 to co-ordinate the activities of the Civilian Conservation Corps, the National Youth Administration, the Office of Education, the Public Health Service, the Social Security Board, the Food and Drug Administration, and minor agencies.   z.

Federal Trade Commission. An independent quasi-judicial commission of five members created by act of Congress, Sept. 26, 1914. Its principal duty is to promote fair competition by preventing illegal combinations in restraint of interstate trade, unlawful price-fixing or price-discrimination agreements among distributors of goods or services or other agreements among producers or distributors not in the public interest. It has the duty of preventing fraudulent or deceptive advertising of foods, drugs, and cosmetics. It may enjoin unfair advertising practices by instituting an appropriate action in a United States district court. In cases of unlawful conspiracies or combinations to restrain or divert trade, the Commission, after a hearing, may issue a cease-and-desist order (*q.v.*) which can only be set aside by a circuit court of appeals after an appeal from the Commission's ruling, and which becomes final if not appealed within 60 days. The Commission often secures voluntary agreements among companies to terminate competitive or trade practices which are of questionable legality. z.

Federal Works Agency. A national agency created by executive order in 1939 to co-ordinate the Public Roads Administration, the Public Works Administration, and the Works Progress Administration, and to administer grants-in-aid and loans made by the United States for the construction of public works. z.

federation. 1. The act of two or more states which, while retaining exclusive control over most public affairs, create a central government with exclusive control over other affairs, the arrangement being maintained under a juridically superior authority such as a written constitution. 2. A federal government. z.

fee. A fixed charge required by law to be paid by a person to defray all or a part of the expense of some public action which confers a special benefit on the payer, and also involves the enforcement of a public policy. s.

fellow-servant doctrine. A common-law doctrine or rule that in an action for damages brought against an employer by an injured employee the employer may plead that the negligence of another employee was partly or wholly responsible for the accident resulting in the injury and, by proving such negligence, reduce or extinguish his own liability. This rule has been generally abrogated by workmen's compensation legislation. z.

fellow traveler. A person who, though not a member of the Communist party, belongs to one of its auxiliary organizations, or sympathizes with its aims, or actively supports its program. z.

felony. Any crime so classified in law and thus distinguished from a misdemeanor; usually a more serious offense than a misdemeanor. z.

fetcher. A slang term for a bill introduced and supported for the purpose of collecting legislative blackmail. s.

few die and none resign. A paraphrase of Jefferson's comment, July 12, 1801, on vacancies in the national civil service: "Those by death are few; by resignation, none." s.

F.H.A. *See* Federal Housing Administration.

fiat money. Paper money issued by government authority and made legal tender. It bears no promise of redemption and is not backed by precious metals or other forms of wealth. s.

Fifteenth Amendment. An amendment to the Constitution of the United States proclaimed Mar. 30, 1870, which forbids a State to deny the suffrage to any person because of race, color, or previous condition of servitude. Several Southern States have circumvented it by imposing taxpaying, educational, and other qualifications.   EES.

Fifth Amendment. An amendment of the federal Constitution, declared in force Dec. 15, 1791, which restricts the powers of the national government by requiring presentment or indictment by a grand jury before judicial trials for "capital or otherwise infamous" crimes; and prohibits double jeopardy, compulsory self-incrimination, the deprivation of life, liberty, and property without due process, and the taking of private property for public use without just compensation. These limitations protect every "person," including corporations and noncitizens, within the jurisdiction of the United States and incorporated territories.   JJR.

fifth columnist. A phrase derived from a remark made during the Spanish Civil War of 1936 by a rebel general who, in advancing with four columns upon the loyalist capital of Madrid, declared that a fifth column of rebel sympathizers existed within the city; hence a traitor or any sympathizer with the enemy in wartime.   z.

Fifty-four forty or fight. A slogan of the Democratic party in 1844, which demanded that the Oregon Country, then jointly occupied by the United States and Great Britain, should be included in the United States to its full extent northward, that is, to 54° 40′, the southern boundary of Alaska.   s.

file. A list of documents arranged for reference particularly in relation to a case pending in a judicial tribunal.   z.

filibuster. 1. An adventurer who led a military expedition against some portion of Latin America with which his own country was at peace. 2. Long-continued speechmaking by a member, or members, of a legislative body, deliberately intended to compel the majority to abandon part of its legislative program. It is of fairly common occurrence in the United States Senate, where the rules make closure almost impossible.   s.

filing fee. A fee collected by about half the States from persons who announce their candidacy for nomination in a primary election to help defray the cost of printing ballots or as an earnest of good faith.   s.

Finality Men. Northerners who, 1850-61, regarded the Compromise of 1850 as a final settlement of the slavery issue and wished to avoid its further discussion.   s.

finance committee. A committee of the United States Senate with jurisdiction similar to that of the Ways and Means Committee of the House; also, the name of the principal financial committee in many State legislative bodies.   s.

finding. A conclusion of fact certified after inquiry by a judicial or other body.   z.

fine. A sum of money which a court may exact from a person as punishment for a proved violation of law.   JWF.

fire department. An administrative department of municipal or local government which controls fire-fighting apparatus and is charged with the prevention and extinguishment of fires and the enforcement of local fire ordinances. JWF.

fire-eater. A violent advocate of Southern interests and constitutional rights in the decade of the 1850's. S.

fire marshal. A State or local officer charged with the enforcement of fire inspection laws and the elimination of fire hazards. JWF.

fireside chat. President F. D. Roosevelt's term for his more informal radio broadcasts addressed to the people. S.

First International. An organization of socialist and labor leaders, officially known as the International Workingmen's Association, formed in London in 1864 by Karl Marx and others. Divergent views of various national contingents distracted its councils from the outset, and personal animosities and doctrinal conflicts of various leaders, in particular of Marx and the anarchist Bakunin, led to a struggle for control which was climaxed by Bakunin's expulsion at The Hague in 1872. The Marxian wing, left in supreme control, moved the headquarters of the International to New York, and the organization was disbanded at a final congress at Philadelphia in 1876. Z.

First in War, First in Peace, and First in the Hearts of His Countrymen. An appellation of Washington which originated in the funeral oration by Richard Henry Lee. S.

first papers. In popular usage, the declaration of intention to become a citizen filed by an alien as the first step in the process of naturalization prescribed by the laws of the United States. Z.

First President of the Southern Confederacy. A title bestowed on John C. Calhoun by a posthumous medal struck by the State of South Carolina. Actually the first (and only) president of the Confederate States was Jefferson Davis. S.

fiscal. Pertaining to finance, especially to problems of public revenue, expenditure, and debt. JWF.

Fiscal Corporation. An institution proposed by Whigs in Congress to meet President Tyler's objections to a recharter of a Bank of the United States. S.

fiscal year. The twelve-month period beginning at any convenient date during which annual appropriations are to be spent, taxes collected, and accounts kept. The fiscal year of the United States begins July 1. Z.

Fish and Wildlife Service. A division of the Department of the Interior created in 1940 as a result of the consolidation of the Bureau of Biological Survey and the Bureau of Fisheries. It carries on the research and wildlife conservation programs formerly entrusted to these bureaus. Z.

fisheries. *See* North Atlantic fisheries.

fishing expedition. A slang term for a legislative investigation instituted by the majority party in the hope that it may unearth information to the detriment of an administration or officer that can be used in a political campaign.   s.

five-minute rule. A rule of the House of Representatives, applying only in committee of the whole, which limits the proposer of an amendment to five minutes in which to explain it, after which "the Member who shall first obtain the floor shall be allowed to speak five minutes in opposition."   s.

Five-Power Treaty. The Washington Naval Limitation Treaty of Feb. 6, 1922, signed by the United States, Great Britain, Japan, France, and Italy, which fixed capital-ship ratios among the signatory powers and limited replacement tonnage.   JWF.

five-to-four decision. A decision of the United States Supreme Court in which the result is sometimes said to be determined by one of nine justices. Criticisms of such decisions in important constitutional cases has occasionally led to a demand that at least six justices be required to concur in holding a statute unconstitutional.   z.

Five-Year Plan. A comprehensive plan for national economic development adopted in 1928 by the government of the Soviet Union and revised and extended later. Similar plans for the same or approximately equal periods have been announced by other states.   z.

Flag of the United States. A standard carried by troops and war vessels and displayed over public and private buildings. It was adopted by the Continental Congress June 14, 1777. From 1795 to 1818 it had fifteen stripes and fifteen stars; but since the latter date it has had thirteen stripes and a number of stars equal to the number of States in the Union.   s.

flexible constitution. A phrase of Lord Bryce descriptive of a constitution which, like the British, can be formally changed or amended without great difficulty; to be distinguished from a rigid constitution, like the American, amendment of which is a complicated and difficult process.   z.

flexible tariff. A tariff law which permits the President, upon ascertaining the existence of certain legally defined conditions, to raise or lower rates within prescribed limits.   z.

floater. 1. A purchaseable voter with no real party affiliation. 2. A person who votes illegally in several election precincts.   s.

floating debt. That portion of a public debt in the form of treasury bills or other short-term obligations which has not been funded, as distinguished from funded debt in the form of bonds or equivalent long-term obligations.   z.

flood control. The erection of dikes, levees, and similar works along rivers and other bodies of water to prevent overflow at flood time; and the construction of dams, canals, and similar installations to permit the regulation of the flow and volume of water in lakes and streams. A systematic policy of flood control also embraces programs of reforestation and afforestation, conversion of some tilled land to pasturage, contour farming, and similar activities designed to regulate drainage, prevent flash floods, and reduce erosion. Large-scale flood control activities are carried on by the Corps of Engineers of the War Department and the Soil Conservation Service of the Department of Agriculture.   z.

floor leader. A member designated by his party caucus to take charge of party interests during legislative sittings. He may plan the course of debate, determine the order in which members of his party may speak, and through the whips, strive to maintain party solidarity. The floor leaders of the two major parties usually decide when debate shall be closed and a vote taken.   EES.

Florida. The 27th State, admitted to the Union Mar. 3, 1845. It was originally purchased from Spain for $5,000,000 by a treaty signed Feb. 22, 1819. It passed an ordinance of secession Jan. 10, 1861, and was readmitted June 25, 1868. Capital, Tallahassee; area, 58,666 sq. mi.; population (1940), 1,897,414; presidential electors, 8. Under the present constitution adopted in 1887 a literacy test is required for the suffrage.   s.

Food and Drug Administration. A division of the Federal Security Agency since 1940, previously under the Department of Agriculture. It is charged with the enforcement of federal pure food, drug, cosmetic, and other laws and for this purpose maintains an inspection service to detect adulterated or misbranded goods.   z.

food stamp plan. A scheme whereby relief clients who purchase stamps redeemable at designated stores for food products may receive free stamps from the government equal in value to 50 per cent of the stamps purchased. The free stamps are good only for items of food declared surplus by the Surplus Commodities Administration. Both kinds of stamps are redeemable at face value through the Federal Reserve System when submitted by merchants.   JMCC.

Foraker Act. An act of Congress Apr. 12, 1900, creating a civil government for the newly acquired island of Puerto Rico under an appointive governor and council and a locally elective lower house of the legislature. Many provisions have since been superseded by the Jones Act. *See* Puerto Rico.   z.

Force Bill. 1. An act of Congress Mar. 2, 1833, which gave the President authority to use the army and navy to enforce the tariff laws of the United States. 2. Any of several bills introduced in Congress, the last in 1890, providing for national supervision of elections.   s.

Fordney-McCumber Tariff. The tariff law of Sept. 21, 1922, which increased the duties on many articles and in which for the first time was introduced the principle of the flexible tariff.   s.

foreign corporation. From the point of view of a State of the Union, any corporation not chartered by that State. Such corporations can do business within the State only with its express approval, but it may not prescribe conditions for entry which deny such corporations the right to resort to federal courts, to engage in interstate commerce, or to act as agents of the national government. They are not "citizens" with "constitutional privileges and immunities"; but they are artificial "persons" protected by the due process and equal protection clauses of the 14th Amendment. JJR.

Foreign Economic Administration. An establishment set up within the Office for Emergency Management by executive order Sept. 23, 1943. It has charge of lend-lease, foreign relief and rehabilitation, economic warfare, procurement of essential commodities from foreign countries, and other foreign economic operations, including plans for future activities of the United States in liberated areas.   s.

foreign policy. A relatively consistent course of conduct pursued by a state over an appreciable period in its relations with other states. American foreign policy has been largely determined by precedent and tradition, international treaties, moral and legal obligations, national interest, and physical circumstances. It is formulated by the President and the Department of State but may be influenced by congressional action or by public opinion.   JWF.

foreign service. The personnel of a state's diplomatic and consular services. *See* Rogers Act.   JWF.

foreign valuation. The valuation placed upon an imported commodity in the country of origin as a basis for levying ad valorem customs duties.   JWF.

Forest Service. A unit in the Department of Agriculture created in 1905 which controls the use and development of national forests, guards them against fire and disease, and conducts research in scientific forestry and wildlife resources.   z.

forgotten man. A phrase apparently derived from the writings of the sociologist William Graham Sumner and applied by President F. D. Roosevelt in the campaign of 1932 to middle-class and laboring elements in the population which the previous Republican administrations had allegedly neglected.   z.

Fortune Bay outrages. Attacks on American fishing vessels by inhabitants of Fortune Bay, Newfoundland, in January, 1878, in violation of privileges guaranteed by treaty. Great Britain paid about $73,000 as indemnity for the damage done.   s.

forty-niner. One who participated in the extensive migration to California in 1849 following the discovery of gold there.   z.

forty-shilling freehold. Real property yielding an annual income of forty shillings, ownership of which was required of every voter in a county constituency in England from 1430 to 1832. This requirement, either in its original form or as capitalized according to value or acreage, was usual in the suffrage laws of the colonial and early federal periods in the United States.   s.

forty thieves. An opprobrious term for members of the Board of Aldermen of New York about 1850 who distinguished themselves by corrupt grants of franchises.   s.

founding fathers. An affectionate name for statesmen of the Revolutionary and Confederation periods, and especially for members of the Convention of 1787.   s.

four freedoms. Freedom of speech, freedom of religion, freedom from want, and freedom from fear — the chief objectives of American and United Nations' policy, as summarized by President F. D. Roosevelt in his message to Congress Jan. 6, 1941.   s.

Four-Power Treaty. A treaty signed at Washington Dec. 13, 1921, by France, Great Britain, Japan, and the United States. The signatories pledged respect for one another's possessions in the Pacific and agreed to settle controversies relating to such possessions by conference or joint discussion.   JWF.

Fourteen Points. President Wilson's proposal for a peace settlement, as presented in a speech to Congress, Jan. 8, 1918. The most important points were: open covenants openly arrived at; freedom of the seas; removal of economic barriers; reduction of armaments; consideration for colonial populations; evacuation of territory occupied by Germany; readjustment of Italian frontiers; autonomy for peoples of Austria-Hungary and Turkey; independence for Poland; and a general association of nations to guarantee independence and integrity to large and small states.   s.

Fourteenth Amendment. An amendment to the Constitution, declared in force July 28, 1868, which superseded the rule of the Dred Scott decision by defining as citizens of the United States and of the States in which they reside "all persons born or naturalized in the United States, and subject to the jurisdiction thereof"; restricted the powers of the States in relation to such citizens and other persons; ordered the reduction of a State's representation in Congress wherever the right of suffrage of adult males was denied; disqualified from office former officeholders who had engaged in rebellion; and validated the war debt of the United States while voiding the war debts of rebellious States and claims for loss or emancipation of slaves. The restrictions on State powers, broadly phrased in the due process, equal protection, and privileges and immunities clauses, though designed primarily to protect freed Negroes, have been judicially interpreted most frequently as constitutional limitations upon State taxing power and State social legislation, especially attempted regulation of economic activity. Since

1923 the due process clause has been increasingly invoked to prevent encroachment by State and local governments upon civil liberties such as freedom of speech, assembly, religion, and the press.   JJR.

fourth estate. The journalistic profession, or the press. z.

Four-Year-Tenure Act. An act of Congress passed in 1820 which limited the terms of most appointive officers of the national government to four years in order to facilitate the retirement of superannuated employees. It was later used to secure rotation in office under the spoils system.   s.

F.P.C. *See* Federal Power Commission.

fractional currency. Coins or notes the face value of which is less than that of the standard monetary unit; in the United States, any coin or note of a face value less than one dollar. JWF.

franchise. 1. A special privilege granted by public authority to an individual or corporation, especially one which permits the use of public property or of the right of eminent domain. Since such a grant has been construed as a contract in the Dartmouth College case (*q.v.*) public authorities limit franchises to a term of years and to minutely specified conditions. They are always strictly interpreted. 2. The privilege of voting. s.

franking privilege. The privilege of sending mail relating strictly to official business, or consisting of excerpts from the *Congressional Record,* free of charge, which is enjoyed by members of Congress and officers and agencies of the national government. The privilege is occasionally extended by law to other persons, such as widows of former Presidents. s.

Franklin, State of. A provisional government organized in 1784 by people residing in what is now the State of Tennessee. s.

fraternity. *See* Democracy.

fraud. An action characterized by deceit, cunning, or misrepresentation. z.

fraud order. An order which may be issued by the Postmaster General which has the effect of withholding all mail service, both outgoing and incoming, from persons against whom there is evidence of the use of the mails for fraudulent purposes. s.

Frazier-Lemke Act. An act of Congress, 1935, which established a three-year moratorium on farm mortgage foreclosures, required the owner to pay rental during the period of the moratorium, and provided for the sale of the property at auction after reappraisal at the expiration of the moratorium if the mortgagor had not been previously satisfied. It superseded an earlier law of the same name which had been declared unconstitutional. z.

Fredonian Republic. A government prematurely proclaimed by American settlers in Texas in 1826. s.

free coinage. The public policy of accepting unlimited amounts of monetary metal such as gold or silver for coinage. z.

free conference. *See* Conference 1.

Free Democracy. The name adopted by the antislavery faction of the Democratic party in New York which nominated Martin Van Buren for President in 1848. The Free-Soil party later nominated him as its candidate. s.

freedman. A former slave who has been emancipated. Congress created a Freedmen's Bureau Mar. 3, 1865, to care for the interests of such persons. s.

freedom of contract. The right of an individual to dispose of his labor, services, or property by contractual agreements to his own best advantage and without arbitrary interference. It is not an absolute right, but subject to regulations in the interests of health, safety, morals, general welfare, and the prevention of fraud. Many laws seeking to limit the hours of labor and in other ways to improve the position of the worker have been declared unconstitutional because they deprived him of the freedom to accept employment under conditions which he believed most beneficial to himself. s.

freedom of debate. The right, essential to representative government, of a legislative body to consider any matter it chooses and to discuss, deliberate, and act under rules of its own making unhampered by the other branches of the government; and of individual members to state their opinions freely without fear of arrest or punishment anywhere, or of being called in question by any authority other than that of the house of which they are members. s.

freedom of religion. The absence of any state-supported or favored religion, every religion being afforded full freedom of organization and worship under the laws so long as it does not violate public order or public morals. The First Amendment of the Constitution states that "Congress shall make no law respecting an establishment of religion, or prohibiting the free exercise thereof." z.

freedom of speech and press. A right guaranteed in American federal and State constitutions to speak or write freely on any subject provided such activity does not affect adversely some superior interest of the state, such as the protection of society against obscene literature, or the advocacy of enemy causes in time of war. Thus the sedition statutes of 1798 and 1918, passed in the exercise of national war powers, and the more recent State criminal syndicalism laws enacted under the police power to promote the public safety and welfare have all imposed limitations upon the right to criticize the government. In this conflict of interests, freedom of expression has received liberal recognition from the courts. Laws limiting such freedom are not always presumed to be constitutional; and justifiable restrictions begin only at the point at which the written or spoken word creates a "clear and present danger" to the fulfillment of some governmental policy of greater concern to the state. Under the 14th Amendment this "clear-and-present-danger rule" is applied by the federal judiciary to protect freedom of speech and press against infringement by State governments. Historically the guarantee of free speech and press was aimed at the institution of direct censorship, but now it protects against subsequent punishment as well as previous restraint, and covers such indirect attempts at invasion as the taxation of publishers or the enactment of ordinances prohibiting the distribution of handbills to prevent littering the streets. With the development of new media for conveying ideas, the scope of the right of free expression is being expanded to include the radio message, the phonograph record, the cinema, the stage, the employer's leaflet, and the laborer's placard in the picket line.   JTC.

freeholders' charter. A municipal charter drafted by a locally appointed charter commission, or board of freeholders, and submitted to the voters of a city for approval under constitutional or legal provisions for home rule.   S.

freeman. 1. A person who is not a serf or a slave. 2. One who, in the colonial period, was admitted to the privileges of a public corporation and who thereby secured certain economic and civil rights, including the suffrage.   S.

free port. A closely guarded district within a country, but not within its customs area, where foreign goods may be unloaded and stored and later transshipped to another foreign port, possibly after a manufacturing process or assembly, without payment of duties.   S.

Freeport Doctrine. The doctrine expressed by Stephen A. Douglas in 1858 at Freeport, Ill., during his famous debates with Lincoln by means of which he attempted to reconcile the opinion of the Supreme Court in the Dred Scott case with his own principle of territorial or "squatter" sovereignty. Douglas conceded that neither Congress nor a territorial legislature could expressly abolish slavery in a territory but insisted that a territory could effectively prevent the existence of slavery by failing to support it with "local police regulations" or by passing unfriendly legislation.   Z.

free silver. The unrestricted coinage of standard silver dollars. S.

Free soil, free speech, free labor, and free men. A slogan of the Free-Soil party in 1848 and of the Republicans in 1856.   S.

Free-Soil party. A minor party opposed to the extension of slavery to the territories which was active in the elections of 1848 and 1852.   S.

free trade. International commerce carried on in the absence of protective tariffs or other legal provisions artificially discriminating against foreign products for the advantage of domestic producers. Free trade does not mean the absence of all customs duties: they may be levied even at high rates if their purpose and effect is to raise revenue.   s.

Free trade and sailors' rights. An American slogan before and during the War of 1812.   s.

French spoliation claims. Claims by American citizens against France for the seizure of ships and goods, 1791-1815. By agreements with France in 1800 and 1803 the United States relinquished prior claims in return for national advantages; but it was not until 1885 that Congress made fully satisfactory arrangements to compensate private claimants. Claims for losses incurred after 1803 were settled by France in Jackson's administration.   s.

friar lands. Lands in the Philippines owned by religious orders but put into the possession of farmers by insurgents about 1896. The United States later extinguished the friars' title by purchase.   s.

Fries' Rebellion. Concerted resistance led by John Fries to the national tax on houses which occurred in eastern Pennsylvania in 1799. Until suppressed by military force, the "rebels" poured scalding water on officers engaged in making measurements. It is also called the Hot Water War.   s.

frontier. 1. A boundary separating two states. 2. The extreme limit of a civilized or inhabited area.   z.

front porch campaign. A dignified, noncommittal, defensive political campaign, such as that conducted by McKinley in 1896 when he made a few addresses to visiting delegations of citizens from the front porch of his home while his opponent was engaged in extensive speaking tours.   s.

F.T.C. *See* Federal Trade Commission.

Fugitive Slave Laws. Acts of Congress, the most important of which were passed in 1793 and 1850, to secure the return of runaway slaves to their masters.   EES.

Full dinner pail. A Republican slogan in the campaign of 1896 designed to appeal to the laboring classes.   s.

full-faith-and-credit clause. Article IV, sec. 1 of the Constitution, which makes it obligatory on a State to recognize and give effect to the legislative acts, public records, and judicial decisions of other States when attested according to the forms prescribed by Congress. This provision makes it unnecessary for a person to reestablish his rights under deeds, wills, contracts, etc., in every State where he has property interests. Judgments of courts in divorce cases are, however, not binding upon other States if the parties were not domiciled in the State in which the decree of divorce was granted, or if the court was without jurisdiction or failed to give proper notice to the defendant.   s.

functional representation. Representation in which a group defined according to the economic or occupational status of its members, rather than the population of a territorial area, serves as a constituency.   JJR.

fundamental law. 1. The Constitution, or such organic statutes or laws as are intrinsically superior to the ordinary law of a state, or which the courts regard as law of superior obligation. 2. Natural law (*q.v.*) which is sometimes deemed to be morally if not juridically superior to positive law.   z.

funded debt. Debt in the form of bonds or other long-term obligations.   z.

funding. The process of converting existing debt into interest-bearing bonds or equivalent long-term obligations, or of creating a sinking fund for the extinction of debt at maturity.   z.

Fur Seal controversy. *See* Bering Sea Arbitration.

fusion. A temporary coalition of two or more parties or organized political groups to support a common ticket.   s.

G

Gadsden Purchase. A tract of nearly 30,000 square miles, lying south of the Gila River and now included in Arizona and New Mexico, which was purchased for $10,000,000 from Mexico by a treaty negotiated by James Gadsden and ratified Dec. 30, 1853.   s.

Gadsden Purchase

gag law. Any law abridging the freedom of speech, or of the press, or the right of petition.   s.

gag rule. 1. A rule of the House of Representatives passed in 1836 which provided that petitions and papers relating in any way to slavery should be laid on the table without further opportunity being given to consider them. 2. Any special closure rule adopted by a legislative body.   s.

galleries. Portions of a legislative chamber separated by a railing from the floor where various classes of persons, including the general public and representatives of the press, may sit and listen to the debates and discussions.   s.

Galveston plan. The commission plan (*q.v.*) of municipal government which originated in Galveston, Texas, in 1901.   s.

game warden. A local official who enforces laws for the protection of game and fish. JWF.

garden city movement. A movement inaugurated by Ebenezer Howard in England about 1900 to decentralize large cities by moving industries to planned sites in rural areas. JMCC.

Garrisonians. Radical abolitionists, followers of William Lloyd Garrison, who denounced slavery, and any government which countenanced it, as immoral. S.

gasoline tax. An excise tax upon each gallon of gasoline sold, originally levied in various States to defray the capital expense and maintenance cost of motor roads and highways and continued as an important source of general revenue. Z.

gavel rule. Exercise of power by the presiding officer of a legislative body in contravention of the rules or in violation of the rights of individual members or the minority. S.

general. The highest rank in the army, corresponding to admiral in the navy. Only a few individuals have held the permanent rank of general, but chiefs of staff and commanders-in-chief in theaters of operations are given the temporary rank of general while performing their duties. Z.

General Accounting Office. An independent auditing office of the national government, created by the Budget and Accounting Act of 1921. Under the direction of its head, the Comptroller General (*q.v.*), the office is empowered to settle all claims in which the United States may be concerned as creditor or debtor and to investigate all matters pertaining to the receipt, disbursement, and use of public funds. It renders binding opinions as to the legal power of disbursing officers of the government to make payments and prescribes uniform accounting procedures for all government departments and establishments. Z.

general appraisers. *See* United States Customs Court.

general court. The official title of the legislature in Massachusetts and New Hampshire. S.

general fund. Monies at the disposal of the fiscal officials of a State which may be drawn upon to cover the legislative appropriations for the normal operating expenses of the State's government; to be distinguished from special funds created by special taxes or reserved for special or extraordinary appropriations. JWF.

general property tax. A tax levied on both real and personal property at a uniform rate according to valuation. It is the chief source of revenue of all local government bodies, and provides a considerable, though declining, proportion of the revenues of the States. S.

general staff.   A group of high-ranking officers associated with a chief of staff, who immediately direct the administration of a state's military forces and are responsible for planning military strategy.   z.

general strike.   Collective cessation of work by the majority of the employees in the chief occupations of a district. The purpose may be to gain some economic or political advantage or to overthrow the existing political and economic system.   JJR.

general welfare clause.   A clause in Art. I, sec. 8 of the Constitution of the United States which declares that Congress may exercise the power of taxation to "pay the debts and provide for the common defense and general welfare of the United States." Strict constructionists have in the past interpreted this clause to mean that Congress may use its taxing power to promote only such functions as are specifically granted to it by the Constitution or properly implied from them. Others, particularly in recent years, have given the clause a broader interpretation, having held in effect that it enables Congress to make appropriations for any subject deemed to affect the public welfare or the national interest.   z.

general will.   According to Rousseau, the summation or collective product of individual wills *with respect to that element of each individual will which strives for the good of the whole.* Other writers use the phrase to denote the general, practically unanimous agreement upon the ultimate objectives of an association which is shared by its members.   JRP.

Geneva Award.   *See Alabama* claims.

Geneva Convention.   An international agreement for the conduct of belligerents drafted in 1864 and ratified by nearly every country. It provides that a belligerent which has enemy sick or wounded in its power shall give them proper care; that the Red Cross shall be the emblem of the sanitary service; and that hospitals and ambulances with their personnel shall be respected and protected. A revision in 1906 brought the convention of 1864 into accord with newer scientific discoveries and methods of warfare. s.

gentlemen's agreement.   An informal understanding or engagement, especially an informal diplomatic agreement arranged by an exchange of notes between the foreign offices of two or more governments or by conversations among heads of state or their emissaries.   z.

geographic determinism.   The theory that climate, the physical features of the earth, the distribution of natural resources, and other geographic phenomena exert a profoundly important, if not controlling, influence in molding human institutions and shaping human culture. Jean Bodin and the Baron de Montesquieu were among the first modern writers to give serious attention to this theory. A number of recent writers have examined with special care the role which geography has played in fostering national and colonial expansion, national maritime power, imperialism, and war. z.

geography, political. A consideration of the facts of geography in terms of their immediate relationship to the physical existence and government of states. z.

Geological Survey. A division of the Department of the Interior which classifies public lands for exploitation, conducts topographic surveys, and engages in geologic and related research. z.

Georgia. One of the original States and the fourth to ratify the Constitution of the United States, Jan. 2, 1788. It passed an ordinance of secession Jan. 19, 1861, and was readmitted July 15, 1870. Capital, Atlanta; area, 59,265 sq. mi.; population (1940), 3,123,723; presidential electors, 12. The present constitution was adopted in 1877. Persons may qualify for the suffrage by paying a poll tax and by meeting any one of the qualifications of property, literacy, honorable service in wartime, descent from a veteran, or good character and an understanding of the duties of a citizen. s.

gerrymander. A redistricting of a State for the election of congressional or legislative representatives which violates the principles of compactness, homogeneity of popular interests, and often equality of population in order to secure the future advantage of the party or group in control of a State legislature. The term is said to have arisen when an artist added wings, claws, and teeth to the map of a sprawling district created in Massachusetts in 1812 and suggested that it be called a salamander, and a Federalist editor changed the title to Gerrymander after Governor Elbridge Gerry. s.

Gettysburg Address. The chief commemorative address, delivered by President Lincoln Nov. 19, 1863, at the dedication of a cemetery on the battlefield at Gettysburg, Pa. It contains the definition of democracy as a "government of the people, by the people, for the people." s.

Ghent, Treaty of. A treaty signed by representatives of the United States and Great Britain at Ghent, Belgium, Dec. 24, 1814, which officially ended the War of 1812. It provided that boundaries should remain as they were before the war and did not confirm American privileges in the North Atlantic fisheries (*q.v.*) s.

gift tax. A State or national tax on the transfer of property by gift, designed chiefly to prevent evasion of inheritance tax laws, and normally assimilated administratively to inheritance or income tax systems. z.

Glass-Steagall Act. An act of Congress June 16, 1933, also known as the Banking Act of 1933, which established the Federal Deposit Insurance Corporation (*q.v.*) and required the separation of commercial and investment banking. z.

gold certificate. A unit of paper currency issued in various denominations from $10 to $10,000 which certifies that an equivalent value of gold has been deposited in the Treasury of the United States. Gold certificates were withdrawn from general circulation in 1934. In denominations of $10,000 they are now chiefly used by national banks as part of their required reserves.   JWF.

Gold Clause cases.   Five cases in which the Supreme Court in February, 1935, held that Congress may invalidate clauses in private contracts calling for payment in gold but may not invalidate gold clauses in United States bonds. Holders of such bonds may not recover, however, if the government refuses to pay in gold unless they can show actual economic loss.   JJR.

Gold Democrats.   Democrats who refused to support Bryan and free silver in 1896. They formed the National Democratic party and nominated a separate ticket.   S.

Gold Reserve Act.   An act of Congress Jan. 30, 1934, under the terms of which the United States bought all gold on deposit with the federal reserve banks, which had previously been called in from circulation; and established it, with other gold authorized to be purchased, as a permanent reserve for outstanding paper money. Most of the gold stock, now valued at about 20 billion dollars, is buried at Fort Knox, Ky.   Z.

gold standard.   A monetary system in which every form of currency may theoretically be converted on demand into its legal equivalent in gold or gold coin. The United States adopted the gold standard in 1900 and abandoned it in 1934.   Z.

good behavior.   1. Proper performance of duties, which is a condition of indefinite tenure of office. 2. Faithful observance of prison regulations, which is often rewarded by reduction in the minimum time to be served by a prisoner.   JMCC.

good-government association.   A nonpartisan organization established to improve the personnel and efficiency of government. JMCC.

good-neighbor policy.   A popular term for the policy adopted by the United States toward other American states under the administration of President F. D. Roosevelt, the principal aims of which were hemispheric diplomatic solidarity and a common system of hemispheric defense. The policy rejected any suggestion of political domination by the United States and stressed the triple conceptions of equal partnership, friendly collaboration, and mutual assistance.   Z.

good offices.   The expediting of communication between the parties to a dispute by a third, neutral, party without suggesting any form of settlement or compromise.   JJR.

good-time law.   A slang phrase for a law permitting the reduction in minimum time served by prisoners as a reward for their faithful observance of prison regulations.   JMCC.

G.O.P. The initials of "Grand Old Party," a familiar name for the Republican party beginning in 1880. When used alone they have a depreciatory sense. z.

Gopher State. A nickname for Minnesota. s.

governance. The method or manner of exercising public or other authority. z.

government. 1. The organization of the state which, in addition to administrative agencies, normally consists of three great branches, executive, legislative, and judicial. 2. The political and administrative activities of the organized state by means of which its powers are exerted and its ends are secured. z.

governmental contract. *See* Contract theory.

government by injunction. An opprobrious term for the injunction in labor disputes which has often been abused by being issued against strikers in general terms or without due notice, sometimes prohibiting acts which were entirely legal, and with long delays before final judicial determination of the legality of the injunction. s.

government-owned corporation. A device first used extensively by the national government during World War I for the administration of functions which are essentially business enterprises. Its stock is wholly owned by the government. It is financed by congressional appropriations and by bond issues which may be sold to private investors. Incorporation permits complete administrative and financial autonomy, better means of handling contracts with private parties, and administration by a board of directors appointed with reference to their technical competence. s.

Government Printing Office. An office created in 1861 and controlled by Congress which provides printing and binding service for all branches, departments, and establishments of the national government and distributes and sells at cost government publications. It occupies the largest and best-equipped printing plant in the world. z.

governor. The chief executive of an American State. Originally elected or controlled by the State legislature, he has acquired practical independence through successive constitutional revisions. His administrative power, however, still must often be shared with other popularly elected officers whose mandate from the people is as good as his own, and with boards a majority of whose members may have been appointed for long terms before his inauguration. Since 1917 a movement to make the governor the real head of the State administration has made considerable progress (*see* Administrative reorganization). His legislative powers are greater. He has the veto power in 47 States; the item veto of appropriations in 39; and may veto sections of general bills in 2. The frequent provision that he may have from six to thirty days in which to sign or veto a bill after the legislature has adjourned tends to make his veto absolute. In calling special sessions of the legislature he may often limit them to the consideration of subjects which he specifies. Through appeals to the people he may compel unwilling legislators to accept his legislative program. His term varies from two to four years, with an increasing tendency toward the longer term. Several State constitutions prohibit his succeeding himself in office. The salaries of governors range from $3,000 to $25,000 a year.   s.

governors, conference of. A meeting of governors held annually since 1908 for the exchange of experience on common problems and the promotion of uniform action by States. It suffers from lack of attendance and platitudinous speeches.   s.

governor's council. *See* Executive council.

gradualism. The reliance of radical parties or political movements upon piecemeal legislative and administrative reforms and upon evolutionary social trends instead of upon violent revolution for the ultimate realization of their programs.   z.

graft. Money or valuable privileges obtained at the expense of the public, or of the public interest, by officeholders, employees, or persons who possess political influence. The term may include actions ranging from downright theft to morally reprehensible acts for which there is no legal penalty.   s.

Grain Futures Act. An act of Congress Sept. 21, 1922, since amended, which empowers the Commodity Exchange Administration of the Department of Agriculture to register brokers in grain and other commodity futures transactions, regulate the amount and duration of their transactions, and prohibit corners in staples, market manipulation, and the dissemination of false information designed to influence commodity prices.   z.

grandfather clause. A clause contained in several of the post-Civil War suffrage laws of Southern States which exempted persons who had voted or whose progenitors had voted prior to 1867 from the fulfillment of educational tests and property qualifications required of other voters. The clause obviously discriminated in favor of whites and against Negroes and because of this was declared void by the United States Supreme Court in 1915.   z.

grandfather's hat. A tall hat of the style of 1840 which was a Republican emblem in 1888, in allusion to the fact that the presidential candidate's grandfather, William Henry Harrison, had been elected President in 1840.   s.

grand jury. A body of from 12 to 23 persons at common law who are summoned to a court to hear witnesses presented on behalf of the state and, after deliberating in secret and by a majority vote, to return indictments or make presentments against all persons whom they find just cause to hold for trial. It may also act concerning nuisances, the prevalence of crime, and neglect of duty by officials. In federal courts, trial for a crime punishable by imprisonment in a penitentiary must be after indictment by grand jury; but in more than half the States, information (*q.v.*) may be substituted for indictment, and the grand jury may be infrequently called. JJR.

Grand Old Party. A phrase applied by Republican orators to their party in 1880 and since used by others, often in a derisive sense, to designate that party. S.

Grange. A popular name for the Patrons of Husbandry, a secret farmers' organization founded in 1867, which by 1874 had 750,-000 members and exerted great influence over State legislation. S.

granger legislation. Laws favoring agricultural interests and named for the Grange, but not necessarily sponsored by it, which were passed, 1870-90, in many Western States. They fixed rates and imposed stringent regulations on railroads, grain elevators, warehouses, etc. S.

Granite State. A nickname for New Hampshire. S.

grant. A tract of land, franchise, or monopolistic privilege given by governmental authority to a private person or corporation. S.

grant-in-aid. An appropriation made by Congress to assist the States, or by a State legislature to assist local government units, in the maintenance of schools, construction of public works, provision for relief, or other public purposes of general interest. Its payment may, or may not, be conditioned upon the maintenance of certain standards fixed by the granting authority; but the temptation to utilize it for regulatory purposes has been almost irresistible. A grant-in-aid is made, strictly speaking, only to supplement appropriations made by the State or locality, and may be proportioned to such appropriations. *Compare with* Subsidy. S.

grass roots. A figure of speech, especially favored by Republican party orators, to identify the allegedly spontaneous or popular origin of party organization or policy. JWF.

Great Pacificator. A nickname of Henry Clay. S.

Great White Father. An American Indian title for the President of the United States. S.

greenback. A popular name for a United States note, a form of irredeemable or fiat paper currency when issued by the United States government in 1862 to aid in financing the Civil War. JWF.

Greenback party. A minor party in elections from 1876 to 1884 inclusive which demanded the continued issuance of fiat money, the eight-hour day for labor, a graduated income tax, and an interstate commerce law; and opposed land grants to railroads. EES.

Green Mountain State. A nickname of Vermont. S.

Gresham's Law. The principle that bad money drives out good; that is, that money with inferior intrinsic value will cause the hoarding of gold or other money with more certain value. The "law" was named for Sir Thomas Gresham, financial adviser to Henry VIII and Elizabeth, though it had been known for centuries by Dutch bankers.   JMCC.

grievance. A ground for complaint or remonstrance against the government resulting either from acts of tyranny or from neglect to remedy an unsatisfactory condition. The right to petition the government for redress of grievances is guaranteed by the First Amendment to the Constitution.   JMCC.

grievance committee. A group composed of employees, or of both employers and employees, to discuss unsatisfactory conditions of employment.   JMCC.

groom for office. To attempt to create a widespread and favorable impression of a potential candidate for office by giving him prominent positions, having him appear frequently in public, and securing publicity for him in newspapers, magazines, and radio broadcasts.   S.

gross income. The total income of a person or corporation from every source before expenses and other deductions allowed under income tax laws have been made.   Z.

group mind. The interpenetration and resultant consensus of the opinions and attitudes of the individual members of a functional group or community.   CS-H.

group pressure. The application of direct or indirect influence by minority interest groups for the purpose of securing their own ends. The influence may be political, economic, psychological, or social, etc.; the focus of application is ordinarily a governmental body or official, a political party, or a leader of prestige and authority.   CS-H.

group representation. 1 (formal). The choice of a legislature or other public body to represent distinct functional interests as opposed to geographical districts. 2 (informal). A system in which, without being formally represented, minority interest groups secure sponsorship of their dominant ideas by officials or public bodies through political or economic influence.   CS-H.

Guadeloupe Hidalgo, Treaty of. The treaty signed Feb. 2, 1848, by Nicholas Trist, an executive agent who had been recalled by President Polk, and representatives of Mexico. As ratified on May 30, it provided for ending the Mexican War, the cession of more than 500,000 square miles of territory to the United States, and the payment to Mexico of $15,000,000.   S.

Guam. The largest of the Marianas Islands, lying in the Pacific Ocean about 1,450 miles east of Manila, which was acquired at the end of the Spanish-American War in 1898. It is governed by a naval officer designated by the President. Its chief importance has been in aiding in naval and air communications. s.

guarantee of deposits. *See* Bank deposits guarantee.

guerrilla warfare. Warlike acts by individuals or groups not immediately under orders of responsible military authorities. Such persons are not always accorded the rights enjoyed by regular armed forces of a belligerent. JWF.

Guffey Coal Act. An act of Congress, 1937, which expired Apr. 26, 1943. It was designed to stabilize the soft-coal industry and to promote conservation and better utilization of coal. It provided for a bituminous coal code to promote fair competition, establish minimum prices, and improve labor relations. Companies subject to the act which refused to become members were liable to a tax of 19.5 per cent of the value of their coal at the mine. z.

guild socialism. A brand of socialism which advocates public ownership of the means of production, control of production by industrial unions or guilds in each industry, and functional representation in legislative bodies. JMCC.

gumshoe campaign. Unobtrusive efforts to secure the support of political leaders and delegates to a political convention. s.

H

habeas corpus. The "great writ of liberty"; a writ directed to a sheriff, jailer, or anyone else holding a person under detention, requiring him to bring the prisoner into court and state the time and the cause of the arrest. If the cause is deemed sufficient the prisoner may be admitted to bail when the offense charged is ordinarily bailable. If the cause is insufficient he is at once unconditionally released. The importance of the writ is that, by guaranteeing judicial intervention and review, it prevents arbitrary imprisonment. It does not apply under martial law or to persons subject to military law. The privilege of the writ may be suspended only when, in times of rebellion or invasion, the public safety requires suspension. Although President Lincoln suspended it on his own authority several times, the best opinion holds that his action, without prior congressional authority, was illegal. s.

habitual offender. A persistent violator of law; an incorrigible criminal. In certain States, under habitual offender acts or so-called Baumes laws (*q.v.*), persons convicted of a certain number of felonies, usually four, are sentenced to imprisonment for life. JWF.

Hague Conferences, The. International conferences which met at The Hague in 1899 and in 1907 to promote disarmament and international peace. The conferences drafted various conventions to regulate warfare and promote the settlement of disputes by arbitration. JAP.

Half-breeds. A faction of the Republican party, 1876-84, which opposed a third term for Grant, and supported the conciliatory policy of Hayes toward the South and the nomination of Garfield in 1880. They were opposed by the Stalwarts.   s.

Halifax Fishery Commission. A joint American and British commission created under the Treaty of Washington of 1871 which sat at Halifax, Nova Scotia, and in 1877 determined that the United States should pay Great Britain $5,500,000 for certain privileges granted by the treaty to American fishermen in Canadian and Newfoundland waters and ports.   s.

Hampton Roads Conference. A meeting of Lincoln, Seward, and three Confederate commissioners at Hampton Roads, Va., Feb. 3, 1865, at which terms of peace between the United States and the Confederate States were discussed.   s.

Hard Cider Campaign. The presidential election of 1840 when a jug of hard cider was one of the Whig emblems.   s.

hard money. A popular term for metallic currency or specie. It originated before the Civil War when the notes of State banks were the principal currency in circulation.   s.

Hards, or Hard-shells. The regular organization of the Hunker faction of the Democratic party in New York, 1852-60. It was extremely conservative and co-operated with slaveholders.   s.

Hare plan. A single-transferable-vote system of proportional representation favored in the United States. Either the Droop quota (*q.v.*) or a fixed quota may be used. All candidates whose vote equals the quota are declared elected. Surplus votes of winning candidates are transferred according to the next choice expressed by the voters. The lowest candidates are then successively eliminated and their votes are transferred until the required number of candidates have received the electoral quota or have been declared elected because no others can possibly receive it.   z.

Hartford Convention. A meeting of delegates from the New England States in secret session at Hartford, Conn., from Dec. 15, 1814, to Jan. 5, 1815. It proposed seven amendments to the Constitution, considered measures for the better defense of New England, and agreed that States ought to interpose for the protection of their citizens against an allegedly ambitious and inept administration of the national government.   s.

Hatch Acts. Two acts of Congress, 1939 and 1940, which limit the annual expenditure of any political committee to $3,000,000 and any individual annual contribution to a national political committee to $5,000. They prohibit any national employee, or State employee partly or wholly paid out of national funds, from using his position to influence political conduct; outlaw coercion of voters in national elections; prohibit solicitation of funds from employees on public relief projects; and forbid efforts to secure political support by the promise or denial of employment on any project made possible by national appropriations.   z.

hat in the ring. Announcement of candidacy for elective office.   s.

Hawaii. A territory of the United States consisting of a group of 21 islands, eight of which are inhabited, lying in the mid-Pacific. Capital, Honolulu; area, 6,435 sq. mi.; population (1940), 465, 339. It was formerly an independent republic, but was annexed to the United States by joint resolution of Congress, July 7, 1898. An organic act, Apr. 20, 1900, provided a complete territorial organization and, by implication, made it an incorporated territory. The governor and judges are appointed by the President and Senate. There is a popularly elective bicameral legislature.   s.

Hawes-Cooper Act. An act of Congress, 1929, which removed the protection of the Supreme Court's original package doctrine (*q.v.*) from prison-made goods shipped in interstate commerce. z.

Hawkeye State. A nickname for Iowa.   s.

Hawley-Smoot Tariff. The tariff act of June 17, 1930, which established some of the highest protective rates in American tariff history. Such rates have, however, been occasionally reduced through the operation of the flexible tariff begun in 1921 or through reciprocal trade agreements (*qq.v.*)   z.

Hay-Bunau-Varilla Treaty. A treaty signed Nov. 18, 1903, by which Panama for a consideration ceded sovereign rights in a ten-mile-wide strip across its territory to the United States to permit it to construct and operate a canal. *See* Panama Canal.   JWF.

Hay-Pauncefote Treaty. A treaty between the United States and Great Britain, proclaimed in 1901, which expressly abrogated the Clayton-Bulwer Treaty (*q.v.*) and allowed the United States to acquire land in Central America for a canal, and to police it when built. It stipulated, however, that the canal should be open on equal terms to all nations.   s.

head tax. 1. A tax on aliens landing at any port of the United States, first levied in 1882. 2. A poll tax.   s.

hearing. 1. An equity trial. 2. A preliminary examination in a criminal case. 3. An opportunity granted by an administrative body or a legislative committee to present evidence before it.   z.

heeler. A party worker who runs errands for a district or precinct leader, distributes literature, canvasses for votes, arranges for open or disguised bribery of individual voters, and gets out the vote on election day.   s.

hegemony. The ascendancy of one state over others acquired by diplomacy or military victory; the position of leadership or superior influence enjoyed by an individual in the government, or by one branch or office of government over others.   JWF.

Helderberg War. Armed resistance to civil authority by anti-renters (*q.v.*) in Albany County, N. Y., in 1839.   s.

henchman. A faithful lieutenant or active supporter of a political boss.   s.

Henry letters. Copies or paraphrases of the letters of John Henry, a British subject, detailing his conversations with leading New Englanders before the War of 1812, which the author sold to President Madison in 1812 for $50,000. They contained quite innocuous material.   s.

Hepburn Act. An act of Congress June 29, 1906, which provided that rate orders of the Interstate Commerce Commission should go into effect 30 days after promulgation and remain in force unless suspended by the courts; increased the Commission's membership to eleven; and extended its jurisdiction to express companies, pipe lines, and sleeping-car companies.   z.

Hero of Appomattox. A nickname of Ulysses S. Grant.   s.

Hero of New Orleans. A nickname of Andrew Jackson.   s.

Hickory Pole Canvass. The presidential election of 1828, when the Democratic emblem was a hickory pole in honor of the party's presidential candidate, Andrew Jackson, whose nickname was "Old Hickory."   s.

high commissioner. The representative of the executive authority of the United States in the Philippine Islands after the establishment of the Philippine Commonwealth in 1935.   s.

high crimes and misdemeanors. Offenses against the law sufficiently grave to warrant impeachment by the House of Representatives and possibly conviction by the Senate.   s.

higher-law doctrine. The doctrine that "there is a higher law than the Constitution," declared in the United States Senate Mar. 11, 1850, by William H. Seward, then the leading spokesman for the abolitionists.   s.

high license. Regulation of the liquor traffic by means of high license fees purposely designed to drive the more irresponsible saloon keepers out of business and limit consumption by raising prices.   s.

High-Minded Men. A nickname for Federalists who disapproved of the alliance of their party with DeWitt Clinton in 1812 and, for a time, acted with Tammany Hall instead.   s.

high seas. The open sea; those portions of the sea which are not enclosed within headlands or recognized as being within the territorial limits of any state; in general, the ocean beyond the distance of three miles from the shore. The Supreme Court of the United States held in *U.S.* v. *Rodgers,* 150 U.S. 249 (1893), that for the purpose of enforcing criminal laws, the open waters of the Great Lakes are high seas.   s.

Hinds' *Precedents*. A digest of Speakers' decisions and actions of the House of Representatives interpreting the rules of the House. It was first published in 1907, as compiled by Asher C. Hinds, and was revised by Clarence Cannon in 1935.   s.

His Excellency. A title sometimes used in referring to the governor of a State.   s.

His Honor. A title sometimes conferred on the mayor of an American city.   s.

His Superfluous Excellency. A title humorously suggested for the Vice President of the United States because of his lack of power.   s.

H.O.L.C. *See* Home Owners' Loan Corporation.

holding company. A corporation which owns stocks of one or more companies, called subsidiaries; especially one whose activities are confined to the ownership of stock, control of management through boards of directors, and the receipt of dividends, interest payments, and management fees from subsidiary companies.   s.

holdover. A member of the United States Senate, or of the upper house of a State legislature, whose term continues beyond the expiration of a Congress or legislature.   s.

hold-up bills. Measures introduced and supported in a legislative body for the purpose of extorting money or favors from corporations or other interests which would be adversely affected by their passage.   s.

Holman rule. A rule of the House of Representatives, first adopted in 1876 and revived in 1911 after long disuse, which forbids the insertion in a general appropriation bill of any provision changing existing laws except such as, being germane to the subject matter of the bill, has the direct effect of retrenching expenditures.   s.

Holy Alliance. An alliance originally (1815) composed of Russia, Austria, and Prussia but subsequently embracing other Continental states, the avowed purpose of which was to apply the principles of the Christian religion to the relations of rulers with their subjects and with each other. It subsequently became identified with the effort to maintain the reactionary political and territorial settlement established by the post-Napoleonic peace treaties, including the reconquest of Spain's colonies in the New World which had achieved independence.   z.

Holy Wednesday. A nickname for Calendar Wednesday (*q.v.*) s.

Home Owners' Loan Corporation. A federal emergency agency which within three years after its creation in 1933 loaned more than 3 billion dollars to home owners who could not finance outstanding mortgages in imminent danger of foreclosure. Since 1936 it has had no power to make loans. It is now under the Federal Home Loan Bank Administration.   z.

home rule. The practice sanctioned by custom or law of allowing local units of government, particularly cities, to determine within the limits of general law their framework of government and to conduct local public affairs with a minimum of legislative or administrative interference by higher State authorities.   AJW,Jr.

home rule charter. *See* Freeholders' charter.

homestead. Real estate occupied by the owner as a residence which, up to a certain fixed value or acreage, is exempted under constitutional and legal provisions in various States from forced sale to pay the owner's debts. Such exemptions do not apply when the debt has been contracted before the constitutional or legal provisions went into effect.   s.

Homestead Act. An act of Congress, 1862, which permitted any citizen to settle on 160 acres of public land and to receive title to it at the end of five years' actual residence or by paying $1.25 per acre six months after taking possession. The act continued in operation until 1910 when public lands were largely removed from entry.   JMcC.

honest graft. A phrase sometimes used by politicians to describe unethical gains which do not render the recipient liable to legal penalties; *e.g.,* those resulting from buying up property about to be taken for a public purpose and profiting from its subsequent appreciation in value.   s.

hoop-la campaign. A campaign characterized by noise and unusual activity.   s.

Hoosier State. A nickname for Indiana.   s.

Hoovercrat. A Southern Democrat who supported Hoover in the presidential campaign of 1928.   s.

Hot Oil cases. Three cases, 293 U.S. 388 (1935), in which the Supreme Court held that Congress had unconstitutionally delegated legislative powers to the President by authorizing him in 1933 to prohibit the shipment in interstate and foreign commerce of oil in excess of the amount permitted to be produced! or withdrawn from storage under the laws of any of the States.   JJR.

hot pursuit. A principle of international law justifying pursuit and arrest of vessels that have infringed the laws of a state, provided such pursuit begins within the territorial waters of the offended state and is continued without interruption. The right of pursuit ceases when the vessel reaches the territorial waters of another state.   JWF.

Hot Water War. Another name for Fries' Rebellion (*q.v.*) s.

House calendar. A calendar of the House of Representatives which lists all bills reported from committee which are of a public character, but which do not raise revenue or directly or indirectly appropriate money or property.   s.

House-Divided Speech. An address by Lincoln accepting the

Republican nomination for United States Senator in June, 1858, which contained the statement, "A house divided against itself cannot stand. I believe this government cannot endure permanently half slave and half free. . . . It will become all one thing or all the other."   s.

House of Commons.   The lower house of the parliaments of the United Kingdom, of Northern Ireland, and of the Dominion of Canada.   JWF.

House of Representatives.   The more numerous of the two chambers of the Congress of the United States. Each State is guaranteed at least one seat, and additional seats are now distributed after each decennial census according to the method of "equal proportions" which guarantees representation approximately in proportion to population. Since 1910 the total membership has been 435, and the ratio of representation to population is now roughly one member for 301,000 persons. The House has the sole powers of impeachment and of initiating revenue bills. When no candidate has received a majority of electoral votes, it may elect a President from the three candidates standing highest in the electoral college vote; but in this case the Representatives from each State have only one vote.   EES.

Howland Island.   A mid-Pacific island near the equator occupied by the United States in 1936 as a meteorological station and for other purposes.   Z.

Hull House.   A social settlement house founded in Chicago in 1888 and made famous because of its association with Jane Addams, pioneer American social-service worker.   JMCC.

Hull trade agreements.   A series of executive agreements negotiated by Secretary of State Cordell Hull under the Trade Agreements Act of 1934, which authorizes the President to enter into reciprocal arrangements with foreign countries for the reduction of tariffs and other trade barriers up to 50 per cent of the existing tariffs. The terms of each agreement apply to all countries to which most-favored-nation treatment has been extended. JWF.

Hunkers.   The conservative faction of the Democratic party in New York, 1845-52, which was willing to co-operate with slaveholders and which was supposed to have no principles except to hunger, or "hunker," for office.   s.

Hydrographic Office.   A unit of the Navy Department charged with hydrographic surveys in foreign waters and the high seas, research in oceanography, and the publication of maps, charts, sailing directions, and other information for the use of navigators and naval air pilots.   z.

hyphenates.   Americans of foreign birth or descent whose sympathies with the country of their origin has led them to oppose, or give only half-hearted support to, the policies of the American government in wartime.   s.

I

I.C.C.   *See* Interstate Commerce Commission.

iceberg patrol.   An international service maintained in the North Atlantic by the United States and other governments to destroy icebergs or warn merchant ships of their presence.   z.

Idaho.   The 43rd State, admitted to the Union July 3, 1890, from territory formerly included in the Oregon Country. Capital, Boise; area, 83,888 sq. mi.; population (1940), 524,873; presidential electors, 4. The original constitution is still in effect. With minor exceptions all adult citizens may vote.   s.

idealism.   A theory which affirms the predominant value and importance of ideas and ideals, external to the individual and derived through reason and insight, as distinguished from empirical reality experienced through the senses alone; applied especially to Kant's doctrine as developed into the theory of the absolute state by Fichte, Schelling, Hegel, Treitschke, and fascist and National Socialist writers; also to the theories of T. H. Green, Bosanquet, and Bradley.   JJR.

Illinois.   The 21st State, formerly part of the Northwest Territory, admitted to the Union Dec. 3, 1818. Capital, Springfield; area, 56,665 sq. mi.; population (1940), 7,897,241; presidential electors, 28. The present constitution was adopted in 1870, and has been amended only seven times. With minor exceptions all adult citizens may vote. Members of the lower house of the legislature are elected under a system of cumulative voting.   s.

I.L.O.   *See* International Labor Organization.

I'm Alone, The.   A rum-running vessel of Canadian registry, but owned by Americans, which was sunk by a United States Coast Guard cutter Mar. 22, 1929, when about 200 miles from shore. A joint commission determined that the United States should apologize and pay indemnity to Canada and to the crew; but the United States refused to compensate the owners.   s.

immigration.   Entrance into a country for the purpose of establishing a permanent residence or obtaining employment. The national government, which has exclusive control over the subject under the Constitution, made no attempt to limit immigration until 1882 when it prohibited the entrance of paupers, lunatics and idiots, and Chinese coolies. Later statutes debarred contract laborers, diseased persons, those convicted of crimes involving moral turpitude, prostitutes, white slavers, anarchists, professional beggars, illiterates, and those likely to become a public charge. These provisions apply to all immigrants from countries of the Western Hemisphere, who are otherwise freely admitted. The immigration of Asiatics from countries east of Iran is prohibited. For other countries the United States adopted a quota system in 1921. The present law limits the number of immigrants from Europe and western Asia to about 153,000 annually, to be distributed among countries in proportion to their respective contributions to the "national origins" of the white population of the United States as of 1920. s.

immunity. Exemption of a person from a duty, obligation, service, or penalty, imposed by law on all others; *e.g.,* presidential immunity from judicial process, the rights and privileges enjoyed under diplomatic immunity (*q.v.*), and, colloquially, exemption from prosecution which is sometimes promised by a prosecutor to a person accused of crime who agrees to "turn state's evidence." s.

immunity bath. A depreciatory term for the exemption from prosecution of an excessive number of accused persons, or of principal defendants, which arose in 1906 when 16 defendants alleged to have been implicated in a beef trust were exempted from prosecution because they had aided the government in obtaining evidence against others. s.

import duty. A tax levied upon foreign goods imported into a country at their arrival at a port of entry and before they have become commingled with domestic goods. z.

impeachment. A formal written accusation by the lower house of a legislature to the upper house for the purpose of removing a civil officer (other than a member of the legislature) for treason, bribery, or other high crimes and misdemeanors. The House of Representatives has the sole power of impeachment of national officers, and through a committee it presents evidence and manages the prosecution. The Senate must try all impeachments; and during the trial Senators must be placed on oath or affirmation. When the President is being tried the Chief Justice of the Supreme Court of the United States presides over the Senate. A two-thirds vote of the Senators, if a quorum is present, is required for conviction. The penalty which the Senate may impose on conviction is limited to removal from office and disqualification to hold any office of honor, trust, or profit under the United States. A convicted person, however, remains liable to trial and punishment in a court of law. The President's pardoning power does not extend to impeachments. The power of impeachment has been little used, only a dozen officers having been impeached by the House of Representatives since 1789; and of these only four have been convicted. In the States, where similar provisions exist, governors and other officers have occasionally been removed from office after conviction on impeachment. s.

imperialism. The policy of extending the sovereignty or dominion of a state, especially the acquisition of territory outside its natural boundaries which is inhabited by an alien race and is not suitable for extensive colonization by its own people. s.

implied powers. Powers not granted in express terms but

existing because they are necessary and proper to carry into effect some expressly granted power. Though such powers had been exercised by the national government almost from its beginning, the Supreme Court first gave them a broad scope in its decision in the case of *McCulloch* v. *Maryland,* 4 Wheat. 316 (1819), when Chief Justice Marshall declared: "Let the end be legitimate, let it be within the scope of the Constitution, and all means which are appropriate, which are plainly adapted to that end, which are not prohibited, but consist with the letter and spirit of the Constitution are constitutional."   s.

impost. A tax, particularly a duty, imposed on imports and exports. Congress has power to collect import duties provided they be uniform throughout the United States.   JWF.

impressment. The "pressing" or drafting of men into the navy for the defense of the state. In Great Britain it was a royal prerogative frequently exercised before 1815. As used in the stopping of American vessels and taking from them of Americans alleged to be British subjects, it was one of the causes of the War of 1812.   JWF.

imprisonment. Confinement in a penal institution for a period specified in the sentence of a court following conviction of a crime.   z.

imprisonment for debt. Detention on civil process for debt, formerly universal but since 1823 when Kentucky abolished it, gradually prohibited or restricted by constitutional provisions in the States. Where it exists it is mostly applied against absconding debtors or those who have deliberately entered into a contract without means of fulfilling their obligations.   s.

inauguration. The ceremony of inducting a President or governor into office, the primary feature of which is the administering of the oath of office.   EES.

incapacitation. Inability to hold office or discharge some public duty because of physical or mental infirmity or legal disqualification.   z.

incidental protection. Tariff duties levied primarily for the purpose of raising revenues which afford some protection for a nation's industries.   s.

income tax. An excise tax levied upon wealth in the process of acquisition in the form of salaries, wages, commissions, rents, royalties, interest, dividends, business profits, or increase in capital actually realized. Such taxes were twice levied by Congress in the Civil War period and were upheld by the Supreme Court; but the income tax provisions of a law passed in 1894 were declared unconstitutional on the ground that a tax on the income from land was indistinguishable from a tax on the land itself, and therefore was a direct tax which must be apportioned among the States according to population. The 16th Amendment, proclaimed in 1913, empowered Congress to lay and collect taxes on incomes "from whatever source derived." During World War I the income tax, levied at steeply progressive rates, became the principal source of revenue of the national government and it has remained so. Income taxes are also levied by many of the States.   s.

incompatible offices. Two or more offices, one of which is ordinarily membership in a legislative body or a court, which may not be held simultaneously by the same person.   z.

incorporated territory. A territory of the United States which Congress, either expressly or by implication, has recognized as a part of the United States, and to which all provisions of the Constitution, both procedural and substantive, apply in full force; to be distinguished from an unincorporated territory (*q.v.*) At present only Alaska and Hawaii are incorporated territories.   z.

incorporation. 1. The creation of a corporation by act of Congress, or by the authority of the legislature of one of the States of the Union. 2. The action of Congress or the treaty-making power in bringing a territory within the full protection of all provisions of the Constitution of the United States.   JJR.

incrimination. The disclosure of facts that render one liable to criminal prosecution. In federal courts and grand juries the accused cannot be compelled to be a witness against himself in a criminal case, but he may waive the privilege and take the stand voluntarily. A witness is immune from self-incrimination in any proceeding, but he may not withhold facts that merely impair his reputation, nor even incriminating facts if Congress has promised immunity from prosecution. *See* Unreasonable searches and seizures.   JJR.

indemnification. Compensation for loss or damage sustained because of improper or illegal action by public authority.   z.

indemnity. 1. Monetary or material compensation for an injury or loss. 2. A legislative act canceling specific debts to a government, assuming personal financial obligations incurred in the public service, or legalizing acts which were illegal when done. JWF.

indentured servant. A person bound to service for a specified number of years to pay off indebtedness. Early American immigrants often paid the cost of passage by indenturing themselves.   JMCC.

Independence League. A reform organization founded in 1905 under the sponsorship of William Randolph Hearst.   s.

Independence party. A minor party, the outgrowth of the Independence League, which in 1908 nominated a national ticket and polled 83,562 votes.   s.

independent. A voter who is not a member of any party or, if formally a member, who is accustomed to vote for candidates of different parties in accordance with his judgment concerning the issues or candidates presented.   s.

independent establishment. A national administrative office or agency not included in any of the ten executive departments. z.

Independent party. The official title of the Greenback party (*q.v.*)   s.

indeterminate permit. An exclusive right or franchise granted to a public utility company for an indefinite period but subject to the right of a governmental authority to take over the enterprise on payment of due compensation.   AJW,Jr.

indeterminate sentence. A sentence of imprisonment the duration of which is not fixed by the court pronouncing sentence but is left to the determination of responsible administrative authorities within minimum and maximum time limits fixed by the court or by law.   JWF.

Indian. A person of an aboriginal American race. For 135 years after the adoption of the Constitution of the United States an Indian born within a tribe was not a citizen of the United States, and could become so only under the explicit terms of a treaty or statute providing for the collective or individual naturalization of members of certain tribes. Under the terms of the Dawes Act, Feb. 8, 1887, Indians who accepted allotments of land, lived on them apart from their tribes, and adopted civilized customs might be naturalized after 25 years. By act of June 2, 1924, all Indians born within the United States were declared to be citizens.   s.

Indiana. The 19th State, formerly part of the Northwest Territory, admitted to the Union Dec. 11, 1816. Capital, Indianapolis; area, 36,555 sq. mi.; population (1940), 3,427,796; presidential electors, 13. Its present constitution was adopted in 1851. With minor exceptions all adult citizens may vote.   s.

Indiana ballot. A form of secret ballot used in 28 States in which names of candidates of different parties are printed in separate columns with the party name and party circle, and sometimes the party emblem, at the top of each column. Three other States have a modified Indiana ballot which omits the party circle.   s.

Indian Affairs. *See* Office of Indian Affairs.

Indian nation. A separate and distinct body of Indians. Though such nations were never recognized as having sovereignty, but were declared to be "domestic dependent nations" (*Cherokee Nation* v. *Georgia*, 5 Pet. 1, 1831), the United States conducted relations with them by treaty until 1871 and regarded them as capable of managing their internal relations subject to the paramount legislative authority of Congress. The national government has sole power to regulate commerce with them and exercises guardianship over their economy.   s.

Indian reservation. A tract of land to which an Indian tribe retains its original title to ownership or which has been set aside for its use out of the public domain. Indian reservations are under the control of the Office of Indian Affairs (*q.v.*)   s.

Indian Territory. A district nearly coterminous with the present State of Oklahoma which was set aside by Congress in

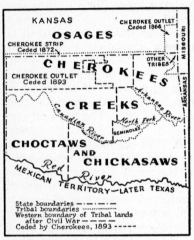

1830 as a permanent home for Cherokees, Creeks, Seminoles, Choctaws, Chickasaws, and other tribes removed from the eastern part of the United States. In 1866 the tribes were forced to retrocede their western lands to the United States in consequence of aid they had given to the Confederacy during the Civil War; though the Cherokees, part of whom had aided the Union, were allowed to retain a western "outlet." The lands thus retroceded were assigned to western Indians, except a portion around Guthrie and Oklahoma City which were opened to white settlement in 1889 and became the nucleus of the Territory of Oklahoma. The Indian Terri-

Indian Territory — Original boundaries, assignment of lands to tribes and reductions of boundaries

tory was never a territory in the strict sense of the word. Each of the Five Civilized Tribes was completely self-governing under a constitution and laws of its own making.   s.

indictment. A formal written accusation, drawn up by the prosecuting officer of a state and returned as a true bill by a grand jury duly summoned and sworn, which charges one or more persons with having committed a felony or misdemeanor.   s.

indignation meeting. A mass meeting called to protest against some public act or policy.   s.

indirect initiative. A form of the initiative (*q.v.*) in which a petition must be submitted to a legislature for action before being placed on the ballot.   s.

indirect tax. An excise or other form of taxation the burden of which may be readily shifted to persons other than those upon whom the tax is levied.   AJW,Jr.

individualism. Theory and practice which emphasizes the worth of human individuality and the rights of persons as against the authority of a group, such as the state, the church, a party, or other collectivity with power over its members. In the economic sphere it is customarily associated with *laissez faire;* in the political sphere, with democratic constitutionalism. JJR.

indoor relief. Maintenance within public institutions of persons who have become public charges; to be distinguished from *outdoor relief,* which is furnishing public assistance to indigent persons within their own homes. JMCC.

Industrial Congress. A convention of laboring men in Philadelphia in 1848 which nominated Gerrit Smith for President and William S. Waitt for Vice President. S.

industrial relations court. A panel of judges empowered to decide labor disputes under compulsory arbitration, as in Kansas, 1920-25. JMCC.

industrial revolution. A historical period beginning in England about 1750, and marked by the introduction of power-driven machinery, unprecedented economic expansion, the wages system, and the corporate form of business enterprise. The terminal date is undetermined. JMCC.

Industrial Workers of the World. An organization of workingmen appearing in America in the early 1900's which endeavored to organize all workers into "one big union" for the purpose of gaining absolute control of economic activity. Known popularly as the "Wobblies," the I.W.W. employed strikes and violence to gain their ends and ignored political activity. JMCC.

ineligible alien. An individual debarred from naturalization in the United States by reason of his not being of the Caucasian race or of African extraction. JWF.

infamous crime. Any crime which carries an infamous punishment such as imprisonment in a penitentiary or elsewhere at hard labor. In the States the meaning of the term varies, but it always denotes a serious offense often resulting in the loss of civil and political rights. JWF.

infant industry. A newly established industry for which the claim is made that, if temporarily protected from foreign competition by high tariff duties, it will attain self-sufficiency through the development of large-scale production. S.

inferior officer. Any officer of the national government whose appointment is vested by law of Congress in the President alone, a court, or the head of a department. Under the Constitution, Congress could probably put any officer into this category except ambassadors, other public ministers and consuls, and judges of the Supreme Court. Z.

inflation. Rapid and extensive increase in the amount of money or credit in circulation, in comparison with the actual needs of trade, which causes prices to rise. Inflation may result from new discoveries of gold, large emissions of paper money, overexpansion of credit, or from sudden decrease in the available supply of consumers' goods. S.

information. A written accusation before a magistrate, made upon oath by a prosecuting officer, which charges one or more persons with having committed a felony or misdemeanor. In more than half the States it may ordinarily be substituted for indictment by a grand jury.   s.

inherent powers. Governmental powers which have not been expressly or impliedly granted by the Constitution or statutes but are presumed to be inherent in a national government or inherent in sovereignty.   JJR.

inheritance tax. A tax or excise levied ad valorem upon the share of the estate of a deceased person which an heir receives. It is sometimes confused with an estate tax, which is levied on the value of the whole estate.   s.

initiative. A device by which a private draft of a constitutional amendment or statute may be formally proposed by a petition signed by a certain number or percentage of the voters of a State, and which must be submitted to the electorate for adoption or rejection before being adversely disposed of. In the form of the *indirect initiative* it is first submitted to the legislature, and goes on the ballot only if the legislature rejects it. In the form of the *direct initiative* it is submitted to the voters without any provision for legislative consideration. The initiative may be used for statutes in 18 States and for constitutional amendments in 13. No additional State has made provision for it in any form since 1918.   s.

injunction. An order issued by a court of equity commanding a person to do, or to refrain from doing, an act which would injure another by violating his personal or property rights. A *mandatory injunction* commands the specific performance of an act; a *preventive injunction* orders a person to desist from an act already commenced or contemplated; a *preliminary, or interlocutory, injunction* may be issued when a danger is immediately threatened and there is inadequate opportunity for a court to determine finally the rights of the parties; and a *permanent injunction* is the final decree of the court. The violation of an injunction is a contempt of court and may be punished by fine or imprisonment. s.

Inland Waterways Corporation. A government-owned corporation chartered under act of Congress in 1924 and transferred from the War Department to the Department of Commerce in 1939. It operates barge lines on several rivers and now derives its funds entirely from operations.   s.

inquest. A legal inquiry to establish some question of fact; particularly an inquiry by a coroner and his jury into a person's death where foul play, violence, or accident is suspected as the cause.   z.

inquiry. *See* Commission of inquiry.

insecurity. Uncertainty about one's economic future, particularly marked among wage earners for whom unemployment, accident, illness, and inadequate provision for old age are constant threats to livelihood.   JMCC.

in-service training. Specialized training offered employees by various administrative agencies. The programs of the Department of Agriculture and of the Bureau of the Census are noteworthy.   Z.

insolvency. The inability to pay debts when due even though assets may exceed liabilities.   JMCC.

inspection laws. National and State laws for the inspection of foods and for controlling human, animal, and plant diseases and parasites. They are administered by various national and State inspection services. Any fees charged by the latter at State boundaries above the cost of maintaining the services, must be paid into the national treasury.   Z.

instruction. **1.** A resolution of a State legislature, town meeting, or other public body directing representatives to support or oppose a certain measure. **2.** A resolution of a party convention directing delegates to a nominating convention to vote for specified candidates. Whether such an instruction is binding on only a few ballots or until the delegates are released by the candidate for whom they were instructed to vote is a matter of frequent dispute.   s.

Insular cases. A group of cases including *De Lima* v. *Bidwell,* 182 U.S. 1 (1901); *Downes* v. *Bidwell,* 182 U.S. 244 (1901); *Hawaii* v. *Mankichi,* 190 U.S. 197 (1903); and *Dorr* v. *United States,* 195 U.S. 138 (1904); in which the Supreme Court distinguished between incorporated and unincorporated territories and held that in the latter only the fundamental guarantees of the Constitution were binding upon Congress; but not those, like equality in taxation or indictment and trial by jury, which were "procedural, remedial, or formal."   s.

insurance. A contract in which for a consideration one party indemnifies another against loss resulting from specified risks. An insurance contract between parties in different States is not subject to regulation by Congress as interstate commerce.   JMCC.

insurgency. Rebellion against a government of such scope and effectiveness that the rebels merit quasi-diplomatic recognition from foreign states and acquire limited belligerent rights.   JWF.

insurgent. **1.** A member of an organized group, especially one not recognized as a belligerent, who rebels against governmental authority. **2.** A person who, while formally retaining his membership in a party, acts in opposition to its decisions and policies; specifically a Republican Congressman who rebelled against Cannonism in 1909-10, or who acted independently after 1921. s.

insurrection. Organized armed rebellion against established political authority.   JWF.

intangible property. Bonds, stocks, mortgages, and other paper titles to wealth, or even less corporeal values such as "good will." z.

inter-Allied debts. The complex network of intergovernmental debts contracted between Allied and Associated governments during and following World War I for the purchase of war equipment and foodstuffs and for economic stabilization. JWF.

interest group. Persons who, whether closely organized or not, have interests in common in the molding of public opinion or in the passage of legislation. *Compare with* Pressure group. JMCC.

interests, the. A term sometimes applied vaguely to corporations or the capitalist class. s.

interim. The period between legislative sessions. s.

Interior, Department of the. A department created by act of Congress Mar. 3, 1849, which now has jurisdiction over a group of subjects including Indian affairs, territories and island possessions, national parks, public lands, reclamation, conservation, the Geological Survey, the Bonneville Power Administration, the Bureau of Mines, and the Fish and Wildlife Service. s.

interlocking directorates. Boards of directors of competing companies or of closely related financial concerns composed in greater or less numbers of the same individuals. The use of this device to restrain trade was prohibited by the Clayton Act. s.

intermediate court. A court in a judicial hierarchy falling between the highest, or supreme, tribunal and the trial court. Known by various names, its jurisdiction is usually appellate, but some States confer original jurisdiction in special cases such as election contests. z.

internal improvement. A highway, railroad, canal, dredged waterway, or other means of transportation constructed within a country at public expense. s.

internal revenue. Income of the national government from taxes other than customs duties. s.

international agreement. A general term applied to all manner of engagements entered into between two or more states, ranging from informal understandings and administrative conventions to formal treaties. JWF.

international boundary commission. A body chosen *ad hoc* by two or more states to determine the location of an international line. The decision may be based on principles of international law or prescription, or it may represent a compromise of conflicting claims. JWF.

international copyright. An exclusive right to copyrighted literary or artistic property in all states with which the author's or artist's state has agreements pledging mutual respect of copyrights. JWF.

International Labor Organization. An institution established at Geneva in 1919 by Part XIII of the Treaty of Versailles to investigate labor problems everywhere and to draft model laws for acceptance by member states. Each member state sent delegates representing labor, capital, and government to the annual Conference which drafted conventions and recommendations embracing such matters as hours of labor, the work of women and children, and dangerous occupations, and submitted them to national legislatures for ratification. The United States became a member of the International Labor Organization in 1934. During World War II a part of its office was re-established in Canada for the purpose of studying labor problems that might arise after the war.   JWF.

international law. An inchoate body of rules which deal principally with relationships between governments or between the government of one state and subjects of another. As states may be at peace or war, rules for various types of relationships are classified as laws of peace, war, or neutrality. Although various usages existed in the relations between peoples of earlier civilizations, modern international law is a product of the European nation-state system. Early jurists, such as Gentilis and Grotius, endeavored to derive an interstate legal system from Roman and mercantile codes, contemporary custom, and reason. As international relationships grew more complex new customary law developed and old rules were elaborated and interpreted in court decisions and studies by learned jurists. In the past century new rules have been decreed by states meeting in conference, thereby adding written international law to customary law. Controversies over the existence of international law are due partly to the Austinian definition of law and partly to the common misconception that international law defines interstate relations as they *ought* to be. Austinian jurists maintain that law must necessarily be handed down by a sovereign authority and be enforced by courts and police; whereas the test of a rule of international law is its universal acceptance by the community of states and their obedience to its mandates. That international law does not always coincide with international ethics is regrettable but irrelevant. *See* Private international law.   JWF.

international legislation. Rules of international law expressed in the form of multilateral agreements formulated by international conferences and later ratified by the principal states. They are to be distinguished from unwritten customary international law discovered by jurists investigating the practice of states.   JWF.

international police. A proposed military force to be recruited from the members of the community of nations for the purpose of enforcing the will of a large majority upon any state failing to fulfill its international obligations or waging offensive war. The possibility of such a force was envisioned in Art. XVI of the Covenant of the League of Nations.   JWF.

international transit. The passage of vehicles from one country to, or through, another. Rules for the conduct of Rhine and Danube river traffic were agreed upon by riparian states as early as the 16th century. Later international agreements have dealt with river, highway, rail, and air transit across state boundaries. JWF.

internment. 1. The confinement of enemy aliens or persons suspected of disloyalty in special camps or designated areas. 2. The custody exercised by a neutral state over the troops, ships of war, or military planes that have sought asylum within its territory or have violated its neutrality. JWF.

interstate commerce. Commerce among the several States which Congress has the power to govern under the commerce clause of the Constitution of the United States, as distinguished from *intrastate* commerce, which is ordinarily subject only to State regulation. It includes traffic, transportation, communication, and intercourse which concern more States than one, and may also embrace certain intrastate operations which affect interstate commerce in a substantial way. The Supreme Court has rejected "the mechanical application of legal formulas" for delimiting federal power over interstate commerce. *See* Commerce. JJR.

Interstate Commerce Commission. An independent commission created by Congress Feb. 4, 1887, and now consisting of eleven members one of whom, chosen by the group, serves as chairman. It has the duty to fix just and reasonable rates, including maximum and minimum rates where necessary, regulate pooling and approve consolidations among carriers, prescribe uniform accounting practices, evaluate carrier property, and approve the issuance and sale of securities. Carriers under its jurisdiction include all railway and express companies, oil pipe lines, sleeping-car companies, and motor carriers operating interstate, and water carriers operating on coastwise, intercoastal, or inland waterway routes. The Commission may also determine intrastate rates where necessary to remove discrimination against interstate rates. Z.

interstate compact. An agreement between two or more States made with the consent of Congress and relating usually to boundaries, control and improvement of rivers for irrigation or water power, conservation of natural resources, penal jurisdiction over boundary rivers and lakes, public utility regulation, development of ports, or uniformity of legislation. Many agreements on minor matters are made without the consent of Congress. S.

interstate rendition. *See* Rendition.

intervention. Forcible interference by one state in the internal affairs of another to restore order, prevent the commission or continuance of acts which shock the moral sense of civilized peoples, or compel a state to fulfill its international obligations. Premature recognition of the independence of insurgents constitutes intervention, but recognition of their belligerency is not so regarded. S.

intimidation. An offense against the purity of elections which consists of threats of physical violence or of the loss of employment or other privileges.   s.

intransigent. Unwilling to compromise on matters of policy; irreconcilable.   s.

intrastate commerce. Trade, transportation, or communication conducted wholly within the boundaries of a single State. It is subject to State regulatory authorities, but rates and standards of service fixed by them must not interrupt or burden the free flow of commerce among the States. In practice, this means that regulations of State commissions can be, and often are, made to harmonize with those of national commissions.   s.

invasion. A large-scale offensive thrust into territory held by another state.   JWF.

investigative power. "An essential and appropriate auxiliary to the legislative function" (*McGrain* v. *Daugherty,* 273 U.S. 135, 1927) which enables a legislative body to obtain information by compelling the attendance of witnesses and the production of books and papers, and which subjects recalcitrant persons to punishment for contempt of legislative authority. The inquiry must relate to a subject within the competence of a legislative house such as an impeachment or the trial thereof, a contested election, or the punishment of a member; or to a subject on which legislation is contemplated; or to a subject like the operation of an administrative or executive office on which remedial legislation may be had. The investigative power does not include a general power to inquire into private affairs. Investigations may be conducted by either house or by joint, standing, or special committees.   s.

Investment Company Act. A law of Congress, 1940, providing for the registration and regulation of investment trusts and companies.   JMCC.

Invisible Empire. Another name for the Ku-Klux Klan. s.

invisible government. The rule of a boss who, having secured the nominations and elections of governors or mayors, legislators, and judges, dictates their general policies and their acts and decisions in specific cases.   s.

involuntary servitude. Slavery, peonage, or compulsory labor to work out a debt. Under the 13th Amendment criminal punishment for breach of a contract in which a person has agreed to render personal service is unconstitutional; but policemen, firemen, members of a train crew, and seamen may be punished for deserting their employment when such an act would jeopardize the public. s.

Iowa. The 30th State, admitted to the Union Dec. 28, 1846, from territory acquired by the Louisiana Purchase. Capital, Des Moines; area, 56,147 sq. mi.; population (1940), 2,538,268; presidential electors, 10. The present constitution was adopted in 1857. With minor exceptions all adult citizens may vote.   s.

ironclad oath. The oath of office prescribed by Congress July 2, 1862, which required a person to swear that he had never voluntarily given aid or encouragement to the enemies of the United States. A similar oath was required in 1867 for voters in the States undergoing reconstruction. s.

irreconcilable. A person who insists on the adoption of the program of his party or group and refuses to make concessions or agree to compromises. s.

irredentism. Activity on the part of a national group to annex territory formerly belonging to their state or inhabited by persons of similar racial stock. JWF.

Irrepressible Conflict Speech. An address by William H. Seward at Rochester, N. Y., Oct. 25, 1858, in which he declared that the slavery controversy was "an irrepressible conflict between opposing and enduring forces, and it means that the United States must and will, sooner or later, become either entirely a slaveholding nation or entirely a free labor nation." s.

irrigation. The artificial watering of arid or semiarid land. *See* Reclamation. s.

isolation. Aloofness in international politics; refusal to participate with other states in efforts to remove causes of international friction and to secure the peace of the world; popularly termed avoidance of "entangling alliances." Based on the alleged self-sufficiency and immunity from attack of the United States and its lack of real interest in European affairs, the policy of isolation prevented our being represented at general international conferences before 1900; our accession to the League of Nations in 1919; and our co-operation in the curbing of aggressor nations until after 1937. s.

itemized appropriations. Appropriations which stipulate in great detail the specific purposes for which even small sums may be spent; opposed to lump-sum appropriations, which may be allocated to specific subjects by heads of departments or bureaus or allotted by the governor to spending agencies. z.

item veto. The power which the governor possesses in 39 States to veto items in appropriation bills without affecting any other provisions of such bills. In some of these States the governor may also reduce the amount of items. s.

I.W.W. *See* Industrial Workers of the World.

J

jackpot. A fund collected before 1912 from interests seeking special favors for distribution at the end of a session to members of the Illinois legislature who "voted right." s.

Jackson Day. The anniversary of the battle of New Orleans Jan. 8, 1815, usually celebrated by the Democratic party with a dinner. It is a legal holiday in Louisiana.   s.

Jacksonian democracy. An equalitarian movement which stemmed from frontier democracy, the rise of cities, and the policies of Jackson's presidency, 1829-37, rather than from any significant American political theory. It was characterized by the virtual disappearance of aristocratic leadership in politics and the demand for universal manhood suffrage, popular election of all State and local officers, rotation in office, the destruction of the United States bank and other monopolies, and vigorous enforcement of national powers which were, however, conceived to be limited in extent by the dogma of States' rights.   s.

Jacobin. 1. A member of a radical republican club in France in the period of the Revolution of 1789. 2. A nickname for democratic societies which opposed some policies of Washington's administration. It was later extended to all Republicans. 3. Radical Republicans in Missouri who during the Civil War wished to proscribe all Southern sympathizers.   s.

jail. A place of imprisonment maintained by local governments for the detention of suspects awaiting trial and the punishment of persons sentenced to less than one year for petty crimes and misdemeanors.   JMCC.

Jamaica. The largest British West Indian island situated in the Caribbean about 100 miles south of Cuba. An area adjacent to Portland Bight was leased by the United States in 1940 for a naval air base.   z.

Jarvis Island. A mid-Pacific island just south of the equator recently occupied by the United States because of its value as a meteorological and air transit station.   z.

jayhawkers. Armed bands of Kansas freesoilers who before and during the Civil War made frequent raids into western Missouri in order to liberate slaves, steal horses, and avenge the deeds of border ruffians (*q.v.*)   s.

Jayhawker State. A nickname for Kansas.   s.

Jay's Treaty. A treaty between the United States and Great Britain negotiated in London by John Jay in 1794. It provided for the British evacuation of Detroit and other northwestern posts, but it was unpopular because it protected what remained of loyalist property in the United States, postponed the settlement of boundaries, debts, and claims for unlawful captures by the British, limited the effect of our Treaty of 1778 with France, and opened our trade to the British West Indies under conditions which the Senate refused to accept.   s.

Jefferson Day. Thomas Jefferson's birthday, April 13, occasionally celebrated by the Democratic party with a dinner. It is a legal holiday in Alabama.   s.

Jeffersonian democracy. Political principles expressed in various writings of Thomas Jefferson. They include natural rights, equal and exact administration of justice, minimum control by government over the affairs of individuals, majority rule, local self-government, preservation of the guaranties of civil liberty, and subordination of the military to the civil authorities. Jefferson had faith in the capacity of the people for self-government, but thought they should be educated and, in the main, be small holders of farm lands. s.

Jefferson's Manual. A compilation of rules of parliamentary procedure made by Thomas Jefferson for his own guidance while presiding over the Senate as Vice President, 1797-1801, and adopted in 1837 as an integral part of the rules of the House of Representatives. s.

Jefferson Territory. A provisional government, 1859-61, in the Pike's Peak region of Kansas Territory, now Colorado. s.

jeopardy. Such an exposure to the possibility of conviction for violation of a provision of criminal law, that State and federal constitutions bar a second prosecution for that same offense; but State and federal governments may prosecute the accused separately for different offenses arising out of the same act, and there is no double jeopardy in retrial after appeal by a prisoner from his own conviction, nor even in appeal by a State government after acquittal, if substantial legal errors are shown. JJR.

Jim Crow law. A popular term for any law requiring the segregation of the white and colored races in a vehicle of transportation or place of public entertainment. s.

jingo. An advocate of war or warlike methods to promote national interests abroad. s.

Johnson Act. An act of Congress Apr. 13, 1934, which prohibited the sale in the United States of securities of foreign governments which were in default in their debts to the United States. s.

joint ballot. A ballot of members of both houses of a legislature voting together, as formerly for the election of a United States Senator. s.

joint commission. In international law, a body composed of commissioners appointed by two states to investigate and make recommendations for the settlement of a particular matter in dispute between them. s.

joint committee. A committee appointed by both houses of the legislature to make a special investigation, administer subjects under direct legislative control, or, as in Massachusetts, Maine, and Connecticut, to study and make recommendations concerning bills to the two chambers. s.

joint rate. A tariff fixed upon the shipment of goods between points where the facilities of two or more carriers are involved. JMCC.

joint resolution. A resolution passed by both houses of a legislative body which, when signed by the executive or passed over his veto, has the full force of an act, though ranking below it in formal dignity. Half the States forbid legislation in the form of a resolution.   s.

joint return. An income tax return filed by husband and wife together and including all income received by either.   z.

joint-stock association. A business organization, not unlike a partnership, the capital stock of which is owned by various shareholders any one of whom may transfer his holdings without the consent of the remainder. It does not enjoy the legal personality of a corporation since it can sue and be sued only through some designated officer; moreover its shareholders do not enjoy limited liability but are individually and collectively responsible for debts. z.

joker. An obscure provision inserted in the body of a bill for the purpose of nullifying other provisions or giving the bill a meaning different from that avowed by its sponsors.   s.

Jones Act. 1. An act of Congress Aug. 29, 1916, which made both houses of the Philippine legislature elective, broadened the franchise, paved the way for a large measure of self-government, and carried the promise of independence as soon as a stable government was assured. 2. An act of Congress Mar. 2, 1917, which liberalized the government of Puerto Rico established by the Foraker Act, 1900. Both houses of the legislature were made elective, their powers were extended, the franchise qualified by a literacy test, was granted to all adults, and American citizenship was collectively conferred upon Puerto Ricans.   z.

journal. The official record of a legislative house kept by the clerk and published as directed by the house. It contains minutes of the introduction and reference of bills, reports of committees, motions, votes, and other actions, but does not report debates.   s.

judge. The principal officer of a court who alone or in concert with colleagues or with a jury, as the law or the rules of the court prescribe, hears and decides cases and controversies and renders judgments.   z.

judge advocate. An officer of a court martial who acts as prosecutor for the government and may act to protect the rights of the accused.   z.

judge-made law. A popular term for decisions of courts which by construction or interpretation declare statutes, or parts of statutes, void; also sometimes applied to the common law because its form and content have been largely developed by judicial decisions.   s.

judge of elections. One of a board consisting of, usually, three persons appointed by local authority to conduct the polling in an election precinct.   s.

judgment. An authoritative determination of the legal rights and duties of the parties to a controversy usually rendered by a court.   JJR.

judicial council. An advisory body of judges and practicing attorneys, or sometimes of judges alone, set up to study the organization and rules of procedure of the courts and recommend improvements to the legislature. Occasionally they have power to reassign judges to districts with crowded dockets.   JWF.

judicial power. The power to hear and decide cases and controversies in accordance with the forms and procedures prescribed by the law of the land and to render judgment consistent with the substantive provisions of law, such judgment being definitive except for the legal right of parties to appeal to a higher judicial tribunal.   Z.

judicial review. The examination or "review" by the courts, in cases actually before them, of legislative statutes and executive or administrative acts to determine whether or not they are prohibited by a written constitution or are in excess of powers granted by it; and if so, to declare them void and of no effect. The power was exercised by several State courts in the Confederation period and was declared inherent in the judiciary by the Supreme Court of the United States in *Marbury* v. *Madison* (*q.v.*) In general the courts do not inquire into expediency or legislative motives; and in cases of doubt the rule is that the statute or act should be sustained.   S.

judiciary. A system of courts; also the judges collectively. The national judiciary consists of a Supreme Court, ten circuit courts of appeals, ninety or more district courts, a court of claims, a court of customs and patent appeals, a customs court and a tax court, besides a number of courts in the District of Columbia and in the territories and dependencies. In the States there is always one supreme court, sometimes called the court of appeals, or the court of errors and appeals; a number of circuit courts with varying titles, holding sessions in every county; and minor courts presided over by justices of the peace or magistrates. Many States also have intermediate courts ranking just below the highest court; county courts with limited jurisdiction ranking below the circuit courts; and special criminal courts, probate courts, domestic relations courts, children's, juvenile, and adolescent courts, etc. Formerly separate courts were organized to administer law and equity, but this distinction has disappeared almost everywhere. Such courts have been merged and in most States both legal and equitable remedies may be used in the same case. *See* Constitutional courts; Legislative courts.   S.

Judiciary, Committee on. A committee in national and State legislative houses which has jurisdiction over bills affecting the organization, jurisdiction, and procedure of courts, or bills which pose a constitutional issue, or raise important questions of private law.   s.

junket. An outing for members of a legislative committee under the guise of making an investigation at a distance from the seat of government.   s.

jurisdiction. 1. The territorial or other limits within which governmental authority may properly be exercised. 2. The authority of a court to hear and decide cases and controversies concerning persons or subjects.   JJR.

jurisdictional dispute. A conflict among labor unions for the exclusive privilege to organize employees in certain industries, or in certain areas, or to control employments in various types of work.   JMCC.

jurisprudence. The science or philosophy of law. In the narrowest sense, it may be considered as applying only to the study of the actual substance of law, as found in judicial decisions. More frequently, it denotes the formal analytical study of legal systems after the fashion established by John Austin. In the broadest sense, it stands for a study of the nature of law and of its relationship to customs and morals, thus involving historical, philosophical, and sociological methods.   JRP.

jury. A body of impartial laymen residing within the territorial jurisdiction of a court who are properly empaneled and sworn to render a true answer to a question of fact submitted to them. In United States courts the petit, or trial, jury must consist of twelve men, and their verdict must be unanimous in both civil and criminal cases; but jury trial may be waived. Seven States provide for trial of criminal cases by less than twelve jurors; and eight States authorize verdicts by three fourths or some other fraction in the trial of cases not involving capital crimes. For civil cases an even greater number of States have relaxed the requirement as to both the size of the jury and the majority necessary for a verdict, and several States provide for no jury except on the demand of one of the parties. A few States make the jury the judge of both the law and the facts of a case. *See* Grand jury.   s.

jus gentium. A body of law developed by Roman jurists for the the trial of cases between Roman citizens and foreigners and provincials; subsequently held by mediaeval jurists to embody principles of right reason applicable to all human relationships; and invoked by Grotius and others as authority for rules of international law.   JWF.

jus sanguinis. The principle implicit in the nationality laws of most Continental European states which holds that a person's citizenship is determined by that of his parents.   JWF.

jus soli. The basic principle of the nationality laws of the United

States, Great Britain, and certain other states which holds that a person's citizenship is determined by the place of his birth.   JWF.

just compensation. The full market value, to be paid in money, when property is taken in eminent domain. Disputes over the amount are determined by administrative tribunals or the courts.   JWF.

justice. 1. The title of a judge. 2. The process of adjudication by which the legal rights of private parties are vindicated and the guilt or innocence of accused persons is established.   Z.

Justice, Department of. A department of the national government created by act of Congress June 22, 1870, with the Attorney General (*q.v.*) at its head. It furnishes legal advice and opinions on request to the President and the heads of other departments, investigates violations of federal laws, conducts all suits in the Supreme Court in which the United States is a party, oversees the work of district attorneys, supervises federal penal institutions, and administers the immigration and naturalization service.   S.

justice of the peace. A subordinate magistrate, usually without formal legal training, empowered to try petty civil and criminal cases, and in some States to conduct preliminary hearings for persons accused of crimes and fix bail for appearance in court. Justices of the peace are usually elective within a minor civil division, although their jurisdiction extends throughout a county. Except in five States, their compensation is derived from fees, with the result that in too many cases judgment is for the plaintiff.   S.

juvenile court. A minor court having jurisdiction in cases of delinquent, neglected, or dependent children which seeks by informal procedure to determine the underlying causes of misconduct and provides for reformation through education, healthful activities, or institutional supervision.   S.

K

Kansas. The 34th State, admitted to the Union Jan. 29, 1861, from territory acquired by the Louisiana Purchase. Capital, Topeka; area, 82,158 sq. mi.; population (1940), 1,801,028; presidential electors, 8. The original constitution, as amended, is still in effect. Provision is made for the recall of officials, including judges. With minor exceptions all adult citizens may vote.   S.

Kansas Industrial Court. A court of compulsory arbitration created by Kansas in 1920 with power to settle labor disputes by mandatory awards on hours and conditions of work and minimum wages. The law creating the court was declared unconstitutional by the United States Supreme Court in *Wolff Packing Co.* v. *Court of Industrial Relations,* 262 U.S. 522 (1923).   S.

Kansas-Nebraska Act. A law of Congress May, 1854, which organized Kansas and Nebraska territories in the region closed to

Kansas-Nebraska Act — Boundaries of
Kansas and Nebraska territories

slavery by the Missouri Compromise of 1820, which it expressly repealed. Either territory might later be admitted as a State "with or without slavery, as their constitutions may prescribe at the time of admission" — a provision which introduced popular, or "squatter," sovereignty. The act angered the abolitionists, resulted in the disruption of political parties, and hastened the outbreak of the Civil War.   s.

Kansas plan. A proposal by Governor G. H. Hodges of Kansas in 1913 to organize the State government on the analogy of the commission government of cities.   s.

Keating-Owen Act. An act of Congress Sept. 1, 1916, which forbade shipment in interstate commerce of the products of mines and factories in which children under certain ages (14 or 16) had been allowed to work. The Supreme Court invalidated it in *Hammer* v. *Dagenhart, 247* U.S. 251 (1918).   z.

Kellogg-Briand Pact. A treaty signed in Paris Aug. 27, 1928, by which adhering states renounced war as an instrument of national policy and declared their intention of seeking pacific means to settle disputes arising among them. By 1939 all independent states except Argentina, Bolivia, Salvador, and Uruguay had adhered.   JWF.

Kentucky. The 15th State, formerly part of Virginia, admitted to the Union June 1, 1792, with the consent of the legislature of Virginia. Capital, Frankfort; area, 40,598 sq. mi.; population (1940), 2,845,627; presidential electors, 11. The present constitution was adopted in 1891. With minor exceptions all adult citizens may vote.   s.

Kentucky Resolutions. Ten resolutions drafted by Thomas Jefferson which were passed by the legislature of Kentucky in 1798 and 1799 and sent to the other States. They declared that the national government was a government of delegated powers, created by compact among the States; that whenever it exercised undelegated powers each State, as a party to the compact, might declare the act void; and, in particular, that the Alien and Sedition acts of Congress were "void and of no effect."   s.

keynote speech. The address delivered by the temporary chairman in opening a national nominating convention.   s.

Keystone State.   A nickname of Pennsylvania.   s.

Kingfish.   A nickname for Senator Huey P. Long.   z.

Kitchen Cabinet.   A group including William B. Lewis, Amos Kendall, Francis P. Blair, and Duff Green whose advice President Jackson was supposed to have followed for a time to the exclusion of consultations with his regular cabinet.   s.

knifing.   Political treachery; secret desertion by a party organization of its own candidates; the pretense of supporting a candidate while actively working for the election of an opponent. s.

Knights of Labor.   A national industrial labor union founded in Philadelphia in 1869 which attained a membership of 600,000 by 1886 and continued to have great importance for a few years thereafter. Its decline has been attributed to political entanglements, rivalry with craft unions, and internal dissensions.   s.

Knights of the Golden Circle.   A secret, semimilitary organization formed in Alabama in 1855 which during the Civil War became the leading Copperhead organization in the Ohio Valley States, claiming 174,000 members in Ohio, Indiana, and Illinois by 1864.   s.

Know-Nothing party.   A secret political party opposed to foreigners which grew out of the Order of United Americans about 1852. Its membership was divided into three classes, the first two of which were alone capable of determining policy or being nominated for party or public office. Members of the third class were pledged to vote the party ticket and to reply "I don't know" to all inquiries concerning the party. It swept the elections in Massachusetts in 1854 and attained great influence in other Northern States. In 1855 its organization was captured by Southerners and its name was changed to American party (*q.v.*)   s.

Know Ye Men.   The paper-money party of Rhode Island, 1783-90.   s.

Ku-Klux Klan.   1. An organization founded in Tennessee in 1866 to reassert white supremacy in the South. Disguised in white masks and robes, members of the Klan rode at night, terrorizing, whipping, and committing other acts of violence, including murder, against Negroes who persisted in voting and against their white leaders. After Congress in 1871 passed the Force Bill (*q.v.*) the Klan adopted less violent, but none the less effective, means to accomplish its purpose. 2. A similar national organization founded in 1915, but directed against Catholics, Jews, and foreigners, as well as Negroes, which was influential in several States for a brief period after World War I.   s.

Kure Island.   The most westerly of the Hawaiian chain of islands which since 1936 has been administered by the United States Navy as a naval air base.   z.

L

Labor, Department of. One of the ten departments of the national government, headed by a secretary of cabinet rank. It was created by act of Congress Mar. 4, 1913, which divided the former Department of Commerce and Labor. It collects statistics concerning employment and other matters concerning labor, promotes the welfare of wage earners, improves their opportunities to obtain employment, and seeks to avert or settle labor troubles by conciliation. Its Women's Bureau looks after the interests of women employed in industry, and its Children's Bureau investigates matters concerning child welfare.   S.

labor leader. One who derives his livelihood from full-time participation in trade-union activities.   JMCC.

labor legislation. Laws regulating the conditions of employment of wage earners and their standard of living. Included are factory inspection laws to promote health and safety, minimum wage laws and maximum hour laws, restrictions upon the employment of women and children, social insurance, and laws regulating collective bargaining. Historically laws regulating the employment of women and minors were enacted first because such persons were not *sui juris,* and their bargaining power in industry was relatively less effective than that of men. But laws safeguarding the labor of men in dangerous occupations were soon enacted, followed by removal of common law impediments to recovery of compensation by workmen injured in the course of their employment, the establishment of compensation funds, provisions for old-age, survivors', and unemployment insurance, and regulations of wages and hours of employment. The most recent type of labor legislation is designed to safeguard the right of workmen to organize into trade-unions and bargain collectively. The power of the national government to enact labor legislation of more or less general scope under its interstate commerce power is fairly well established. Labor legislation in the States is justified under the police power.   JMCC.

labor reformer. One who seeks to improve the conditions of employment and the economic condition of labor as a social class by state regulation, collective bargaining, or the transformation of the social system in accordance with such revolutionary doctrines as Marxian socialism or syndicalism.   JMCC.

Labor Reform party. A minor party formed in 1869 which advocated the exclusive use of greenbacks for currency, an eight-hour day on government contracts, abolition of the contract system in prison labor, and Chinese exclusion.   S.

Labor's Nonpartisan League. A body created Aug. 10, 1936, to unite organized labor for political action. It aided in the re-election of President F. D. Roosevelt in 1936 and organized the American Labor party.   S.

labor union. An unincorporated and voluntary association of employees which acts as their collective bargaining agent with employers to determine wages and the conditions of employment. Labor unions are roughly classified as *craft,* or *horizontal,* unions; and as *industrial,* or *vertical,* unions. The former exercise jurisdiction over all workers of a particular craft, trade, or skill, wherever they may be employed; the latter may include all workers in a given industry regardless of their craft, trade, or skill. JMCC.

LaFollette Seamen's Act. An act of Congress Mar. 4, 1915, which regulated wage scales, the payment of wages, conditions of employment and size of crews on merchant ships, and established minimum standards for the victualing and quartering of crews on shipboard. z.

laissez faire. A phrase coined by French physiocrats which has come to stand for noninterference by government in economic life. z.

lame duck. A former officeholder who has failed of re-election. s.

lame duck session. Before the adoption of the 20th Amendment, the short session of Congress beginning in December of even-numbered years and ending March 4, in which a number of Senators and Representatives sat who had failed of re-election. s.

land-grabber. A person who obtains public land by bribery or collusion with officials, or by taking advantage of loopholes in the land laws. s.

land grant. A gift of public land to an individual, corporation, local government division, or State to aid in accomplishing some public purpose. s.

land-grant college. An independent agricultural and mechanical college, or equivalent division of a State university, created by the distribution, under the Morrill Act of 1862, of public lands to the States roughly in proportion to their representation in Congress, and aided by further grants of land and money under later acts. s.

landslide. An overwhelming triumph of a party in a popular election. s.

Lanham Act. An act of Congress Oct. 14, 1940, amended in June, 1941, which authorized the Federal Works Agency, in cooperation with other national agencies, to provide housing for persons employed in war plants and to acquire land for the construction of necessary community works and services, such as hospitals, schools, streets, and water works. z.

Lansing-Ishii Agreement. An executive agreement between Japan and the United States signed Nov. 2, 1917, and ended Apr. 14, 1923, by which the United States recognized Japan's "special interests" in China, and Japan assented to the principle of the open door (*q.v.*) in that country. JWF.

larceny. Theft of personal property.   z.

last-minute lie. A falsehood concerning a candidate's public record or private life circulated on the eve of an election when refutation is impossible.   s.

Lausanne Treaty. 1. A Turco-Italian treaty, Oct. 18, 1912, by which Turkey ceded Tripoli, Rhodes, and the Dodecanese Islands to Italy. 2. The final peace treaty between the Allies and Turkey, signed July 24, 1923. It provided for a settlement of boundaries, exchange of minority groups between Greece and Turkey, and the practical abolition of capitulations by which foreigners in Turkey had been free from the jurisdiction of Turkish courts. JWF.

law. 1. A general rule for the conduct of members of the community either emanating from the governing authority by positive command or approved by it, and habitually enforced by some public authority by the imposition of sanctions or penalties for its violation. 2. The whole body of such rules, including constitutions, the common law, equity, statutes, judicial decisions, administrative orders, ordinances, etc., together with the principles of justice and right commonly applied in their enforcement.   s.

Law and Order party. 1. The group supporting the constitution of Rhode Island during the Dorr Rebellion (*q.v.*) 2. The proslavery party in Kansas Territory, 1854-61.   s.

law of nations. *See* International law.

laying pipes. Colonization (*q.v.*) of voters, especially when they are introduced from other States.   s.

leader. The actual, if not the titular, head of a party organization in a city, county, or other subdivision. Though nominally elected directly or indirectly by party voters, he is often actually chosen by a small coterie or by his immediate party superior. The distinction between boss (*q.v.*) and leader depends largely on method of choice and manner in which power is exercised.   z.

league. Two or more states bound together by treaty or other form of agreement for the accomplishment of some purpose, usually war or defense; also the covenant which binds them. JWF.

League of Nations. An organization of most of the states of the world created by the Treaty of Versailles in 1919 "to promote international co-operation and to achieve international peace and security." The League Covenant provided for an Assembly of member states meeting annually for general debate, a Council of larger states devoted to the settlement of international disputes, and a Permanent Secretariat to act as a statistical clearing agency for the member states. Various international administrative and judicial agencies were identified with the League organization. The United States never joined the League although it occasionally co-operated with its agencies.   JTC.

League of Women Voters. An organization founded in 1918 to provide information and instruction for women in public affairs. It maintains a staff for research, publishes bulletins, and conducts study groups. s.

lease system. The employment of the inmates of public institutions by private persons who provide food, clothing, and shelter for the leased workers and pay a stipulated sum to the institution for their labor. It is no longer in use by either national or State governments. JMCC.

leave to print. Permission, freely granted by both houses of Congress, to print undelivered speeches of members, or almost any other kind of material, in the *Congressional Record*. s.

Lecompton Constitution. A proposed constitution for Kansas drafted by a convention at Lecompton in 1857 in which freesoilers refused to be represented. Efforts of Southern Congressmen to admit Kansas under this constitution were assailed by Stephen A. Douglas and others as a breach of faith. s.

left. Those political groups whose views are considered radical or in advance of the general norm of political action and thought at a given time and place; so called because in Continental European legislative chambers such groups are seated to the left of the presiding officer. CS-H.

legal aid. Counsel and advice in matters of law furnished free or at small charge by private or semipublic organizations to those who cannot afford the services of an attorney. JMCC.

legal fiction. A condition assumed to be true in law, regardless of its actual truth or falsity, so that something may be embraced by rules of law established before its existence was contemplated; *e.g.,* in some jurisdictions automobiles were considered as horsedrawn vehicles until legislation especially applicable to them was passed. JWF.

legal personality. The legal status accorded a corporation or other artificial person entitling it to hold and administer property, to sue in the courts, and to enjoy many of the rights and assume many of the liabilities of a natural person. z.

legal sovereign. The person or collective body or bodies (in the United States, both houses of Congress and the State legislatures, or national and State conventions) which is formally endowed with unlimited power to amend the fundamental law, as distinguished from the political sovereign which expresses the public will through the electorate. JWF.

legal tender. Any kind of money which a creditor is required by law to accept when offered in payment of a debt expressed in terms of the monetary unit of the country or forfeit interest and compulsory process for collection. The States are forbidden by the Constitution (Art. 1, sec. 9) to make anything but gold and silver

coin a legal tender. The power of the national government to issue
fiat legal tender notes long remained in doubt. The Supreme Court
held in *Hepburn* v. *Griswold,* 8 Wall. 603 (1870), that the legal
tender provision of notes issued by the national government during
the Civil War could not be applied to debts previously contracted;
but the Court, with a somewhat different composition, reversed its
position by declaring in the *Legal Tender cases,* 12 Wall. 457
(1871), that the legal tender provision was constitutionally applicable to all debts, under the power of Congress to adopt necessary
and proper means to conduct the War. Finally, in *Juilliard* v.
Greenman, 110 U.S. 421 (1884), the Court conceded the power of
Congress to emit legal tender notes at any time under its currency
and borrowing powers.   s.

legation.   1. A diplomatic agent of the rank of minister with
his staff, retinue, servants, etc.   **2.** The official residence of the envoy in the country to which he is sent. *See* Diplomatic immunity. s.

legation, right of.   The right of states to send and receive diplomatic representatives.   s.

legislation.   1. Rules of law enacted by the legislative authority and enforced by courts and administrative agencies.   **2.** The
process of law making.   cs-h.

legislative blackmail.   An attempt by one or a group of legislators to extort money or favors from some person, corporation,
or group by threatening to introduce or secure the enactment of
unfavorable legislation.   z.

legislative council.   A body composed of members of the legislature, or jointly of legislators and administrative officers, which
exists in several States to meet between legislative sessions, study
the needs of the State, and formulate a comprehensive legislative
program.   s.

legislative counsel.   An attorney employed by a legislative
body to give legal and constitutional advice on proposals for legislation, draft bills, and amendments, and in some States to assist
in the codification of the laws.   s.

legislative courts.   Courts established by Congress under
powers other than those granted in the judiciary article (Art. III)
of the Constitution. In creating them Congress is not bound by limitations concerning the tenure of judges or the imposition of duties
which are not strictly judicial. The United States Courts of Claims,
and of Customs and Patent Appeals, the United States Customs
Court, the Tax Court of the United States, the United States Court
for China, and the territorial and consular courts are legislative
courts. The Court of Appeals for the District of Columbia and the
district court there, in addition to being constitutional courts (*q.v.*)
are also legislative courts in the sense that they have additional
powers conferred by Congress.   s.

legislative day. A period not interrupted by an adjournment. It may include several calendar days during which, by recessing from day to day, a legislative house may continue its discussions uninterrupted by the regular order of business which is required by the rules to be considered at the beginning of each day.   s.

legislative drafting bureau. A body of technical experts employed by a legislative body to aid in securing precision in stating the legislative intention.   s.

legislative reference bureau. A specialized library for use by members of a legislature. It contains in easily accessible form information on subjects of legislation, codes of laws, copies of bills introduced in other States, etc.   s.

legislative supremacy. 1. The doctrine that the legislature is sovereign, characteristic of British constitutional law and theory. 2. The theory implied in most State constitutions and upheld by State courts that the legislature, though less than sovereign, enjoys an undefined residuum of power in contrast to other major branches of government whose powers are constitutionally prescribed and defined.   z.

legislature. A body of persons invested with power to make, revise, and repeal statutes and other ordinary laws, to determine the amount and rate of taxes, to appropriate funds and, as corollaries of all these powers, to conduct investigations and to supervise in greater or less degree the conduct of officers who execute or administer the laws. It usually participates in constitutional revisions and may supervise the election of, or sometimes elect, public officers. Generally the lower house has the sole powers of impeachment and the initiation of revenue bills; the upper house tries impeachments and consents to executive acts like appointments and treaties. State legislatures are bicameral in every State except Nebraska. In one or both houses rural interests generally are predominant. Each house chooses its own officers, except that the lieutenant governor presides over the senate; and makes its own rules of procedure subject, in most States, to numerous constitutional restrictions such as limited length of sessions, requirement of three readings of bills and roll call on final passage, prohibitions of local and special legislation and of riders on bills, and provisions as to the number of members who must be present or participate in legislation. Procedure is dominated by the presiding officer and committees to an even greater degree than in Congress. In most States legislative power is construed to extend to every subject not prohibited by federal and State constitutions.   s.

Lend-Lease Act. An act of Congress Mar. 11, 1941, which authorizes the manufacture or procurement of munitions (later amended to include foodstuffs and industrial products) for any country whose defense the President deems vital to the defense of the United States. It authorizes him to sell, transfer title to, lend, or lease such articles under terms which he deems satisfactory, such as payment or repayment in kind or in property, or any other direct or indirect benefit.   s.

letter of acceptance. An elaborate statement of campaign issues formerly prepared by a presidential or vice presidential candidate in accepting his nomination.   s.

letter of marque and reprisal. An authorization formerly granted by a government to the owner of a private vessel to capture enemy vessels and goods on the high seas. The signatory powers to the Declaration of Paris in 1856 agreed to stop issuing such authorizations.   s.

libel. 1. The plaintiff's written statement, which is the first proceeding in an admiralty case. 2. A defamatory writing, picture, or effigy published without lawful justification which imputes to a person the commission of a criminal act, tends to injure him in his trade or profession, or exposes him to ridicule, contempt, or odium. The injured person may bring action for damages. Where malice is shown, the act of publication may constitute a crime.   s.

liberal. A believer in liberalism (*q.v.*)

liberal construction. *See* Construction.

liberalism. In the broadest sense, a philosophy which stands for an attitude favorable to the freest and fullest development of the individual, and to the elimination of laws, institutions, and beliefs which restrict human development. It holds that men are sufficiently reasonable to be able to modify an older order in favor of more progressive institutions without resort to violence. Thus it stands midway between conservatism and radicalism. In the 19th century liberalism stood both for a form of government and for a governmental policy judged most favorable to individual liberty. The form came to mean constitutionalism, with stress laid upon written constitutions, bills of rights, the separation of powers, and checks and balances. The policy became identified with *laissez faire*. As it became evident that the chief obstacles to human development were by no means all governmental, liberalism was reinterpreted to allow for a positive program of governmental action to provide the conditions, economic and otherwise, without which mere freedom from restraint is insufficient for individual development. Similarly, the liberal concept of government is undergoing modification to allow for governmental forms more conducive to positive action than are those of the traditional liberal state.   JRP.

Liberal Republican party. A group of Republicans, opposed to the reconstruction and other policies of Grant's first administration, which in 1872 nominated Horace Greeley for President. The Democrats also nominated Greeley, but the two parties together elected only 66 presidential electors.   s.

Liberia. A republic in West Africa settled in 1822 by the assisted emigration of emancipated Negroes from the United

States, and independent after 1847. In World War I its finances came under the control of an officer appointed by the American government, and in World War II it became an advanced base for American troops. s.

liberty. The privileges and immunities enjoyed by an individual in the state; particularly the freedom of private action which is protected from governmental interference by the constitution and the laws. *See also* Democracy. z.

Liberty League. A minor abolitionist party which nominated Gerrit Smith for President in 1848. s.

Liberty League, American. *See* American Liberty League.

Liberty loan. One of several bond issues floated by the United States Treasury in 1917 and 1918 to finance American participation in World War I. JWF.

Liberty party. A minor party in the elections of 1840 and 1844 which demanded the abolition of slavery and the equality of human rights. EES.

liberty pole. An emblem of American patriots before and during the Revolutionary War. s.

Library of Congress. A national library, one of the greatest in the world, created by Congress in 1800. Designed chiefly for the use of Congress, it now serves the entire governmental establishment and the public as well. Its administrative head, the Librarian of Congress, is appointed by the President and Senate. A division of the Library, the Copyright Office, has charge of the issuance of copyrights. z.

license. Permission granted by public authority to perform a specific act or type of activity for which privilege a fee is usually exacted or special qualifications are required. JWF.

licensing. A system of public regulation which requires liquor vendors and certain other establishments to secure a license to operate from the public authorities and to conduct their business in an approved manner, failure to do so resulting in the revocation of the license and possibly other penalties. JWF.

lien. A claim upon property arising out of an unsatisfied debt or judgment. The holder may foreclose the lien by court action if the debt is not paid. z.

lieutenant governor. An executive officer in most American States who usually presides over the State senate, succeeds to the governorship when it becomes vacant, and often may perform the duties of the governor during that official's temporary absence from the State. EES.

Lifesaving Service. A former division of the Treasury Department whose function of rescuing sailors in distress is now performed by the Coast Guard. s.

Lily-whites. A faction of the Republican party in the Solid South which stands for the exclusion of colored voters from public office and from membership in party conventions and committees. They are opposed by the Black and Tans (*q.v.*)　　s.

limitation. *See* Constitutional limitations; Statute of limitations.

limitation of armaments. Restriction by international agreement of the quantity of each nation's war equipment. The desirability of a program of action was recognized by the Treaty of Versailles in 1919, and a beginning was made by the United States, Great Britain, Japan, France, and Italy during the Washington Conference, 1921-22. Later efforts to extend the program were less successful.　　JWF.

limited vote. A crude system of minority representation under which a voter may vote only for a certain number of candidates which is less than the total number of seats to be filled. It has been used occasionally for the election of members of municipal councils.　　s.

line of succession. The succession of Secretaries of State to the Presidency after two terms, which was customary in the first quarter of the 19th century.　　s.

line organization. That part of a public service which carries out orders and performs day-to-day duties of administration, as contrasted with the staff (*q.v.*)　　s.

liquor legislation. Laws regulating the liquor traffic. Since the repeal of the 18th Amendment (*q.v.*) such regulation has again become primarily a State matter. A few States prohibit the traffic entirely or permit local option (*q.v.*); others have established a public monopoly of the liquor business and sell liquor through State-operated dispensaries; still others license private dispensaries.　　z.

list system. A method of proportional representation used on the Continent of Europe under which a voter casts a vote for a list of candidates usually without the privilege of marking a preference among individuals on the list. Any seats to which the list is entitled by the balloting are given to persons in the order in which their names appear on the list.　　s.

literacy test. A qualification for the suffrage in 18 States, seven of which are in the South, which requires that a voter be able to read or write. Its administration, by local election officials, often leads to discrimination. In New York such tests are given by school authorities.　　s.

Little Giant. A nickname of Stephen A. Douglas.　　s.

Little Group of Willful Men. A term applied by President Wilson to a bipartisan group of eleven Senators who, by conducting a five-day filibuster ending Mar. 4, 1917, prevented the passage of a bill for arming American merchant ships.　　s.

Little Mac. A nickname of General George B. McClellan. s.

Little Magician. A nickname of Martin Van Buren. s.

living wage. A theoretical money income without exact definition which is believed adequate to maintain standards of health and decency prevalent among a certain group or within a given area. JMCC.

lobby. The main corridor of a capitol frequented by persons interested in legislation; hence, by extension, the persons collectively, whether principals or agents, who appear before a legislative body or any of its committees, or seek to influence individual members in order to accomplish the passage or defeat of bills. Congress has tried to curb the sinister aspects of lobbying by investigations and by requiring the registration of utility lobbyists and detailed statements from those representing shipping and foreign interests. Several States require registration with statements as to the specific measures in which lobbyists are interested, names of their employers, and amount of compensation; and have prohibited payment of lobbyists on a contingent basis. s.

local. A branch of the Socialist party in a geographical or other area; also the basic administrative unit of a labor union. s.

local government. The regulation and administration of matters, chiefly of local concern, which under general laws or the grant of charters by the State are confided to counties, towns, townships, special districts, or municipalities. Each subdivision is nearly always either a public corporation or a quasi corporation (*q.v.*) which may hold property, levy taxes, sue, and be sued; and it is responsible for torts arising from its acts or from neglect of its duties. Its powers are strictly interpreted. For rural local government the county is the principal division in the South, and the town, in New England. Elsewhere functions are more evenly divided between the county and its minor subdivisions. There is a growing tendency toward State centralization and supervision of matters of state-wide interest formerly left almost exclusively under local control. s.

local legislation. Statutes of State legislatures applying only to counties, cities, or other places specifically named or clearly described, which impose special duties, grant special authority, create public corporations, or alter the provisions of charters. To mitigate the evil of legislative interference in purely local concerns local legislation is forbidden by State constitutions, either absolutely or whenever general legislation can be made to apply, in three fourths of the States for cities; and in a few States for counties. One result of such constitutional restrictions has been classification of cities and home rule (*qq.v.*) z.

local option. The determination by popular vote in a county, city, or township as to whether or not saloons or bars may be licensed or dispensaries opened for the sale of liquor within its limits. s.

Locarno Treaties. Seven interrelated agreements signed in October, 1925, in which a procedure to settle disputes by conciliation and arbitration was agreed upon by Germany, on the one hand, and Belgium, France, Poland, and Czechoslovakia, on the other. The existing German-French and German-Belgian boundaries were guaranteed by the states concerned and by Great Britain and Italy. France promised to aid Poland and Czechoslovakia if the arbitration procedure between either country and Germany should fail to solve any dispute between them. JWF.

lockout. A weapon of employers in labor disputes which consists of excluding employees from shops or mines to prevent unionization, forestall a strike, or hinder union activities. s.

Locofocos. Independent Democrats in New York City who were opposed to monopolies and the corrupt methods used in chartering State banks. One of their meetings in October, 1835, was plunged into darkness by Tammany men; but it proceeded with candles lighted by "locofocos," a trade name for a friction, or "self-lighting," match. The name was applied to the Equal Rights party organized by this group, and later to all Democrats. s.

Lodge Reservations. Fifteen modifications of the Versailles Treaty proposed by Senator Henry Cabot Lodge of Massachusetts and supported by a group of Senators opposed to the incorporation of the Covenant of the League of Nations into the Treaty. JWF.

Log Cabin Campaign. The presidential election of 1840 in which a log cabin was one of the emblems of the Whig party. s.

logrolling. Mutual aid by members of a legislative body in the passing of laws of local or personal interest, especially those containing appropriations beneficial to a particular constituency. s.

London Economic Conference. A conference held in London in 1933 to ameliorate the world economic crisis by stabilizing the principal national currencies. Its failure is generally ascribed to President F. D. Roosevelt's policy, announced at the time of the conference, that internal economic reorganization of the participant states should precede stabilization. JWF.

London Naval Conference. A conference of representatives of the United States, Great Britain, Japan, France, and Italy, held in London in 1930 which resulted in a treaty limiting the cruiser-building programs of these states and reducing slightly the battleship, destroyer, and submarine tonnages of their respective fleets. JWF.

Lone-Star State. A nickname of Texas. The flag of the Republic of Texas bore a single star. s.

long-and-short haul. Pertaining to a former practice, now illegal, under which railroad companies charged lower rates between points at which there was competition than from intermediate points, under the principle of charging all that the traffic would bear.   s.

Long Convention. The constitutional convention elected in Missouri in 1861 which deposed secessionist State officials, appointed others in their places, and acted as a legislature until the fall of 1864.   s.

long session. Before the adoption of the 20th Amendment, the session of Congress which began in December of the odd-numbered years.   s.

loose construction. *See* Construction.

lottery. A form of gambling by which some States, cities, and the District of Columbia formerly financed public improvements. The sending of lottery tickets through the mails and by other instrumentalities of interstate commerce is now prohibited.   s.

Louisiana. The 18th State, admitted to the Union Apr. 8, 1812, from territory acquired by the Louisiana Purchase, plus a part of West Florida. It adopted an ordinance of secession Jan. 26, 1861, and was readmitted June 25, 1868. Capital, Baton Rouge; area, 48,506 sq. mi.; population (1940), 2,363,880; presidential electors, 10. The present constitution adopted in 1921 provides for the recall and for a literacy test for voters.   s.

Louisiana Purchase. A tract of 885,000 square miles, mostly west of the Mississippi River and extending thence to the Spanish

Louisiana Purchase

possessions or the Continental Divide, which was purchased from France for $15,000,000 by a treaty ratified Oct. 21, 1803. Under the claim that the Purchase embraced West Florida, the United States asserted its title to the strip west of the Pearl River in 1810 and to the area west of the Perdido River (the present western boundary of Florida) in 1813. The western boundary was fixed at the Sabine River and thence irregularly northwestward to the Rocky Mountains by treaty with Spain in 1819. The northern boundary with Great Britain was fixed at the 49th Parallel in 1818.   s.

lower chamber. Usually the more popular house of a bicameral legislature.   z.

loyalist. One of a numerous group who espoused the cause of the King and opposed the American Revolution. Because of confiscations of their property and the passage of harsh laws against them by the American States, many loyalists sought refuge in Great Britain, Canada, or the British West Indies.   s.

Loyal League. An organization of Union men formed in the North during the Civil War to combat the activities of Peace Democrats, and extended to the South in the Reconstruction period. s.

Loyal Legion. A hereditary organization formed in 1865, membership in which was open to officers of the Union Army and Navy and their eldest sons.   s.

lump-sum appropriation. An appropriation which does not stipulate in detail how funds are to be spent but grants them in "lump sum" to heads of departments and other major administrative units, permitting them to determine how they shall be allocated for various objects or to subordinate spending agencies.   z.

lunatic fringe. A term used by Theodore Roosevelt to characterize adherents of reform movements who refuse to recognize the difficulties of practical administration and insist upon the immediate fulfillment of an extreme program.   s.

Lusitania, The. A British passenger liner sunk by the German submarine *U-20* off the southern coast of Ireland May 7, 1915, entailing the deaths of 1,198 persons, including 128 American citizens. The German government refused to disavow the act, and public opinion demanded war; but after the dispatch of three notes Germany made promises of future good conduct which were accepted.   s.

lynch law. The punishment of persons by mob violence without waiting for the orderly processes of law. The term is derived either from Charles Lynch, a Virginia justice of the peace, who meted out summary punishment to loyalists during the Revolution; or from John Lynch, a North Carolina planter, who took the law into his own hands against criminals who infested the Dismal Swamp.   s.

M

mace. The symbol of the authority of the House of Representatives displayed during all sessions, except in committee of the whole, after a Speaker is elected.   s.

machine. An organization controlled by a boss or a small coterie of leaders which subjects party organization and public officials to its will and operates efficiently and ruthlessly in exploiting governmental activities of nearly every sort for the private gain of its members.   s.

McCulloch v. Maryland. A case in the United States Supreme

Court, 4 Wheat. 316 (1819), which arose from the refusal of the cashier of the Baltimore branch of the Bank of the United States to pay a tax levied by Maryland on the issuance of bank notes. In an opinion which contains the classic exposition of the doctrine of implied powers, Chief Justice Marshall declared that Congress had power to create a bank as a "necessary and proper" means to carry out its financial and other powers. He also held that Maryland could not tax the operations of the bank because such a power, in the hands of a State, threatens the supremacy of the national government in matters committed to its jurisdiction.   s.

McKinley Tariff Act. The tariff act of Oct. 1, 1890, which provided protection for numerous "infant" industries, raised rates generally to new high levels, offered a bounty for the production of sugar within the United States, and empowered the President to enter into limited reciprocal trade agreements in order to remove barriers imposed by other countries on the admission of American products.   z.

McLeod case. An international incident resulting from the arrest of Alexander McLeod, a Canadian deputy sheriff, in New York in 1840 on charges of murder and arson at the time of the destruction of the ship *Caroline* (*q.v.*) The State authorities refused to release him on demand of the British government and national authorities. He was tried and acquitted. To meet such contingencies in the future, Congress empowered national courts to issue writs of habeas corpus for aliens held by State courts.   s.

McNary-Haugen Bill. A bill twice vetoed by President Coolidge, 1927, which proposed to raise farm prices by dumping surplus staples abroad and compensating farmers for losses thus sustained by payments from the proceeds of an equalization fee (*q.v.*)   z.

Madison's *Journal*. Extensive notes kept by James Madison of debates and resolutions of the Convention of 1787, and first published in 1840 after his death. It remains the chief source of information of the Convention's deliberations.   z.

Mafia incident. The lynching of eleven Italians, allegedly members of a secret criminal society, by a mob in New Orleans, Mar. 15, 1891, for which Italy demanded an indemnity and the punishment of those responsible; and recalled her ambassador when informed that only the State authorities had jurisdiction to punish the lynchers. Congress voted an indemnity of $25,000 for the deaths of the victims who were of Italian nationality.   s.

magistrate. A public official, especially one exercising jurisdiction of a summary judicial nature over police court offenses or minor criminal cases.   z.

Magna Charta. The Great Charter wrung by the barons from King John at Runnymede, June 15, 1215, confirming privileges and rights which had been violated by royal order. Because of its express recognition of trial by jury and other procedural guaranties, it has long been regarded as a cornerstone of English and American liberty. s.

Magnetic Statesman. A nickname of James G. Blaine. s.

Maine. The 23rd State, formerly part of Massachusetts, admitted Mar. 15, 1820, with the consent of the Massachusetts legislature. Capital, Augusta; area, 33,040 sq. mi.; population (1940), 847,226; presidential electors, 5. The original constitution is still in effect. As amended, it provides for the initiative and referendum and for literacy and poll tax requirements for the suffrage. s.

Maine, The. An American battleship sunk in the harbor of Havana, Cuba, Feb. 15, 1898, following an explosion of undetermined cause. The incident hastened the outbreak of war with Spain. s.

Maine law prohibition. Prohibition of the manufacture and sale of intoxicating liquors by constitutional amendment and stringent laws, such as existed in Maine after 1851. s.

majority. More than one half. Unless an absolute majority is legally required for a decision, a majority consists of more than one half of those present and voting. s.

majority rule. An accepted principle of democratic politics, resting logically on force or the weight of superior numbers, that the decisions arrived at by a majority of those voting should be binding upon all. EES.

malfeasance. The performance of an illegal act, especially on the part of a public official. JWF.

malpractice. An offense against law which consists of ignorant or wrongful practice of a profession resulting in injury to client or patient. JWF.

manageable voter. A voter who is willing to vote as he is instructed in return for money or other consideration. s.

manager. 1. One who conducts the primary or election campaign of a candidate for elective office. 2. The executive head of a city government under the commission-manager plan. 3. A member of one legislative house appointed to represent it in a conference (*q.v.*) for the adjustment of differences with the other house. s.

mandamus. A writ issued by a superior court having jurisdiction at law and directed to a public officer, corporation, individual, or lower court to compel the performance of an act where there is a clear legal duty to act in a certain way. It may be applied to ministerial, but not to discretionary, duties. s.

mandatary. A state which administers a mandate (*q.v.*) s.

mandate. 1. Authority granted to Great Britain, certain British Dominions, France, or Japan to establish orderly governments in certain of the former German or Turkish possessions under the supervision of the League of Nations. 2. An instruction issued by a constituency to its representative in a legislative body. s.

mandatory law. A law which imposes a duty upon some public official, agency, or local government body, and requires that it be executed forthwith in accordance with the terms which the law prescribes. z.

mandatory referendum. A popular referendum required in nearly every State for the ratification of a constitutional amendment and generally required in cities and other local areas for bond issues, charter amendments, and annexation of territory to another unit. z.

manhood suffrage. Full, free, and equal suffrage granted to all adult male citizens not under a legal disability on account of lunacy, idiocy, or the commission of a crime. s.

manifest destiny. A phrase originating in 1845 which expressed the belief that the territory of the United States would eventually include the whole continent of North America. s.

Mann Act. *See* White Slave Act.

Marbury v. Madison. The case, 1 Cr. 137 (1803), in which the Supreme Court of the United States first elaborated the principle of judicial review. William Marbury applied directly to the Supreme Court, as provided by the Judiciary Act of 1789, for a writ of mandamus to compel Secretary of State James Madison to deliver a commission as justice of the peace for the District of Columbia which had been signed and sealed by the previous Secretary of State. The Court through Chief Justice Marshall declared that under Art. III, sec. 2 of the Constitution it could issue a writ of mandamus only when exercising appellate jurisdiction; hence the provision of the Judiciary Act authorizing the writ of mandamus in original jurisdiction, on which Marbury had relied, was void. The Constitution, said the Court, was the fundamental law; and in cases of conflict between it and a statute, the judges were bound by their oaths to uphold the Constitution and disregard the statute. s.

marginal sea. *See* Territorial waters.

Marine Corps. A corps of trained soldiers first created by the Continental Congress, June 25, 1776, and permanently established by act of Congress July 11, 1798, as a separate unit for amphibious service under the Department of the Navy. s.

Marine Hospital Service. A service, now incorporated in the Public Health Service, which provides treatment and hospitalization for American merchant seamen in various United States marine hospitals and other designated institutions. z.

maritime belt. *See* Territorial waters.

maritime boundary. *See* Territorial waters.

maritime jurisdiction. The power to try cases arising under national regulations or international usages relating to ships, seamen, or merchants engaged in maritime trade which, in the United States, is vested in the national courts.   JWF.

maritime law. The law and usages governing the conduct of men and ships engaged in peaceful commerce. Though maritime law is international in scope, national codes vary with local judicial interpretations and statutory additions.   JWF.

marque. *See* Letter of marque and reprisal.

marshal. **1.** An appointive officer in each judicial district of the United States who executes the processes of the court and performs duties similar to those of a sheriff. **2.** An officer sometimes attached to a magistrate's court.   S.

martial law. Government by military commanders over the civilian population in designated areas during which military decrees may, as far as necessary, supersede ordinary laws; and military tribunals, the agencies of civil government. Properly speaking, martial law should only be proclaimed during war or threatened invasion in the vicinity of actual hostilities where the local government ceases to function, though the term is often applied by State governors to a qualified form of military control during domestic disturbances.   JTC.

Martling Men. A faction of the Democratic party in New York about 1804, led by Aaron Burr and opposed to Jefferson and the supporters of George Clinton.   S.

Marxism. A political and economic doctrine originating with Karl Marx which aims at the interpretation of all significant human relationships in terms of dialectical materialism. The varieties of opinion and application of this doctrine have resulted in a great number of separate schools of thought.   JMCC.

Maryland. One of the original States, and the seventh to ratify the Constitution, Apr. 28, 1788. Capital, Annapolis; area, 12,327 sq. mi.; population (1940), 1,821,244; presidential electors, 8. The present constitution was adopted in 1867. The statutory referendum may be invoked.   S.

Mason and Dixon's line. The boundary between Pennsylvania and Maryland, and hence between free and slave States, which was surveyed, except for the western 36 miles, by Charles Mason and Jeremiah Dixon, 1763-67.   S.

Masons. *See* Antimasonic party.

Massachusetts. One of the original States, and the sixth to ratify the Constitution of the United States, Feb. 6, 1788. Capital, Boston; area, 8,266 sq. mi.; population (1940), 4,316,721; presidential electors, 16. The present constitution was adopted in 1780 and, as amended, provides for the constitutional and statutory initiative and referendum and a literacy test for the suffrage.   S.

Massachusetts ballot. The "office block" type of Australian ballot in which, under each office, the names of candidates with party designations are printed in alphabetical order.   s.

masterly inactivity. John C. Calhoun's characterization of his policy as Secretary of State, 1843-45, concerning the acquisition of Cuba.   s.

Maximilian. An Austrian archduke who was made Emperor of Mexico with French support during the American Civil War, but was executed by a Mexican revolutionary government, June 19, 1867, after French troops had been withdrawn at the insistence of the United States.   s.

Mayflower Compact. A written agreement drawn up by the Pilgrim Fathers in the cabin of the *Mayflower,* Nov. 21, 1620, which served as the basis of civil government in the Plymouth Colony until 1691.   s.

mayor. The chief executive of a municipal corporation. In the colonial and early federal periods he was generally appointed by the governor or elected by the council, and his powers were hardly more than those of an alderman. By 1850 he had become popularly elective, and in some places had a limited veto over ordinances, the appointment and removal of officers with the consent of the council, and supervision over administrative officers. Toward the end of the 19th century the strong-mayor plan *(q.v.)* was introduced in which the mayor had real control over municipal administration. Under the commission and commission-manager plans *(qq.v.)* there is sometimes a mayor with duties mainly of a ceremonial nature. In many small municipalities the mayor has judicial powers.   s.

Mecklenberg Declaration of Independence. A document resembling the Declaration of Independence but probably written long afterward in an effort to reproduce from memory some resolutions passed at Charlotte, Mecklenberg County, N.C., May 31, 1775, which declared that commissions issued by the Crown were null and void and "the constitution of each particular colony wholly suspended."   s.

mediation. Counsel to the parties to a dispute by a neutral third person suggesting to them a form of settlement. They are not obligated to accept the proposal.   JJR.

mediation board. A panel established to mediate industrial disputes either as a voluntary service to labor and management, or as a compulsory step in the settlement of railroad labor disputes. JMCC.

medical examiner. A qualified physician appointed to perform autopsies of persons who are supposed to have met violent deaths and to investigate the causes and circumstances of death. In a few States he has supplanted the coroner.   z.

melting pot. A phrase descriptive of the assimilation of races and cultures to a common pattern in America; derived from a play of that name by Israel Zangwill.   z.

member bank. Any private banking institution which has purchased stock in, and become affiliated with, one of the twelve federal reserve banks. National banks are required to become members; State banks may do so.   z.

mending fences. Quiet preparations in his State or district by a member of Congress in advance of the formal opening of his campaign for renomination or re-election.   s.

mercantilism. A term designating various policies and practices of European states between the 16th and 18th centuries, the chief aim of which was to unify and strengthen the state in competition with other states through public control over economic activities, thus securing a "favorable" balance of trade, exporting commodities and importing specie and gems, building a merchant fleet, extending colonies, and planning the domestic economy to conserve and increase wealth.   JJR.

mercenaries. Citizens or subjects of one country hired as soldiers by another.   JWF.

merchantman. A commercial vessel used to transport passengers or freight overseas or along the coast.   JWF.

merchant marine. The ships and personnel of a state's commercial fleet whether publicly or privately owned.   JWF.

merit system. *See* Civil service.

message. A formal communication from the chief executive to a legislative body either in person or in writing.   s.

Metals Reserve Company. A United States government corporation created and capitalized by the Reconstruction Finance Corporation in 1940 to acquire and accumulate metals of strategic importance to national defense.   z.

Me Too. A nickname of Senator Thomas C. Platt of New York because he resigned as United States Senator, along with Senator Roscoe Conkling in 1881, in a controversy with President Garfield over national appointments in New York.   s.

metropolitan area. Any large city and the numerous satellite urban communities which surround it and which, though administratively distinct, are physically and economically closely identified with it.   z.

Mexican cession. Land acquired by the United States from Mexico under the terms of the Treaty of Guadeloupe Hidalgo, 1848, which closed the Mexican War. After allowing for the rather extravagant claims of Texas, the cession

Mexican cession of 1848

amounted to 523,802 sq. mi., including the entire area of California,

Nevada and Utah, nearly all of Arizona, and parts of New Mexico, Colorado, and Wyoming. *See* map, page 196.

Mexican War. A war which began Apr. 24, 1846, when Mexican forces attacked a detachment of an American army which had been sent into the strip between the Nueces and Rio Grande rivers claimed by both the United States and Mexico; and which ended, after American troops had entered Mexico City, with the ratification of the Treaty of Guadeloupe Hidalgo, May 30, 1848.   s.

Michigan. The 26th State, formerly part of the Northwest Territory, admitted to the Union Jan. 26, 1837. Capital, Lansing; area, 57,980 sq. mi.; population (1940), 5,256,106; presidential electors, 19. The present constitution, adopted in 1909, provides for the constitutional and statutory initiative and referendum and the recall.   s.

Middle-of-the-Road Populists. Members of the Populist party who disliked their party's endorsement of Bryan in 1896, and who nominated separate tickets in 1900 and afterward.   s.

midnight judiciary. A derogatory term applied to the judges appointed in the closing days of John Adams's administration under the Judiciary Act of 1801.   s.

Midway Islands. A group of small islands in the North Pacific owned by the United States which, with Kure Island, form the westernmost link of the Hawaiian chain. They are the site of important naval installations and a way station for trans-Pacific airplanes.   z.

migration. Transference of residence from one place to another. z.

Migratory Bird Act. An act of Congress July 3, 1918, to enforce a treaty of Aug. 16, 1916, between the United States and Great Britain for the mutual protection of migratory birds. It was upheld by the Supreme Court in the case of *Missouri* v. *Holland,* 252 U.S. 416 (1920).   s.

Milan Decree. An order issued by the Emperor Napoleon at Milan, Dec. 17, 1807, ordering the seizure of every neutral ship which had stopped at a British port in compliance with British orders in council.   s.

mileage. An allowance for traveling expenses of members of a legislative body going to and from their homes to attend legislative sessions. Congressmen receive 20 cents a mile.   s.

militarism. Maintenance of excessive armaments; elevation of military men over civil authorities and the substitution of military for civilian institutions and ideals.   s.

military government. Temporary government by the military forces of a state over conquered or occupied territory.   jwf.

military indemnity. A sum of money or other valuable consideration exacted by a victorious state from a defeated enemy after resort to war.   JWF.

military intelligence. The acquisition and interpretation of data concerning the defensive strength or vulnerability of actual or potential enemies by espionage, interception of messages, questioning of prisoners, aerial observation, study of maps, photography, and documents, and like methods.   JWF.

military law. That branch of jurisprudence governing the discipline and administration of the army and navy and pleaded before military tribunals. Codes of military law are derived from statutes, executive orders, and time-honored military usages. JWF.

militia. All able-bodied male citizens, and male aliens who have taken out their "first papers," between the ages of 18 and 45, whether members of the organized militia (National Guard) or of the reserve militia. The States retain power to appoint officers, to train the militia according to the discipline prescribed by Congress, and to call them out for defense and the preservation of order in emergencies. The national government may provide for their organization, arming, and discipline, and may call them into the national service in time of war or other emergencies.   S.

milk control. The action of New York in setting up a State board to regulate the retail price of milk, which was upheld by the Supreme Court in *Nebbia* v. *New York,* 291 U.S. 502 (1934), in a decision which appears to justify regulation for the public welfare even though the business regulated does not fall within the classical category of "businesses affected with a public interest." z.

Miller-Tydings Act. An act of Congress, 1937, actually a rider to an appropriation bill of that year, which exempted from the operation of the antitrust laws such agreements as prescribed minimum resale prices for trade-marked goods in interstate commerce whenever such minimum price agreements were valid under the laws of the State where the goods were sold.   z.

Milligan case *(Ex parte Milligan).* The case of a civilian who was sentenced to be hanged by a military commission sitting at Indianapolis in 1864, and who applied to the Circuit Court of the United States for a writ of habeas corpus. The Supreme Court, 4 Wall. 2 (1866), declared that conviction by a military commission was illegal in any community in which the courts were open and their processes unobstructed.   S.

Millions for defense but not one cent for tribute. An American rallying cry during the informal war with France in 1798, said to have been the reply of Charles C. Pinckney to a suggestion of agents of the French foreign office that the United States should make a loan to France and a present to the agents before a treaty could be negotiated. *See* XYZ Papers.   S.

mines. *See* Bureau of Mines.

minimum rates. The lowest rates for any particular service which national or State regulatory commissions permit a public utility, such as a railway or grain elevator, to charge, the purpose being to prevent cutthroat competition. z.

minimum-wage legislation. Laws passed by both the State and national governments forbidding the employment of workers, especially women and children, at wages less than those found necessary for the maintenance of health and morals. The Supreme Court of the United States refused to recognize the validity of such laws until the case of *West Coast Hotel Co.* v. *Parrish,* 300 U.S. 379 (1937). s.

minister. 1. A diplomatic representative of a grade inferior to that of ambassador. 2. The title of the head of an administrative department in many foreign countries. s.

ministerial powers. Powers of an administrative official precisely stipulated in the instrument granting the powers which permit of little or no discretion in their execution. z.

minister plenipotentiary. A diplomatic agent with full powers. s.

minister resident. A diplomatic agent of lower rank than a minister, who may be accredited to one of the less important states, like Liberia. s.

ministry. 1. In a parliamentary government, the entire body of ministers and their immediate political subordinates who are likely to lose office with a change in the political complexion of the cabinet. 2. In Great Britain and elsewhere, any major administrative department or office. z.

Minnesota. The 32nd State, admitted to the Union May 11, 1858, from territory carved out of the Northwest Territory and the Louisiana Purchase. Capital, St. Paul; area, 84,286 sq. mi.; population (1940), 2,792,300; presidential electors, 11. With minor exceptions, all adult citizens may vote. s.

Minnesota press case. A decision of the Supreme Court in *Near* v. *Minnesota,* 283 U.S. 697 (1931), annulling a Minnesota statute of 1925 for the suppression of newspapers publishing malicious or defamatory statements on the ground that the statute contravened the due process clause of the 14th Amendment. z.

Minnesota rate cases. Several cases, 230 U.S. 352 (1913), in which the Supreme Court first suggested that where intrastate and interstate commerce were so thoroughly commingled as to render segregation impossible or difficult Congress might regulate both in order to make effective its power over interstate commerce. This suggestion was subsequently applied in the Shreveport and Wisconsin rate cases (*qq.v.*) z.

minority. Any racial, religious, occupational, or other group constituting less than a numerical majority of the population whose interests need protection from an overpowering majority controlling the government. National minorities in post-Versailles Europe were protected by treaties, while minorities in the United States are protected by the due process and equal protection clauses of the Constitution. JTC.

minority report. A written statement prepared by members of a legislative committee or a commission who disagree with the conclusions reached by the majority. S.

minority representation. Any electoral or representative scheme such as cumulative voting, the limited vote, or proportional representation, designed to permit minority groups to be represented in a legislature or similar body. Z.

minor party. A party with only local or widely scattered support, which has little influence in an election. S.

mint. A public establishment for the coining of money. The Bureau of the Mint supervises the mints at Philadelphia, Denver, and San Francisco, the assay offices at New York and Seattle, and the bullion depositaries at Fort Knox, Ky., and West Point, N.Y. S.

minuteman. Before the American Revolution, a volunteer ready for military service at a minute's notice from a patriotic committee. Z.

minutes. A recorded summary of proceedings at a meeting of a legislative committee or other organization. JWF.

misconduct in office. Negligent, improper, dishonorable, or unlawful behavior on the part of an individual holding a position of public trust which may result in impeachment and removal from office. JWF.

misdemeanor. An indictable offense not serious enough to constitute a felony; any offense so classified by statute, but usually not including minor violations punishable by summary proceedings. JWF.

misfeasance. The performance of a lawful act in an improper or illegal manner, to the detriment of another person. JWF.

Mississippi. The 20th State, admitted Dec. 10, 1817, from territory ceded by Georgia, plus a portion of West Florida. It adopted an ordinance of secession Jan. 9, 1861, and was readmitted Feb. 23, 1870. Capital, Jackson; area, 46,865 sq. mi.; population (1940), 2,183,796; presidential electors, 9. The present constitution, adopted in 1890, has literacy, property, and poll tax requirements for the suffrage. S.

Missouri. The 24th State, admitted Aug. 10, 1821, from territory included in the Louisiana Purchase. The northwestern corner of the State, or "Platte Purchase," was added in 1837. Capital, Jefferson City; area, 69,420 sq. mi.; population (1940), 3,784,664; presidential electors, 15. The present constitution was adopted in 1875. Provision is made for the constitutional and statutory initiative and referendum and practically unlimited adult citizen suffrage. S.

Missouri Compromise. An agreement between members of Congress representing free and slave States under which Maine was admitted as a free State and Missouri as a slave State, and the further existence of slavery in the region north of the parallel of 36° 30′ (the southern boundary of Missouri) was to be forever prohibited.　　　　　　　　　　　　　　　　　　　　　**s.**

mixed caucus. A nominating body, early in the 19th century, which was composed of all members of a political party in both houses of a State legislature and, in addition, of delegates elected by party conventions from counties and districts not represented by members of the party in the legislature.　　　　　　　　　**s.**

mobilization. The action of placing armies, fleets, and other public forces in readiness for immediate duty; in a more general sense, the process of placing a nation on a war footing, including the establishment of emergency governmental controls over manpower, production, and resources.　　　　　　　　　　　　**z.**

moderator. The presiding officer of a town meeting.　　　**s.**

modus vivendi. An arrangement or understanding between the foreign offices of two or more countries pending final settlement of an international problem.　　　　　　　　　　　　　　**JWF.**

monarchy. Any form of polity which vests public powers in a king or equivalent regal potentate. The kingship may be either hereditary or elective although the former type now prevails; if elective, the tenure is for life. Where royal powers are subject to enforceable constitutional limitations or where their exercise is shared with other public organs, such as a parliament, or requires the assent of advisers or ministers responsible to the law or to the people, the monarchy is said to be *limited* in form. In some limited monarchies, the powers of the king have become so circumscribed by law or constitutional practice as to render him little more than a titular authority. Where limitations are not imposed or where such limitations are merely a form involving no serious restrictions upon the personal discretion of the monarch, the monarchy is said to be *absolute.*　　　　　　　　　　　　　　　　　　　　**z.**

money. Coins of such metals as gold or silver or paper certificates to represent coins, or a certain value of bullion, or promissory notes of the government, or of authorized banks, which serve as media of exchange and are accepted as legal tender.　　　**z.**

money bill. Any bill to raise revenue; in Congress such a bill must originate in the House of Representatives.　　　　　　**z.**

mongrel caucus. Another name for mixed caucus (*q.v.*)　　**s.**

monopoly. The ability to fix the price of a service or a commodity without reference to a competitive market. This ability may result from exclusive control of the supply, control of patents, a public franchise, or from co-operative action of erstwhile competitors which tends to eliminate competition.　　　　　　　**z.**

Monroe Doctrine. A cardinal principle of American foreign policy first announced in President Monroe's message to Congress Dec. 2, 1823, when Russia was extending her settlements southward from Alaska and seemed about to join with other members of the Holy Alliance in attempting to force the newly independent Spanish-American republics to return to their allegiance to Spain. President Monroe declared that "we should consider any attempt on their part to extend their system to any portion of this hemisphere as dangerous to our peace and safety. With the existing colonies or dependencies of any European power we have not interfered and shall not interfere. But with the Governments who have declared their independence and maintained it, and whose independence we have, on great consideration and on just principles, acknowledged, we could not view any interposition for the purpose of oppressing them, or controlling in any other manner their destiny, by any European power in any other light than as the manifestation of an unfriendly disposition toward the United States." The principal later applications of the Doctrine were in 1867 when we secured the withdrawal of French troops who had established the Emperor Maximilian in Mexico; in 1895 when we brought pressure to bear on Great Britain to settle the boundary between British Guiana and Venezuela by arbitration; and in 1912 when the Senate adopted a resolution against a reported Japanese colonization scheme at Magdalena Bay in Lower California. On several occasions we have sought to forestall European intervention by ourselves intervening in the affairs of minor American countries to restore order or compel the observance of international obligations. Recently the United States has followed the policy of collaboration with the other principal American states.   s.

Montana. The 41st State, admitted Nov. 8, 1889, from territory formerly included in the Louisiana Purchase and the Oregon Country. Capital, Helena; area, 146,997 sq. mi.; population (1940), 559,456; presidential electors, 4. The original constitution is still in effect. Provision is made for the statutory initiative and referendum. With few exceptions all adult citizens may vote.   s.

Mooney case. The conviction and imprisonment of Thomas J. Mooney, on evidence increasingly regarded as trumped up, for having caused a bomb explosion in the course of a Preparedness Day parade at San Francisco, July 22, 1916. He was pardoned, Jan. 7, 1939.   s.

Moore's *Digest*. *A Digest of International Law* in eight volumes, valuable especially for American precedents, which was prepared by John Bassett Moore and published by the Government Printing Office in 1906.   jwf.

moratorium. The postponement for a stated time of the date for the payment of a debt, as by law in Minnesota and elsewhere, or by action of a creditor nation.   jwf.

Morey Letter. A forged letter published Oct. 20, 1880, and purportedly written by Garfield to a fictitious "H. L. Morey," advocating the continued immigration of Chinese labor.   s.

Mormon War. A series of disorders between Mormons and non-Mormons at Nauvoo, Ill., 1844-46, which resulted, after some bloodshed, in the removal of the Mormons to Utah.   s.

morning hour. Under the rules of the House of Representatives, an hour following the disposition of unfinished business during which standing committees may call up public nonfinancial bills for consideration. Because of priority granted to other kinds of business, the morning hour is seldom observed.   s.

Morrill Act. A law of Congress, 1862, making large land grants to the States for the endowment of agricultural and mechanical colleges.   s.

Morrill Tariff. The tariff law of Mar. 2, 1861, which greatly increased duties and embodied many protective features.   s.

mortgage moratorium. *See* Moratorium.

most-favored-nation clause. A provision often contained in treaties by which one state agrees to grant to another all privileges in certain matters that have been, or may in the future be, granted to any other country.   s.

Mother of Presidents. A nickname of Virginia.   s.

Mother of States. A nickname of Virginia. Kentucky, West Virginia, and the States of the Old Northwest were carved out of territory formerly included in Virginia.   s.

mothers' pension. Public assistance granted by nearly all the States to widows and deserted wives with no other means of support to aid them in rearing their children.   s.

motion. 1. A proposal by a member of a parliamentary body to secure some specific action. 2. The application of a party or his counsel in a case at law for a ruling or order from the court.   z.

motion-picture censorship. Review by a State board of a motion picture before exhibition for the purpose of eliminating or revising scenes deemed offensive to public morals.   z.

Motor Carrier Act. An act of Congress Aug. 9, 1935, which extended the rate-making and regulatory powers of the Interstate Commerce Commission to all motor trucks and busses in interstate commerce except taxicabs, the trucks of newsvendors, and a few other vehicles.   z.

motor vehicle taxation. A State license tax on motor trucks and passenger cars usually levied according to weight, value, or horse power. In many States, the proceeds are paid into a special fund for road construction and maintenance.   z.

Motor Vehicle Theft Act. An act of Congress, 1919, which

made it a national offense to transport across a State boundary line
a motor vehicle known to have been stolen.   z.

muckraker. A term applied by President Theodore Roosevelt in 1906 to journalists who made sweeping, and often untrue,
charges of corruption against public officials.   s.

mudslinging. The offensive injection of personalities into a
political discussion.   s.

mugwump. A Republican who refused to support James G.
Blaine in 1884; an independent member of a political party.   s.

Mulligan Letters. A series of letters between James G. Blaine
and Warren Fisher, Jr., read in the House of Representatives by
Blaine in 1876 after one Mulligan had been ordered to present them
before an investigating committee. They aroused the suspicion that
Blaine had used the Speakership for his own financial advantage. s.

multiple-party system. A condition, usual in the politics of
continental European states, in which there are several parties, no
one of which is strong enough alone to establish or maintain a ministry in office.   s.

municipal. 1. Pertaining to an incorporated city or town.
2. Pertaining, in international law, to the purely internal affairs of
a country.   s.

municipal corporation. A subordinate unit of government created under the authority of the State for convenience in administration in a thickly populated area. It has a corporate name, a charter,
and delegated powers, strictly interpreted. It has a dual character,
first, as an agency of the State with responsibility for the fulfillment
of public policy; and secondly, as a *quoad hoc* private corporation
with proprietary rights, powers, and responsibilities.   s.

municipal ownership. Ownership by municipalities of water
supply systems, passenger transit facilities, gas and electric generating and distributing systems, and other utilities.   z.

municipal socialism. A term applied to the extension of municipal ownership and operation to enterprises normally under private
management, particularly to electric generating and distributing
systems, surface or subway transit facilities, retail markets, docks,
and warehouses.   z.

municipal veto. A veto, usually suspensive in character,
which, in a few places, may be exercised by the mayor, governing
body, or voters of a city against an act of a State legislature applying exclusively to it.   z.

munition. Any weapon of war, including arms, equipment,
stores, and any other product necessary for waging war.   z.

Murchison Letter. A letter stating that Cleveland was more
friendly to England than Harrison, which Lord Sackville-West,
the British minister, was tricked into writing in September, 1888.
He was dismissed by President Cleveland.   s.

Muscle Shoals. The site of a hydroelectric development during World War I, practically unused until control over it was given to the Tennessee Valley Authority in 1933. s.

mutiny. Revolt against, or concerted disobedience to, the lawful orders of constituted authority by persons in the armed services or by members of a ship's crew. JWF.

Myers case. The case of *Myers* v. *United States,* 272 U.S. 52 (1926), in which the Supreme Court upheld the power of the President to remove at pleasure any person appointed by himself and the Senate; since qualified by the Rathbun-Humphrey case (*q.v.*) *See also* Removal of officers. z.

N

Nansen passport. An identity certificate provided by the League of Nations Advisory Commission for Refugees to White Russians and other persons who lost their nationality during and after World War I. JWF.

Nashville Convention. A meeting of delegates from nine Southern States at Nashville, Tenn., in June and November, 1850. Though called to concert action for secession, it adopted resolutions of a conservative character. s.

nation. Any people who possess a sense of unity because of common race, language, or religion or because of common political traditions or experiences; sometimes loosely used as a synonym for state. z.

national. A person who owes allegiance to, and is entitled to protection from, a state, though he may not be a citizen. Natives of certain unincorporated territories are nationals but not citizens of the United States. s.

National Archives. An agency created by Congress in 1934 to inspect records and archives of the government including recordings and films and to preserve and administer all such materials as are committed to its care. The Archivist of the United States is also chairman of the Administrative Committee for the *Federal Register* (*q.v.*) and administrator of the Franklin D. Roosevelt Library at Hyde Park, N. Y. z.

National Association for the Advancement of Colored People. An organization founded prior to World War I to combat discrimination against colored persons in the economic and political life of the nation and thereby raise their economic and social positions. JMCC.

national banks. Commercial banks chartered under the act of Congress of Feb. 25, 1863, and later acts. They were empowered to issue bank notes up to 90 per cent (after 1900, 100 per cent) of the par or market value of United States bonds which they purchased and kept on deposit with the United States Treasury. A monopoly of note issues was assured them by the imposition in 1866 of a 10 per cent tax on the issue of bank notes by State banks; but national bank notes are now being retired from circulation. All national banks are under the supervision of the Comptroller of the Currency and are required to be members of the Federal Reserve System (*q.v.*)   z.

National Bureau of Standards. A bureau of the Department of Commerce established in March, 1901. Its research and testing laboratories establish and maintain all the basic scales and units of reference used for testing and measuring in commerce, industry, science, and engineering.   z.

national chairman. The chairman of the national committee of a party, who is designated by the presidential candidate and formally elected by the committee. He establishes headquarters, raises and allocates funds, manages the campaign, and promotes the interests of the party between campaigns.   s.

national committee. The permanent executive body of a national party composed of one man and one woman from each State, territory, important island possession, and the District of Columbia. Members are chosen by the national convention on nomination of the State or territorial delegation, or sometimes of the voters in a primary election. Its most important duty — to supervise the presidential campaign — is performed by the national chairman (*q.v.*) It determines the place and date of the national convention, issues the call, chooses a temporary chairman, makes up a temporary roll of delegates, and performs other duties imposed by the convention.   s.

national convention. A party gathering which meets every four years to nominate candidates for President and Vice President, adopt a platform, elect a national committee, and adopt rules regulating party affairs. It is composed of delegates chosen in primary elections or by conventions. In the Democratic convention each State is entitled to twice as many delegates as it has presidential electors, plus two delegates at large if it went Democratic at the last presidential election. In the Republican convention each State is entitled to four delegates at large; two for each Congressman at large; one for each congressional district casting at least 1,000 Republican votes, and an additional one if it cast 10,000 Republican votes; and a bonus of three delegates at large if it went Republican at the last presidential election or if it later elected a Republican United States Senator. Both conventions have delegates from territories and insular possessions. Special committees report on the right of delegates to their seats; nominate the chairman and other permanent officers; recommend rules of procedure to be followed; and draft the platform. Voting on candidates is by call of the States in alphabetical order. In the Democratic convention the unit rule (*q.v.*) may be applied. In both conventions a majority vote of all delegates is required to nominate candidates. s.

national debt. *See* Public debt.

National Defense Mediation Board. *See* National War Labor Board.

national government. In a federal system, the government whose authority over certain defined subjects extends throughout the territory of a country, as contrasted to a State or provincial government. s.

National Guard. The volunteer militia of the States which in 1916 was organized as an auxiliary of the regular army and substantially controlled by the national government. In peace time it may be used by the States under conditions beyond the control of the regular police forces. s.

national income. The total annual income in all categories of production and service including profits, wages and salaries, dividends, rent, and interest. In the United States in 1941 it was 94 billion dollars; in 1942, 120 billions; and substantially higher in 1943. z.

National Industrial Recovery Act. An act of Congress, June 16, 1933, which authorized the President to approve or formulate codes of fair competition for business and industry and enforce such codes in order to promote national economic recovery. The codes were expressly exempted from the provisions of the antitrust acts. The act was invalidated by the Supreme Court in the Schechter case (*q.v.*) z.

nationalism. The sentiment or theory that every people who constitute a separate nationality ought to be independent and united in a separate state. s.

nationality. 1. The legal condition which binds an individual to a particular state. In the United States it includes citizenship as well as the subordinate status of Indians or Puerto Ricans before they were naturalized by law. 2. A group of people supposedly descended from common ancestors and having common physical, cultural, or linguistic traits. JWF.

nationalization. The transference of control over property, services, or productive enterprises from private persons or local governments to a national government. JWF.

National Labor Relations Board. An independent establishment of three members created by the Wagner Act of 1935. Examiners of the board are authorized to try cases involving allegations of unfair labor practices affecting interstate commerce; and if such practices are found to exist, the board may issue "cease-and-desist" orders and petition a federal Circuit Court of Appeals to enforce such orders. Unfair labor practices which the board may proceed against include interference by the employer with the employees' right to organize and bargain collectively, discrimination against employees by employers because of union activity, and refusal of the employer to bargain collectively. The board may also supervise elections to determine employee representation for collective bargaining.   z.

National Mediation Board. A board of three members created by Congress in 1934 to promote collective bargaining among employees engaged in interstate rail or air commerce and to mediate disputes affecting their compensation or working conditions.   z.

national minority. People of one nationality domiciled in a state controlled by another. Provision for the protection of such groups was made by treaties after World War I.   JWF.

national origins. A term used in recent immigration laws to denote the probable descent of the population of the United States as a means of fixing the proportions of new immigrants who may be admitted from a given country.   JWF.

National Park Service. A division of the Department of the Interior which administers the national park system and the parks in the District of Columbia.   z.

National Recovery Administration. An independent national agency created by presidential order in June, 1933, to secure and enforce codes of fair competition in industry in accordance with the provisions of the National Industrial Recovery Act (*q.v.*) The agency was abolished Apr. 1, 1936.   z.

National Republican party. The name adopted by the followers of Adams and Clay in the election of 1832. It was one of the groups which formed the Whig party in 1834.   s.

National Research Council. A scientific body which investigates and reports upon "any subject of science or art" for any department of the national government. It is a creation of the National Academy of Sciences incorporated by Congress in 1863. z.

National Resources Planning Board. A division established within the Executive Office of the President by executive order, Sept. 8, 1939, and discontinued in July, 1943. It prepared reports for the planned development and exploitation of the nation's resources and issued recommendations to the President and Congress.   z.

national self-determination. A principle enunciated by Woodrow Wilson and others which found application in the use of plebiscites to determine the boundaries of many European states after World War I and in the creation of many small sovereign national states.   JTC.

National Silver party. The name adopted by seceders from the Republican party in 1896 who endorsed Bryan and free silver. s.

National Socialism. The authoritarian, totalitarian, and imperialistic doctrine of German Fascism developed by Adolf Hitler and his followers after 1923. z.

national supremacy. The doctrine, formally developed by Chief Justice John Marshall in the case of *McCulloch* v. *Maryland* (*q.v.*), that the authority and power of a State cannot be interposed as a bar to the effective prosecution of any legitimate power of the national government. z.

National Union party. The name adopted by the Republican party in the campaign of 1864. s.

National War Labor Board. A board of 12 members, representing labor, employers, and the public, established by executive order in 1942 within the Office for Emergency Management. It supplanted the National Defense Mediation Board. It is charged with the settlement of all labor disputes affecting the nation's war effort in World War II after failure of direct negotiation between the parties involved. z.

National Youth Administration. A national agency established by executive order in June, 1935, to provide part-time employment assistance for youths attending school; for youths 16 to 24 years old who were members of relief families; and for job training, placement, and constructive leisure-time activities. JMCC.

Native American party. An anti-Catholic minor party which had a brief existence about 1845. s.

nativism. The idea that the institutions established by Americans of older stock should be protected from the influence of the newer immigrant stock. It was manifested in the Know-Nothing party after 1850; in the Ku-Klux Klan after World War I; and in movements to restrict immigration, increase the period of residence required for naturalization, and deprive foreign-born residents of civil and political privileges. s.

Nat Turner's Insurrection. An uprising of slaves in Virginia in 1831 in which about 60 white persons were killed. s.

naturalization. The process by which an alien becomes a citizen. The inhabitants of a territory or dependency or other designated groups of people may be collectively naturalized by law of Congress. The privilege of individual naturalization may be granted under present laws to persons of white or African nativity or descent who are not polygamists, pacifists, illiterates, opponents of organized government, or advocates of violence or sabotage. The first step is the declaration of intention to become a citizen, or "first papers," which must be filed with a national, State, or territorial court of record at least two years before citizenship may be granted. From two to seven years thereafter the applicant must file a petition certifying that he has resided within the United States five years, and within a State or territory six months, and that he intends to reside permanently within the United States. It must be accompanied by affidavits of two responsible citizens testifying to his moral character and the truthfulness of his statements. After 90 days he must appear in court for a public hearing and examination. His record will have been investigated by the Immigration and Naturalization Service of the Department of Justice, which may file objections in writing or by one of its examiners in person. If all requirements are satisfied, the judge administers the oath of allegiance and grants final papers. In war time the naturalization of members of the armed forces is speeded up. Alien wives of American citizens may be naturalized after only one year's residence. The naturalization of either parent automatically naturalizes all legitimate children under 18 years of age.   s.

natural law. The law, allegedly discoverable by human reason, which, it is assumed, would govern human relations in the absence of positive law and still exists as supplementary to positive law and as a standard by which the conduct of government may be judged. The theory was originated by Stoic philosophers. In the 18th century the law was variously derived from reason, from the Bible, and from the fundamental principles of the common law. Nowadays, with the abandonment of the concept of an original state of nature, natural law is identifiable with the sense of justice, of changing content, which pervades a community.   s.

natural monopoly. A monopoly which results from the possession of virtually the entire supply of some natural resource or from some strategic location; also a business inherently monopolistic in that duplication of its product or service would be economically wasteful.   z.

natural resource. Any raw material in its native state which has economic value or any facility or advantage which nature has provided unaided by man.   z.

natural rights. Individual rights, including those to life, liberty, and the pursuit of happiness, which are regarded as inalienable, and the violation of which by the British government was a justification for the Declaration of Independence.   s.

naval academy. *See* United States Naval Academy.

naval base. An area which serves permanently or temporarily as a focal point for naval operations and has facilities for provisioning, equipping, repairing, or providing protection for naval units. The number of United States naval bases was greatly expanded in 1940 through leases acquired in British possessions in the western Atlantic and the Caribbean.   z.

Naval Observatory. An observatory at Washington, D.C., under the jurisdiction of the Bureau of Navigation of the Navy Department, which collects and publishes astronomical data. It broadcasts signals every hour which officially establish standard time.   z.

Naval War College. An advanced school at Newport, R.I., for the study of naval tactics and strategy maintained by the Bureau of Navigation of the Department of the Navy.   z.

navigable waters. Rivers, lakes, inlets, etc., capable of bearing useful commerce. The beds of such waters are the property of the State. National regulation extends over such as form a continuous highway for the passage of foreign or interstate commerce. jwf.

navigation acts. A series of British ordinances from 1651 to 1750, designed to stimulate British commerce and encourage British colonial production by judicious tariffs, subsidies, and regulations. They ultimately hurt American interests and were in no small part responsible for the Revolution.   jwf.

Navy, Department of the. A department of the national government created by act of Congress Apr. 30, 1798, and headed by a secretary of cabinet rank. It has charge of the maintenance and operations of the Navy, the Marine Corps, and the Coast Guard, including their personnel, ships, aviation, and bases. It maintains the Hydrographic Office and the Naval Observatory and administers the government of several small island possessions like American Samoa.   s.

Near v. *Minnesota.* *See* Minnesota press case.

Nebbia v. *New York.* *See* Milk control.

Nebraska. The 37th State, admitted to the Union Mar. 1, 1867, from territory acquired by the Louisiana Purchase. Capital, Lincoln; area, 77,510 sq. mi.; population (1940), 1,315,834; presidential electors, 6. The present constitution was adopted in 1875 and, as amended, provides for the constitutional and statutory initiative and referendum, the recall, and a unicameral legislature. s.

necessary-and-proper clause. Art. I, Sec. 8, par. 18 of the Constitution, which authorizes Congress to make all laws necessary and proper to carry out the enumerated powers of Congress and all other powers vested in the government of the United States or any department or officer thereof; often used to justify the doctrine of implied powers (*q.v.*)   z.

negligence. Failure to exercise due care to avoid injury to others, usually entailing civil liability on the part of the culpable party.   z.

negotiation. Discussion among heads of state or diplomats of two or more countries with a view to arranging a treaty or arriving at some international understanding.   z.

Negro suffrage. The privilege of voting by persons of color which, under the 15th Amendment, the States are forbidden to deny or abridge on account of race, color, or previous condition of servitude. During the Reconstruction period many Negroes were prevented from voting by intimidation by private persons and groups. Beginning about 1890 the States of the Solid South imposed property, taxpaying, educational, or other requirements which, administered unequally between the races, legally accomplished the practical exclusion of Negroes from the polls.   s.

net income. Income subject to taxation after allowable deductions and exemptions have been subtracted from gross or total income.   z.

neutrality. The condition of a state which during a war between other states takes no part in the contest. It must abstain from rendering direct aid, such as the building and fitting out of ships and the recruitment of soldiers and sailors, to either belligerent; and in cases where indirect aid is permissible, such as the limited coaling of vessels, repair of storm damage, or export of munitions, it must treat both belligerents impartially.   s.

neutralization. An agreement among several states to respect the integrity of a particular state or region and its neutrality in time of war as, for example, Switzerland.   JWF.

Nevada. The 36th State, admitted to the Union Oct. 31, 1864, from territory acquired by the Mexican cession of 1848. Capital, Carson City; area, 110,690 sq. mi.; population (1940), 110,247; presidential electors, 3. The original constitution still is in effect. As amended, it provides for the constitutional and statutory initiative and referendum. With minor exceptions, all adult citizens may vote.   s.

Newberry case. A case, *Newberry* v. *United States,* 256 U.S. 232 (1921), in which the Supreme Court declared unconstitutional that part of the national Corrupt Practices Act of 1910 which set a maximum limit of expenditures for a candidate for the Senate in a primary election. This case was practically overruled in *United States* v. *Classic,* 313 U.S. 299 (1941).   s.

New Deal. A phrase used by Franklin D. Roosevelt in his acceptance speech at the Chicago Democratic convention in 1932 to characterize his personal platform as a presidential candidate; subsequently used as a label for the reformist social and economic policies of his administration as President.   z.

New England Confederation. A league, 1643-84, for offensive and defensive military operations against the Dutch and Indians, composed of the colonies of Massachusetts Bay, Plymouth, New Haven, and Connecticut.   s.

Newfoundland. A large island off the eastern coast of Canada, formerly a British Dominion but since 1933 governed by a mixed British-Newfoundland Royal Commission, on which the United States in 1940 leased sites for military and air bases.   z.

New Freedom. The title of a book by Woodrow Wilson published at the time he became President in which he elucidated his economic philosophy and particularly his proposed policy of securing economic freedom by breaking up trusts and combinations and restoring competition.   z.

New Hampshire. One of the original States, and the ninth to ratify the Constitution of the United States, June 21, 1788. Capital, Concord; area, 9,210 sq. mi.; population (1940), 491,524; presidential electors, 4. The present constitution was adopted in 1784. With minor exceptions, all adult citizens may vote. s.

New Hampshire grants. A former name for the part of New York colony now included in Vermont, in which Governor Benning Wentworth of New Hampshire made extensive land grants. s.

New Harmony. The site of a colony in Indiana founded in 1825 by Robert Owen to apply his co-operative social theories. z.

New Jersey. One of the original States, and the third to ratify the Constitution of the United States, Dec. 18, 1787. Capital, Trenton; area, 8,224 sq. mi.; population (1940), 4,160,165; presidential electors, 16. The present constitution was adopted in 1844. With minor exceptions, all adult citizens may vote. s.

New Jersey plan. *See* Paterson plan.

Newlands Act. An act of Congress, 1902, which authorized the Reclamation Service of the Department of the Interior to construct irrigation and other works for the reclamation of arid and semiarid public lands and sell such improved lands to settlers. z.

New Mexico. The 47th State, admitted to the Union Jan. 6, 1912, from territory acquired by the Mexican cession of 1848, plus a small portion of the Gadsden Purchase. Capital, Santa Fe; area, 122,634 sq. mi.; population (1940), 531,818; presidential electors, 4. The original constitution, which is still in effect, provides for the referendum. s.

New Roof. A nickname for the Constitution of the United States, 1787-88, when it was before the people for ratification. s.

New York. One of the original States, and the eleventh to ratify the Constitution of the United States, July 26, 1788. Capital, Albany; area, 49,204 sq. mi.; population (1940), 13,479,142; presidential electors, 47. The present constitution was adopted in 1894. Suffrage is limited by educational or literacy requirements administered by school authorities. s.

Niagara Falls Conference. *See* A.B.C. Mediation.

nihilism. The doctrine that established standards and institutions have no objective validity, at times accompanied by advocacy of their destruction by any effective means, including "propaganda by deed," terrorism, and violence. JJR.

Nine-Power Pact. A treaty concluded at the Washington Conference in 1922 by the United States, Great Britain, France, Italy, Japan, China, Belgium, Portugal, and the Netherlands. It reaffirmed the open door in China, renounced the so-called "spheres of influence," and provided for the relinquishment by France, Great Britain, and Japan of some of their Chinese holdings. JWF.

Nineteenth Amendment. An amendment to the Constitution proposed to the States June 4, 1919, and proclaimed in effect Aug. 26, 1920. Its principal provision, that the right to vote shall not be denied because of sex, had the effect of giving the ballot to women. z.

nisi prius court. A court in which trial by jury is held. Originally the words "nisi prius" appeared in the writ summoning the jury. JJR.

N.L.R.B. *See* National Labor Relations Board.

nominating convention. *See* Convention 4; National convention.

nomination. 1. The designation by a party of a candidate for elective office, as, historically in the United States, by secret caucus, committee of correspondence, legislative or congressional caucus, mixed or mongrel caucus, convention, direct primary election, or petition. 2. Part of the process of appointment, which consists in an executive officer's submitting the name of an appointee for confirmation by the Senate or other body. s.

nonassembled examination. *See* Assembled examination.

noncombatant. A civilian or a member of the armed forces such as a chaplain or medical attendant not authorized to bear arms. JWF.

non-co-operation. A form of civil protest involving refusal of individuals or groups to pay taxes or perform normal civic duties. JMCC.

Nonimportation Act. A law of Congress Apr. 18, 1806, which prohibited the importation of certain commodities from Great Britain or the British Empire. s.

nonimportation agreement. Any of several agreements made by residents of American colonies or towns, 1768-74, not to import goods from Great Britain. s.

Nonintercourse Act. A law of Congress, Mar. 1, 1809, prohibiting the entry of British or French ships or goods into the territorial waters or ports of the United States. s.

nonpartisan ballot. A ballot containing no party designations. s.

nonpartisan board. A board, usually in reality bipartisan, nominally appointed without reference to party affiliations. s.

nonpartisan election. An election, usually for local or for State judicial offices, from which the nominees of national political parties, as such, are excluded by law. s.

Nonpartisan League. A farmers' organization founded in North Dakota in 1915 which sponsored State ownership and operation of grain elevators, flour mills, packing plants, etc. It gained control of several State governments in the Northwest through the Republican or Democratic primaries and the organization, in Minnesota, of the Farmer-Labor party. s.

nonpartisan primary. A direct primary for the nomination of candidates without recognition of parties. The two candidates receiving the highest vote oppose each other in the general election. In some States, if one candidate has a clear majority in the primary, he is declared elected. s.

nonquota immigrants. Immigrants to the United States who do not come within the immigration quota restrictions. They include: the wife or unmarried child, under 18, of a resident citizen of the United States; an alien, previously lawfully admitted, who is returning from a visit abroad; a visiting professor or minister of two years' standing; a bona fide student; a native of a country of the Western Hemisphere. s.

nonresistance. Protest against the imposition of authority, particularly of a conqueror, which takes the form of popular acceptance of such regulations as force or circumstances may dictate but which denies the legitimacy of the authority and rejects any form of uncoerced collaboration. jmcc.

nonsovereign state. A state whose foreign or domestic policies are controlled by another, though outwardly the puppet state may appear autonomous and independent. jwf.

nonviolence. A policy adopted by an opposition group which refrains from the use of force as a matter of principle or expediency. jwf.

normalcy. The period of readjustment to peace time conditions under President Harding's administration. The phrase "back to normalcy" occurred in one of Harding's speeches. s.

Norris Amendment. The 21st Amendment (*q.v.*) to the Constitution so called because of Senator George W. Norris' long effort to secure its adoption. z.

North Americans. Antislavery men who seceded from the convention of the American party in 1856 and made separate nominations, endorsing the Republican candidate, John C. Frémont. s.

North Atlantic fisheries. Rich fishing grounds off Newfoundland where Americans had the privilege of fishing and of drying their catch on near-by uninhabited shores by the Treaty of 1783 and a convention with Great Britain in 1818. The privileges of obtaining bait and water in near-by ports were granted by reciprocal treaty, 1854-67, by the Halifax Fishery Commission (*q.v.*), 1877-85, and finally by arbitration in 1909. s.

North Carolina. One of the original States, and the twelfth to ratify the Constitution of the United States, Nov. 21, 1789. It adopted an ordinance of secession May 21, 1861, and was readmitted June 25, 1868. Capital, Raleigh; area, 52,426 sq. mi.; population (1940), 3,571,623; presidential electors, 14. The present constitution, adopted in 1876, makes no provision for an executive veto. Suffrage is limited by a literacy test. s.

North Dakota. The 39th State, admitted to the Union Nov. 2, 1889, from territory acquired by the Louisiana Purchase. Capital, Bismarck; area, 70,837 sq. mi.; population (1940), 641,936; presidential electors, 4. The original constitution, which is still in effect, as amended, provides for the constitutional and statutory initiative and referendum, and the recall.   s.

Northeast Boundary Dispute. A controversy between the United States and Great Britain concerning the identification of the source of the St. Croix River, of highlands between tributaries of the St. Lawrence and "rivers which flow into the Atlantic Ocean," and of the "North-western most head" of the Connecticut River mentioned in the Treaty of 1783. In 1827 the question was referred to the King of the Netherlands for arbitration, but neither country accepted the award. A compromise line was fixed by the Webster-Ashburton Treaty of 1842. s.

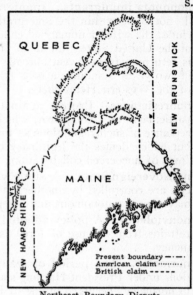

Northeast Boundary Dispute

Northern Securities case. A case, *Northern Securities Co.* v. *United States,* 193 U.S. 197 (1904), in which the Supreme Court ordered the dissolution of a holding company controlling northwestern railways on the ground that such a company constituted a restraint of interstate trade prohibited by the Sherman Antitrust Act.   z.

northwest boundary. The western part of the boundary between the United States and Canada. By the Treaty of 1783, it was to be drawn from the northwest corner of the Lake of the Woods due west to the Mississippi River. After the purchase of Louisiana, and when it was found that the Mississippi did not rise so far north, Great Britain and the United States agreed in 1818 that the line should be drawn south from the northwest corner of the Lake of the Woods to the 49th parallel, and thence westward to the Rocky Mountains. In 1846 it was extended to Puget Sound (*see* Oregon Country). A dispute over the ownership of the San Juan Islands which lie in Puget Sound was settled in favor of the United States by the arbitration of the German Emperor in 1872.   s.

Northwest Conspiracy. A Copperhead plot, exposed in June, 1864, to detach the Northwestern States from the Union.   s.

Northwest ordinances. Three laws passed by the Congress of the Confederation for the organization of the territory between the Ohio River, the Great Lakes, and the Mississippi. The Ordinance of 1784, later repealed, envisaged the admission of nine or ten new States; that of 1785 provided for the survey of all lands in townships six miles square, with one square mile in each township reserved for educational purposes; and that of 1787, for an appointive governor, council, and judiciary, an elective assembly when the population reached 5,000, the abolition of slavery, guarantees of civil rights, and the eventual admission of from three to five new States with minimum populations of 60,000.   s.

notary public. A public officer authorized to authenticate and certify documents such as deeds, contracts, and affidavits with his signature and seal.   JWF.

notification. A ceremony in which a committee of the national convention officially informs a presidential or vice presidential candidate of his nomination.   s.

nuisance. Any establishment or practice which offends public morals or decency or menaces public health, safety, or order. Usually it may be summarily abated by a competent police or other administrative officer.   z.

nuisance tax. Any tax of negligible yield which causes undue irritation and annoyance among the taxpayers.   z.

nullification. An alleged right of a State in the American Union, acting in a sovereign capacity through a convention of its people, to declare an act of Congress "null, void, and no law, not binding upon [the] State, its officers or citizens." South Carolina acted in this manner in opposing the tariff acts of 1828 and 1832.   JTC.

Nutmeg State. A nickname of Connecticut.   s.

N.Y.A. *See* National Youth Administration.

O

oath. A solemn declaration in the presence of witnesses as to the truth of a statement or intent, sometimes accompanied by the invocation of a Supreme Being.   JWF.

oath of allegiance. *See* Allegiance, oath of.

oath of office. An oath administered to persons entering public office or employment in the United States, in which they promise to uphold the Constitution and faithfully to perform their official duties.   JWF.

obiter dictum. A statement of opinion by a judge on some point not argued in a case, or not a part of the conclusions necessary to support the judgment. It is not binding on the court in later cases.   s.

obligation of contracts. The promise to perform or refrain from performing a certain act, given in contracts for a valid consideration. The Constitution declares that no State may impair the obligation of any contract. *See* Contract clause.   z.

obstruction. Dilatory tactics used for the purpose of delaying or defeating a legislative measure.   s.

occupational disease. A disease contracted during the course of employment and attributable to the effects of certain poisonous or other dangerous substances exposure to which is a necessary, or at least a customary, hazard of such employment; *e.g.,* silicosis, or phosphorus or radium poisoning. Victims usually receive workmen's compensation (*q.v.*)   z.

occupational representation. A system of representation in which the constituencies represented are aggregates of persons of common vocational or professional interests rather than geographical areas.   z.

occupation tax. A license tax, often for regulatory purposes, levied upon individuals engaged in a particular occupation or profession, or in managing a particular business.   z.

O.C.D. *See* Office of Civilian Defense.

October States. A few States in which gubernatorial and congressional elections were formerly held in October.   s.

O.D.T. *See* Office of Defense Transportation.

O.E.M. *See* Office for Emergency Management.

offense. Any violation of the law of a state. The Constitution, Art. I, sec. 8, authorizes Congress to define and punish "offences" against the law of nations.   z.

offensive partisan. A holder of a civil service position who engages in political campaigns to an extent contrary to the spirit, if not the letter, of civil service laws.   s.

office. A position under the government held by the incumbent by virtue of election, or appointment, or operation of law and not as a result of a contract of employment; and which has legally defined tenure, emoluments, and duties.   z.

office-block ballot. A form of ballot in which the names of candidates, with or without party designations, are grouped under the offices for which they are contesting.   s.

State Ticket

GOVERNOR
Vote for ONE
☐ Terry Carpenter ....Democrat
☐ Dwight Griswold ....Republican
☐ ....

LIEUTENANT GOVERNOR
Vote for ONE
☐ William H. Diers ....Democrat
☐ William Edward Johnson ...Republican
☐ ....

SECRETARY OF STATE
Vote for ONE
☐ Harry R. Swanson ....Democrat
☐ Frank Marsh ....Republican
☐ ....

AUDITOR OF PUBLIC ACCOUNTS
Vote for ONE
☐ William H. Price ....Democrat
☐ Ray C. Johnson ....Republican
☐ ....

STATE TREASURER
Vote for ONE
☐ Walter H. Jensen ....Democrat
☐ L. B. Johnson ....Republican
☐ ....

Office-block ballot
(Nebraska)

Office for Emergency Management. A division of the Executive Office of the President established by presidential order in

May, 1940. It serves as an advisory and clearing instrument by means of which the President may more effectively discharge executive responsibilities created by World War II and co-ordinate agencies, public and private, whose activity is directly related to the war effort. z.

Office of Censorship. A wartime agency headed by the Director of Censorship established by presidential order Dec. 19, 1941, which has absolute discretion to censor any sort of communication passing between the United States and any foreign country. The Director is advised by a Censorship Policy Board consisting of high officials with the Postmaster General as chairman. z.

Office of Civilian Defense. A wartime agency of the national government created within the Office for Emergency Management by the President in May, 1941. In co-operation with State and local defense agencies, it supervises and directs measures for the protection of civilian life and property and the fostering of civilian morale during wartime emergency. z.

Office of Defense Transportation. A national agency created by executive order Dec. 18, 1941, within the Office for Emergency Management to co-ordinate and secure the most effective use of railways, motor transport, and other domestic transportation facilities during the military emergency created by World War II. z.

Office of Education. A national office created in 1867 and now under the Federal Security Agency. Headed by the Commissioner of Education, it conducts educational surveys and supervises miscellaneous national educational institutions and services. z.

Office of Indian Affairs. A unit of the Department of the Interior responsible for the exercise of special guardianship over the economic, educational, and moral welfare of Indians and other aborigines. z.

Office of Lend-Lease Administration. A national agency created by executive order Oct. 28, 1941, within the Office for Emergency Management to administer the Lend-Lease Act of Mar. 11, 1941. The office was made a part of the Foreign Economic Administration by executive order Sept. 25, 1943. z.

Office of Price Administration. A wartime agency of the national government, established by executive order of the President Apr. 11, 1941, as the Office of Price Administration and Civilian Supply and given its present title Aug. 1, 1941. Its primary purpose is to prevent inflation and maladjustment of markets owing to wartime conditions. For this purpose it is authorized to fix price ceilings for commodities and ration consumers' goods. z.

Office of Production Management. *See* War Production Board.

Office of War Information. A national wartime agency created by executive order June 13, 1942, in which were consolidated the activities formerly carried on by the Office of Facts and Figures, the Office of Government Reports, and other information services. An Overseas Operations Branch carries on foreign propaganda and information activities.   z.

Office of War Mobilization. An establishment within the Office for Emergency Management created by executive order May 27, 1943, to develop and establish programs for the maximum utilization of the nation's natural and industrial resources for military and civilian needs, the effective use of civilian manpower, and the maintenance and stabilization of civilian economy. It has power to unify the activities of federal agencies and departments concerned with production, procurement, distribution, or transportation of military or civilian supplies and materials, and to determine controversies among such governmental units. Its head, the Director of War Mobilization, is sometimes familiarly called the "Assistant President."   s.

Ohio. The 17th State, formerly part of the Northwest Territory, admitted to the Union Feb. 19, 1803. Capital, Columbus; area, 41,040 sq. mi.; population (1940), 6,907,612; presidential electors, 25. The present constitution was adopted in 1851. As amended, it provides for the constitutional and statutory initiative and referendum. With minor exceptions, all adult citizens may vote.   s.

Ohio Company. A New England company which obtained a large grant of land in southeastern Ohio from Congress and settled Marietta in 1788.   s.

Ohio Gang. A group of Ohio politicians, chief of whom was Harry M. Daugherty, later Attorney General, who aided in securing the nomination and election of Warren G. Harding as President in 1920 and whose influence, allegedly sinister, continued throughout his administration.   z.

Ohio Idea. A proposal by George H. Pendleton of Ohio in 1868 to pay the national debt in greenbacks.   s.

oil scandal. The transfer in May, 1921, of certain naval oil reservations from the Navy to the Interior Department; the leasing of the Elk Hills reservation to interests represented by E. L. Doheny who had made a large loan to Secretary of the Interior Albert B. Fall, on account of which Fall was convicted of bribery in 1931; and the leasing of the Teapot Dome reservation to interests controlled by Harry F. Sinclair, who was later acquitted of the charge of conspiracy.   s.

Oklahoma. The 46th State, admitted to the Union Nov. 16, 1907, from territory acquired by the Louisiana Purchase. Capital, Oklahoma City; area, 70,057 sq. mi.; population (1940), 2,336,434; presidential electors, 10. The original constitution, still in effect, provides for the constitutional and statutory initiative and referendum, and a literacy test for voters.   s.

Old Abe. A soldiers' nickname of Abraham Lincoln.   s.

old-age security. A public pension system or other form of material aid for persons who are no longer capable of gainful employment because of advanced age.   z.

Old Bullion. A nickname of Senator Thomas H. Benton of Missouri.   s.

Old Colony. A nickname of the Plymouth Colony.   s.

Old Dominion. Virginia, because in the colonial period it was referred to as a dominion of the British Crown.   s.

Old Fuss and Feathers. A nickname of General Winfield Scott.   s.

old guard. A title assumed by delegates to the Republican national convention of 1880 who supported Grant; and since applied to conservative or reactionary Republicans.   s.

Old Hickory. A nickname of Andrew Jackson.   s.

Old-Line Whig. A member of the Whig party about 1850 who wished to ignore the slavery issue and base political campaigns on economic questions.   s.

Old Man Eloquent. A nickname of John Quincy Adams during his service in the House of Representatives, 1831-48.   s.

Old North State. A nickname of North Carolina.   s.

Old Public Functionary. A nickname of James Buchanan. s.

Old Rough-and-Ready. A nickname of Zachary Taylor.   s.

Old White Hat. A nickname of Horace Greeley.   s.

oleomargarine tax. A tax of ten cents a pound levied by Congress in 1902 on oleomargarine colored to imitate butter. Though attacked as regulative, the Supreme Court, in *McCray* v. *United States,* 195 U.S. 27 (1904), upheld it as being ostensibly a revenue measure.   s.

oligarchy. 1. A government in which authority constitutionally reposes in a few individuals or families. 2. A small coterie of individuals who, because of economic or other power, can measurably influence the policy of government even though they lack formal authority.   z.

omnibus bill. A bill, such as the Compromise of 1850 when first proposed, or pension or appropriation measures combining the provisions of several bills into one.   s.

O.P.A. *See* Office of Price Administration.

open covenants openly arrived at. One of the Fourteen Points (*q.v.*) proposed by President Wilson, Jan. 8, 1918, which would have outlawed secret peace treaties.   s.

open door. An extension of the principle of the most favored nation, first applied to China in Secretary of State John Hay's note to the powers of Sept. 6, 1899, and later applied to all so-called "backward" countries. It demands equal opportunities for commercial and other intercourse for all nations and the abolition of spheres of influence and special rights and privileges.   s.

Open Market Committee. A committee of the Board of Governors of the Federal Reserve System and five federal reserve bank representatives which seeks to stabilize the general credit situation by dealing in government and other securities on the open market. z.

open primary. A primary election open, without any test of party affiliation, to any qualified voter.   s.

open sea. Waters in which vessels of all nations may navigate without restriction, as distinguished from territorial waters and straits adjacent to the coast which are usually under the limited jurisdiction of the littoral state.   JWF.

open shop. An establishment which hires employees without reference to their union or nonunion status.   z.

opinion. The reasoning by which a court explains and justifies its decision in a particular case or controversy.   z.

opportunist. One who is inclined to take advantage of circumstances or events for his, or his party's, immediate advantage without much regard for long-run consequences or political principles.   s.

opposition. 1. The members of a minority party in a legislature. 2. Members of a party in Congress, whether in a minority or majority, politically opposed to the President and his administration.   z.

optional charter plan. A system in use in several States by which cities or counties may select any one of several fully-drawn charters prepared by the State legislature for their local government.   s.

optional clause. A clause in the Statute of the Permanent Court of International Justice which gave that tribunal compulsory jurisdiction over specified classes of disputes among states which had elected to sign the clause.   JWF.

order. A command or regulation emanating from the executive authority or an administrative officer.   z.

order in council. In Great Britain, an executive order issued by the advice of the privy council either under the royal prerogative or under the authority of a statute.   s.

order of business. The order in which business before a legislative body is transacted, whether the regular order or an exceptional order provided for in the rules.   s.

ordinance. 1. A regulation or bylaw of purely local application issued by an American municipal corporation. It must be made under authority granted in the corporation's charter and in conformity with national and State constitutions and laws. 2. An act or resolution of a constituent assembly or of a public deliberative body which lacks statute-making authority as normally understood. The Confederation Congress and State constitutional conventions in the South formerly passed ordinances.   s.

Ordinance of 1787. *See* Northwest ordinances.

ordinance power. The authority of the President and certain executive officials or governmental agencies, conferred by the Constitution or the laws, to issue administrative directions or such orders and regulations as may be necessary to apply and enforce the law.   z.

Oregon. The 33rd State, admitted to the Union Feb. 14, 1859, from territory included in the Oregon Country. Capital, Salem; area, 96,981 sq. mi.; population (1940), 1,089,684; presidential electors, 6. The original constitution has been amended to provide for the constitutional and statutory initiative and referendum, the recall, and a literacy test for voters.   s.

Oregon Country. The Pacific Northwest extending from the northern boundary of California (the 42nd parallel) to the southern boundary of Alaska (54° 40′). The title of the United States

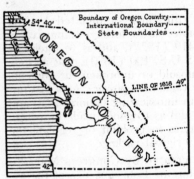

Oregon Country 42° to 54° 40′

to the region was derived from the discovery of the mouth of the Columbia River by Captain Gray in 1792, the explorations of Lewis and Clark, 1803-05, the settlement of Astoria, 1811, the cession of Spanish claims by treaty signed in 1819, the activities of missionaries after 1834, and numerous settlements after 1840. Great Britain had a claim derived from the voyage of Drake, 1577, the establishment of trading posts by the Hudson's Bay Company, and settlements in what is now British Columbia. A convention in 1818 provided for joint occupation of Oregon by the two countries. In 1846, despite American rallying cries of "Fifty-four forty or fight" and "The whole of Oregon or none," President James K. Polk negotiated a treaty with Great Britain extending the boundary along the 49th parallel from the Rocky Mountains to the Strait of Juan de Fuca and thence to the Pacific Ocean.   s.

organ. A partisan newspaper reflecting the views of a politician, a factional group, or a political party.   s.

organic act. An act of Congress creating a territory, conferring powers of self-government, and determining the duties of officers and the rights of individuals.   s.

organic law. The fundamental law or constitution.   s.

organization. The official system of party committees. The word is sometimes used in the sense of a party "machine."   s.

organized reserves. Officers and enlisted men who have received some training in the armed services and who, while engaged in civilian pursuits, are subject to call to active duty in time of emergency.   z.

organized territory. A territory with definite boundaries for which Congress has provided a system of laws and a settled government, with usually an elective legislature, as a condition precedent to a grant of statehood.   z.

Orientals, exclusion of. The general policy of the United States of barring immigration from certain Asiatic countries. Chinese, except for certain classes, were first excluded in 1882 although the prohibition has now been relaxed; Japanese were excluded in 1924. The rule with respect to other nations in eastern Asia is not clear although none is assigned a quota under recent immigration laws.   z.

original jurisdiction. The power of a court to hear and determine cases in the first instance.   s.

original package doctrine. A rule, first enunciated by the Supreme Court of the United States as to foreign commerce in *Brown* v. *Maryland,* 12 Wheat. 419 (1827), and as to interstate commerce in *Leisy* v. *Hardin,* 135 U.S. 100 (1890), that as long as the original package remains unsold or unbroken the contents are not subject to State taxing or regulative power. Acts of Congress have abrogated the rule as to intoxicating liquors, 1890 and 1913; as to oleomargarine, 1902; and as to goods made by prison labor, 1929; thus allowing the States to prohibit or regulate the entry of such articles even in the original package.   s.

Orleans Territory. A territory created by Congress Mar. 26, 1804, embracing all the present State of Louisiana except the region north of Lake Pontchartrain and east of the Mississippi. s.

Ostend Manifesto. A statement by American ministers to Great Britain, France, and Spain at Ostend, Belgium, Oct. 15, 1854, advising the United States to offer to purchase Cuba from Spain, and if Spain refused, to seize the island if its further possession by Spain appeared inimical to American domestic interests. s.

Our federal union, it must be preserved. A toast volunteered by President Jackson at a Jefferson Day dinner, Apr. 13, 1830, which dampened the ardor of advocates of nullification.   s.

outdoor relief. Public assistance in the form of food, money, clothing, or medical services rendered to needy persons in their own homes.   jwf.

outlawry of war. The denunciation of war as illegal. Some opinions hold that the Kellogg-Briand Pact (*q.v.*) outlawed war, but it does not expressly debar defensive warfare. JWF.

overt act. An open and manifest act of hostility. The requirement of the Constitution that in prosecutions for treason such an act must be proved by the testimony of two witnesses prevents a person from being convicted merely for hostile words or designs. z.

Owenism. The philosophy of Robert Owen, 1771-1858, British philanthropist and social reformer. Owen attempted unsuccessfully to apply his social theories in a colony which he established at New Harmony, Ind., in 1825. z.

O.W.I. *See* Office of War Information.

oyer and terminer. A court in certain States with jurisdiction over serious crimes; traditionally a royal order directing judges on circuit to hear and determine certain causes. z.

P

pacific blockade. A blockade instituted by one nation over the ports of another for the purpose of obtaining redress for some alleged injury without other hostile intentions. s.

pacific settlement. The adjustment of an international controversy by peaceful means such as conciliation or arbitration. JWF.

pacifism. Advocacy of settlement of international disputes by arbitration, collective action, or other peaceful means; disbelief in force because of the human and material costs of war and alleged historical experience of the temporary nature of military settlements. s.

packed caucus. A party primary meeting filled with supporters of a boss or machine, sometimes to the complete exclusion of other voters. s.

pact. An agreement between two or more states usually less elaborate than a treaty but practically equivalent thereto. JWF.

pains and penalties, bill of. A legislative conviction similar to an attainder (*q.v.*) except that it imposes a penalty of less than death. It is prohibited in the United States. s.

pairing. An agreement between members of a legislative body on opposite sides of an issue that in case of the absence of one the other will also be absent or will refrain from voting. Where a two-thirds vote is required two members for, may be paired with one against, a measure. s.

Palisades Interstate Park. A public park system of some 44,000 acres including the Palisades on the west bank of the Hudson from Fort Lee, N.J., to Newburgh, N.Y., under the jurisdiction of a commission jointly created by New Jersey and New York in 1937 with the consent of Congress. z.

Palmyra Island. An island in the Pacific, about 900 miles south of the Hawaiian group, owned by the United States. It is of strategic importance as a weather and naval station.   z.

Panama Canal. An interoceanic waterway extending from Colon, on the Atlantic Ocean, to Panama, on the Pacific, a distance of 49 miles. Construction was begun in 1883 by a French company which afterward failed. In 1903 the United States negotiated a treaty with Colombia for a 99-year lease of a right of way on payment of $10,000,000 down and $250,000 annually, but the Colombian congress refused to ratify it. Panama then declared her independence of Colombia, Nov. 4, 1903, and was recognized by the United States two days later. She agreed to cede a right of way ten miles wide for the amount previously offered to Colombia. The canal was opened in 1915. In 1921 the United States made a compensatory payment to Colombia of $25,000,000. *See* Canal Zone. s.

Panama Congress. A meeting of representatives of several American republics held at Panama in 1826 on the call of the South American general Simon Bolívar to concert plans for an American league. Representatives of the United States were appointed, but were unable to attend.   s.

Pan-Americanism. A movement to foster the economic, cultural, and political solidarity of the nations of the Western Hemisphere. The Inter-American Institute, held at intervals since 1930, and the Pan American Union (*q.v.*) with headquarters at Washington, D. C., are effective instruments for promoting the aims of the movement.   JMCC.

Pan American Union. The official international organization of the 21 republics of the Western Hemisphere, founded in 1890 as the International Bureau of American Republics, and operating under its present name since 1910. Its governing board is composed of the diplomatic representatives in Washington of all the Latin American governments and the Secretary of State of the United States. The Union maintains a research staff and prepares and distributes illustrated monthly bulletins in English, Spanish, and Portuguese.   s.

***Panay* incident.** The sinking by Japanese planes of the United States gunboat *Panay* in the Yangtse River, Dec. 12, 1937. Although Japan later apologized and paid reparations, the action was apparently deliberate and part of a campaign directed against American interests in China.   JWF.

Panhandle State. A nickname of West Virginia.   s.

panic. Sudden widespread fright over business conditions resulting in the dumping of securities on the markets, and later usually in business depression.   s.

paper blockade. A blockade declared by one country against the ports of another and not enforced, or insufficiently enforced. s.

paper money. Notes or certificates issued by a government or authorized central bank, and generally used as a convenient medium of exchange. JWF.

parcel post. A division of the post office engaged in transmitting parcels, first established by an act of Congress which took effect Jan. 1, 1913. It provides for special handling, a C.O.D. service, and insurance of parcels. S.

pardon. A release from the legal consequences of a crime or a remission of penalties imposed, which may be issued as an act of grace by the competent executive authority before or after indictment or conviction. The President's pardoning power is complete except that he may not remove disabilities imposed as a result of conviction after impeachment. In some States the governor may grant pardons only with the consent of the State senate or council or on recommendation of a pardon board; or the pardon board, of which the governor may or may not be a member, is the sole authority. A conditional pardon becomes effective on compliance with conditions set forth. A general pardon, or amnesty (*q.v.*), applies to a class of persons. S.

Paris, Treaty of. 1. The treaty signed Feb. 10, 1763, which closed the French and Indian War, and by which Great Britain received Canada from France and Florida from Spain. 2. The treaty signed Sept. 3, 1783, which ended the American Revolution, recognized the independence of the United States, fixed its boundaries, gave Americans certain rights to the North Atlantic fisheries, and provided that the United States should place no impediment to the collection of debts owed by Americans to British creditors. 3. The treaty signed Dec. 10, 1898, which ended the Spanish-American War. Spain ceded Puerto Rico, the Philippines, and Guam to the United States on payment of $20,000,000 for public works in the Philippines, and relinquished her sovereignty over Cuba. S.

parish. 1. A local government unit in Louisiana corresponding to a county in other States. 2. A minor governmental unit for ecclesiastical and other subjects in Great Britain and several British colonies. S.

parity. Equality, as for naval ships or tonnage of different nations; for prices of farm products in relation to those existing at some former date or to the general cost of living; or for the standard of money in foreign exchange. S.

parliamentary procedure. The transaction of business in a deliberative body in accordance with established rules, usages, and precedents. S.

parliamentary system. A government such as those of Great Britain or the British dominions in which the executive, consisting of a prime minister and ministerial colleagues in a cabinet, directs the administration and exercises political leadership on condition that it shall at all times command the support of a majority of the legislature or parliament. Withdrawal of such support necessitates the resignation or reconstitution of the executive.   z.

parlor caucus. A secret meeting of party leaders for the purpose of agreeing on candidates or policies.   s.

parochial school. A local educational institution conducted by an ecclesiastical organization.   jwf.

parole. A conditional release, generally under supervision of a parole officer, of a person who has served part of the term for which he was sentenced to prison. It is revocable if he fails to observe the conditions.   s.

particularism. Devotion to the special interests of a State or section, rather than to the country as a whole.   s.

party. A body of voters organized for the purpose of influencing or controlling the policies and conduct of government through the nomination and, if possible, the election of its candidates to office. In some States a party is legally defined as a group which cast a certain number or percentage of votes at the last election for President or governor. A party is distinguished from other groups by its nomination of candidates and its tacit willingness to assume responsibility for the whole conduct of public affairs. Parties provide a means by which public sentiment may be expressed and ascertained and the policies of various branches of the government may be made consistent.   s.

party affiliation tests. Various conditions in State laws imposed as a prerequisite to participation in a closed primary. They require a voter to declare that he has generally supported the candidates of a party in past elections, that he intends to do so in the future, or that he has not voted in the primary of a different party within a given period.   s.

party circle. A circle at the top of a party column on some ballots. By marking a cross in it, a voter may vote a straight party ticket.   s.

party column. A vertical division on the Indiana type of ballot in which is printed, under the name of a particular party, all the candidates nominated by it for office. *See* illustration, page *229*. s.

party committee. A group of persons chosen by a party convention or by voters in a primary election in practically every area in which one or more executive, legislative, or judicial officers are popularly elected. It assists in conducting an election campaign, and between sessions of the convention, it serves as a general executive committee for the party.   s.

party convention. *See* Convention 4; National convention.

party emblem. A device, such as the Democratic Statue of

Liberty or the Republican elephant, printed at the top of the party column or opposite the names of candidates on some ballots to assist voters in identifying candidates of their party. s.

DEMOCRATIC PARTY	REPUBLICAN PARTY	SOCIALIST PARTY	SOCIALIST-LABOR PARTY	PROHIBITION PARTY
○	○	○	○	○
For President and Vice-President — FRANKLIN D. ROOSEVELT / HENRY A WALLACE	For President and Vice-President — WENDELL L. WILLKIE / CHARLES L. McNARY	For President and Vice-President — NORMAN THOMAS / MAYNARD C. KRUEGER	For President and Vice-President — JOHN W. AIKEN / AARON M. ORANGE	For President and Vice-President — ROGER W. BABSON / EDGAR V MOORMANN
For Senator in Congress — HARRY S. TRUMAN	For Senator in Congress — MANUEL H. (Cap) DAVIS	For Senator in Congress — W. F RINCK	For Senator in Congress — THEODORE BAEFF	For Senator in Congress —
For Governor — LAWRENCE McDANIEL	For Governor — FORREST C. DONNELL	For Governor — JED A. HIGH	For Governor — WILLIAM W. COX	For Governor —
For Lieutenant-Governor — FRANK G. HARRIS	For Lieutenant-Governor — WM P. ELMER	For Lieutenant-Governor — A M DEMAREE	For Lieutenant-Governor — MICHAEL L. HILTNER	For Lieutenant-Governor — WILLIAM J. CADY
For Secretary of State — DWIGHT H BROWN	For Secretary of State — LOYD (Boody) MILLER	For Secretary of State — HENRY SIROKY	For Secretary of State — HENRY W. GENCK	For Secretary of State —
For State Auditor — FORREST SMITH	For State Auditor — J T WADDILL	For State Auditor — HELEN NICHOLS	For State Auditor —	For State Auditor —
For State Treasurer — WILSON BELL	For State Treasurer — SCOTT PETERS	For State Treasurer — LUCY HENSCHEL	For State Treasurer —	For State Treasurer —
For Attorney-General — ROY McKITTRICK *	For Attorney-General — RAY MABEE	For Attorney-General — EDWARD J. FLYNN	For Attorney-General —	For Attorney-General —
For Judge Supreme Court (Div. No. 2) — GEORGE ROBB ELLISON	For Judge Supreme Court (Div. No. 2) — FRANK E. ATWOOD	For Judge Supreme Court (Div. No. 2) —	For Judge Supreme Court (Div. No. 2) —	For Judge Supreme Court (Div. No. 2) —
For Judge of Court of Appeals —	For Judge of Court of Appeals —	For Judge of Court of Appeals —	For Judge of Court of Appeals —	For Judge of Court of Appeals —
For Judge of Court of Appeals (unexpired term) —	For Judge of Court of Appeals (unexpired term) —	For Judge of Court of Appeals (unexpired term) —	For Judge of Court of Appeals (unexpired term) —	For Judge of Court of Appeals (unexpired term) —
For Representative in Congress —	For Representative in Congress —	For Representative in Congress —	For Representative in Congress —	For Representative in Congress —

Party column ballot — Showing party circle and party emblem (Missouri)

party finance. *See* Campaign fund.

party line. The line across the face of a voting machine occupied by names of candidates of one party. s.

party organ. A newspaper which is supposed to reflect the official or dominant views of a party. s.

pass examination. A noncompetitive examination used in the national civil service for a few positions to determine whether or not the applicant possesses minimum qualifications. s.

passive resistance. A form of direct but nonviolent opposition to action of the government by a group of people. It usually takes the form of mass civil disobedience, the disruption of traffic by crowding thoroughfares and entrances to public buildings, and the sit-down strike. JMCC.

passport. An official document issued by competent authority of a government (in the United States, the Secretary of State) to one of its citizens or nationals, identifying him, permitting him to leave the country and travel abroad, and requesting protection for him from foreign states.   s.

paster. A gummed strip of paper bearing a candidate's name which a voter may paste on a ballot in some States as an alternative to writing in a name.   s.

patent. A grant made by public authority to the first inventor or discoverer of a new or useful process, machine, manufacture, composition, design, or variety of plant growth, entitling him to the exclusive right to make, use, sell, or lease it. Patents are granted for a term of 17 years.   s.

Patent Office. A national agency headed by a Commissioner of Patents, established in 1790 and transferred to the Department of Commerce in 1925. Some 66 divisions of the Office examine applications for patents on useful inventions. Applications which are denied may be appealed to the Office's own Board of Appeals and thence may be carried to the Court of Customs and Patent Appeals or to a United States district court. More than 2,225,000 patents have been granted since 1790. A division of the Office hears and decides upon applications for trade-mark registration. z.

paternalism. The practice of a government of intervening in affairs ordinarily deemed to be of private interest, as for the protection of persons from the consequences of their own ignorance; or by supplying economic and social services on the theory that they would not be supplied at all, or supplied as well, by private initiative.   s.

Paterson plan. A series of seven resolutions to amend the Articles of Confederation by giving Congress more power, submitted to the Convention of 1787 by William Paterson of New Jersey. They expressed the desires of the small States and were designed to counter the Virginia plan (*q.v.*), which was considered too nationalistic.   z.

Pathfinder. A nickname of John C. Frémont.   s.

patronage. The power to make appointments to office, especially when not governed by civil service laws or rules; also the power to grant contracts and various special favors.   s.

Patronage, Committee on. A committee appointed by the majority party caucus in each house of Congress to insure the equal distribution among members of the party of appointments of congressional employees.   s.

Patrons of Husbandry. *See* Grange.

pauper's oath. A formal declaration by a person that he is destitute and incapable of self-support, required in certain States in order to be eligible for public relief. Such an oath normally operates to deprive a person of the vote.   z.

Payne-Aldrich tariff. The strongly protectionist tariff law of 1909 which was an important cause of the Progressive revolt of 1912. s.

pay-roll patriot. An opprobrious term for a civilian employee of the government who takes advantage of his position during wartime to advance his private interests. s.

pay-roll tax. A national excise tax of 3 per cent paid by employers in defined categories hiring eight or more employees upon all wages paid amounting to $3,000 or less per employee per annum. The purpose is to finance unemployment benefits under the Social Security Act. A credit of as much as 90 per cent of the tax is allowed employers for their contributions to a State unemployment system. Employers also pay a pay-roll tax of 1 per cent to finance old-age and survivors' insurance for employees. z.

peace. A condition of domestic tranquillity within a state and of normal relations with other states. s.

peace conference. A meeting of representatives of belligerents to discuss and formulate terms of peace. s.

Peace Democrat. A Northern Democrat during the Civil War who opposed the continuance of hostilities and was in favor of a settlement by conference between the sections. s.

peaceful penetration. Extension of the influence of a powerful state over a weak state by means of commercial investment, government loans, the institution of strong diplomatic posts and technical advisers, the planting of nationals as colonists, and similar devices. JWF.

peace without victory. A phrase which occurred in President Wilson's address to the Senate, Jan. 22, 1917, when he was still hopeful of bringing World War I to a close and avoiding American participation in it. s.

peanut politics. Attention to trivial matters, to the neglect of urgent public business, for the purpose of winning votes. s.

Pearl Harbor. A primary American naval base in the Pacific with adjacent army installations situated near Honolulu on Oahu, the Hawaiian Islands. It was the objective of the surprise Japanese attack, Dec. 7, 1941, which brought the United States into World War II. z.

pear tree, shaking the. Distributing the spoils of office. s.

peer. An equal. An accused man must be tried by a jury of his peers. JWF.

Peerless Leader. A nickname of William Jennings Bryan. s.

penal administration. The maintenance and management of institutions and programs, such as probation and parole, for the punishment and correction of criminals. The personnel of such an administration consists of prison and parole boards, wardens, guards, medical and psychiatric staffs, and probation and parole officers.   JMCC.

penalty. The punishment, especially a pecuniary exaction, inflicted for violation of a law.   S.

Pendleton Act. The civil service reform act of Congress, Jan. 16, 1883. *See* Civil service.   S.

penitentiary. A State or national maximum-security institution designed for the punishment and correction of adult criminals serving terms of more than one year ; usually accepted as a synonym for prison.   JMCC.

Pennsylvania. One of the original States and the second to ratify the Constitution of the United States, Dec. 12, 1787. Capital, Harrisburg ; area, 45,333 sq. mi. ; population (1940), 9,900,180 ; presidential electors, 35. The present constitution was adopted in 1874. With minor exceptions, all adult citizens may vote.   S.

Pennsylvania system. A penal system originated about 1790, the principal feature of which was the solitary confinement of inmates in cells arranged along corridors radiating from the center to the circumference of a prison.   JMCC.

pension. A stated allowance paid at regular intervals to a former soldier or sailor or to a retired employee from a general fund ; or to a disabled or retired employee or aged person from an insurance fund.   S.

peonage. A condition of servitude in which persons are bound to perform personal service on account of a debt ; any involuntary service prohibited by the 13th Amendment.   S.

people's lobby. A voluntary organization formed for the purpose of combatting, in the interests of the general public, the activities of special-interest groups.   S.

People's party. The official name of the Populists.   S.

People's Power League. An organization in Oregon about 1900 which worked for the adoption of direct legislation, the primary election, and other governmental reforms.   S.

per capita. For each inhabitant ; a phrase used to express the statistical ratio between the whole population of a community and some community resource or liability such as its wealth, its tax burden, or its public debt.   JWF.

performance test. The test of the ability of an applicant to do the tasks required in a position under actual or simulated conditions of employment.   S.

periodic registration. Registration of voters before every election.   S.

permanent appropriation. An appropriation for a public institution or a fixed expense which does not require re-enactment every year, but continues in effect until repealed.   S.

Permanent Court of International Justice. A court with a panel of eleven justices established at The Hague in 1920 under the provisions of Art. XIV of the Covenant of the League of Nations. It has a limited jurisdiction to hear disputes between members of the League and is open to other states.   s.

Permanent Joint Board on Defense. A joint American-Canadian board of ten members, set up by the President and the Canadian prime minister Aug. 17, 1940, to study and correlate common measures for the defense of the Western Hemisphere.   z.

permanent registration. A system of registration of voters under which a completely new registration is made only at long intervals and the list is kept continuously up to date by a permanent staff in each county.   s.

permissive powers. Powers conferred by a State legislature upon a municipal corporation or other local agency which may be exercised at its discretion; to be distinguished from mandatory powers so conferred which must be exercised.   z.

permit. An official paper identifying a person as one who is entitled to exercise some privilege under the law; a license.   s.

perquisite. An emolument supplementing the regular salary of an official and acquired in the course of duty, such as a fee paid an officer for performing a marriage ceremony.   jwf.

persecution. A persistent attack of a prejudiced dominant group in a community upon a weaker group, usually because of national, racial, or religious differences, or economic rivalry. jwf.

personal liberty laws. Laws passed by the legislatures of several Northern States which impeded the enforcement of national fugitive slave laws by denying the use of jails and securing to alleged fugitives the writ of habeas corpus and trial by jury. s.

Personal Politics, Period of. The decade between 1820 and 1830, so called because, after the disappearance of the Federalist party, the chief contests were among adherents of rival Republican leaders like Jackson, Adams, and Clay.   s.

personal property. Money, chattels, and other movable goods or things separable from real estate.   s.

personal union. The relationship between countries the governments of which are independent but share the same sovereign. jwf.

persona non grata. A diplomatic or consular official not acceptable to the country to which he is sent.   jwf.

personation. An offense against the law which consists in acting under the title or name of another, as impersonating an officer, or casting, or attempting to cast, a vote under the name of a registered voter.   s.

personnel. The whole body of employees in the public service, in any division or branch thereof, or in any specified governmental or private enterprise.   jwf.

pet bank. A bank in which public funds are deposited as a result of official favor. s.

petition. A formal written request addressed to some governmental authority. The right of the people to petition for redress of grievances is guaranteed by the First Amendment. Petitions signed by a certain number or percentage of voters are often required to place the name of a candidate on a primary or general election ballot; and to initiate, or invoke the referendum on, legislation. s.

petition jobbing. Professional solicitation of signatures to electoral petitions. s.

Petition of Right. A declaration of the rights of the English people presented by Parliament to King Charles I and signed by him June 7, 1628. s.

petit jury. *See* Jury.

Pewter Muggers. A faction of the Democratic party in New York City about 1828 opposed to Tammany Hall. s.

Philippine Commonwealth. A group of more than 7,000 islands lying off the southeastern coast of Asia with an area of 114,-400 sq. mi. and a population (1939) of 16,000,303. They were acquired by the United States at the close of the Spanish-American War, and were governed under military authority until 1901, and under a governor and appointive commission, 1902-16. A popularly elective lower house was established in 1907. Under the Jones Act, 1916, both legislative houses were popularly elective and the chief executive power was vested in a governor general appointed by the President and Senate. In 1934 Congress enacted, and the Philippine legislature accepted, a law providing for independence in 1946, with in the meantime a large degree of self-government except as to foreign affairs. Under a constitution adopted in 1935 the people choose their own president. Certain acts of their legislature are subject to disapproval by the President of the United States, who is represented in Manila by a high commissioner. Before the Japanese occupation of the islands, 1941-42, it seemed likely that the date of independence might be advanced beyond 1946 to allow for economic readjustments. The Philippine Commonwealth is represented at Washington by a resident commissioner. s.

phosphorus match tax. *See* White Phosphorus Match Act.

picketing. Patrolling the entrance to a business establishment or public place with placards in an effort to persuade persons about to enter to take some specific action concerning an industrial dispute or public controversy. JMCC.

pie. A slang term for patronage or the spoils of office. s.

pigeonholing. The practice of congressional and most State legislative committees of withholding and failing to report out bills referred to them of which they disapprove. s.

Pinckney's Treaty. A treaty negotiated by Thomas Pinckney at San Lorenzo, Spain, Oct. 27, 1795, by which Spain relinquished her claim to territory north of the 31st parallel, opened the Mississippi River to free navigation by American citizens, granted them the right of deposit at New Orleans for a period of three years with the privilege of renewing the right either at New Orleans or another port, and agreed to make compensation for spoliations of American commerce. s.

pipe laying. A slang term for colonization (*q.v.*) of voters. s.

Pipe-Line cases. A series of cases, 234 U.S. 548 (1914), in which the Supreme Court held that the transportation of oil by pipe line across State boundaries was interstate commerce and subject to congressional legislation. z.

piracy. An act of violence committed at sea by persons or armed vessels not acting under the authority of a state or organized community. JWF.

pitiless publicity. A phrase coined by Woodrow Wilson in the course of his gubernatorial campaign in New Jersey in 1910. He promised to give the people full information of public affairs regardless of the effect on private interests. s.

pivotal State. A doubtful State having a large number of electoral votes. In a closely contested presidential election its vote may decide the result. s.

plank. A section of a party platform referring to a distinct subject. s.

planning. The process of devising a basis for a course of action. It may or may not include specific procedures and methods. If systematically done the process involves analysis of historical data pertinent to the purpose and nature of the plan, continuous research yielding information concerning future matters bearing upon the plan, and a tentative course of action. Scientific planning is an ongoing process wherein all tentative aspects are continuously tested and retested in the light of developments. The fundamental nature of planning may range from the most democratic to the most authoritarian. CS-H.

platform. A statement of principles and of policies to be followed concerning a great number of public questions, adopted by a party convention as a basis for the party's appeal for public support. Platforms nearly always result from compromises among conflicting sectional and economic interests and contain many "weasel" words which suck the life blood from apparently binding pledges. They are regarded as of less importance than a candidate's statements during his campaign. s.

platoon system. The division of policemen and firemen into two or three shifts, or "platoons," each of which is on duty during certain hours of a twenty-four-hour day. s.

Platt Amendment. A rider on an army appropriation bill passed in 1901 and repealed May 29, 1934, which provided that Cuba should allow the United States to intervene to preserve her independence and maintain order, grant the United States land for naval bases, continue sanitary improvements, contract no excessive debt, and make no agreement with a foreign power that would impair her sovereignty.   S.

Platte Purchase. The northwestern corner of Missouri which was purchased by the United States from the Pottawatomie Indians in 1836 and added to Missouri by act of Congress Mar. 28, 1837.   S.

Platte Purchase

pleadings. Formal statements made in court by parties or their counsel to establish the issue of a controversy.   z.

plebiscite. The submission of an important issue to a vote of the people concerned. It was used in some parts of Europe after World War I to determine which of two or more countries should include disputed territory.   JWF.

plenary session. A fully assembled meeting of a conference or congress as distinguished from committee meetings of the same body.   JWF.

plenipotentiary. A diplomat with full powers to negotiate for his state with the government of another state or in an international conference.   JWF.

plum. A desirable appointment or political reward.   S.

Plumed Knight. A nickname of James G. Blaine.   S.

plumping. Giving more than one vote for a candidate, as under the system of cumulative voting used in Illinois.   S.

plunder bund. A corrupt combination of politicians and economic interests to profit at the expense of the public.   S.

pluralism. The doctrine that governmental authority within a community should be distributed among various functional groups and neither monopolized nor — according to some writers — shared by a sovereign power in the state.   JJR.

plurality. The number by which the leading candidate's vote exceeds that cast for the next highest candidate, usually sufficient for election to office.   S.

plural voting. The casting, under provisions of law, of more than one ballot at a voting precinct, or of one ballot in each of several precincts.   S.

plutocracy. A government dominated by men of wealth; also the wealthy class. s.

pocket borough. An English term for an electoral area controlled by the influence of one man, sometimes applied to certain American constituencies. s.

pocket veto. The failure of the President to sign and return a bill within ten days if, at the end of ten days, Congress is in adjournment. Such an unsigned bill does not become law. s.

point of order. A question raised by a member of a legislative body as to the propriety of a motion or proceeding under the rules. The presiding officer is required to rule on it immediately and his ruling is subject to appeal to the floor. s.

police. An organized body of municipal, county, or State officers engaged in maintaining public order, peace, and safety, and in investigating and arresting persons suspected or formally accused of crime. z.

police court. A municipal tribunal of lowest grade which tries those accused of violating local ordinances or acts as a tribunal for the preliminary examination and commitment of those accused of graver offenses. z.

police jury. The administrative board of a parish in Louisiana, equivalent to a county board elsewhere. s.

police power. The power of the State to place restraints on the personal freedom and property rights of persons for the protection of the public safety, health, and morals or the promotion of the public convenience and general prosperity. It is a residuary power of the States. It extends over a multitude of subjects, and may involve taking or destroying property, as in the abatement of a nuisance, or debarring a person from pursuing a trade, or forcing him to submit to vaccination; and it may affect the movement of interstate commerce through quarantine regulations, requirements of safety devices on trains, adequate service to a community, etc. The police power is subject to limitations of the federal and State constitutions, and especially to the requirement of due process (*q.v.*) The need of the general public for legislation must be relatively great; the inconvenience to the individual must be relatively slight; and the restraints imposed must be adapted to secure the end in view. In balancing these principles, court decisions tend to vary with the judge's knowledge of the social situation which a statute is designed to improve and the probable burden of the restraint on the individual. Similar powers of regulation, sometimes called the federal police power, are derived from the national commerce, postal, and other powers. s.

political bargain. An agreement between two factions or parties, as for the withdrawal of a candidate in consideration of a division of appointments or other spoils of office. s.

political clearance. The influence and support of party leaders, including letters and endorsements from county or local chairmen, commonly required as a prerequisite for appointment to unclassified or "spoils" positions. Civil service reform attempts to substitute "merit" for "clearance."   GHD.

political departments. The executive and the legislature. *See* Political question.   s.

political disability. Any condition, such as physical or mental incapacity, minority, conviction of crime, or lack of citizenship, which disqualifies a person from holding public office.   z.

political offense. An offense against public security committed for the purpose of changing the form of government, or the persons in office, or altering the laws.   s.

political party. *See* Party.

political prisoner. A person held in custody for a political offense. Such a person cannot usually be extradited.   s.

political question. A problem of state the solution of which the courts regard as belonging exclusively to the discretion of the executive or legislative branch. Such questions as the territorial extent of the United States, whether or not a State has a republican form of government, the recognition of a foreign state, the existence and end of a war, and the continued existence of treaties, are political, and are not subject to review by the courts.   JWF.

political science. A branch of the social sciences dealing with the theory, organization, government, and practice of the state. It embraces both politics and administration, the two parts being co-ordinate, rather than exclusive.   CS-H.

political theory. Generally the entire body of doctrine relating to the origin, form, behavior, and purpose of the state. Somewhat arbitrarily, this body of doctrine may be given a fivefold classification: (1) ethical; (2) speculative; (3) sociological; (4) legal; and (5) scientific. The first of these classifications is sometimes termed "political ethics" or "political philosophy" and is fundamentally a branch of ethics. It deals with what ought to be in the realm of matters political and its method consists of systematic rational analysis of common-sense notions and relevant data. *Speculative political theory* consists of imaginative constructions of ideal or utopian states such as may be found in Plato's *Republic,* More's *Utopia* (1516), and Campanella's *City of the Sun* (1623). *Sociological political theory* may well be described as a part of the broader theory of society. Its method is analytical and empirical and it seeks to determine the relation of the state to other aspects of society and to analyze the state as a form of social organization. *Legal political theory* deals with the nature of law, the juristic concept of sovereignty, and legal situations arising out of the institutions and devices for distributing and controlling the exercise of political power. Finally, *scientific political theory* consists largely of empirical observations of political phenomena to ascertain probable trends or generalizations, the equivalent of "laws" in the empirical sciences. The study of the course and nature of political change, the relative efficiency of various governmental and administrative forms and processes, and the probable effect of given political institutions upon human liberty and social well-being, fall into this category. Although there is a vast and rich literature on the subject, political theory is not a well-integrated body of doctrine. JRP.

politician. 1. A person versed in public affairs and skilled in adjusting conflicting interests within a state and in the creation and guidance of public policy. 2. In a disparaging sense, a manager of party affairs or a mere manipulator of public sentiment for private gain. S.

politics. That part of political science dealing with policy making. It concerns itself with the agencies and instrumentalities which establish policy, including the legislature and all but the purely administrative functions of the executive, together with the electorate, political parties, etc. It is also concerned with the results which flow from this stage of government activity. Politics is primarily identified with public objectives and administration with method, although there is a growing interpenetration between the two branches of political science. CS-H.

polity. A state. Z.

poll. The counting of individual voters as they announce their preference for different candidates; the result of such a count; in the plural, the election precinct. S.

poll book. The register of voters at an election precinct. S.

poll tax. A direct personal tax usually levied by a local government unit at a stated rate per head upon all adult male persons (and sometimes upon women). Exemptions are often granted to war veterans, paupers, or physically or mentally disabled persons. In a few States its payment is a prerequisite for voting or obtaining an automobile license. S.

Pomeroy Circular. A letter sent out early in 1864 in the interest of Salmon P. Chase's candidacy for the presidency in which Lincoln's policies were attacked. S.

pooling. An agreement among competitors to avoid the detrimental effects of unhampered competition by fixing common prices, or by allocating available markets or their common income or profits according to a fixed ratio. Z.

poor farm. A farm maintained by its produce and by public funds as a shelter for the destitute of a community. JWF.

poorhouse. A public institution usually maintained by a

county or town, for the shelter of aged poor, orphans, and sometimes incapacitated or mentally defective persons.   JWF.

poor man's dollar. A term for the silver dollar used by advocates of free and unlimited coinage of silver about 1896.   S.

poor relief. Organized private or public assistance to needy families.   JWF.

Poor Richard. A pen name assumed by Benjamin Franklin. S.

Popocrat. A nickname given by Republicans to a Democrat who, in the campaign of 1896 or 1900, espoused Populist issues. S.

popular assembly. 1. A gathering of the citizens of a local community or of their representatives for the transaction of public affairs. 2. A legislative body consisting of representatives elected by the people.   JWF.

popular sovereignty. 1. Supreme and unlimited power on the part of the indeterminate mass of the people to create and alter the fundamental structure of a government. The idea of popular sovereignty has been asserted by many writers including the Monarchomachs, Rousseau, and the draughtsmen of the Declaration of Independence. Several State constitutions declare that all power resides in the people. 2. In the disputes over Kansas, the power of the people, represented in the territorial legislature, to admit or exclude slavery.   S.

popular vote. The vote of the qualified electorate, as distinguished from that of the electoral colleges.   S.

population. According to the census of 1940 the population of continental United States, not including Alaska, was 131,669,275. Classified according to race, the numbers are:

White	118,214,870
Negro	12,865,518
All other	588,887

Classified according to citizenship, the numbers are:

Citizens	127,354,644
Native born	120,074,379
Naturalized	7,280,265
Alien	3,479,652
First papers	924,524
No papers	2,555,128
Foreign born — citizenship not reported	834,979

The total population of noncontiguous territory (Alaska, Hawaii, Puerto Rico, etc.) was 2,495,956; in addition, the population of the Philippine Commonwealth was 16,356,000, making a grand total of 150,621,231.   S.

Populists. Members of the People's party, which was organized in 1891 by agricultural and labor groups. They demanded the free and unlimited coinage of silver, an increase in the amount of greenbacks to $50 per capita, public ownership of railroads, telegraphs, and telephones, recapture of lands formerly granted to railroads, and a graduated income tax. In 1892 they cast 1,027,329 popular, and 22 electoral, votes for James B. Weaver for President. In 1896 and 1900 they endorsed Bryan. They disappeared after 1908.   s.

pork. Appropriations, appointments, and favors obtained by a representative for his district.   s.

pork barrel. The national treasury from which, by logrolling (*q.v.*), Congressmen vote appropriations for river and harbor improvements, public buildings, navy yards, army posts, and government offices which are of special benefit to their districts and to their campaigns for re-election.   s.

port authority. An administrative commission charged with regulating and facilitating the water, rail, and other traffic of a seaport.   JWF.

portfolio. A brief case in which official papers may be carried; hence, symbolically, the office or administrative department of a minister.   JWF.

port of entry. A place where a customhouse is established. JWF.

positive law. Law as defined by John Austin and others of the so-called "positive school of jurisprudence" which owed much of its inspiration to the French social theorist Auguste Comte. According to this school, law consists of definite rules of human conduct with appropriate sanctions for their enforcement, both prescribed by a determinate human superior or sovereign.   z.

posse comitatus. The power of the county. The whole body (under the common law all male persons over 15 years of age) whom the sheriff may summon to assist him in law enforcement; also the body he summons.   s.

postal money order. A device for safely transferring funds from place to place through the facilities of the postal system. The payer, specifying amount and the payee, may purchase an order at any post office and send it to the payee who may cash it at a post office or elsewhere.   JWF.

postal savings system. A division of the Post Office Department created by Congress June 25, 1910, to receive savings deposits from individuals at designated post offices and invest the funds received.   s.

post-audit. Periodic examinations of the financial records of government departments to determine whether their expenditures have been made in accordance with law.   z.

Postmaster General. The head of the Post Office Department. His tenure, unique among cabinet officers, is during the term of the President who appoints him and for one month thereafter unless sooner removed. The national chairman of the successful party is usually appointed to the office in a new administration. The Postmaster General has wide discretion in the extension and curtailment of the postal service, the exclusion of fraudulent and immoral material from the mails, and in the letting of contracts. With presidential approval he makes postal agreements with foreign governments.   s.

Post Office Department. The division which handles the mails and conducts a registry, postal savings, money order, and parcel post service. It was created a department in 1829 although its origins can be traced in an unbroken line from the appointment of Alexander Spotswood in 1727 as deputy postmaster general for the colonies. At its head are the Postmaster General (*q.v.*) and four assistant postmasters general.   z.

post road. Originally a road designated as a mail route. The power of Congress to establish such routes has been extended by implication to include the construction of roads.   JWF.

power politics. The exaction of concessions in international political bargaining by threatening to use force, by economic reprisals, or similar tactics.   JWF.

practical examination. A civil service examination which seeks to determine training and fitness of an applicant for a particular position rather than general knowledge and mental aptitude.   z.

Prayer of Twenty Millions. A title given by Horace Greeley to a letter he wrote to President Lincoln Aug. 19, 1862, demanding the enforcement of laws under which many slaves were free.   s.

preamble. An introductory statement prefixed to a constitution or statute setting forth the circumstances or reasons which led to its adoption or passage. It is not a part of the law; but in case of ambiguity in the body of the document, the courts may refer to it to ascertain the intentions of the framers.   s.

pre-audit. Determination by a comptroller or equivalent officer of the existence of a legislative appropriation for a claim before authorizing its payment.   z.

precedent. A judicial, administrative, or legislative act or decision deemed of sufficient weight to be followed in subsequent cases. The conclusiveness of a precedent depends greatly upon the authority and prestige of the body which established it, and upon its adherence to just principles, its reasonableness, and the length of time it has stood unchallenged.   s.

precinct. A minor division for casting and counting votes in elections or for police administration in a city or ward.   s.

pre-emption. Under former land laws, the right of a person who first marked a tract of land to acquire a legal title to it.   s.

preference primary. *See* Presidential primary.

preferential shop. An industrial establishment in which preference is given to union men in hiring and layoff.   JJR.

preferential voting. A scheme under which a voter marks first, second, third choices, etc., opposite the names of candidates on a primary or general election ballot. If no candidate has a majority of first choices the second and later choices become effective, as under the Bucklin or Ware plans (*qq.v.*)   s.

prejudice. A preconceived attitude in favor of or against one side of a controversy or one of a class of objects otherwise regarded impartially.   JWF.

preliminary canvass. An investigation of the probable outcome of an election conducted by a party organization through its ward, district, or precinct leaders.   s.

preparedness. Readiness, through adequate naval and military establishments, for a possible war.   s.

preprimary convention. A party convention held in advance of a primary election to present platform planks or endorse a slate of candidates.   s.

prerogative. An arbitrary power; a right inherent in an office which may be exercised without responsibility to any other authority. Certain powers of the President, as in the field of foreign affairs, and of the Speaker of the House of Representatives, as in the recognition of members, are often loosely called prerogatives.   s.

prescription. 1. Acquisition of sovereignty over a territory by reason of continuous and undisturbed possession over a long period. 2. Acquisition of an inheritable personal right to use a way, water, light and air, etc., by reason of immemorial usage or long-continued enjoyment.   JJR.

presentment. A formal accusation against a person or persons made by a grand jury on its own motion. *See* Grand jury. s.

President. The chief executive of the United States. The Constitution vests in the President virtually complete control of the nation's foreign relations, including the conduct of diplomacy, the leadership of the armed forces, the making of international agreements, and, with the consent of two thirds of the Senate, the making of treaties. His general administrative powers include the appointment, by and with the advice and consent of the Senate, of principal officers of the government; exclusive power to appoint many other officers; general supervision of the "executive" departments and agencies; and the power to see that the laws are faithfully executed. The last prerogative has been greatly expanded owing to presidential control of law enforcement agencies and the discretionary authority committed to him by statute. The President may also pardon offenses against the United States. The President's legislative powers include authority to interpose a veto to the enactment of any bill or resolution, a two-thirds vote of each house of Congress being necessary to override the veto; the power to call Congress or either house into special session; and the power to recommend policy to the Congress by message or oral address. The prestige of the office, the President's ready access to information- and opinion-molding media such as the radio and the press, his power to dispense patronage, and, above all, his position as leader of the party to which he belongs, have all contributed toward making the more recent Presidents the real leaders of Congress and the molders of the nation's domestic policy. Hence the President has become the political leader of the government. Electoral colleges choose the President by a majority vote from among candidates selected by the major parties at quadrennial conventions, but in practice the choice of the electoral colleges is almost uniformly the choice of a plurality of the voters. Usage restricted an incumbent President to two terms of four years each until 1940 when precedent was broken by the re-election of President Franklin D. Roosevelt for a third term. The President receives a salary of $75,000 per annum and various allowances.   z.

presidential elector. A person chosen within a State (now always by popular vote of the State at large, though formerly sometimes by the State legislature or the voters of a congressional district) who meets with other electors at the State capital and casts one vote for a presidential, and one vote for a vice-presidential, candidate.   s.

presidential government. A system, in contradistinction to cabinet or parliamentary government, in which the real head of the executive power is chosen by an authority independent of the legislature; and in which his cabinet, who are not members of the legislature or subject to dismissal by it for lack of confidence, are appointed by the chief executive and subject to his direction.   s.

presidential primary. An adaptation of the primary election to enable voters to express a preference among candidates for President by voting either directly for a candidate or for delegates to a party convention who may, or may not, be pledged. It is mandatory in 15 States and optional in 4 others. The result is morally, but not legally, binding on delegates.   s.

presidential short ballot. A form of ballot which omits the names of individual candidates for presidential elector and allows a voter, by making one mark, to vote for all the electors nominated by one party. *See* illustration, page 245.   s.

presidential succession. The order in which officials succeed to the presidency in case of the removal, resignation, death, or legal disability of the President. The Vice President is next in line; and after him Congress at first, by act of 1792, provided for the succession of the president pro tempore of the Senate and then of the Speaker of the House; but in 1886 this law was repealed and the succession devolved in order upon the Secretary of State, the Secretary of the Treasury, the Secretary of War, the Attorney General, the Postmaster General, the Secretary of the Navy, and the Secretary of the Interior, provided they possess the qualifications listed in the Constitution. The 20th Amendment provided for the succession to the presidency in certain unusual circumstances. s.

A vote for the Candidates for President and Vice President shall be a vote for the electors of such party, the names of whom are on file with the Secretary of State.

USE X ONLY IN MARKING BALLOT

Presidential short ballot (Ohio)

president pro tempore. A member of the Senate chosen by that body to preside over its sessions when the Vice President is absent or is serving as President. The position has been permanent since 1876. s.

President's Re-employment Agreement. The "blanket code" authorized by the National Industrial Recovery Act and signed by nearly all employers of labor after July 27, 1933. The signers agreed to observe maximum weekly hours and minimum wages for employees, the maintenance of wages and of prices for their products, and the abolition of child labor. s.

press. *See* Freedom of speech and press.

press gallery. That portion of the gallery of a legislative house reserved for journalists in order that reports of proceedings may appear in the press. s.

pressure, social. The force of organized public opinion brought to bear upon legislatures and public officials in support of a particular policy or program. JMCC.

pressure group. An organization which promotes specific economic, moral, or other causes by employing paid agents or lobbyists to influence legislators and public officials, by endorsement of candidates nominated by political parties, or by conducting systematic educational or propaganda campaigns among the general public. JMCC.

previous question. The principal substantive motion. In the House of Representatives it may be moved on the passage of a bill, an amendment, or a motion or series of motions. It is not debatable. If passed, it has the effect of stopping all debate and amendment and of bringing the question to an immediate vote. If there has been no debate in the House or in committee of the whole when the motion is made, each side is allowed twenty minutes before a vote is taken. s.

price ceiling. Legally established maximum prices for any commodity or service. z.

price fixing. 1. An agreement among producers or distributors to maintain an arbitrary price for a commodity or service, normally illegal although occasionally countenanced by law. 2. The establishment of a scale of maximum prices for selected commodities or services by legislation or administrative order, a normal part of a government rationing system or of a public plan to encourage production, distribution, or export of certain commodities such as agricultural staples. z.

primary. A mass meeting or primary assembly of voters belonging to one party; also, loosely, a primary election. s.

primary election. A preliminary election for the nomination of candidates for office, designed to wrest power from the bosses and return it to the people. Primary elections are classified as *closed* or *open* depending on whether or not tests of party affiliation are required for participation; as *mandatory* or *optional,* depending upon whether the State law requires a primary or leaves to each party discretion to adopt it or not and merely provides machinery for its operation; and as *nonpartisan* if party designations do not appear on the primary ballot. The first primary laws, beginning in 1871, were optional. About 1890 the adoption of the Australian ballot prepared by State authority encouraged the passage of mandatory laws, though it was not until 1904 that the first mandatory state-wide law was passed. At present 46 States require the primary election in some form, though, as in New York, only a limited number of officers may be affected by it. The open primary has gradually lost ground to the closed primary. In a few Southern States the primary election is held under party rules and is optional for parties casting a small percentage of the total vote. *See* Presidential primary; Runoff primary. s.

prime minister. The chief minister in a government; the official or unofficial title of the head of a council of ministers in a cabinet or parliamentary form of government. JWF.

primogeniture. The right of the eldest son under English law to inherit all real property. It was abolished in America either by colonial legislatures or by the States in the Revolutionary or Confederation periods. s.

prison. An establishment for the incarceration of persons convicted of crime. *See* Penitentiary. JWF.

prisoner. A person held in custody or imprisoned by lawful
authority. JWF.

prisoner of war. A member of the armed forces of a belligerent state who has been captured by the enemy. JWF.

prison labor. Work performed by convicts. Although sometimes intended as punishment for crime, it is usually designed to
teach convicts useful skills and promote their rehabilitation. JWF.

private bill. A bill for the relief or special benefit of an individual or a local government unit. Those presented in Congress
mainly concern claims against the government or Civil War pensions. Many State constitutions prohibit legislation except by general law. S.

private calendar. A calendar of the House of Representatives,
officially styled the Calendar of the Committee of the Whole House,
containing all private bills. It is called on the first Tuesday of each
month in the numerical order of bills, and unless a bill is deferred
by the objection of two members it is immediately considered as a
whole under the five-minute rule. Deferred bills may be similarly
considered on the third Tuesday of each month. S.

privateer. An armed private vessel formerly commissioned
by letter of marque and reprisal to cruise against enemy naval or
merchant vessels. Privateering was abolished by the Declaration
of Paris, 1856, which the United States observed; but not being a
signatory, it could not effectively protest against Confederate privateering. S.

private international law (conflict of laws). The usages adopted
by the municipal courts of a country in dealing with cases involving
individuals whose private problems are international in scope and
are affected by conflicting regulations or are subject to the jurisdiction of two or more states. JWF.

private law. The law which regulates the relations of individuals with each other. S.

private property. *See* Property.

private rights. Rights enjoyed by the individual under law.
Many such rights are enumerated in the Bill of Rights of the federal and State constitutions. Z.

privilege. 1. Any favor or exemption granted by law, as to be
protected by the government, to enjoy life and liberty, to acquire
property, to travel from place to place, or to have access to courts
and government offices. 2. The right of freedom of debate in a
legislative body and the exemption of its members from arrest for
words spoken there. S.

privileged question. A motion which under the rules of a legislative body has precedence over other motions. S.

privy council. An organ of the British government that once possessed wide legislative, executive, and judicial powers. Today, aside from the work of its committees (such as the judicial committee) its principal function is to give formal expression to administrative orders and proclamations.   JWF.

Prize cases. Four cases, 2 Black 635 (1863), in which the Supreme Court upheld the action of President Lincoln in imposing a blockade of ports of the Southern States.   s.

prize court. A tribunal before which the legality of the capture of a vessel or other private property by a belligerent at sea is determined by condemnation (*q.v.*) proceedings.   JJR.

probate. Proof before the proper judicial officer that a document is the last will of a deceased person. It establishes *prima facie* that a will is in proper form, and that the testator was competent. s.

probate court. A court having general supervision over the administration of estates and sometimes empowered to appoint guardians or approve the adoption of minors.   s.

probation. The status of a person who is allowed his freedom after conviction for a crime subject to the condition that for a stipulated period he shall conduct himself in a manner approved by a special officer to whom he must make periodic reports.   JWF.

probe. A slang term for an investigation by a legislative committee or a grand jury.   s.

procedural right. The right of a person to have his case determined before a judicial or administrative tribunal according to the forms set forth in a constitution or law. All procedural provisions of the Constitution of the United States must be observed by national courts in the States and incorporated territories, but are not essential to due process of law in unincorporated territories if other methods insuring fairness and impartiality are followed. s.

processing tax. A tax levied on millers, packers, and other processors of agricultural products, such as was incorporated in the Agricultural Adjustment Act of 1933.   s.

proclamation. A public pronouncement or an order by a chief executive authority, which has general application in a state or community.   JWF.

production tax. A tax levied upon the producer of goods at the time they are sold. *See also* Severance tax.   s.

pro forma **amendment.** An amendment — *e.g.*, to strike out the last word — proposed for the purpose of allowing a member to continue a discussion in a legislative body.   s.

progressive. 1. One who favors the gradual introduction of political and social reforms. 2. A member of the national Progressive party of 1912, or of the present Wisconsin party of that name, or a supporter of the independent candidacy of Robert M. LaFollette for the presidency in 1924.   JWF.

Progressive Labor party. A socialist party in New York in 1887. s.

Progressive party. A third party composed largely of dissatisfied Republicans which in 1912 nominated Theodore Roosevelt for President and Hiram Johnson for Vice President, and demanded primary elections, direct election of Senators, woman suffrage, limited recall of judicial decisions, abolition of the injunction in labor disputes, enactment of child labor, minimum wage, and employers' liability laws, scientific tariff making, etc. Its ticket received 4,119,507 popular, and 88 electoral, votes. s.

progressive taxation. Taxes, especially those on income and inheritances, levied upon different amounts at percentage rates which increase more sharply than the increase of the tax bases. s.

prohibition. The public policy of entirely forbidding, by national or State law or constitutional amendment, the manufacture, transportation, or sale of intoxicating beverages except for medicinal or scientific purposes. s.

Prohibition party. A minor party advocating prohibition, and sometimes other reforms, founded in 1869 and in continuous existence since that date, though its highest popular vote for a presidential candidate was 271,058 (1892) and it rarely influenced the outcome of an election. s.

prohibition, writ of. *See* Writ of prohibition.

proletariat. The working class. s.

promotion. Advancement to a higher rank with duties of greater responsibility usually, but not necessarily, accompanied by an increase in salary. The basic standards for promotion are seniority and ability as measured by efficiency ratings or new examinations. The latter are justified as a means of removing political influence. s.

propaganda. The utilization of words, objects, or persons in an attempt to influence or control the opinion and overt actions of groups and individuals. cs-h.

property. Exclusive possession and enjoyment of something which has economic value including anything tangible or an idea, process, privilege, or interest. The extent of any property right is determined by the law. z.

property qualification. The requirement that a voter must be the owner of real (later personal) property of a certain acreage or value. It existed in all the colonies, but disappeared by 1856, only to be revived by several Southern States after 1890 as an alternative to other qualifications. s.

proportional representation. A system of minority representation based on the theory that interests, opinions, and party affiliations should be represented rather than geographical areas. Large political subdivisions are the unit for elections, and they are entitled to three or more representatives as fixed by law or determined by total popular vote. Under the list system voters may express a preference for a whole list of candidates, and representatives are apportioned among various lists according to the number of votes each list receives. Under the single transferable vote, or Hare, system each voter expresses a first choice for a single candidate, and second and other choices for as many candidates as there are seats to be filled. The first choices are counted and an electoral quota is determined (*see* Droop quota). All candidates whose vote equals the quota are declared elected, and surplus votes cast for them, selected at random, are transferred to candidates named as second choices. If anyone's vote at this point equals the quota, he is declared elected and his surplus votes are transferred according to the third choices indicated by the voters. The weakest candidates are then successively eliminated and their votes are transferred, as indicated above, until all seats

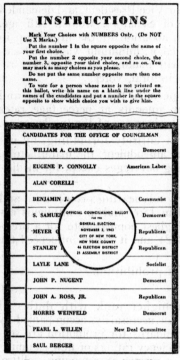

INSTRUCTIONS

Mark Your Choices with NUMBERS Only. (Do NOT Use X Marks.)

Put the number 1 in the square opposite the name of your first choice.

Put the number 2 opposite your second choice, the number 3, opposite your third choice, and so on. You may mark as many choices as you please.

Do not put the same number opposite more than one name.

To vote for a person whose name is not printed on this ballot, write his name on a blank line under the names of the candidates and put a number in the square opposite to show which choice you wish to give him.

CANDIDATES FOR THE OFFICE OF COUNCILMAN

WILLIAM A. CARROLL	Democrat
EUGENE P. CONNOLLY	American Labor
ALAN CORELLI	
BENJAMIN J.	Communist
S. SAMUE	Democrat
MEYER	Republican
STANLEY	Republican
LAYLE LANE	Socialist
JOHN P. NUGENT	Democrat
JOHN A. ROSS, JR.	Republican
MORRIS WEINFELD	Democrat
PEARL L. WILLEN	New Deal Committee
SAUL BERGER	

OFFICIAL COUNCILMANIC BALLOT

GENERAL ELECTION
NOVEMBER 2, 1943
CITY OF NEW YORK,
NEW YORK COUNTY
46 ELECTION DISTRICT
21 ASSEMBLY DISTRICT

Proportional representation ballot
(New York City)

are filled. Experience with proportional representation on the Continent of Europe indicates that it tends to divide the electorate, create "splinter" parties, and make less certain the establishment of a responsible and durable government.   s.

proprietary colony. One of several English colonies founded and administered by private individuals or companies under a grant by royal authority.   s.

prorogation. Deferment or termination of the session of a deliberative assembly by royal authority. It has been unknown in the United States since the colonial period.   JWF.

prosecuting attorney. A locally elected officer who represents the State in securing indictments or informations and in prosecuting criminal cases before a court. He sometimes serves as the legal adviser of local government bodies concerning their official duties and powers.   JWF.

prosecution. 1. The conduct of a criminal proceeding before a judicial tribunal including all steps from the indictment or information to the final decision. 2. The party, usually the State, which conducts a criminal proceeding against an accused person. JWF.

protection. 1. Favor granted to economic interests within a country through the imposition of tariffs on imported goods so high as to exclude them from effective competition with domestic products: usually justified for the public reasons of encouraging the establishment of new industries or preserving those in existence, of making a country self-sufficient in case of foreign war, or of maintaining or increasing employment, wages, and the standard of living. 2. Immunity from prosecution granted for partisan or corrupt reasons to criminals or underworld characters engaged in gambling, prostitution, or other illegal transactions. S.

protective tariff. A rate of duty imposed under the principle of protection (*q.v.*); or a tariff law containing many protective rates, as opposed to a revenue tariff which is enacted primarily for the purpose of yielding revenue from duties on goods imported. S.

protectorate. A state which by treaty has placed itself under the protection of a stronger power, yielding up its control over foreign affairs, but retaining self-government in domestic matters, though the protecting state is usually granted the right to intervene in certain circumstances. A colonial protectorate is a district controlled by a state to the exclusion of other states but not claimed as part of its territory. S.

protest vote. A vote cast, generally for the candidates of a minor party, because of a voter's dislike for a measure or policy pursued by his own party. S.

protocol. 1. A memorandum of negotiations or of preliminary conclusions arrived at by diplomacy. Ratification of a protocol gives it the force of a treaty. 2. Diplomatic or state ceremonial etiquette. JWF.

province. A territorial unit of a state, as in Canada and certain European countries; before the American Revolution, one of the colonies governed directly under royal authority. S.

provisional appointment. An appointment to a civil service position made prior to the applicant's taking an examination or the certification of the results. It is supposed to be vacated if the applicant does not qualify within a reasonable time. S.

provisional government. A temporary government set up during, or immediately after, a revolutionary overturn of the established order and functioning until a new definitive regime has been provided. JWF.

provisional order. An administrative order issued by a British minister or subordinate in anticipation of parliamentary authority which may subsequently be given in an omnibus statute called a Provisional Orders Confirmation Bill. JWF.

proxy. A person who casts a vote in place of another; or the instrument which authorizes him to do so.   s.

prudent investment theory. A theory of the valuation of public utilities based on the historical cost of property minus the amount represented by imprudent expenditures.   s.

public administration. *See* Administration.

public bill. A bill concerning a subject of general public interest, as opposed to a private bill (*q.v.*)   s.

Public Buildings Administration. A division, created in 1939, of the Federal Works Agency which, under the direction of the Commissioner of Public Buildings, supervises the construction, maintenance, and repair of public buildings of the national government.   z.

public corporation. An artificial person created for convenience in the administration of purely public affairs. Unlike a private corporation it has no protection against legislative acts altering or even repealing its charter.   s.

public crib. The pay roll of a national, State, local, or municipal government.   s.

public debt. The principal amount and unpaid interest of all outstanding bonds, notes, bills, and other evidences of a government's indebtedness resulting from past borrowings. In 1932, the gross national debt of the United States was about 19½ billion dollars; a decade later it had mounted to somewhat less than 77 billion dollars as a result of the unprecedented borrowings made to finance the depression and military requirements. It is freely predicted that before the end of World War II, the national debt will total upwards of 300 billion dollars. The gross public debt of States and local subdivisions (1943) is upwards of 20 billion dollars.   z.

public defender. An official in a few cities and counties of the United States whose duty it is to defend persons accused of crime. z.

public domain. Lands over which the United States exercises proprietary rights. The original public domain included areas ceded to the United States by some of the original States of the Union and all accessions of continental territory after the Revolution except Texas. Many generous grants of public lands have been made to States for educational purposes, and the liberal homestead policy pursued after 1862 has resulted in the transfer of vast areas to private ownership. What remains of the public domain now totals approximately 411,000,000 acres. It includes national parks, forests, grazing areas, and Indian reservations.   z.

public finance. A science lying along the border between political science and economics and partaking of some of the characteristics of both, which deals with governmental expenditures, taxation and borrowing, and public financial policy and administration.   s.

public health laboratory. A laboratory maintained by a State or municipality to produce, or test the purity of, vaccines and biological products used in the treatment of disease and to conduct research in the prevention of epidemic diseases.   z.

Public Health Service. A service, the origins of which go back to 1798, first known by its present title in 1912 and since 1939 a part of the Federal Security Agency. It engages in research in the causes and prevention of human disease; issues health information to the public; enforces quarantine laws at ports of entry; provides hospitalization for various classes of patients eligible under national laws; and co-operates with State and local authorities in public health programs.   JMCC.

public health work. Activities of both public and private agencies to safeguard and improve the health of the people. Public activities include health education, physical examination of school children, research in the causes of disease, quarantine, enforcement of health and sanitary regulations, collection of vital statistics, and provision of facilities for treatment. Private agencies engage principally in health education, medical research, and treatment of special diseases.   JMCC.

public interest. *See* Business affected with a public interest.

publicity laws. Laws requiring the publication of certain facts, enacted on the theory that publication will alleviate evils. Examples of such laws are "blue-sky" laws (*q.v.*); national and State laws requiring the filing by candidates or party committees of statements concerning campaign funds and expenditures; and laws requiring lobbyists to file statements of the conditions of their employment. s.

publicity pamphlet. A pamphlet prepared and distributed by State authority before a primary or election which contains information concerning candidates and party programs.   s.

public lands. *See* Public domain.

public law. The law which regulates the organization of government, the powers and duties of its departments and officers, and its relations with individuals.   s.

Public office is a public trust. A statement of President Grover Cleveland which became a slogan of civil service reformers. s.

public opinion. In an operational sense, in any given area or situation, the common will or attitude of a sufficient number of persons or groups to have a determining influence on a person or thing within a given period or at a specific time. The influence may be negative, positive, or neutral; the attitude or will may or may not be formally registered or expressed. In a psychological sense, public opinion is the collective response to given stimuli.   CS-H.

public purpose. The constitutional requirement that the purpose of any tax, police regulation, or particular exertion of the power of eminent domain shall be the convenience, safety, or welfare of the entire community and not the welfare of a specific individual or class of persons. The distinction between private and public purpose is determined largely by usage or by the courts. z.

Public Roads Administration. A division of the Federal Works Agency which, in co-operation with State highway departments, administers national grants-in-aid and other national appropriations for the construction and maintenance of arterial highways and, in co-operation with other national agencies, constructs national park and forest roads. z.

public school. An elementary or high school established and maintained by authorities of local school districts in accordance with State law and financed by local property and other taxes and by direct grants from the State. z.

public service commission. An administrative agency of three or more members set up by the State legislature to regulate rates and services of public utilities. z.

public utility. A privately owned and operated business whose services are so essential to the general public as to justify the grant of special franchises for the use of public property or of the right of eminent domain, in consideration of which the owners must serve all persons who apply, without discrimination except where such discrimination is required by law. It is nearly always a natural or virtual monopoly. It may be for the production and distribution of a commodity like gas, electricity, water, or steam; for transportation, as a railroad, street railway, bus line, taxicab company, ferry, or oil pipe line; for communication, as a telegraph or telephone company; or it may be a dock, wharf, grain elevator, or stockyard. It is subject to a great variety of public regulations, especially as to its financial structure, the rates it charges, and the standards of its services. s.

Public Utility Holding Company Act. An act of Congress Aug. 26, 1935, which placed virtually all gas and electric utility holding companies under the jurisdiction of the Securities and Exchange Commission and gave it authority to bring about geographic and corporate simplification and supervise security transactions, dividends, loans, and contracts between the holding company and its subsidiaries. s.

public works. Highways, bridges, levees, or similar constructions, or major engineering developments such as irrigation, power, drainage, or navigation projects financed or undertaken by government for the convenience and welfare of the community. z.

Public Works Administration. A division of the Federal Works Agency which, in co-operation with local governments, provided loans and subsidies for public works built by private contractors. Its organization and activities were liquidated after June, 1943. JMCC.

Puerto Rico. An unincorporated territory of the United States with an area of 3,434 sq. mi. and a population (1940) of 1,869,255, lying east of Hispaniola in the West Indies. It was acquired from Spain in 1898 and governed under military law until 1900, and under a governor, commission, and popularly elected lower house, 1900-17. The organic act passed by Congress in 1917 made the people citizens of the United States and granted a bill of rights not including indictment or trial by jury. The governor, judges, and three other officers are appointed by the President. The acts of the popularly elective bicameral legislature are subject to the veto of the governor and the President and to disallowance by Congress. If it fails to make appropriations for any year, the appropriations for the preceding year are continued. Puerto Rico is represented in Washington by a resident commissioner who may speak but not vote in the House of Representatives. s.

Pujo Committee. A special committee created by the House of Representatives in 1912 to determine whether or not there was a "money trust." s.

pull. A slang term for hidden influence with an official or organization that is in a position to grant favors. s.

Pullman Strike. A strike of Pullman employees in 1894 actively supported by the American Railway Union. Their stoppage of trains in Chicago and consequent interference with interstate commerce and the mails led President Cleveland to send federal troops to the area over the protest of Governor Altgeld of Illinois and to the issuance of an injunction against the strikers by the federal Circuit Court. Defiance of the injunction by Eugene V. Debs and other union leaders resulted in their conviction and subsequent incarceration for contempt of court. z.

pump priming. Huge government expenditures financed mainly by borrowing for the purpose of stimulating production, employment, and general economic activity during a depression. s.

punishment. The penalty imposed upon a convicted person by a court in accordance with the law. The Eighth Amendment to the Constitution prohibits national courts from inflicting "cruel and unusual punishments." z.

purge. The elimination of troublesome members of the party in power by officially ordered assassination, as in contemporary dictatorships; or use of executive influence to encompass their defeat in primary or election campaigns. s.

Purple Heart, Order of the. A decoration established by General George Washington at Newburgh, N.Y., Aug. 7, 1782, and revived by an order of the War Department Feb. 22, 1932, as a recognition for soldiers wounded in action or cited for gallantry. s.

pussyfooting. The action of a candidate or official in making general or ambiguous statements, or none at all, on some issue on which a straightforward statement is expected. s.

Q

qualification. A requirement or condition, as of age, citizenship, residence, character, or education, which an individual must possess before he is eligible for an office or participation in the suffrage, jury service, etc. s.

quarantine. The isolation of persons afflicted with, or suspected of having been exposed to, a contagious disease; the stoppage of the travel of persons or the transportation of plants or animals from an infected area; also the place where persons are detained. Both national and State governments may establish quarantines. State quarantines may be sustained even though they affect foreign or interstate commerce. s.

quartering. The billeting of soldiers or the commandeering of billets for soldiers. The Third Amendment to the Constitution declares that no soldier shall be quartered in any house in time of peace without the owner's consent; nor in time of war, except as prescribed by law. z.

Quartermaster Corps. A division of the War Department charged with feeding, clothing, and transporting the army. z.

quarter sessions. A court with criminal jurisdiction in some States which sits at intervals of three months. s.

quasi corporation. A local government unit, such as a county, township, or special district; or officers therein, such as a school board, which, though not given general corporate powers, have acquired by statute or prescription a corporate personality at least to the extent that they may sue or be sued. s.

quasi-judicial. Resembling a judicial action or procedure; specifically the action of an administrative body with limited powers to make decisions affecting the rights of persons under the law. jwf.

quasi-legislative. Resembling a legislative body or lawmaking procedure but lacking the general competence of a legislature or the power to clothe decisions with legislative finality. jwf.

quasi-public corporation. A private corporation engaged in rendering essential services to the public and therefore allowed to acquire rights of way under eminent domain. s.

Quebec Act. An act of Parliament, 1774, organizing the government of Quebec and extending its boundaries southwestward to the Ohio and Mississippi rivers. *See* map, page 257. s.

question. A motion; the chief point of inquiry or discussion. s.

question of privilege. A matter concerning the privileges of a legislative body or one of its members.   s.

Quids. Members of the Jeffersonian Republican party led, 1804-08, by John Randolph, who opposed some of Jefferson's policies and favored the nomination of Monroe to succeed him.   s.

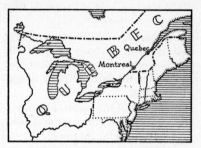

Boundaries of Quebec, 1774

quisling. A sympathizer with a foreign country and potential traitor to his own who may become an actual traitor in wartime — so called from Major Vidkun Quisling, head of the Nazi party in Norway and subsequently head of the German puppet government in that state. s.

quorum. The number of members who must be present in a deliberative body before business may be transacted. In both houses of Congress a quorum consists of a majority of those chosen and sworn. A smaller number may adjourn from day to day and compel the attendance of absent members. In 1890 Speaker Reed instituted the practice of counting a quorum in the House of Representatives by ordering the clerk to add to the roll the names of those present but refusing to vote.   s.

quota. A number or proportionate share which may be assigned; as, under the immigration laws of 1921, 1924, and 1929, the number of immigrants of a certain nationality who could be legally admitted every year. *See also* Electoral quota.   s.

quo warranto, writ of. A writ issued on behalf of the state to inquire into the validity of the title by which a person holds an office or a public corporation its franchise as the first step in legal proceedings to vacate it.   s.

R

rabble rouser. One who seeks support for a political or social program chiefly by means of pageantry and spellbinding calculated to arouse the emotions rather than to appeal to the reason of the masses.   jwf.

race. A body of people believed to be of common descent, or distinguished from others by physical characteristics, the most important of which is color.   s.

race discrimination. *See* Discrimination, racial; Equal protection.

race-track legislation. State statutes regulating horse racing, usually administered by a State racing commission. Payment of a fee for operating a track or holding a race meeting is usually required, and either betting may be prohibited or — what is more often the case — the proceeds of a pari-mutuel pool must be shared with the State.   z.

racketeering. Activities of organized gangsters or other criminal elements who systematically extort money from legitimate business enterprise by violence or other forms of intimidation, or by similar methods exploit illegal enterprises such as gambling or prostitution.   z.

radical. **1.** One who advocates immediate and fundamental changes in governments and laws, especially laws relating to economic and social matters. **2.** A Republican opposed to Lincoln's or Johnson's policy of reconstructing the seceded States, 1864-69. s.

Radical Democracy. The name adopted by Republican opponents of President Lincoln who in 1864 nominated John C. Frémont for President. He withdrew Sept. 21, 1864.   s.

rag baby. A nickname for greenback currency about 1876. s.

raid on the treasury. Large appropriations of public funds for the benefit of localities or special interests.   s.

railroad. A permanent double line of rails on which locomotives and cars operate for the transportation of passengers and goods. Many early railroads were partly financed by subscriptions of stock or bonds by States, municipalities, and other local subdivisions, and transcontinental lines by land grants from the national government. They are regulated by the Interstate Commerce Commission and public service commissions (*qq.v.*) and may be subject to other agencies in wartime.   s.

Railroad Retirement Board. A board of three members created by Congress in 1935 to administer retirement pensions, unemployment benefits, and a placement service for railroad employees.   z.

Rail Splitter. A campaign nickname of Abraham Lincoln. s.

rally. A party mass meeting held before election day for the purpose of getting out a large vote.   s.

Randolph plan. *See* Virginia plan.

rank. Official standing in the army or navy.   s.

ranking member. The member of a congressional committee next below the chairman in point of seniority.   s.

ranking minority member. The member of the minority party of longest continuous service on a congressional committee.   s.

rate. The unit cost of a service supplied to the public by a utility. Such cost may either be fixed in a utility's franchise or it is established by a public service commission or subject to its approval.   z.

Rathbun-Humphrey case. The case of *Rathbun* v. *United States*, 295 U.S. 602 (1935), in which the Supreme Court declared that the President's power to remove principal officers of the government at pleasure, recognized in the Myers case (*q.v.*), does not extend to members of the independent administrative commissions or to officers not performing an "executive" function.   z.

ratification. Confirmation by a state's constitutional authorities of an international agreement previously negotiated and signed by its diplomatic representatives.   JWF.

rationing. The policy of distributing available goods and services equitably among the population in time of war or other emergency when total supply has been drastically curtailed. During World War II the government limited individual consumption for particular periods and required the use of ration coupons.   z.

raw material. Any material after extraction from its natural source, but before being converted into a finished or semifinished article of commerce by processing or manufacture.   JWF.

reactionary. One who favors a return to an outmoded system. s.

reading. An essential step in the passage of a bill which used to consist in having the clerk read each bill in full on three different days. At present only the second reading in the House of Representatives, and the third in the Senate, are in full, at which time amendments may be proposed and voted on. The requirement for two other readings in each body is usually met by reading by title only.   s.

Readjusters. A party in Virginia, 1878-83, which had as its chief issue readjusting, or scaling down, the principal and interest of the State debt. It was successful in one election.   s.

real estate. Property consisting of lands and buildings.   s.

reappointment. Issuance of a new commission to an incumbent whose term of office has expired.   z.

reapportionment. A new apportionment (*q.v.*) of legislative seats among States or other units. It is required by the Constitution of the United States for seats in the House of Representatives after every decennial census.   s.

rebate. A part of the stated transportation charge refunded to the shipper. Rebates were forbidden by the Interstate Commerce Act of 1887.   s.

rebel brigadier. A Southern Democratic member of Congress during the Reconstruction period.   s.

rebus sic stantibus. A controversial doctrine of international law which holds that treaties remain valid only while "things stand as they are," and that unexpected circumstances, rendering their terms oppressive or obsolete, justify repudiation by one party.   JWF.

recall. A procedure by which a public officer may be removed from office, but usually only after six months of his term has expired, by vote of the people. It may be invoked by petition of from 10 to 35 per cent of the qualified voters (usually 25 per cent) ; and at the election the questions of removal and of the election of a successor both appear on the ballot. It may be used as to executive and legislative officers in eleven States and as to judges in eight. Many municipal charters provide for it.   s.

recall of judicial decisions. A proposal by Theodore Roosevelt in 1912 that the decision of a court might be prevented from becoming a precedent in the decision of later cases under the same law by an adverse vote of the people.   s.

recapture. 1. The retaking from the enemy of ships or goods captured by him. Recaptured private property is usually restored to the owner. 2. The taking by the public, under the provisions of a franchise or statute, of the earnings of a public utility beyond a certain fixed percentage of profit.   s.

receiver. A person appointed by a court to manage the affairs of a bankrupt or property in litigation.   z.

recess. 1. An intermission in the course of a legislative day. 2. The period during which Congress is adjourned.   s.

recess appointment. An appointment of an officer of the United States made by the President on his sole authority when the Senate is not in session. It expires on the last day of the succeeding session of the Senate.   s.

recess committee. A legislative committee appointed to conduct an investigation in the interim between sessions.   s.

reciprocal legislation. Legislation separately enacted by two or more states which establishes a common policy on some issue or insures a mutually beneficial exchange of some prerogative or right.   z.

reciprocal trade agreement. An arrangement between two countries in which one agrees to lower certain tariff rates, buy the other's produce, or supply its wants in exchange for equivalent favors.   JWF.

reciprocity. The granting by one nation to another of special commercial privileges, such as lower tariff duties on its products, in consideration of special privileges granted by it.   s.

reclamation. The draining of marshy or swampy land or the irrigation of desert areas, with electric power occasionally an incidental product.   s.

recognition. Acknowledgment by one state of the existence of another state or government. The President may recognize a foreign country by receiving its diplomatic envoy, sending a diplomat to it, negotiating a treaty with it, or issuing an appropriate proclamation.   JAP.

recognizance. A bond recorded with a magistrate guaranteeing appearance of an accused person before a court or the fulfillment of some other legal obligation under penalty of forfeiting the bond so recorded.   z.

recommittal. The action of a legislative body in sending a measure back to a committee with or without instructions.   s.

reconsideration. Renewed discussion and vote upon a legislative measure already passed.   s.

reconstruction. The process by which the national government, during and after the Civil War, reorganized the governments of the seceded States, generally under military authority; forced the adoption of provisions in their constitutions guaranteeing the rights and privileges of their colored populations and recognizing their obligations to the Union as a prerequisite to readmission; and finally readmitted them.   s.

Reconstruction Finance Corporation. A corporation of the national government chartered in 1932. Its management is confided to a board of five directors appointed by the President and the Senate of whom the chairman and two other members constitute an executive committee. The Corporation may make emergency or distress loans to banks, insurance companies, railroads, and mortgage companies, taking their stocks, bonds, or other evidences of indebtedness as security; it extends its credit to local government bodies and to a great variety of public and semipublic co-operative associations; it has lent at least a half billion dollars to the Export-Import Bank of Washington to aid in stabilizing Western Hemisphere markets; and it is authorized to charter and capitalize public corporations for producing, buying, selling, storing, or dealing in strategic or critical materials. The Corporation issues its own bonds, notes, and debentures; it has a capital stock of $325,000,000 and outstanding loans totalling several billion dollars.   z.

record. The official stenographic account of the proceedings of a court of justice or similar tribunal.   z.

recorder. 1. A judicial officer in some cities. 2. A local government officer in whose office deeds, mortgages, liens, and other documents are registered.   s.

record vote. A vote in which the response of each individual is required to be recorded, as in either house of Congress by yeas and nays on roll call on the demand of one fifth of the members, or when voting on a bill after a presidential veto.   s.

recruiting. The whole process, including examinations and practical tests, by which a civil service commission or personnel officer attempts to secure an adequate and competent staff of public employees.   z.

red. A popular designation for an adherent to socialism or communism, derived from the red flag, symbol of international Marxism.   z.

Red Cross. *See* American National Red Cross.

redemption. The payment of principal and unpaid interest on bonds or other obligations that have matured.   z.

rediscounting. A second discounting (advancing of principal less interest) on a promissory note: the process by which one bank, as, *e.g.,* a federal reserve bank, advances funds to another bank on the security of commercial paper originally discounted by it.   z.

redistricting. The action of a State legislature in abolishing old, and creating new, congressional districts following a reapportionment of Representatives in Congress or at other times; also the readjustment of the boundaries of State senatorial and assembly districts.   s.

redress of grievances. The correction of abuses in the government of a state. The right of the individual to petition for redress of grievances, one of the oldest of British constitutional rights, is guaranteed in the First Amendment of the Constitution of the United States.   z.

red tape. Rigid observance of official routine, including the routing of requests and orders "through the regular channels" and other procedures which result in delay and inaction.   s.

re-eligibility. Eligibility for election or appointment to an office after a certain period of service: generally assumed to exist unless provided to the contrary by a constitution, statute, or custom.   s.

re-entry permit. Permission given to an alien who has previously resided in the United States to return to this country after a brief sojourn abroad.   jwf.

referee. 1. An official appointed by a court to act for it in some aspects of a pending proceeding. 2. A member of an arbitral or similar body.   z.

reference. The action of a legislative body, usually by, or at the direction of, its presiding officer, in sending a bill to a committee; or of a court in referring a matter to a referee.   s.

referendum. The act or process of referring to the electorate for approval or rejection the draft of a proposed new State constitution or amendment (constitutional referendum) or of a law passed by the legislature (statutory referendum). The constitutional referendum is mandatory in practically every State, and often an extramajority vote is required for adoption. The statutory referendum is provided for in 20 States. It may be invoked during a period of, usually, 90 days between the passage of a measure and the date it goes into effect by a petition signed by a certain number or percentage (ordinarily 5 or 6 per cent) of the voters. In the general or special election which follows, an adverse majority of the total vote cast on a measure suffices for its rejection. The referendum may not be invoked on laws which the legislature declares to be emergency measures. In many States and municipalities a legislative body may of its own motion refer a controversial measure to a popular vote (optional referendum) ; or the law may provide that certain kinds of measures, like those for the creation of bonded indebtedness, must be submitted (mandatory referendum). s.

reforestation. The scientific replanting of denuded forest lands, an activity carried on in the United States under the supervision of the Department of Agriculture and other national and local agencies. z.

reformatory. A penal institution for the incarceration and rehabilitation of young or first offenders or those not deemed incorrigible. z.

refugee. One who has fled his native land to escape discrimination or persecution. JWF.

refund. The return of that portion of a tax or other payment which was in excess of what the law or contractual obligation required. z.

refunding. The process of issuing new bonds to replace previous obligations that are retired: a means of postponing debt redemption. s.

regent. One who assumes the duties of a monarch during his minority, absence, or incapacity. JWF.

regents, board of. A body of officials appointed to direct and supervise an educational institution or, as in New York, the whole educational system. JWF.

regionalism. Any theory of territorial decentralization of power in a state; in the United States, the view that the existing 48 States should be superseded by nine or more great districts or regions. z.

register. 1. A list of the personnel of an organization. 2. An official record of vital or other statistics. 3. A local official who keeps a record of vital and related statistics. z.

registered bond. Any bond the number of which is recorded by the seller in the name of the purchaser and which only the latter or those legally authorized to act for him can redeem. z.

registered mail. Valuable mail given special protection against loss in transmission on payment by the sender of a special fee, a record of which is stamped on the envelope or container. z.

registration. Official enrollment of persons with various data concerning them, for the administration of election, selective service, rationing, lobbying, or other laws. Registration of voters is now required in all parts of the United States except in rural regions in a few States. It is either by personal appearance of the voter before a board, or by official canvassers. The process may be repeated before each election (periodic registration) or lists may be made up at longer intervals and kept up to date by a permanent staff (permanent registration).   S.

registration area. That part, now comprising nearly the whole, of the United States in which the official recording of births and deaths conforms to standards set by the Census Bureau.   S.

registry. The compulsory listing of a ship in the register or record of ships subject to the maritime regulations of a particular country.   JWF.

regressive taxation. The imposition of any tax which bears relatively more heavily upon poorer, than upon more wealthy, taxpayers.   S.

regular. A voter or office holder who consistently follows the decisions of his party organization.   S.

regulation. 1. An official clarification of a statute or administrative order or ordinance issued usually by the official charged with its enforcement. 2. Generally the activity of government in controlling the affairs, and particularly the economic affairs, of the community.   JWF.

regulator. 1. A North Carolinian who, 1767-71, engaged in riotous acts against extortionate lawyers and officials. 2. One of a self-constituted band of law enforcers in a frontier community. 3. A bill introduced for the purpose of extorting money from a company but ostensibly for regulating it.   S.

rehabilitation. Restoration of a person to productive earning power.   S.

rehearing. Formal presentation of part or all of the testimony and pleadings in a particular cause a second time.   Z.

reinstatement. Restoration of a person to an office.   S.

rejection. Refusal, as by the Senate of the United States, to confirm an appointment or to ratify a treaty.   S.

religious test. The legal requirement that in order to hold an office or exercise some legal privilege a person shall publicly proclaim that he supports a particular religious faith or belief. The Constitution (Art. VI, par. 3) states that "no religious test shall ever be required as a qualification to any office or public trust under the United States."   Z.

remand. The act of returning an accused person to custody. Z.

Remember Pearl Harbor. An American rallying cry in World War II. Pearl Harbor, a naval and army base in the Territory of Hawaii, was perfidiously attacked by Japanese naval and air forces Dec. 7, 1941.   S.

Remember the Alamo. A rallying cry of Texans in their war for independence, recalling the massacre by Mexican forces of a Texan garrison at the Alamo, a mission near San Antonio.   S.

Remember the Maine. An American rallying cry during the Spanish-American War. *See Maine, The.* s.

Remember the River Raisin. An American rallying cry recalling the murder by Indians of American prisoners who fell into the hands of the British at the battle of the River Raisin, Jan. 22, 1813. s.

remission. A return of part of a fine, or reduction or abatement of some other penalty inflicted by a court. z.

remonstrance. A formal protest against the policy or conduct of the government or certain officials and a demand for reform, drawn up and presented by aggrieved citizens or their representatives; *e.g.,* the Grand Remonstrance of 1641 addressed to the Crown by the British Parliament. JWF.

removal from office. Dismissal from office by competent authority. The Constitution of the United States makes no specific provision for removal except when an officer is convicted after impeachment. From the beginning of the national government it was generally conceded that the President was vested with the removal power. But the Tenure of Office Act (*q.v.*) of 1867 (repealed in 1887) and an act of 1876 relating to certain postmasters required the consent of the Senate to the removal of an officer whose appointment was made with its consent. In 1926 the Supreme Court determined in the Myers case (*q.v.*) that the President alone had power to remove officers appointed with the consent of the Senate because of the general grant of executive power and as a necessary adjunct to his duty to "take care that the laws be faithfully executed." Under the decision in the Rathbun-Humphrey case (*q.v.*), his power does not extend to members of such bodies as the Federal Trade Commission created by Congress to exercise quasi-legislative and quasi-judicial powers. Congress may by law regulate the removal of inferior officers appointed by heads of departments. The provisions of State constitutions and laws rarely grant to the governor an unrestricted power of removal, even of officers appointed by him. s.

removal of cases. The transfer of cases prior to a decision from a State to a national court, as may be done in a civil case on application of the defendant when the parties are of diverse citizenship or when a federal question is involved, if the amount in controversy is $3,000 or more; or in a criminal case if the accused claims that he was acting under color of federal authority. s.

rendition. The return of a fugitive from justice to the State in which he is accused of having committed a crime, by the order of the governor of the State to which the fugitive has gone. The duty of rendition is imposed by the Constitution, but the courts have found no appropriate means to enforce it. Occasionally governors have refused to grant it. s.

reparations. Monetary or material compensation for loss or damage paid by the party held responsible to the injured party.   JWF.

repatriation. Restoration of prisoners of war or refugees to their own country.   s.

repeal. The abrogation of a law by legislative action, either by express declaration or by the passage of a later act which contains provisions repugnant to the terms of existing law.   s.

repeater. A voter who illegally casts more than one vote. s.

replacement cost. The amount required to buy new equipment of up-to-date design which would perform the identical function of the equipment already in use.   s.

report. 1. The official printed record of the court reporter of a case or controversy. It contains a statement of the principal facts, the opinion, decision, and judgment of the court and sometimes arguments in counsel's brief. 2. Findings and recommendations of a legislative committee appointed to examine a bill or make an investigation.   z.

representation. The function of a member of a legislative assembly who is assumed to speak for, and safeguard, the interests of the people of a geographic or other constituency which elected him. The origin of the theory of representation is traced by some writers to the Teutonic folkmote and by others to the practices of the monastic orders, particularly of the Dominican Order. In mediaeval assemblies, representation had primarily a class or corporate character; that is, members were selected by classes or estates of the realm and they were expected to concern themselves exclusively with the interests of the constituencies which chose them and even be guided in their endeavors by explicit instructions issued by their principals. In most contemporary democratic parliaments, on the other hand, members are chosen from geographic districts rather than by occupational or social groups. Members of such assemblies are not regarded as mere agents of their constituents, subject to explicit instructions, but as stewards who exercise their discretion and attempt to identify local interests with those of the state as a whole. The doctrine of agency nevertheless persists, particularly in the United States. Members of Congress are compelled by usage to reside in the districts they represent; they attempt to secure patronage and administrative favors for their constituents; and their legislative attitude is greatly affected by the temper of electoral and public opinion in their respective districts.   z.

representative. 1. One chosen to act for a popular or other constituency in a legislative assembly. 2. A member of the House of Representatives or of a State legislative chamber so named. z.

representative government. A government in which there is an independent legislature composed of representatives freely elected by a numerous body of the people and endowed with substantial legislative and fiscal powers. s.

reprieve. A delay for a certain time in the execution of a sentence, granted either by a court or, more usually, by the pardoning power. s.

reprimand. A public reproof for indecorous conduct or for inefficiency or dereliction of duty directed to a subordinate by an administrative superior or by a judge to some officer or attendant of the court. z.

reprisal. A retaliatory punishment inflicted by one country upon another for an allegedly illegal act. JWF.

reproduction cost. The amount required to purchase new equipment identical in design with existing equipment at current market prices. s.

republic. A government in which the generality of adult citizens determine policies and laws through elected officials and representatives and in which no individual has a vested right to office. z.

republican form of government. A government which is administered under the forms of law by responsible officers chosen directly or indirectly by a numerous electorate. The determination as to whether or not a State has a republican form of government within the meaning of the Constitution is a political question. Either house of Congress may refuse to admit members chosen from a State, or Congress or the President may determine which of two rival governments in a State is the rightful authority and intervene in its behalf. s.

Republican party. A major party which arose in 1854 out of the widespread dissatisfaction with the Kansas-Nebraska Bill and quickly gained adherents among former Whigs and Democrats in all the Northern States. At first devoted to preventing the spread of slavery into the territories, it added to its platform, in 1860, advocacy of protective tariffs and free homesteads for settlers. It was later identified with the adoption of the Civil War amendments; the harsh reconstruction policy toward the Southern States; the maintenance of "sound money" through the resumption of specie payments and, by 1900, the gold standard; high protective tariffs to aid American business and provide a "full dinner pail"; acquisition and retention of territory outside the continent of North America; and a self-centered foreign policy, including opposition to entry into the League of Nations. In the main it has been a sectional party supported by business interests in the East and by farmers in the West. Though it received the electoral votes of several States of the Solid South during the Reconstruction period, it received none after the withdrawal of troops from the South, 1877, until the election of 1928. From 1860 to 1928 inclusive it won all but four presidential elections, and suffered only one severe defeat, in 1912, when it was split by the Progressive movement. In the last three presidential elections it has been badly defeated; but it made substantial gains in the off-year elections in 1942.   s.

Republican party, Jeffersonian.   A major party led by Jefferson and Madison which arose about 1791 in opposition to the assumption of State debts, the chartering of the United States Bank, the excise tax, the foreign policy, and other centralizing and loose construction tendencies of Washington's administration. It lost the election of 1796 by three electoral votes; but carried all subsequent elections until, by 1820, it had no national opposition. Long tenure in office caused it to relax, in practice, many strict construction principles on which it had been founded. It was dispersed in 1824 into several personal followings; and in 1828 split into National and Democratic-Republican wings.   s.

repudiation.   Refusal to honor an obligation, particularly the declaration of a state that it considers itself no longer bound to pay a debt it has contracted.   JWF.

res adjudicata.   A matter upon which a competent court of law has passed judgment and which it will therefore not re-examine.   JWF.

reservation.   1. An area set aside for exclusive public use, particularly for military or naval purposes or for occupancy by an Indian tribe.   2. A special condition attached to a state's accession to a multilateral treaty or convention.   3. A modification by the United States Senate of the draft of a treaty submitted to it for ratification. Such a "reservation" has the effect of rejecting the draft treaty, but carries an implied promise that if a new treaty embodying the "reservation" is negotiated by the President with a foreign power it will be ratified by the Senate.   JWF.

Reserve Officers' Training Corps.   A student corps for training in military science and tactics maintained by the War Department in various American colleges and other educational institutions. Students who qualify after pursuing the course of instruction may become reserve officers in the army.   z.

residence.   The place where a person habitually lives, though he may be temporarily absent or lodge elsewhere.   s.

resident commissioner.   An official agent sent to the national capital by an unincorporated territory such as Puerto Rico. He may speak but not vote in the House of Representatives.   JWF.

residuary powers.   Powers of government which remained under the control of the States after the adoption of the Constitution of the United States.   s.

resignation.   Relinquishment of an office by one who has qualified for it. It should be tendered to the person who has power to fill the vacancy, and becomes valid only upon acceptance.   s.

resolution.   A measure proposed or passed by one or both houses of Congress or of a State legislature or by each acting separately (*see* Joint resolution; Concurrent resolution) which expresses legislative policy or opinion, censure, thanks, condolence, etc.; or provides for subsidiary or procedural matters. A joint resolution has the effect of law. It ranks in formal dignity below a bill and is supposed to be used only for minor or transient matters; but this principle has frequently been violated.   s.

responsibility, legal. Accountability under the law for the proper performance of a duty.   jwf.

responsibility, political. Accountability of legislative and executive officers to the electorate, enforced in the United States by such means as popular election of officers, requirements for the publicity of proceedings, publication of reports, free access to public records, and provision for impeachment or recall, or the initiative and referendum.   s.

restraint of trade. A concerted effort by private persons or organizations to limit the free flow of trade or commerce or to reduce or hamper competition.   z.

restricted district. Under zoning regulations, an area in which the use of land for certain purposes is not permitted.   s.

restriction. A governmentally imposed restraint or limitation upon erstwhile free or relatively free action; *e.g.,* a statutory limitation upon immigration.   z.

resulting powers. Powers of the national government derived, not from any single express or implied grant of powers, but from a combination of several grants or the aggregate of power granted to the national government.   s.

Resumption Act. A law of Congress Jan. 14, 1875, providing for gradual reduction in the amount of greenbacks outstanding and resumption of specie payments on Jan. 1, 1879.   s.

retired list. Members of the armed forces who, because of advanced age, long service, or disability, are relieved of active duty but still receive some pay and allowances.   jwf.

retirement. Permanent withdrawal of a person from public employment as a result of advanced age, disability, or illness, usually with a retirement allowance or pension.   s.

retrenchment. Abolition of offices or curtailment of services in order to reduce expenditures.   z.

retroactive legislation. Laws applying to conditions or circumstances before their enactment. The constitutional prohibition against ex post facto laws (*q.v.*) applies only to retroactive criminal laws which operate to the disadvantage of the accused. It does not apply to civil laws. The chief protection of the individual against retroactive civil laws is the constitutional provision that no State may impair the obligation of a contract.   s.

returning board. A body, usually ex officio, which canvasses the results of an election.   s.

returns. The results of an election as certified by the proper election officials.   s.

revenue. A government's income from all sources, the principal one being taxation.   z.

revenue cutter. An armed patrol boat used to pursue and investigate craft suspected of smuggling.   jwf.

reversal. The action of an appellate court in rendering judgment in a case under review contrary to the judgment of the court or tribunal in which the case originated.   z.

review. A re-examination of some matter, such as the decision of a lower court, the findings of a board, or the valuation of property for the purpose of assessing taxes, by a higher court or administrative officer or tribunal.   s.

Revised Statutes. A collection of the general and permanent laws of the United States enacted by Congress, June 22, 1874.   s.

revolt. 1. A violent uprising against public authority, usually confined to a district or province, for the correction of intolerable wrongs or to obtain autonomy or independence (*see also* Revolution). 2. Separation of a minority group from a political party whose policies it can no longer support.   jwf.

revolution. The overthrow of a constitution or government as a result of armed rebellion of the citizens or by peaceful extra-legal means generally acquiesced in.   s.

Revolution, American. A war between thirteen British North American colonies and the mother country resulting partly from British acts in imposing taxes and regulations which were regarded as tyrannical in America, and partly from a growing sense of American nationality and power. Hostilities began with a skirmish at Lexington, Mass., Apr. 19, 1775, and virtually ended, after substantial military and naval help had been extended by France, with the surrender of Cornwallis at Yorktown, Va., Oct. 19, 1781. Preliminary articles of peace between the United States and Great Britain were signed at Paris, Nov. 30, 1782, and the definitive treaty, Sept. 3, 1783. It was ratified by Congress Jan. 4, 1784. s.

revolving fund. A special fund set up by appropriation to provide working capital for a public business enterprise. Amounts paid out or loaned are theoretically expected to return to the fund without diminution and to provide the basis for continuing payments or loans.   s.

R.F.C. *See* Reconstruction Finance Corporation.

Rhode Island. One of the original States, though it did not ratify the Constitution of the United States until May 29, 1790. Capital, Providence; area, 1,300 sq. mi.; population (1940), 713,-

346; presidential electors, 4. The present constitution was adopted in 1843. With minor exceptions all adult citizens may vote in national and State elections. s.

riches and reform. An epithet invented by Charles F. Murphy, former leader of Tammany Hall, and used by machine politicians to ridicule reform movements. s.

rich man's dollar. A term for the gold dollar used by advocates of greenbacks and the unlimited coinage of silver. s.

rider. An amendment, in reality a separate and extraneous measure usually of a highly controversial nature, which is added to a bill in the course of its passage in order that congressional opponents and the President will have to accept the bill with its rider or do without the bill. Riders are most frequently attached to appropriation bills despite House and Senate rules prohibiting them. s.

right. 1. A privilege or prerogative conferred upon a person or group by usage or law. A legal right may be vindicated and protected in the courts. 2. A popular designation for conservatives derived from the custom in continental European legislatures of seating members of conservative parties to the right of the presiding officer. z.

right of way. 1. A prescriptive legal right of one or more persons to traverse property belonging to another. 2. A route acquired by a public utility as a result of a public franchise or through the power of eminent domain. z.

rigid constitution. A term used by Lord Bryce to describe a constitution which sets up a complicated, involved, and difficult procedure for its formal amendment. z.

ring. The inner circle of a party machine; a group of spoilsmen who loot the public treasury for their own personal or political gain. s.

riot. The tumultuous disturbance of the peace by three or more persons unlawfully acting together for the accomplishment of some purpose by violence and terror. s.

ripper act. A law making drastic changes in administrative organization or procedures which is enacted from motives of obtaining partisan advantage or revenge usually by a party recently come to power; *e.g.,* a law abolishing existing offices and creating new ones with slightly different titles and duties; increasing or decreasing the appointing and removal power of the executive; altering the terms of a city charter; or transferring authority to grant franchises from a city to a State board, or vice versa. s.

river and harbor bills. Bills making appropriations for the improvement of rivers and harbors, long the outstanding examples of logrolling and pork-barrel tactics in Congress. s.

roads. Public rights of way for vehicular traffic. The building and maintenance of roads have been the responsibility of national, State, and local governments. The national government advanced funds for the construction of the Cumberland Road as early as 1806; but this early national interest in road building declined after 1830. The modern system of free, hardsurface, interconnected highways, called forth by the development of the motor car, has largely come into existence since 1910 and has been financed by national grants-in-aid and State contributions derived largely from the taxation of motorists. National grants began in 1916 under the terms of the Federal Highway Act; and subsequent appropriations, including direct national expenditures for work relief projects, ultimately brought the annual national contribution, prior to 1940, to about $300,000,000. Funds are expended through State highway departments under the supervision of the Public Roads Administration in the Federal Works Agency.   z.

Robinson-Patman Act. An act of Congress, 1936, the so-called "Anti-Chain Store Act," which prohibits special or disguised discounts to purchasers of commodities or any price discrimination among such purchasers where it would tend to lessen competition or create a monopoly.   z.

Rogers Act. A statute of 1924 consolidating the American diplomatic service and the consular service into a single corps. It provided for the transfer of personnel from the diplomatic to the consular ranks and vice versa and established a salary and service classification and pensions.   JWF.

roll call. The calling of the names of members of a legislative body to ascertain the presence of a quorum or for a record vote. s.

roorback. A campaign falsehood. The name is derived from the publication in 1844 of extracts from the supposed "Travels" of a fictitious Baron Roorback reflecting on James K. Polk.   s.

Roosevelt Doctrine. *See* Stewardship theory.

rooster. An emblem of the Democratic party dating from about 1842.   s.

Root-Takahiri Agreement. An executive agreement of 1908 between Japan and the United States in which each promised to respect the other's Pacific possessions, to preserve the independence of China, and to respect the equal opportunity of all nations to trade with China.   JWF.

rotation in office. Rapid turnover in the personnel of appointive offices, a characteristic of the spoils system introduced under President Jackson in 1829, and contemporaneously justified as a means of educating a large number of citizens in political affairs.   s.

rotten borough. An English term for a parliamentary constituency containing few voters which has sometimes been applied to certain States or districts in the United States.   s.

Roughrider. A nickname of Theodore Roosevelt. s.

royal colony. Historically a British possession administered by a royal governor whose council was appointed by the Crown. Royal colonies in America achieved some degree of self-government through popularly elected assemblies. JWF.

Rubber Reserve Company. A corporation of the national government organized by the Reconstruction Finance Corporation in June, 1940, to accumulate a reserve of raw rubber for defense purposes. z.

rubber stamp. An opprobrious term for an official with discretionary powers whose acts are supposed to be dictated by a superior officer or a political boss. s.

rule. An authoritative regulation or standard to be followed; a regulation adopted by a legislative body to secure adequate debate, freedom of expression, full consideration, protection of the minority against surprise or fraud, and the orderly and prompt disposal of business. s.

rule-making power. The power of a court to make regulations for its procedure or to devise a formula for the construction or interpretation of statutes. s.

rule of reason. A doctrine of the Supreme Court of the United States, first announced in 1911 in the American Tobacco and Standard Oil cases, that the Sherman Antitrust Act applied not to monopolies as such but to those which used their power for "unreasonable" restraints of trade. s.

Rules, Committee on. A committee of the House of Representatives with power to propose modifications in the general rules and to propose special orders for the consideration of separate bills out of turn with limitations on the number and scope of amendments and the time for consideration. s.

ruling. An authoritative interpretation of a provision of a statute, order, regulation, or ordinance, rendered by a superior administrative official or tribunal. z.

rum fleet. Vessels of foreign registry engaged in smuggling liquors into the United States during the prohibition era. s.

rum, Romanism, and rebellion. *See* Burchard incident.

runoff primary. A second primary election between the two highest candidates for an office, provided for in all the States of the Solid South except Virginia as a means of obviating nominations by a mere plurality. s.

Rural Electrification Administration. A division of the Department of Agriculture, created in May, 1935, whose principal function is to make loans for the construction of electric power distribution systems in rural areas. z.

rural free delivery. The delivery of mail along certain rural highways and roads, first begun in 1902. s.

S

sabotage. Malicious waste, destruction of property, or other acts designed to hamper production. It may occur in a deliberate effort of labor to weaken an employer or of fifth columnists to impede a nation's war effort. JMCC.

Sacco-Vanzetti case. The case of two aliens who were convicted of the murder of a paymaster in Massachusetts on April 15, 1920. The introduction of evidence showing their radicalism, and certain questions of the prosecutor and remarks of the judge created a widespread impression that the defendants were being tried for their political opinions. After legal resources had been exhausted, Governor Fuller appointed a commission of laymen, who reported that the trial had been fair. Both defendants were executed Aug. 22, 1927. S.

safety appliance. Any mechanical device or other instrument, installation of which, often required by law, is designed to prevent accidents to operators of machines or to workmen in mines and factories or to insure safety of passengers and employees on railways or other public media of transportation. Z.

Sagebrush State. A nickname of Nevada. S.

Sage of Greystone. A nickname of Samuel J. Tilden. S.

Sage of Monticello. A nickname of Thomas Jefferson. S.

St. Lawrence Waterway. A long-contemplated joint American-Canadian project to make the St. Lawrence River navigable for ocean-going vessels as part of a deep waterway from the Great Lakes to the Atlantic and for exploiting the potential power resources of the river. A treaty calling for this development was signed at Washington July 18, 1932. z.

The upper course of the St. Lawrence River

salary. Payment made to a public official or other person at fixed intervals for services rendered. Z.

salary grab. An act of Congress Mar. 3, 1873, which increased the salaries of members of Congress from $5,000 to $7,500 a year and made the increases retroactive to the Congress just expiring. It was repealed by the next Congress. S.

sales tax. A tax upon the sale of commodities, usually a fixed percentage of the selling price and normally paid by the purchaser. Although opposed by fiscal experts as regressive, general sales taxes were imposed in many States in the 1930's and remain an important source of State revenue. Z.

Salt River. The supposed oblivion of defeated candidates or parties. s.

Samoan Islands. *See* American Samoa.

sample ballot. A facsimile of the official ballot distributed before an election for the information of voters. s.

sanction. 1. That portion of a law which is designed to secure its enforcement either by a reward for its observance or by punishment (penal sanction) ; or by withholding a reward, making restitution, or righting a wrong (civil sanction). 2. Any action, such as military intervention or economic embargo, undertaken by several countries to prevent aggression by another. JWF.

Sand-Lot party. A workingmen's party in California, 1877-81, formed through the agitation of Denis Kearney. s.

sanitary district. A special governmental district set up by a State to provide sewage disposal service and a water supply to a large metropolitan area. z.

Santo Domingo. *See* Dominican Republic.

satellite city. A suburban area geographically and industrially a part of an adjacent metropolis but having a separate corporate existence. z.

savings bank. An institution for safeguarding and investing small amounts of money deposited by the public. Its investments are more closely scrutinized by the State than investments of commercial banks. JWF.

savings bonds and stamps. Securities issued by the United States Treasury designed primarily for purchase by the general public, their chief purpose being to encourage direct lending by the citizen to his government and to promote thrift. Bonds of varying rates of interest are issued in denominations of $25 or more. Stamps are issued in denominations as low as ten cents; they bear no interest but may be used to purchase bonds. JWF.

scalawag. A white Southerner who assisted radical Republicans in their reconstruction policies after the Civil War. s.

Schechter case. A decision of the Supreme Court, 295 U.S. 495 (1935), which declared the National Industrial Recovery Act (*q.v.*) unconstitutional because it delegated powers legislative in nature to the President and attempted, under the guise of the interstate commerce power, to regulate aspects of a business, in this instance the slaughtering and sale of poultry, which fell within the jurisdiction of the States. z.

schedule. 1. That part of a constitution which contains detailed arrangements for its becoming effective. 2. A section of a tariff law. s.

Scottsboro cases. The cases of nine Negro youths tried for statutory offenses at Scottsboro, Ala., and later appealed to the

Supreme Court of the United States. The Court held in *Powell* v. *Alabama*, 287 U.S. 45 (1932), that the guarantee of due process of law was violated by the failure of the lower court to make adequate provision for counsel for the defendants; and in *Norris* v. *Alabama*, 294 U.S. 587 (1935), that failure to summon qualified Negroes for jury service for a generation or more within the county was sufficient evidence of an intent to deny equal protection of the laws.   s.

scratch. To strike out the names of one or more candidates on a party ticket and insert other names.   s.

scrip. Fractional paper currency; also a substitute for legal tender currency issued in periods of emergency by clearinghouses and banks to be redeemed by legal currency when available.   z.

Seabury Commission. A legislative committee, of which Samuel Seabury was chief counsel, appointed to investigate maladministration in the government of New York City. Its disclosures resulted in the resignation of Mayor James J. Walker, Sept. 1, 1932, the ousting of Tammany Hall from control of the city, and the adoption of a new city charter.   z.

seamen, impressment of. *See* Impressment.

search warrant. Documentary permission from a magistrate or court to a peace officer to enter and search designated premises and take into custody persons, papers, and other effects described in the warrant. The warrant is issued only when there is good reason to believe that the person or thing sought may be found on the premises to be searched. *See* Unreasonable searches and seizures.   z.

S.E.C. *See* Securities and Exchange Commission.

secession. Voluntary withdrawal from an organization, especially the action of eleven Southern States which, between Dec. 20, 1860, and June 8, 1861, withdrew from the Union.   JAP.

second chamber. Except in the Netherlands, the less numerous and usually the less powerful legislative house.   s.

Second International. The international organization of Marxian parties founded at Paris in 1889 and known since 1921 as the Second and Labor International to which most moderate or gradualist socialist parties of the past half century, including the American, have nominally belonged.   z.

second papers. A popular term for the certificate of naturalization granted by a court to an alien.   JWF.

Second War for Independence. A name sometimes given to the War of 1812.   s.

secretariat. An office or body of officials charged with keeping records and fulfilling secretarial functions for a deliberative council or assembly.   JWF.

secretary. A part of the official title of most of the heads of the ten great administrative departments of the national government; also a part of the title of certain State officials. z.

secret service. A division of the Treasury Department established in 1860 which suppresses counterfeiting, protects the person of the President, and investigates violations of various laws, thefts of government property, and the forging of government checks. JWF.

secret session. A legislative session at which the galleries are cleared and members are placed under obligation not to reveal the proceedings; often called an executive session. s.

sectionalism. Excessive devotion to a geographical region to the prejudice of the unity of a country. s.

Securities and Exchange Commission. An independent commission created by Congress, 1934, to enforce the provisions of the Securities Exchange Act (*q.v.*) It enforces the Act's requirement of publication of stock prospectuses and its regulation of stock market practices and transactions. Subsequent legislation has given the Commission power to dissolve uneconomic corporate structures among public utility holding companies, supervise financial transactions and contracts among the subsidiaries of such companies, and scrutinize their dividend payments to stockholders. The Commission is also responsible for registering and regulating all types of investment trusts and companies. The five-year terms of its five members are staggered so that one commissioner retires every year. z.

Securities Exchange Act. An act of Congress, 1934, supplementing the earlier Securities Act, 1933. Together they require corporations or others wishing to sell stocks or other securities on exchanges or through interstate media to furnish a prospectus giving the public complete and accurate information concerning the securities offered for sale. They also regulate the use of credit for stock exchange transactions, particularly purchases on "margin"; prohibit market "rigging" and other questionable manipulations of exchanges or exchange transactions; and establish a Securities and Exchange Commission (*q.v.*) z.

Sedition Act. 1. A law of Congress July 14, 1798, which imposed severe penalties for conspiracy against the government or the writing or printing of false or malicious statements concerning the President or Congress. 2. A similar act passed May 16, 1918, against anyone who hindered the prosecution of World War I. s.

segregated appropriations. *See* Segregation 1.

segregation. 1. Determination in minute detail as to the purposes for which monies, appropriated by a legislature, are to be spent. 2. The allocation of certain taxes or their proceeds to the use of local political subdivisions. 3. The practice, especially prevalent in certain Southern States and often required by law, of providing "separate and equal" educational, amusement, transport, and other facilities for members of white and colored races.   z.

seigniorage. 1. A fee charged by a mint for the coining of precious metal. **2.** The difference between the face value of a coin and the value of the metal it contains, representing a profit to the government.   s.

Seismological Union. An international society for the study and exchange of information about earthquakes. It was directed from Strasbourg Observatory and existed from 1903 to 1922. JWF.

Selective Service System. A bureau in the War Manpower Commission, organized in 1940 to carry into effect the provisions of the Selective Service and Training Act of that year and amendments thereto. Under the supervision of a national headquarters staff, headed by a Director, local civilian boards throughout the United States and its territories register and classify males for military service. Males between the ages of 18 and 64 are required to register; those between 20 and 44 are eligible for active service. The local boards place these into a class available for immediate duty or into various deferred or exempt classes.   z.

selectman. A member of the governing board of a New England town except in Rhode Island.   s.

self-determination. *See* National self-determination.

self-government. 1. Government in which there is a substantial measure of participation by the generality of the citizens through a system of elections and representation. **2.** The autonomy enjoyed by municipalities and local political subdivisions in the management of purely local governmental affairs.   z.

self-incrimination. *See* Incrimination.

self-perpetuating board. A board with power to fill up its membership by electing new members to fill vacancies as they occur.   JWF.

selling out. Abandoning one's party or political friends in return for an appointment or pecuniary reward.   s.

semi-sovereign. Possessing limited or partial sovereignty. JRP.

senate. The upper legislative house of the national government, of all States, and of many foreign countries. The United States Senate was designed to give the States, as such, equality of representation, and each State has two Senators. Under the terms of the 17th Amendment, adopted in 1913, Senators are elected by popular vote, and not by State legislatures, as formerly. The term is six years. Vacancies are filled by special elections, though the State legislatures may empower the governor to make temporary appointments until an election can be held. The Vice President is normally the presiding officer of the Senate, but he may vote only when it is equally divided. A president pro tempore, elected by the

Senate from its own membership, presides when the Vice President is absent or has become President. The special powers of the Senate are to try all impeachments, ratify treaties, confirm appointments, and, when no candidate for Vice President has received a majority of electoral votes, to elect a Vice President from the two receiving the highest electoral votes. A two-thirds vote is required for conviction after impeachment or the ratification of a treaty. The legislative power of the Senate is practically co-ordinate with that of the House of Representatives; for, though the House alone may originate revenue bills, the Senate may amend any part of such a bill after the enacting clause.   s.

Senator. A member of the Senate of the United States or of similarly named chambers in State legislatures.   z.

senatorial courtesy. A long standing custom of the Senate that it will refuse to approve nominations submitted by the President if the Senators representing the State in which the nominee resides, and belonging to the majority party, have not given their prior approval of the nomination. In effect the custom transfers to such Senators the distribution of patronage from their States. The rule does not apply to cabinet positions.   s.

seniority rule. The custom, nearly always observed in both houses of Congress, of promoting to the chairmanship of a committee the member of the majority party who has had the longest period of continuous service on it.   s.

sentence. A judgment pronounced by a court of law, particularly the penalty imposed upon a convicted defendant in a criminal case.   JWF.

separation of powers. The allocation of lawmaking, law-enforcing, and law-interpreting functions of government to different bodies in order to preserve liberty from the tyranny thought to result from combining legislative, executive, and judicial powers in the same hands. Derived from European writers, especially Montesquieu, and supported by colonial experience, this theory, as applied in American State and national constitutions, grows out of the assumption that the only effective restraints upon arbitrary governmental power — "paper guarantees" to the contrary notwithstanding — are those internal checks woven into the machinery of government itself. The separation of legislative, executive, and judicial powers becomes a convenient medium for establishing a check and balance system within the government. That this was the major objective behind the separation of powers theory is evidenced by the fact that nowhere is the separation complete; for each of the three departments does exercise powers logically belonging to the other two as a means of controlling them more effectively. The recent creation of numerous independent boards and commissions, each exercising combined legislative, executive, and judicial powers, has tended to discredit the separation of powers theory as such, although it has not seriously impaired the efficacy of the check and balance system for which separation of powers became the convenient foundation stone.   JTC.

sergeant at arms. An officer, but not a member, of a legislative body who is present at all sessions and executes its orders to compel the attendance of absent members, preserve order, make arrests, and serve subpoenas.   S.

serial bond. One of an issue of bonds which mature at different specified dates, thus enabling the borrowing authority to redeem them without recourse to a sinking fund.   S.

service rating. A civil servant's record of proficiency and other qualities upon which his future promotion is supposed to be based.   Z.

servitude. A restriction upon ownership or sovereignty. A *private servitude* qualifies ownership by a right enjoyed by a non-owner; a *state servitude* enables one state to use the territory of another for a specific purpose.   JWF.

session. 1. The period during which a legislature or court is sitting. A session of Congress begins on a day fixed by the Constitution, by law, or by call of the President; and ends when the terms of Representatives expire or at a time fixed by concurrent resolution. **2.** A sitting during one legislative day.   S.

session laws. A pamphlet collection of acts and resolutions of Congress which, before 1937, was published at the end of each session; since superseded by the *Statutes at Large* (*q.v.*) which, published at the end of each Congress prior to 1937, is now published at the end of each session.   Z.

Seventeenth Amendment. An amendment to the Constitution submitted by Congress to the States May 16, 1912, and proclaimed May 31, 1913. It vests the election of United States Senators in the voters of a State qualified to vote for the more numerous branch of the State legislature but provides that a State legislature may empower the governor to make a temporary appointment to fill a vacancy until an election can be held.   Z.

Seventh-of-March Speech. An address by Daniel Webster in the Senate of the United States Mar. 7, 1850, urging the compromise of differences between North and South.   S.

severance tax. A tax, levied either ad valorem or according to amount, on mineral or forest products at the time they are removed or "severed" from the soil. It is usually regarded as a form of property taxation.   S.

shakedown. A forced contribution exacted by a political machine from underworld characters and others who have benefited from its special favors.   S.

Share the wealth. A slogan taken from President Franklin D. Roosevelt's speech of acceptance in 1932 by Huey P. Long, Louisiana political boss and United States Senator, to describe his social philosophy and his campaign against corporations and vested interests. z.

Shays' Rebellion. An armed revolt in western Massachusetts, 1786-87, led by Daniel Shays, which had for its object the relief of the debtor class. s.

Sheppard-Towner Act. A law of Congress Nov. 23, 1921, providing for grants-in-aid to the States for the care and protection of maternity and infancy. s.

sheriff. The chief law enforcement officer of a county who conserves the peace, serves court processes, usually has the duty of maintaining the jail and feeding its inmates, and sometimes collects taxes. He is popularly elective in all States except Rhode Island and is usually not re-eligible. The fees and perquisites ordinarily belonging to the office make it unusually lucrative, but not necessarily efficient. s.

Sherman Antitrust Act. An act of Congress July 2, 1890, which forbade "every contract, combination in the form of trust or otherwise, or conspiracy, in restraint of commerce among the several States," under severe penalties, and provided for its enforcement by injunction, criminal prosecution, confiscation of property used in the unlawful conspiracy, and the award of threefold damages to injured parties. It was held not to apply to manufacturing (*United States* v. *E. C. Knight Co.,* 156 U.S. 1, 1895), and was further limited by the rule of reason (*q.v.*) It was supplemented and strengthened by the Clayton Act (*q.v.*) s.

Sherman Silver Purchase Act. An act of Congress passed in 1890 and repealed in 1893 which required the Secretary of the Treasury to purchase 4,500,000 ounces of silver a month. s.

shinplasters. Fractional paper currency issued by the United States, 1862-76, or notes in small denominations formerly issued by private bankers. s.

shipping board. *See* United States Maritime Commission.

shipping subsidy. Public financial aid granted to private builders or operators of merchant ships either in the form of outright payments or as favorable contracts for carrying mails, etc., for the purposes of building up a merchant marine, expanding foreign commerce, and having auxiliary vessels available for use in time of war. s.

shirt-sleeve diplomacy. The conduct of diplomatic relations by direct and relatively informal methods. s.

short-ballot movement. Agitation for the elimination of many elective offices with ministerial duties and making them appointive, in order that the attention of voters may be concentrated on legislative and policy-determining executive officers. The movement has borne fruit in numerous State, municipal, and county reorganizations.   s.

short session. The session of Congress which formerly met on the first Monday in December of even-numbered years and ended the following March 4, when terms of members expired. s.

Show Me State. A nickname of Missouri.   s.

Shreveport Rate case. A case, *Houston E. & W. Texas Ry. Co. v. United States,* 234 U.S. 342 (1914), in which the Texas Railway Commission was found to have fixed unreasonably low rates between distributing centers in Texas and points near the State borders, to the disadvantage of distributors in other States. The Supreme Court of the United States ordered the Texas Commission to raise its rates to conform with those fixed by the Interstate Commerce Commission for interstate shipments.   s.

sick leave. Leave of absence granted to ill or injured officials or employees pending recovery.   jwf.

sifting committee. A committee appointed in some State legislatures, or one branch, to determine the priority of bills.   s.

silk-stocking district. An election district inhabited chiefly by people of wealth.   s.

silver. A precious metal which in the early period of the nation had a fairly stable value in relation to gold, but which declined greatly following the Civil War. Congress stopped the coinage of silver dollars in 1873; and a little later there arose an insistent demand from advocates of cheap money for the remonetization of silver which, though partly satisfied by a limited coinage of silver after 1878 and the Sherman Silver Purchase Act (*q.v.*) of 1890, culminated in Bryan's campaign for the free and unlimited coinage of silver at the ratio of 16 to one. His defeat temporarily settled the question; but in 1933 Congress remonetized silver and in 1934 in effect nationalized new production by requiring the Secretary of the Treasury to purchase silver until the total value held by the Treasury represented one fourth of the total bullion reserve.   s.

silver certificate. United States paper currency issued in varying denominations and based on equivalent value of silver bullion or silver currency held by the Treasury.   z.

Silver Grays. The more conservative members of the Whig party who supported the Compromise of 1850 and Fillmore's administration.   s.

simple conference. A conference between legislative houses in which managers are bound by instructions of one or both houses.   s.

sinecure. A public office providing an emolument but having no duties or only nominal ones.   z.

sine die. Without fixing a date for reassembling.   s.

single-member district. An electoral district which returns one member, chosen by a plurality, to a legislative assembly; characteristic of the United States. z.

single standard. A system of currency in which the value of the basic unit is a fixed weight of only one precious metal. z.

single tax. The proposal of Henry George and other economists that rent from land, as distinct from income from use of land or improvements thereon, should be diverted to the public treasury in the form of a tax, the proceeds of which, it was argued, would alone be sufficient to pay the cost of government. z.

single transferable vote. *See* Hare plan; Ware plan.

sinking fund. A separate fund set aside out of revenues, usually at yearly intervals, to be invested and eventually applied to the redemption of public debt or a certain bond issue. s.

sit-down strike. A work stoppage accompanied by occupation of company premises by workers attempting to compel their employers to accede to their demands. After a wave of sit-down strikes in 1937, they lost favor because of their violation of property rights. JWF.

Sixteenth Amendment. An amendment to the Constitution of the United States proclaimed Feb. 25, 1913, which permits Congress to levy taxes upon incomes from whatsoever source derived. It canceled the decision in the case of *Pollock* v. *Farmers' Loan and Trust Co.*, 158 U.S. 601 (1895), in which the Supreme Court had held that an income tax was a direct tax within the meaning of the Constitution and that, in consequence, the burden of such a levy had to be apportioned among the several States according to population. JAP.

Sixteen to one. A slogan of the Democratic party in 1896 when it demanded the free and unlimited coinage of silver at the value ratio of 16 ounces of silver to 1 of gold. s.

slate. A list of candidates informally agreed upon in advance of a primary election, convention, or election. s.

Slaughterhouse cases. Several cases in which butchers in New Orleans appealed for the protection of the 14th Amendment against an act of the Louisiana legislature passed under the police power of the State. The Supreme Court of the United States, 16 Wall. 36 (1873), held that, though the Amendment created a national citizenship, the rights guaranteed against impairment were rights of national, and not of State, citizenship; and that its adoption did not indicate any purpose to destroy the main features of the federal system. In later cases, however, the Supreme Court has gradually extended its protection over the field of civil rights against State impairment. s.

slavery. A legal status of a person, involving ownership as a chattel by a master, subjection of person and activities to his commands, and obligation to perform labor without consent or compensation. Slavery existed in all the colonies, but it was abolished everywhere in the North between 1774 (Rhode Island) and 1804 (New Jersey). Fears of slaveholders that the abolitionist movement would interfere with the institution of slavery in the South were chiefly responsible for the policy of keeping an even balance in admitting new States, 1820-60, and for the doctrine of State sovereignty, secession and the Civil War. Slavery was abolished in the United States by the 13th Amendment (*q.v.*)   s.

slave trade. The seizure and transportation of Negroes for the purpose of selling them as slaves. Under various international conventions, ships of all nations have the right to search vessels suspected of carrying slaves.   JWF.

slum clearance. Large-scale razing of outmoded, unsightly, and unsanitary dwellings and other buildings in the congested or slum districts of large cities and the construction on the cleared site of modern low-cost housing and community facilities for low-income families. Such activity is now encouraged by loans and capital grants by the United States Housing Authority to State and local public housing authorities which carry out the specific projects.   z.

slush fund. A fund collected for purposes of bribery or improperly influencing public opinion.   s.

small claims court. A municipal or other local court which provides expeditious, informal and inexpensive adjudication of small contractual claims.   z.

small loan law. A law enacted by more than one half of the States fixing the maximum legal rate of interest, normally from 3 to 3½ per cent per month, on short-term "distress" loans of $300 or less made by banks and finance companies.   z.

smelling committee. A name given to a legislative investigating committee which is alleged to have been created from partisan motives to unearth unpleasant facts about the conduct of an office for use in a political campaign.   s.

Smith-Hughes Act. An act of Congress, 1917, which provided federal grants-in-aid to States for vocational training in agriculture, home economics, trade, and industry.   z.

Smith-Lever Act. An act of Congress, 1914, which supplied federal funds to the States, partly as grants-in-aid, to support extension work carried on chiefly by county agricultural agents under the joint auspices of the Department of Agriculture and State agricultural colleges.   z.

Smithsonian Institution. An establishment created by act of Congress Aug. 10, 1846, under the terms of the will of James Smithson, of London, and governed by a board of regents consisting of the Chief Justice, the Vice President, three members each of the Senate and the House of Representatives, and six citizens appointed by joint resolution of Congress. It has jurisdiction over the National Museum, the National Gallery of Art, the National Collection of Fine Arts, the Freer Gallery of Art, the Bureau of American Ethnology, the National Zoological Park, and the Astrophysical Observatory. s.

smothering. An action, such as referring a bill to an unfriendly committee or abuse of power by a committee or its chairman, which prevents a bill from coming to a vote. s.

smuggling. The shipment of goods or persons into or out of a country in defiance of its regulations taxing or prohibiting such shipment. JWF.

snap. Pertaining to a meeting called or a vote taken without sufficient notice to all those entitled to participate. s.

Snapper. A New York Democrat opposed to the renomination of Grover Cleveland in 1892. *See* Antisnapper. s.

soap. Political slang for money, particularly money used for corrupt purposes. s.

soapbox. The small platform used by street-corner speakers; hence statements on public questions and criticism of the political and social order emanating from irresponsible persons, agitators, or radicals. s.

social compact. *See* Contract theory.

social control. The direction, modification, or restraint of the behavior of groups of people, especially that form of control exercised by beliefs, myths, mores, slogans, and public opinion. JMCC.

social convention. A usage or practice which governs human behavior without the force of law. It may be of a political or economic character; usually, however, it concerns matters of morality or personal deportment. JMCC.

social insurance. A contractual relationship in which the government indemnifies members of certain economic classes against loss from specified risks such as unemployment, illness, or accident. The payment of a premium (tax) is not always required of the insured and if paid the amount is never graduated according to risk. JMCC.

Socialism. Marxian doctrines of social ownership of the productive mechanism, and production for use instead of profit; a program advocated by one or more minor parties in the United States since 1876. Z.

Socialist Labor party. An uncompromising Marxist party organized as the Workingmen's party in 1876 and called by its present name since 1877. Though it has nominated presidential candidates since 1892, none of them has received as many as 40,000 popular votes. s.

Socialist party. A minor party with moderate Marxian objectives which has nominated candidates in every presidential election since 1900, except in 1924 when it endorsed LaFollette. It cast somewhat more than 900,000 popular votes in 1912 and 1920. *See* Socialism. z.

socialized medicine. A somewhat loose term applied to almost any proposal for public regulation of the services and fees of the members of the medical profession or to co-operative or governmentally subsidized projects to supply medical treatment to the public at nominal cost. z.

social legislation. Laws designed to improve living standards of persons who are unable to better themselves because of physical handicap, poverty, or the lack of economic or political opportunity. Such laws may relate to social insurance, public welfare activities, the protection of workers and consumers, minority rights, land tenure, indebtedness, education, and dependency. Social legislation in the United States may be enacted under the police power of the States or under the taxation, commerce, and other powers of the national government. JMCC.

social science. Any organized body of knowledge which deals with man's environment, history, and political, economic, or other social institutions; such bodies of knowledge considered collectively. z.

Social Security Board. A board of three members which, since 1939, has formed part of the Federal Security Agency. It administers the national old-age insurance plan, examines and approves State plans for unemployment compensation, old-age assistance, and other types of State aid to social dependents, and certifies federal grants-in-aid to the States for these purposes. JMCC.

society. A group of individuals united by common interests who possess a sense of corporate unity and discipline and an organization to promote common aims. z.

Softs or Soft-shells. The antislavery and reform wing of the Hunkers (*q.v.*) in New York about 1848. s.

soil conservation. Various activities of the Department of Agriculture, carried on in co-operation with State agencies and farmers. They include efforts to maintain soil fertility by crop rotation, prevention of erosion by reforestation, afforestation, and flood control, provision of increased water supply for arid lands, and the public purchase and scientific exploitation of submarginal agricultural lands. z.

solicitor. In England a lawyer who may conduct all processes of litigation except pleading in open court. In America the term is synonymous with attorney and is often the official designation of a legal officer in government service. JWF.

solicitor general. An official of the Department of Justice who has special charge of the business of the United States before the Supreme Court and represents it in person there. When requested by the Attorney General he may appear in any United States court or represent the interests of the United States before a State court. His approval is necessary before the United States may take an appeal to an appellate court. s.

Solid South. The States of Virginia, North Carolina, South Carolina, Georgia, Florida, Alabama, Mississippi, Louisiana, Texas, and Arkansas, in which, since the Reconstruction period, Republican opposition to the Democratic party has usually been ineffective or negligible. s.

Sons of Liberty. Any one of several secret and informally organized groups of Americans who opposed the Stamp Act, 1765-66, and later other oppressive acts of the British government, and who aided in enforcing nonimportation agreements. s.

Sons of the South. Societies organized in Missouri after the passage of the Kansas-Nebraska Bill, 1854, to take possession of Kansas on behalf of slavery. s.

Sooner State. A nickname of Oklahoma. s.

sorehead. A defeated candidate who refuses to accept the result of a primary election or a convention; or a disappointed office seeker who refuses to support his party. s.

South Americans. The proslavery faction of the American or Know-Nothing party; or the American party after the North Americans (*q.v.*) seceded from it. s.

South Carolina. One of the original States, and the eighth to ratify the Constitution of the United States, May 23, 1788. It adopted an ordinance of secession, Dec. 20, 1860, and was readmitted June 25, 1868. Capital, Columbia; area, 30,989 sq. mi.; population (1940), 1,899,804; presidential electors, 8. Under the present constitution adopted in 1895 the suffrage is limited by literacy or property and poll tax requirements. s.

South Dakota. The 40th State, admitted to the Union Nov. 2, 1889, from territory acquired by the Louisiana Purchase. Capital, Pierre; area, 77,615 sq. mi.; population (1940), 642,961; presidential electors, 4. The original constitution is still in effect. The statutory initiative and referendum were adopted in 1898. s.

Southern Confederacy. *See* Confederate States of America.

sovereign. 1. The person or body possessing legal sovereignty. 2. The body in whom political sovereignty is thought to reside. 3. Pertaining to, or possessing the quality of, sovereignty. JRP.

sovereignty. As defined by Bodin in 1576, the "supreme power over citizens and subjects unrestrained by laws." Bodin ascribed to the concept the qualities of inalienability and indivisibility. Although he recognized certain limits upon sovereignty, his definition emphasized the obvious need for a center of final authority in the modern state. Later writers, notably Hobbes, practically discarded all limitations upon the sovereignty of the ruler or rulers and made the power of the state absolute. Today confusion can be avoided only by sharply distinguishing the concept of *legal* sovereignty, which is finality of legal authority, and *political* sovereignty, which is political supremacy; and by insisting that neither concept carries with it any necessary implication of ethical justification for the acts of the sovereign. In international law, sovereignty stands for independent statehood and complete freedom from direct external control.   JRP.

Spanish-American War. A war with Spain which was declared by Congress Apr. 24, 1898, to have begun three days earlier; and which ended with the ratification by the Senate of the Treaty of Paris, Feb. 6, 1899.   S.

Spar. The popular name of a member of the Women's Reserve of the Coast Guard, created during World War II, derived from an abbreviation of the Coast Guard's motto, *semper paratus.* Z.

speaker. The presiding officer of the lower house of the legislature in English-speaking countries who conducts the business of the house in accordance with the rules, recognizes members who wish to speak, preserves order and decorum in debate, puts questions to a vote, authenticates by his signature all bills, resolutions, warrants and subpoenas, and is the sole organ of communication between the house and persons outside it. The Speaker of the House of Representatives early became its political leader and at times exercised autocratic control over it largely through his power to appoint standing committees and his position as chairman of the Committee on Rules — powers that were taken from him by the Congressional Revolution of 1910-11. He may still affect the fate of measures through his powers of recognition, especially in unanimous consent and suspension of the rules; of referring bills to committee; and of ruling on points of order; for though his references and his rulings are subject to appeal to the floor, a partisan majority ordinarily sustains him. The Speaker retains all the rights of a member of the House, though he rarely participates in debate and may refrain from voting except to give a casting vote (*q.v.*) Speakers in State legislatures usually possess the powers exercised by the Speaker of the House before 1910. The British speaker, who observes a studied nonpartisanship, has more power than American speakers to halt dilatory tactics.   S.

special assessment. A levy upon the owners of property adjacent to a contemplated public improvement to defray the capital cost thereof. It differs from a tax in that it is levied for a specific purpose and in an amount proportioned to the direct benefit of the property assessed.   JMCC.

special committee. A legislative committee whose jurisdiction is limited to investigation, consideration, and report on a particular subject or bill. **s.**

special legislation. Private bills (*q.v.*) passed for the relief or benefit of an individual or local government unit. **s.**

special order. A legislative rule applying to only one bill, or a military order applying to one or a few individuals, and not of general concern. **s.**

special session. An extraordinary session (*q.v.*) **s.**

Specie Circular. An order of President Jackson, July 11, 1836, directing that government agents receive only gold, silver, or Virginia scrip in payment for public lands. **s.**

specific performance. The execution of the specific terms of a contract which may be required by a court of equity when an award of damages to the injured party at common law would be inadequate. **z.**

specific rate. A customs or other tax rate fixed upon articles according to their weight, volume, or other physical characteristics, rather than ad valorem (*q.v.*) **s.**

speech. *See* Freedom of speech and press.

speech of acceptance. The address of a presidential or gubernatorial candidate in response to the formal notification of his nomination in which he outlines the policies he intends to follow if elected. **EES.**

speeding. Operation of a motor vehicle or other conveyance at a rate of speed in excess of the maximum allowed by law or ordinance. **z.**

spellbinder. A convention or campaign orator who is addicted to spread-eagle oratory. **s.**

sphere of influence. A politically backward, economically under-developed region, in which a powerful state claims, often with the concurrence of other states, special rights of economic exploitation, colonization, and possible ultimate annexation. **JWF.**

split session. A legislative session, such as that required by an amendment to the constitution of California, which consists of two parts: the first devoted to the appointment of committees and the introduction and reference of bills, after which an extended adjournment occurs for consultations between members and their constituents; and the second, to the consideration of bills already introduced or of new bills introduced only by consent of an extra-majority vote. **s.**

split ticket. A ballot marked for candidates of more than one party. **s.**

spoils system. The practice of regarding appointive offices as booty for a party which comes to power, under the principle "To the victor belong the spoils of the enemy"; of turning out the incumbents; and of distributing offices, public contracts, and a long list of other official favors to persons, regardless of their competence, who have worked for the success of the party: opposed to the merit system (*q.v.*)   s.

square deal. President Theodore Roosevelt's characterization of his own legislative and administrative policies, particularly those concerning corporations and big business.   z.

squatter. One who settles on land to which he has no legal title.   z.

squatter sovereignty. The doctrine, 1854-61, that the settlers of a territory of the United States had the right to organize a government and admit or exclude slavery as they chose.   s.

S.S.B. *See* Social Security Board.

S.S.S. *See* Selective Service System.

stabilization fund. A fund of about $2,000,000,000, the profit accruing to the United States Treasury as a result of the devaluation of the dollar in terms of gold in 1933. It may be used by the Treasury to manipulate foreign exchange rates or influence the domestic money market.   JWF.

staff. That portion of an administrative organization which has mainly investigative, advisory, or planning functions, in contrast to the line organization which is engaged directly in administrative action.   s.

stalking-horse. A candidate who is put forward by the party organization, or in the interest of another candidate, for the purpose of dividing the opposition, and who withdraws when the purpose is accomplished.   s.

Stalwarts. The self-assumed title for the "regular" or "machine" faction of the Republican party who were responsible for many of the scandals of Grant's administration, 1869-77; who opposed the reform policies of President Hayes; and who in 1880 tried to obtain a third nomination for Grant.   s.

Stamp Act. An act of Parliament, 1765, imposing taxes and requiring the affixing of stamps as evidence of payment on all legal and commercial documents, newspapers, etc., issued in the American colonies. It was repealed in 1766 because of colonial and British opposition.   s.

Stamp Act Congress. A meeting of delegates from nine North American colonies at New York, Oct. 7, 1765, which, though admitting the power of Parliament to make general regulations concerning the colonies, denied its power to tax them.   s.

stampede. A sudden tumultuous movement in a political convention when the great mass of delegates break away from various candidates they have previously supported and concentrate their votes on the winning candidate.   s.

Standards, Bureau of. *See* National Bureau of Standards.

standing army. The professional army of a country as distinguished from a volunteer, or temporarily conscripted, army or militia. JWF.

standing committee. A committee appointed at the beginning of a Congress and having jurisdiction over all bills which may be introduced concerning a certain subject matter. s.

standing order. A legislative rule which is valid until repealed by the legislative body which made it. s.

standpatter. A member of the conservative faction of the Republican party about 1900; any conservative or reactionary in politics. s.

star-chamber proceeding. A secret proceeding in which a person whose interests are affected is given inadequate or no opportunity to present his case, and in which the proceedings are conducted and conclusions reached in derogation of the usual forms. The name is derived from the Star Chamber, an ancient court abolished by Parliament in 1641 which had no jury and was permitted to apply torture. s.

stare decisis. To stand by decided cases; a principle of Anglo-American jurisprudence that a precedent once established in the decision of a case should be followed in other like cases unless it is found to be in conflict with established principles of justice. s.

Star Route Frauds. The establishment of unnecessary mail services operated under extravagant contracts which was exposed early in 1881. s.

Stars and Bars. A familiar name for the flag of the Confederate States of America. s.

Stars and Stripes. A familiar name for the flag of the United States. s.

Star-Spangled Banner. 1. The title of a poem composed by Francis Scott Key while detained on a British man-of-war off Fort McHenry in 1814, long used as a national anthem, and officially adopted as such by act of Congress in 1931. 2. A familiar name for the flag of the United States. s.

state. 1. A politically organized body of people occupying a definite territory and living under a government entirely or almost entirely free from external control and competent to secure habitual obedience from all persons within it — in other words, possessing both external and internal sovereignty. 2. The title of a component of the federal systems of the United States, Australia, and several Latin American republics. s.

State aid. Subsidies or grants-in-aid made by a State to one of its subdivisions for educational or other purposes. s.

State central committee. The principal party committee within a State generally composed either of one member from each congressional district or of one member from each county.   s.

State centralization. The process by which a State assumes direct administrative control over subjects formerly administered by counties or other local subdivisions.   s.

State, Department of. 1. A department of the national government created as the Department of Foreign Affairs July 27, 1789, and given its present title and many duties of a domestic character, including the authentication of official documents, Sept. 15, 1789. It supervises the Foreign Service, conducts negotiations with foreign governments, promotes friendly relations with other countries, including trade and cultural relations, and issues passports and visas. Separate divisions on European, Near Eastern, Far Eastern, American Republics, and Philippine affairs concentrate their attention on relations with different geographical areas. In the emergency before and during World War II, it was given authority over the allocation of exports to countries of the Western Hemisphere, responsibility for matters of foreign policy under lend-lease, foreign-funds control, and world trade intelligence. 2. A department of State government which has the custody of the State seal and control of other functions, including the administration of election laws, the issuance of charters to corporations, and the admission of foreign corporations.   s.

State examiner. A State official who inspects accounts of local governments or who is charged with the examination of persons who wish to secure a license or certificate to practice a regulated profession.   z.

State Guards. Organized militia established by act of Congress Oct. 21, 1940, to replace the National Guard for service within their respective States. They are expected to meet domestic emergencies, protect war industries and suppress fifth column activities.   s.

statelessness. The condition of being without nationality under the laws of any existing state.   jwf.

state of nature. The condition of mankind, assumed to exist by many writers on political theory, before the establishment of organized government. It was a brutish existence, according to Thomas Hobbes, who wanted to establish strong governmental power; but an idyllic condition, according to Rousseau, who set out to show that "man is born free, and everywhere he is in chains."   s.

State police. An organized professional police force maintained and directly commanded by a State authority for the enforcement of law, the suppression of disorder, the patrolling of highways, and guarding public property.   s.

State's attorney. An officer, usually locally elective within a county, who represents the State in securing indictments and in prosecuting criminal cases; a prosecuting attorney.   s.

state's evidence. The evidence given by an accomplice against his confederates in crime under an implied promise of pardon. s.

statesman. A political leader who consistently shapes public policy with foresight, or administers public affairs with wisdom and integrity. JWF.

State sovereignty. A doctrine of constitutional construction maintained by many writers before the Civil War that the States were sovereign before the adoption of the Constitution of the United States; that the Constitution was a compact among the States; and, sovereignty being inalienable, that the States retained the power through their conventions to secede from the Union or to nullify acts of Congress. s.

States' rights. A generic term applied to various theories of strict construction and interpretation of the Constitution ranging from State sovereignty to present-day opposition to concentration of power in the national government. s.

state succession. A partial or complete change in the identity of a state resulting from its absorption by another state, its division into independent states, or any similar development. JWF.

State use system. The system of employing prison labor in the production of articles exclusively for use in State institutions or by local subdivisions of a State. s.

status. 1. The condition of a person who is not *sui juris, i.e.,* one who lacks the fullest measure of freedom of action under the law; *e.g.,* a minor. 2. The legal position of a member of a group upon whom the law confers special privileges or imposes special limitations. z.

status quo ante bellum. "The situation prevailing before the war" — an expression used in effecting a restoration to conditions temporarily altered by war. JWF.

statute. A formal written expression of the legislative will whether couched in the form of an act or joint resolution. Statute law is to be distinguished from unwritten or common law. s.

statute of limitations. A law which fixes a period during which existing claims may be collected, judgments enforced, or crimes prosecuted. After the lapse of the prescribed period, the law serves as a legal bar to action. z.

Statutes at Large. An official compilation of the acts and resolutions of each session of Congress. It consists of two parts, the first comprising public acts and joint resolutions, the second, private acts and joint resolutions, concurrent resolutions, treaties, and presidential proclamations. z.

stay-at-home voter. A voter who by remaining away from the polls tacitly aids an opposing party or faction. s.

stay law. A law to prevent or delay collection of a debt or the application of a judgment against a debtor. z.

stealing thunder. Appropriating an important issue of another candidate or party.   s.

steamboat inspection. The public inspection of steam plant, boilers, machinery, equipment, and hulls of commercial vessels, a function at present confided to the Bureau of Marine Inspection and Navigation (*q.v.*)   z.

steam roller. A political force which ruthlessly crushes opposition in disregard of established rules or principles.   s.

steering committee. A committee of the party caucus, generally with the floor leader as chairman, which determines the order in which measures will be considered in a legislative house.   s.

sterilization law. A law effective in a number of States which empowers appropriate authorities to deprive feeble-minded or congenitally insane persons in public institutions of the power of reproduction.   z.

stewardship theory. A theory, first enunciated by James Wilson and revived by Theodore Roosevelt, that the President may take any action in the general interest which is not interdicted by the laws or the Constitution.   z.

still hunt. A canvass for votes or the support of delegates to a convention carried on unobtrusively or stealthily.   s.

storm troopers. A German quasi-military organization begun as a private army of the Nazi party and used to enforce Hitler's will after he became dictator in 1933.   JWF.

straddle. To take an equivocal position; to be on both sides of a question at the same time.   s.

Straight-out Democrats. Democrats who, disapproving their party's endorsement of Horace Greeley in 1872, nominated Charles O'Conor for President. They cast about 30,000 votes.   s.

straight ticket. A vote for all the candidates regularly nominated by one party.   s.

strategic material. A material essential to national defense for the supply of which, in war, dependence must be placed in whole or substantial part on sources outside the continental limits of the United States.   s.

straw vote. An unofficial poll taken by a newspaper or private organization to forecast the result of an election.   s.

strict construction. *See* Construction.

strike. A concerted work stoppage by employees in a plant or industry in an effort to compel the management to make concessions or redress grievances.   z.

strike bill. A bill introduced in a legislative body for the purpose of extorting a bribe from an individual or corporation which would be harmed if it were passed.   s.

strong-mayor plan. A form of municipal government in which the mayor has effective control over the administrative services of a municipality with usually, though not necessarily, budget-making authority and veto power over municipal legislation, grants of franchises, and alienation of municipal property.   s.

stump. A platform often used by campaign speakers in frontier communities. A stump speech is a campaign address of a rough-and-ready sort.   s.

subjugation. The process of compelling a people by force of arms to yield to the will of a conqueror.   JWF.

Submission Man. An opprobrious nickname for an American who opposed the War of 1812.   s.

subpoena. An order of a court, tribunal, or legislative house requiring the attendance of a witness; the subpoena *duces tecum* requires the witness to bring with him certain specific documents or papers.   z.

subsidiary coinage. Coins issued in denominations representing fractions of the monetary unit.   s.

subsidiary motion. A motion for the adoption of a particular method of considering or disposing of a matter proposed in a legislative body.   s.

subsidy. A gift of money or property made by the national government, or by a State or a local government unit, to assist a private party in the establishment or operation of a service deemed beneficial to the public at large, such as a railroad or shipping line, or a manufacturing establishment, or the production of certain foodstuffs. In a controlled economy subsidies may be paid to producers in lieu of allowing increases in prices.   s.

subsistence homestead. A house and a plot of ground sufficient to provide a supply of food for a family, established and financed by the Farm Security Administration of the Department of Agriculture.   z.

substantive law. That part of the law which determines rights and duties, as distinguished from procedural, or adjective, law which determines judicial and administrative procedures.   s.

substantive rights. Rights to the enjoyment of fundamental privileges and immunities equally with others, as distinguished from procedural rights (*q.v.*)   s.

subtreasury system. The system of depositing the funds of the national government in the treasury of the United States or in subtreasuries located in various cities, which prevailed from 1840 to 1920, when federal reserve banks became the depositaries.   s.

subvention. A grant of money or property made by a government or one of its agencies to a private institution usually for educational, scientific, or literary purposes. *Compare with* Grant-in-aid.   s.

Sucker State. A nickname for Illinois.   s.

suffrage. The right granted to certain individuals by constitution or statute to express a choice among candidates for elective office or to register a vote for or against a proposed constitutional amendment, statute, bond issue, etc., submitted to the electorate according to law. The suffrage in 1776 was restricted to property holders, but has since been extended to nearly all adult citizens. The determination both as to the persons entitled to the suffrage and the manner of its exercise is left to the States, subject to the provisions of the 15th and 19th Amendments to the national Constitution that no person shall be denied a vote on account of race, color, previous condition of servitude, or sex. Infancy, insanity, alienage, and insufficient period of residence in a State, county, or election district are disqualifications in all States. Many States impose educational or literacy tests, and in the South taxpaying qualifications are frequent.   cs-h.

suffragette. A feminine advocate of votes for women and the eligibility of women for political offices.   jwf.

Sugar Frauds. Frauds in the weighing of sugar in the New York customhouse which were exposed in 1909.   s.

suit. Traditionally any litigation following the rules and procedures of equity, distinguished from common law litigation which is known as an "action."   z.

summary. Descriptive of court procedure lacking usual judicial formalities, characteristic of a court-martial, police court, or court which does not keep a record.   z.

summons. A judicial order addressed to a defendant in a civil action commanding him to appear and make answer to a complaint made against him.   z.

sumptuary legislation. Laws designed to regulate the expenditure of persons in order to promote frugality and temperance, and prevent ostentatious or vulgar display.   jmcc.

superannuation. The retirement of public employees and officials on account of advanced age.   z.

superintendent. Part of the title of certain national, State, and local officials, *e.g.*, Superintendent of Documents, Superintendent of Instruction, Superintendent of Schools.   z.

Supervising Architect. An official, formerly of the Treasury Department and now of the Federal Works Agency, whose office is responsible for designs and specifications for all authorized national building projects.   z.

supervisor. In some States the popularly elective chief administrative officer of a township, and a member, with other supervisors, of the administrative and fiscal board of a county.   z.

supplementary appropriation. An appropriation made after the enactment of the regular appropriations for a fiscal period to defray unexpected or extraordinary expenditures.   z.

Supreme Court. The highest court in the American federal system and the only one which the Constitution directly provided for. The number of justices was fixed by Congress at six in 1789; at five in 1801; at seven in 1807; at nine in 1837; at ten in 1863; at seven in 1866; and at nine in 1869, where it has since remained. Its original jurisdiction, as fixed by the Constitution, extends to "all cases affecting ambassadors, other public ministers, and consuls, and those in which a State shall be a party"; but, since the enactment of the 11th Amendment, not to cases in which a State is sued by a citizen of another State. Its appellate jurisdiction, as determined by Congress, has varied greatly and now extends to fewer subjects than formerly; but the popular impression that it is confined to cases involving the construction or interpretation of the Constitution (*see* Judicial review) is erroneous. All cases in which the Circuit Court of Appeals declares a State law unconstitutional must be appealed; and others may be brought to the Supreme Court by writ of certiorari or under certification of division from circuit judges. A miscellaneous group of cases involving criminal law, determinations of commissions created under the interstate commerce power, etc., may be appealed directly by writ of error or otherwise from special sessions of district courts. Decisions of the highest State courts may be appealed if rights under the Constitution of the United States or national laws or treaties are asserted to have been denied or ignored; or if a State constitution or statute is alleged to be in conflict with the Constitution, laws or treaties of the United States. The Supreme Court sits from October to May and hears about a thousand cases annually, nearly all of them involving novel questions of constitutional or statutory interpretation. Decisions and opinions may be found in the *United States Reports*. The highest State courts are often called "supreme courts"; but, as in New York, the term may be applied to a lower court.   s.

Surgeon-General. The official title of the head of the Public Health Service (*q.v.*)   z.

surplus. An amount held in the treasury representing the excess of ordinary revenues over expenditures.   s.

Surplus Commodities Corporation. A United States government corporation chartered under the laws of Delaware in 1933 to stabilize and improve markets for agricultural products; since merged with the Agricultural Marketing Administration.   z.

Surplus Marketing Administration. A unit of the Department of Agriculture charged with developing by-product uses for agricultural products, expanding their internal consumption by "food stamp" and similar plans and encouraging foreign sales by export bounties; recently merged with the Agricultural Marketing Administration.   z.

surrogate. A local judicial officer in New York with jurisdiction over the probate of wills, the disposition of estates, and the guardianship of orphaned minors.   z.

surtax. A tax levied upon certain classes of taxpayers or goods in addition to the normal or general tax.   s.

suspending clause. A clause in a constitution, statute, or other public document identifying certain contingencies under which temporarily the document is not effective or some right or privilege granted in it may be denied.   z.

suspension. The action of an executive or administrative officer in barring a person from a position or employment pending final determination of his case by the authority which has power to remove him.   s.

suspension of rules. The temporary abrogation of the rules of a legislative body for the consideration of a particular measure. In the House of Representatives the motion is usually "to suspend and pass" and requires a two-thirds vote.   s.

suspensive veto. An executive veto which has the effect of suspending the operation of a law until it is reconsidered by the legislature and repassed by an ordinary majority.   s.

suzerainty. A relationship between two states in which one is overlord of the other, although the vassal state may retain most of the prerogatives of an independent state; *e.g.,* the British Crown is suzerain of the Indian native states.   JWF.

sweating. 1. The employment of labor at low wages, long hours, and under unsanitary conditions, including the employment of women and children on piecework to be done in tenement homes. 2. Plying a prisoner with threats for the purpose of extorting information or a confession from him.   s.

swing round the circle. An extensive speaking tour in which a President or presidential candidate attempts to obtain popular support for his policies.   s.

symbol. An object or pattern representing an intangible concept, *e.g.,* the mace as a symbol of parliamentary authority. JWF.

sympathetic strike. A strike called among workmen who themselves have no direct grievances but who wish to support a strike called in another plant or industry.   z.

system, the. The combination of politicians with underworld characters or with businessmen seeking advantage from the public by underhand means.   s.

T

Tammany Hall. A nickname for the regular Democratic organization of New York County, bestowed because from an early date until recently it held its meetings in the hall of the Tammany Society, a benevolent society founded in 1789. s.

tangible property. Real or personal property having a corporeal existence, as distinguished from intangible property which consists of securities, mortgages, and other instruments of credit representing wealth. s.

tariff. 1. A series of schedules or rates of duties on imported goods. Tariffs are *for revenue* if their objects are wholly or mainly fiscal; *protective* if they are designed to relieve domestic producers from effective foreign competition; *discriminatory* if they apply unequally to products of different countries; and *retaliatory* if they are designed to compel a foreign country to remove artificial trade barriers against the entry of a country's products. The first tariff law of the United States, passed July 4, 1789, was designed partly to raise revenue and partly to protect certain industries, though the rates were so low as hardly to afford protection in fact. It was not until after the War of 1812 when many "infant industries" were threatened with extinction by foreign importations that Congress, in 1816, effectively applied the protective principle. Still greater protection was afforded in the act of 1824 and in the "Tariff of Abominations," 1828, in which duties were so high as to bring about the nullification movement. A downward adjustment was made in 1832, and the Compromise Tariff of 1833 provided for further gradual adjustment downward over the next ten years. The law of 1842 generally restored the rates of the tariff of 1832; but the process was again reversed in the Walker Tariff, 1846, which introduced the principle of free trade, subsequently extended in the act of 1857. The Republicans, when they came to power in 1861, reintroduced the protective principle in the Morrill Tariff, and continued it in later piecemeal revisions and in the act of 1883 and the McKinley Tariff of 1890. The revisions made by a Democratic Congress in the Wilson-Gorman Act, 1894, were disappointing to sincere free traders. The Republicans passed the thoroughly protective Dingley Tariff, 1897, and in general maintained the high rates, with only slight concessions, in the Payne-Aldrich Act, 1909. The Underwood Tariff, 1913, reduced duties in attempting to reach a point where foreign competition might be effective in curbing monopolies. The Fordney-McCumber Tariff, 1922, again raised duties; and further increases were made by the Smoot-Hawley Tariff of 1930; but reductions have since occurred through reciprocal trade agreements. 2. A rate of duty on a single product. 3. A published statement of charges by a common carrier. s.

Tasmanian dodge. An electoral fraud by which a vote buyer, having obtained a blank official ballot, marks it, and gives it to a bribed voter with instructions to cast it and bring back a blank official ballot from the polling place; upon which, he receives his bribe. The process is continued throughout election day. Many election laws seek to prevent this practice by providing a detachable numbered stub which can be compared with the number on the ballot cast by the voter.　　　　s.

Tattooed Man. A nickname of James G. Blaine, inspired by a cartoon by Thomas Nast.　　　　s.

tax. A compulsory contribution or payment, usually in the form of money, levied according to law upon a person for the support of government, or for regulation or the promotion of certain social objectives. It must be for a public purpose and it must be uniform upon all taxpayers of a given class. It is levied without reference to the benefit which an individual receives from a government or his ability to pay, though consideration of both benefit and ability may strongly influence tax policies. Congress is forbidden to tax exports; to levy direct taxes unless apportioned among the States according to population (except income taxes); to expend the funds raised by taxation for purposes other than the common defense or general welfare; or to show a preference among the ports of different States, which in effect means that taxes must be uniform throughout the States and incorporated territories.　　s.

Taxation without representation is tyranny. An American rallying cry in the period before the Revolution, based on the theory that taxes could be levied only by colonial assemblies.　　s.

tax avoidance. The action of a taxpayer in legally using alternative rates or methods of assessment of taxes for his own advantage.　　　　s.

tax base. The unit of taxation, such as annual net income, the value of property or of a decedent's estate, or the number, weight, volume, or value of articles of a certain kind.　　s.

tax commission. A State fiscal body, consisting usually of three appointive or elective members, which supervises local tax officials, assesses public utility and other property, collects most taxes not collected locally, and often serves as a State tax equalization board.　　　　z.

Tax Court of the United States. A special judicial tribunal of eight members, created by Congress in 1924 as the Board of Tax Appeals, which hears and decides cases appealed by taxpayers from the decisions of the Commissioner of Internal Revenue in which insufficient payment is alleged in income, and certain other internal revenue, taxes. Its decisions are subject to review by the regular courts.　　　　z.

tax dodging. Tax evasion or tax avoidance, especially the practice of establishing a legal residence in a State or other area where tax rates are low.　　　　s.

tax evasion. The action of a taxpayer in illegally escaping the payment of taxes by such methods as failure to report taxable property or income.　　　　s.

tax exempt. Pertaining to property used for educational, religious, or charitable purposes which is ordinarily exempted by law from assessment for taxes; or to certain bonds issued by the national government or a State, or one of its subdivisions which, in order to secure ready marketability or a lower rate of interest, has relieved them from taxation. A long-established canon of constitutional construction that neither the national nor State governments could tax the other's instrumentalities was broken down as to salaries of public employees in 1939.   s.

taxpayer's suit. A suit which, under the laws of nearly all the States (but not of the United States), may be brought by any taxpayer, no matter how little his pecuniary interest may be, to enjoin the illegal expenditure of public funds.   s.

taxpaying qualification. A requirement that a person pay taxes in order to participate in elections. It was introduced in the Revolutionary period as a substitute for the property qualification and, after practically disappearing, was revived by Southern States after the Reconstruction period.   s.

teacher's certification. Issuance by a State department of public instruction or equivalent agency of credentials to an individual attesting his legal qualification to teach in the public schools of the State.   z.

teacher's oath. The sworn declaration of a teacher in a public school or other educational institution that he will uphold the Constitution of the United States and of his State, and that he will neither teach subversive doctrines nor participate in organizations preaching them.   JWF.

Teapot Dome. *See* Oil scandal.

technocracy. A social philosophy popular in the United States in 1932 which was based on the assumption that machine production had rendered existing forms of social and economic control obsolete and which proposed the construction of a rational social organization by scientists and engineers.   JWF.

tellers. Persons appointed from either side of a question to count the members of an assembly as they rise when their names are called. A vote by tellers is not a record vote.   s.

temperance. Habitual restraint in indulgence, especially in intoxicating liquors.   s.

temporary chairman. A person appointed by a party committee to call a convention to order, deliver a keynote speech, and preside until a permanent chairman is elected.   s.

Tennessee. The 16th State, admitted to the Union June 1, 1796, from territory ceded by North Carolina. It seceded from the Union June 8, 1861, and was readmitted June 24, 1866. Capital, Nashville; area, 42,246 sq. mi.; population (1940), 2,915,841;

presidential electors, 12. The present constitution was adopted in 1870. With minor exceptions all adult citizens are legally entitled to vote.   s.

Tennessee Valley Authority. A corporation chartered by Congress in 1933 to construct dams and other works along the Tennessee River and its tributaries and promote the development

Tennessee Valley Authority — Drainage area and dams

of the Tennessee Valley, an area of some 41,000 sq. mi. inhabited by some 2,500,000 persons. The Authority distributes electric power to consumers at low rates through private utility companies, local governments, and co-operatives; distributes fertilizers to farmers through the Department of Agriculture; and produces nitrates for defense purposes. It is managed by a board of three directors appointed by the President and the Senate, employs some 30,000 persons, and is financed by public appropriations, the sale of its own bonds, and proceeds from the sales of its products and services.   JMCC.

Tennis Cabinet. A group consisting of James R. Garfield, Gifford Pinchot, and other bureau chiefs with whom President Theodore Roosevelt played tennis, and who were influential in determining his conservation and other policies.   s.

Tenth Amendment. An amendment to the Constitution of the United States, proclaimed along with nine other amendments constituting the Bill of Rights on Dec. 15, 1791. This amendment formulates the doctrine that the Constitution delegates powers to Congress and reserves all other powers not so delegated or expressly denied the States, to the States or the people.   CHS.

tenure. An individual's continuance in office. The tenure of an appointive office may be during good behavior, as in the case of the national judiciary, or during pleasure, *i.e.*, at the discretion of the administrative superior having the power to remove. Tenure during pleasure has in the past been controlled largely by political considerations. With the rise of the merit system in the national civil service, safeguards have been erected for all so-called "classified" positions to prevent removal except for incompetence or other good cause. CHS.

Tenure of Office Act. A law of Congress passed Mar. 2, 1867, and repealed Mar. 3, 1887, which required the approval of the Senate for the removal of an officer appointed by a President with the consent of the Senate. Alleged disregard of this act by President Johnson led to his impeachment. An act of like purport, passed July 12, 1876, applying to postmasters, was declared unconstitutional in the Myers case (*q.v.*) S.

term. A fixed period of time, especially the period for which a public official is elected or appointed. JWF.

Terrapin War. A derisive term applied by Federalists to the Embargo and Nonintercourse acts. S.

territorial waters. The marginal sea or maritime belt extending outward three miles from the shore, measured from headland to headland, which is considered within the boundaries of the littoral state and hence subject to its jurisdiction. They may include bays and gulfs or broader belts of marginal seas where the jurisdictional claim of the littoral state is supported by international convention or general acquiescence. JTC.

territory. A portion of the United States not included within any State or the District of Columbia, whether organized or unorganized. An organized territory at first had a lower house of the legislature elected by the people and other officials appointed by the President and Senate; but in all territories created since 1836 both legislative chambers have been popularly elective. *See* Incorporated territory; Unincorporated territory. S.

testimony. Information or evidence offered by witnesses under oath at a judicial or similar proceeding. Z.

test oath. A declaration of past loyalty to the United States required of teachers, clergymen, and former public officials by certain State constitutions during the Reconstruction period following the Civil War. It was declared unconstitutional as both an ex post facto law and a bill of pains and penalties in *Cummings* v. *Missouri,* 4 Wall. 277 (1867). JWF.

Texas. The 28th State, admitted to the Union Dec. 29, 1845. It became independent of Mexico in 1836 and was annexed to the United States under a joint resolution of Congress in 1845. Its boundaries were undefined until 1850. It adopted an ordinance of secession Feb. 1, 1861, and was readmitted Mar. 30, 1870. Capital, Austin; area, 265,896 sq. mi.; population (1940), 6,414,824; presidential electors, 23. The present constitution was adopted in 1876. Suffrage is limited by a poll tax requirement. *See* map, page 304. S.

Texas Primary cases. Four cases in the Supreme Court of the United States involving the right of Negroes to vote in Democratic primary elections in Texas. *Nixon* v. *Herndon,* 273 U.S. 536 (1927), held void a State law excluding them, as in violation of the equal protection clause of the 14th Amendment. A new law providing that the State executive committee of the party might exclude them met a like fate in *Nixon* v. *Condon,* 286 U.S. 73, (1932). When the State party convention, of its own authority, excluded them, the Court declined to interfere, *Grovey* v. *Townsend,* 294 U.S. 45 (1935), because the discrimination was by private persons, a political party being a voluntary association under Texas laws. But this decision was reversed in the Lonnie Smith case in which the Court held in April, 1944, that Negroes were entitled, under the 15th Amendment, to participate in primary elections; and

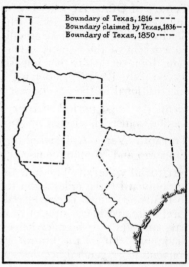

Texas — Disputed boundaries of Republic of Texas

that their right to do so could not be nullified by a State through casting its electoral process in a form which permits a private organization to practice social discrimination.   s.

Texas v. White. A case, 7 Wall. 700 (1869), in which the Supreme Court denied the existence of the alleged right of secession and declared that "the Constitution, in all its provisions, looks to an indestructible Union composed of indestructible States."   s.

thalweg. The middle of the navigable channel of a boundary river or strait. It marks the exact legal boundary line unless an agreement between the riparian states stipulates otherwise.   JWF.

Thanksgiving Day. An American holiday annually proclaimed by the President and State governors to acknowledge and express gratitude for divine favor.   JWF.

theocracy. A state in which political authority is concentrated in the clergy or in which public officials are closely controlled by an ecclesiastical hierarchy, *e.g.,* Geneva in the time of Calvin, or perhaps Massachusetts Bay Colony.   JWF.

third degree. The process of extorting a confession or information from a prisoner by prolonged questioning, the use of threatening words or gestures, or actual violence.   s.

third house. A term sometimes applied to the lobby.   s.

Third International. The international organization of Marxian communist parties of various countries, sometimes known as the Communist International, or Comintern, founded at Moscow in March, 1919, by Russian Soviet leaders to counter efforts of moderate Socialists elsewhere to revive the Second Marxian International originally established in 1889. The dissolution of the Comintern was announced in July, 1943.   z.

third party. A party, such as the Know-Nothing party or the Progressive party of 1912, which occasionally rises in a two-party system and attains sufficient strength to have a decisive effect on the result of an election. It should be distinguished from a minor party (*q.v.*)   s.

third-term tradition. An unwritten custom of the American Constitution, begun by Washington and established by Jefferson and other early Presidents, that a President should not serve more than two terms. President Grant failed of a third nomination in 1880 though his friends argued that the tradition applied only to *consecutive* terms; and the same was true of Theodore Roosevelt in 1912 with the additional argument that he had not already served two *full* terms. The tradition was broken by the re-election of President Franklin D. Roosevelt in 1940 after he had completed two constitutional terms.   s.

Thirteenth Amendment. The first of the three so-called "Civil War Amendments" to the Constitution, proposed to the States by Congress Jan. 31, 1865, and proclaimed in effect Dec. 18, 1865. It provides that neither slavery nor involuntary servitude except as a punishment for a crime shall exist anywhere in the United States or its territories.   z.

Three acres and a cow. A slogan of the Populists who demanded equal treatment of all persons regardless of wealth.   s.

three-fifths compromise. A decision of the Convention of 1787 that in estimating a State's population for representation in Congress and apportioning direct taxes, only three fifths of the whole number of slaves were to be counted. The decision was a compromise between Southern and Northern States.   z.

three-mile limit. The distance of one marine league or three miles offshore which, in the absence of international agreements to the contrary, is recognized as the limit of a littoral state's territorial jurisdiction.   JWF.

tidal wave. An overwhelming popular majority in an election. s.

tin box. An expression, originating in the testimony of former sheriff Thomas M. Farley before the Seabury Committee Oct. 6, 1931, which denotes the questionable source of a politician's income over and above his salary.   s.

Tippecanoe and Tyler too. A slogan of the Whig party in the campaign of 1840 in which the presidential candidate was William Henry Harrison, victor over Indians at Tippecanoe, Ind., and the vice presidential candidate was John Tyler.   s.

tissue ballot. A ballot printed on very thin paper. The depositing of several such ballots, folded together to look like one ballot, was formerly a favorite means of stuffing the ballot box. s.

token coin. A coin with a face value greater than that of the metal it contains.   s.

Toledo War. A dispute between the State of Ohio and Michigan Territory, 1835, as to the boundary between them which involved the town of Toledo. It was settled by the act of Congress admitting Michigan as a State in 1837 which gave the disputed district to Ohio, but added the Upper Peninsula to Michigan.   s.

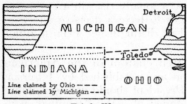

Toledo War

tonnage. A tax on ships based on weight of goods carried or cubic capacity and often discriminatory as between vessels of domestic and foreign registry.   s.

Too proud to fight. A phrase used by President Wilson in an address May 10, 1915, and immediately seized upon by his opponents who desired a more vigorous foreign policy.   s.

Torrens system. A system of registration of land titles devised by Sir Robert R. Torrens and used in Australia, Canada, and several of the United States. On payment of a fee the purchaser of a tract of land may secure a valid title after a court hearing. Later claimants with valid titles are compensated in cash from an insurance fund created and maintained from the registration fees. s.

tort. Any wrongful act, not including breach of contract, for which an injured party may bring a civil action against the alleged wrongdoer.   JWF.

Tory. 1. A member of an English political party, 1679-1832, which supported the royal prerogative and the Established Church. 2. An American who, during the period of the Revolution, adhered to the Crown or did not join the revolt against it. 3. An epithet often applied by politicians to their conservative opponents.   s.

totalitarian state. A state with a dictatorial or other authoritarian form of government to which constitutional law and usage ascribe power without limit over all spheres of human organization and activity, political, economic, intellectual, and moral.   z.

town. 1. The principal unit of local government in New England except in more populous places which have been incorporated as cities. It is governed by a town meeting and administered through selectmen and other officers elected by it. 2. The official title for a township (*q.v.*) in some States. 3. A small urban place whether incorporated or not.   s.

town meeting. An assembly of the qualified voters of a town or, occasionally, of their representatives, in whom all local governmental powers are vested. It is characteristic of New England but not limited to that section. JWF.

Townsend plan. The proposal of Francis E. Townsend that substantial pensions be granted by the national government to elderly people with the proviso that the payments be spent quickly to circulate money and thus stimulate business; hence sometimes called the "revolving pension plan." JWF.

Townshend Acts. Three acts of Parliament passed in 1767 when Charles Townshend was Chancellor of the Exchequer which levied duties on American imports of glass, paper, paints, and tea; created a commission to enforce trade laws; and suspended the legislature of the Colony of New York. S.

township. 1. A unit of local government comprising part of a county and often a mere subdivision of it. It is governed in a few States by boards of commissioners or trustees; in others, by a supervisor elected by popular vote. The functions of townships vary greatly in different States. They usually include the maintenance of local roads and the administration of elementary schools and poor relief. 2. An area, sometimes called a congressional township, approximately square and containing nearly 36 square miles, which is the unit of public land surveys in States not included in the original thirteen and in northern Maine. Its boundaries may or may not coincide with those of the civil township. S.

trade association. A voluntary nonprofit association of competitors in a branch of industry for dealing with mutual business problems, such as accounting practices, trade promotion, and relations with organized labor, the public, and public officials. There were about 8,000 such associations in the United States in 1942. JJR.

trade dollar. A United States silver coin — of slightly greater weight than the silver dollar — minted 1873-85 for use in trade with China and Japan. It was not a legal tender. S.

trade-mark. An emblem, symbol, trade name, or similar device used to distinguish the goods or services of a particular manufacturer or dealer. On payment of a fee, it may be registered with the Trade-Mark Division of the United States Patent Office; but ownership and use of the trade-mark are regulated chiefly by the laws of the States. Z.

trading. Mutual exchange of support for candidates or measures between rival politicians or party organizations. S.

trading-with-the-enemy act. Any statute passed after the outbreak of war prohibiting citizens from transacting business with enemy persons except under special license. JWF.

traffic court. A municipal court of summary jurisdiction responsible for the disposition of offenses against laws and ordinances regulating motor vehicle traffic. Z.

Transportation Act. **1.** A law of Congress, passed Feb. 28, 1920, shortly after the return of railroads from wartime government operation to private operation. It provided that railroad rates should be high enough to enable the companies to earn a reasonable return and that surplus earnings should be subject to partial recapture and use as a loan fund to aid needy companies; for the creation of a railway labor board; and for the eventual consolidation of the railroads into several large systems. **2.** An act of Congress Sept. 18, 1940, extending the jurisdiction of the Interstate Commerce Commission to transportation on intercoastal and inland waterways in order to develop a unified rail, water, and motor transportation system.   s.

treason. A violation of the allegiance which a person — whether a citizen or an alien resident — owes to the state under whose protection he lives. "Treason against the United States shall consist only in levying war against them, or in adhering to their enemies, giving them aid and comfort. No person shall be convicted of treason unless on the testimony of two witnesses to the same overt act, or on confession in open court" (*Constitution*, Art. I, sec. 3). To be considered treasonable, there must be, at the least, an overt assemblage of persons with intent to overthrow the government or the laws. Neither a riotous resistance to officers nor a mere conspiracy to commit treason is treason; but supplying a public enemy with materials or information of military value does constitute treason. The penalty for treason, as fixed by Congress, is death. The States may also punish treason against themselves under the provisions of their own constitutions and laws.   s.

treasurer. An officer of a State, municipal, or local government who is responsible for the receipt and custody of public funds, makes payments on the warrant of a comptroller or equivalent officer, and sells and retires bonds and debt certificates.   z.

Treasurer of the United States. An officer of the Department of the Treasury who is the official custodian of the public money and of miscellaneous securities and trust funds. He receives and disburses public funds, and is fiscal agent for the issuance and redemption of paper currency and for the payment of principal and interest on the public debt.   s.

Treasury, Department of the. A department of the national government created Sept. 2, 1789, which superintends and manages the national finances and is especially charged with the improvement of public revenues and the public credit. It collects customs duties and internal revenue taxes, floats loans, keeps government accounts, supervises the national banks, coins money, prints paper money, negotiates contracts for supplies and services for the general requirements of the government, and administers the narcotic laws. Its secret-service division protects the President, suppresses counterfeiting and violations of the revenue laws, and investigates thefts of government property. **S.**

treasury note. 1. A piece of paper currency issued in various denominations by the United States Treasury under the provisions of the Sherman Silver Purchase Act of 1890, and since retired. 2. A promissory certificate sold in various denominations by the United States Treasury to meet emergency or short-term fiscal needs. **Z.**

treaty. A solemn agreement or compact between two or more sovereign states for the purpose of creating, altering, or extinguishing mutual rights and reciprocal obligations. Treaties are made by negotiation, followed by formal ratification by the head of the treaty-making power. They may be ended by the accomplishment of the purposes for which they were made, by the expiration of a time limit, or by the creation of a new treaty. Denunciation (*q.v.*) by one state, unless provision is made for it in the treaty, may be regarded as a breach of faith. A war between states is usually held automatically to end all treaties between them. For the enforcement of their provisions, treaties depend on the honor and interest of the governments which are parties to them. If these fail, an aggrieved state may make diplomatic protests, apply economic or other sanctions, or, as a last resort, declare war. Treaties are classified as *bilateral,* if only two states are parties; *multilateral,* if more than two accede; *executed,* or *transitory,* if they relate to a single object which is at once disposed of; and *executory,* or *permanent,* if they relate to acts to be performed whenever the conditions specified in the treaty are present. In the United States, treaties are negotiated under the direction of the President and must be ratified by a two-thirds vote of the Senate. A President often takes leading members of the Senate into his confidence during negotiations. According to the Constitution (Art. VI), "All treaties made, or which shall be made under the authority of the United States are a part of the supreme law of the land." In domestic law, they take precedence over State constitutions and statutes and are on an equal footing with valid laws of Congress; *i.e.,* a treaty may void the provisions of a prior statute and vice versa. But the action of Congress in passing statutes repugnant to the terms of treaties or in failing to carry out the provisions of a treaty may result in strained international relations. No treaty has been declared unconstitutional; and the completion of a treaty may actually increase the powers of Congress, as when that body was enabled to pass the Migratory Bird Act (*q.v.*) to enforce a treaty with Great Britain. **S.**

Trent **Affair.** An international incident caused by the stopping and search of the British mail steamer *Trent* by the American ship *San Jacinto,* Nov. 8, 1861, and the seizure of two of her passengers, James M. Mason and John Slidell, who were Confederate commissioners bound for London and Paris respectively. Responsible persons in both the United States and Great Britain acted to avert war, and the commissioners were subsequently put on board a British vessel.   s.

trial. A judicial procedure for examining and deciding the merits of a controversy or establishing the guilt or innocence of a person accused of crime.   z.

trial court. A judicial tribunal having original jurisdiction over cases and controversies, *i.e.*, the power to hear and decide such cases or controversies in the first instance.   z.

tribunal. A court or other body in which decisions binding on litigants are made.   z.

tributary state. A state which has submitted to a stronger state by making payments in money, goods, or services in order to ward off threatened aggression and preserve the semblance of its sovereignty; loosely used for any dependent state.   JWF.

tribute. Valuable commodities such as gold, raw materials, or manufactured goods, or labor or military service, exacted from a weak state as the price of the continued observance of its formal sovereignty or the "protection" rendered by a stronger state. JWF.

trimmer. A political opportunist who readily changes his opinions or loyalties for his own advantage.   s.

Trinidad. A British crown colony, the most southerly of the West Indies, on which the United States leased a site for a naval-air base in 1940.   JWF.

truant officer. A local official concerned with the enforcement of compulsory school attendance laws.   JWF.

truce. An agreement between belligerents to suspend hostilities for a specific purpose such as the celebration of a holiday or the burial of the dead.   JWF.

trust. A form of business combination, now illegal, by which stockholders of corporations or firms assigned their stock to a small board of trustees with voting or managerial powers, receiving in return trust certificates on which payments similar to dividends were made from time to time; loosely, any cartel, pool, conference, or syndicate of companies, or any holding company or integrated corporation powerful enough to exercise monopolistic control.   s.

trust busting. The vigorous prosecution of monopolies under the terms of the Sherman Antitrust Act, especially during the administration of President Theodore Roosevelt.   s.

Tutuila. An island of American Samoa, the site of a naval station.   JWF.

T.V.A. *See* Tennessee Valley Authority.

Tweed Ring. A small group of spoilsmen, led by the notorious boss, William Marcy Tweed, which captured the Democratic organization in New York City in 1863 and subsequently came into complete control of the government of the city. Between 1868 and 1871, the various forms of graft practiced by members of the ring and their outright thefts from the municipal treasury are estimated to have been more than $75,000,000. z.

Twelfth Amendment. An amendment to the Constitution of the United States, proclaimed Sept. 25, 1804, which provides that the electors shall vote for the President and Vice President on separate ballots; and if no candidate has a majority, reduces the range of choice of the House of Representatives from the five highest to the three highest candidates in the electoral vote for President and the range of the Senate in choosing a Vice President to the two highest candidates. AJW,Jr.

Twentieth Amendment. The so-called "lame duck" Amendment to the Constitution, proclaimed Feb. 6, 1933. It changed the beginning of presidential and vice presidential terms from Mar. 4 to Jan. 20; and of congressional terms from Mar. 4 to Jan. 3, thereby eliminating the short, or "lame duck," sessions of Congress; and provided for the succession to the presidency in case the President-elect dies, or no President is duly elected, or an elected President fails to qualify. CHS.

Twenty-first Amendment. An amendment to the Constitution of the United States, proclaimed Dec. 5, 1933. It effectively repealed the provisions of the 18th, or Prohibition, Amendment but prohibited the importation of intoxicating beverages into any State where delivery or use of such beverages constitutes a violation of law. CHS.

twenty-four-hour rule. The requirement that belligerent warships entering a neutral harbor for shelter, repairs, or supplies leave within twenty-four hours unless a longer period is needed to render them seaworthy. JWF.

twilight zone. An undefined area along the boundary between subjects or jurisdictions, such as that lying between the constitutional powers of the States and of the national government. s.

twisting the British lion's tail. Political acts or statements against Great Britain generally made to gain applause among certain elements of the American public. s.

two-party system. The condition which obtains when the political loyalties of the voters of a state are, for any considerable period of time, rather evenly divided between two great political parties, additional parties being either nonexistent or powerless to affect popular or representative decisions on public issues. The system has been traditional in Great Britain, in some of the British dominions, and in the United States, although there have been periods in all these countries when the biparty system was seriously disturbed by the rise of third parties. Because it facilitates the establishment of cohesive electoral and parliamentary majorities, disciplines political opposition, and simplifies the voters' problem in making electoral decisions, the biparty system is generally regarded as essential to stable popular government.   z.

two-thirds rule. A rule of Democratic national conventions, adopted in 1832 and rescinded in 1936, which required that nominations of presidential and vice presidential candidates be made by a two-thirds vote of the delegates.   s.

tying contract. An agreement which requires distributors to maintain fixed resale prices, or to obtain supplies exclusively from one source, or to purchase goods of a specified quantity or quality in addition to those they actually wish to purchase.   s.

tyranny. Government by a despot; the arbitrary or capricious exercise of power in a state; hence government uncontrolled by law or custom.   z.

U

ultra vires. Pertaining to acts done by a public or private corporation which are void for want of legal power conferred in their charters.   s.

umbrella agency. A slang term for an agency of the national government created to prevent overlapping and duplication of activities among a number of other agencies, some of which may themselves be "umbrella" agencies.   s.

unanimity. The agreement or consent of all members of a group.   z.

unanimous consent. Consent, indicated by the absence of objection on the part of any member of a legislative body, for proceeding contrary to a rule or rules. It is a time-saving device frequently used in a variety of minor matters. The House of Representatives has a special consent calendar for such matters called the first and third Mondays of each month. The objection of one member causes a matter to lie over for two weeks, at which time it will be considered unless there are objections from three members.   s.

Uncle Sam. A familiar personification of the government of the United States which originated about 1813.   s.

Unconditional Surrender. 1. A nickname of General U. S. Grant. 2. The terms announced at the Casablanca conference of Prime Minister Churchill and President Franklin D. Roosevelt, 1942, for the capitulation of the Axis powers.   s.

unconstitutional. Contrary to the accepted principles and practices of the state; repugnant to the provisions of a written constitution.   z.

unconstitutional conditions. Conditions imposed by a State of the Union upon a foreign corporation seeking entry to do business therein, which violate the constitutional rights of the corporation as a person. JJR.

underground railroad. Organized secret assistance to fugitive slaves before the Civil War which often enabled them to escape to the North or to Canada. S.

under secretary. An officer of each of seven executive departments in the United States ranking next to the Secretary. An equivalent official in Great Britain represents his department in the house of Parliament to which the minister does not belong. JWF.

Underwood Tariff. The tariff law of Oct. 3, 1913, which substituted ad valorem for specific and compound duties, extended the free list, and reduced the rates on many manufactured articles to a point where foreign competition might become effective as a means of curbing monopolies. S.

undistributed profits tax. A graduated federal tax, ranging from 7 to 27 per cent, levied in 1936 upon corporate surplus, *i.e.*, upon earnings not distributed as dividends. Z.

unearned income. Income derived from interest, dividends, gifts, certain types of royalties, or the like. Z.

unearned increment. Increase in the value of land or economic goods resulting from factors other than the efforts or economic risks of the owner. CHS.

unemployment insurance. A system whereby unemployed workers who meet qualifications receive a stipulated weekly income from a tax-supported fund or reserve during unemployment. JMCC.

unfair trade practice. Any deceptive or discriminatory business practice, including a false or misleading advertisement, the misbranding of a product, or an agreement among business enterprises to fix prices, to discriminate among buyers of their goods or services, to divert business from competitors, or to establish monopoly conditions and interfere with the free flow of commerce. Z.

unicameral. Pertaining to a legislature which consists of only one chamber. S.

uniformity. A constitutional requirement that national tax laws shall operate in the same manner upon persons and property in all the States of the Union. It applies also to the District of Columbia and incorporated territories. Z.

uniform State laws. Statutes of common content enacted on diverse subjects by various States of the United States as a result of the efforts of the Conference of Commissioners on Uniform State Laws (*q.v.*) CHS.

unincorporated territory. A territory or possession of the United States whose inhabitants, under the doctrine of the Insular cases (*q.v.*), can claim only the substantive rights of the Constitution and not such procedural rights as a common law jury trial or indictment by a grand jury before being held for trial. The constitutional requirement that taxes shall be uniform does not apply to such a territory.   z.

union. 1. The combination of two or more states to form a single state. 2. Colloquially, the United States of America. 3. A labor organization.   CHS.

union calendar. An abbreviation for the "Calendar of the Committee of the Whole House on the State of the Union" which lists bills raising revenue, general appropriation bills, and bills of a public character directly or indirectly appropriating money or property.   S.

union label. A tag or stamp placed upon goods to inform purchasers that such goods were produced by union workmen operating in shops observing the conditions of a contract with a labor union.   JMCC.

Union Labor party. A minor party organized in 1887 by various farm and labor groups and the remnants of the Greenback party. It cast 146,897 votes in 1888.   S.

Union League. A secret political organization formed in the North in 1862 to assist the national government and to combat the activities of Southern sympathizers and Copperhead societies. During the Reconstruction period it extended its activities into the South for the protection of freedmen.   S.

union maintenance clause. A clause, required by the War Labor Board in many collective contracts, stipulating that although non-union men may be hired or continued in employment, all who were members of a union when the contract was signed or join voluntarily thereafter must maintain membership as a condition of employment.   JJR.

Union Now. A movement inaugurated by Clarence K. Streit in 1939 to unite the United States and other democratic nations on the analogy of the American federal system.   CHS.

Union party. 1. The name adopted in Ohio Valley States at the beginning of the Civil War by fusions of Republicans and War Democrats, and widely used by Republicans elsewhere. *See* National Union party. 2. A minor party in the election of 1936 composed of advocates of the Townsend plan, "share the wealth," and other movements. Its presidential nominee, William Lemke, received 882,479 popular votes.   S.

Union saver. A contemptuous epithet applied before the Civil War to an advocate of concessions and compromises as a means of averting the disruption of the Union.   S.

union shop. A place of employment in which new employees must become union members after a certain period and continuously maintain their membership. JJR.

unitary state. A state having a unitary government, *i.e.,* one lacking federal features or one in which the institutions of regional and local government lack constitutional or legal guarantees of autonomy. JWF.

unit costs. Inclusive costs per unit of service or production. Unit costs are utilized to compare costs of operating an institution at different times, to compare the cost of operating different institutions performing similar functions, and to assist in foreseeing costs. CHS.

United Labor party. A single-tax party which, with Henry George as its candidate, ran second in the New York mayoralty election in 1886. It cast 2,818 votes in the national election of 1888, after which it disappeared. S.

United Nations. An official designation for the states opposed to the Axis powers in World War II. JWF.

United Nations Relief and Rehabilitation Administration. An international agency created Nov. 9, 1943, to give effect to the determination of the United Nations and powers associated with them to aid the people of regions liberated from the Axis powers. It provides relief, food, clothing, shelter, medical and sanitary assistance, and help in securing the return of exiles and prisoners of war, and the restoration of agriculture, industry, and essential services. The Administration is composed of a council consisting of one representative from each signatory power and a central committee representative of China, Russia, Great Britain, and the United States. Administrative expenses are shared by all member governments. Operating funds are contributed by member nations which have not been invaded at a recommended rate of one per cent of the national income. S.

United States Coast Guard. An essentially autonomous unit of the public forces of the United States, subject to the jurisdiction of the Department of the Treasury in time of peace and of the Department of the Navy in time of war or national emergency. Although it is especially charged with the enforcement of the customs, navigation, and neutrality laws, it serves as a general law enforcement agency upon navigable waters and the high seas and protects life and property at sea. Z.

United States Conciliation Service. A unit of the Department of Labor which investigates the cause of labor disputes and seeks to bring about a settlement by mediation and the use of good offices. Z.

United States Court of Customs and Patent Appeals. A legislative court established in 1910 as the United States Court of Customs Appeals and given its present title and duties in 1929. It consists of five justices, and has a specialized appellate jurisdiction to determine disputes over customs, patents, and trade-marks. s.

United States Customs Court. A legislative court created in 1890 as the Board of United States General Appraisers and given its present title in 1926. It consists of nine judges sitting in New York City, and has sole jurisdiction over the interpretation of tariff laws, the classification of merchandise, and the determination of the dutiable valuation of imported goods. s.

United States Employees Compensation Commission. An independent quasi-judicial commission of three members, created in 1916 to administer workmen's compensation legislation for federal civil employees and employees in private enterprises operating under the jurisdiction of the national government. z.

United States Government Manual. An official publication appearing at intervals of about six months which contains statements of the duties, functions, and activities of all Administrations, Agencies, Authorities, Boards, Bureaus, Commissions, Committees, Corporations, Councils, Courts, Departments, Divisions, Institutions, Offices, Services, Units, and other establishments of the national government in existence as of the date when it goes to press. An Appendix of more than 25 double-column pages lists, with brief notes, all Administrations, etc., which have been abolished, transferred, or terminated since Mar. 4, 1933. Organizational charts were included until recently when they were omitted in order to conserve strategic metals and provide space for important additions to the text. s.

United States Housing Authority. A small government-owned corporation operating within the National Housing Agency, which was created in 1937 to make loans to the States or to their political subdivisions for slum clearance and the construction of dwelling units for low-income families. z.

United States Maritime Commission. An independent national agency of five members, established by Congress in 1936 as the successor to the United States Shipping Board and given the powers and properties of that board along with other functions. It is charged with the development of an American merchant marine owned and operated as far as practicable by citizens of the United States, of sufficient tonnage to carry all domestic waterborne commerce, and of practical utility as a combat auxiliary in time of war or emergency. The commission grants subsidies to American citizens for the construction and operation of vessels engaged in foreign trade to permit them to meet adverse foreign competition, and enforces the labor provisions of national maritime legislation in contracts between operators and crew on ships receiving operational subsidies. Its functions with respect to operations, purchase, and charter were transferred to the War Shipping Administration (*q.v.*) Feb. 7, 1942. z.

United States Military Academy. An institution at West Point, N.Y., for the training of junior officers of the nation's military establishment, under the supervision of the War Department. z.

United States Naval Academy. An institution at Annapolis, Md., under the supervision of the Bureau of Navigation for training junior naval officers. z.

United States Office of Education. An administrative unit established in the Department of the Interior in 1867 and transferred to the Federal Security Agency in 1939. It collects statistics, disseminates information, and supervises vocational education under federal grants and the training of civilians in occupations essential to war. s.

United States Reports. The official printed record of cases heard and decided by the United States Supreme Court. They usually contain a statement of the essential facts of each case, occasionally an abstract of counsel's briefs, the opinion of the Court and concurring and dissenting opinions, if any, and the disposition made of each case. Originally a series of *Reports,* with volumes numbered consecutively, was issued during the incumbency of each successive Court reporter and these are cited as Dallas (1790-1800) ; Cranch (1801-1815) ; Wheaton (1816-1827) ; Peters (1828-1843) ; Howard (1843-1860) ; Black (1861-1862) ; and Wallace (1863-1874). By 1874, the number of volumes so identified totalled 90. At that time the practice began of eliminating the reporter's name and citing them merely as *United States Reports;* and all volumes since issued are identified in that fashion. The latest volume (Apr., 1944) is number 320. z.

United States Tariff Commission. A national administrative body of six members, not more than three of whom may belong to one party. Created in 1916, its principal functions are to study the operation and effect of American customs laws, conduct research in the field of domestic and international commercial policy, and supply Congress and the President with pertinent information on tariff and related matters. It advises the President in the negotiation of reciprocal trade agreements and in the exercise of his discretionary power to raise or lower tariff duties by as much as 50 per cent; and supplies him with the requisite data for the exercise of his statutory power to limit or otherwise regulate the importation of agricultural goods when such importation threatens benefits secured by law to domestic agriculture. z.

unit instruction. A resolution of a party convention which requires all delegates to a higher convention to vote in accordance with the will of the majority of the delegation. s.

unit rule. A rule of Democratic national conventions that whenever a delegation is under unit instructions from its State party convention, its vote on the call of the States must be cast and counted as if it were unanimous, notwithstanding the existence of a minority within the delegation which desires to vote otherwise. Delegates chosen from congressional districts by mandatory direct primary elections and not subjected by law to the authority of the State party convention may vote as individuals; and so, of course, may delegates who are not under unit instructions from a State party convention.   s.

Universal Postal Union. An organization constituted by an international convention in 1874 in which the signatory states agreed reciprocally to deliver foreign mail without charge. A permanent bureau to administer the Union was set up in Bern, Switzerland, and congresses of national delegates meet periodically to decide problems and policies. All independent states except Afghanistan are members.   JWF.

unofficial observer. A title formerly given to a representative of the United States appointed to attend meetings of commissions set up by the League of Nations.   s.

unreasonable searches and seizures. Searches of persons and houses, and seizures of papers and effects, without search warrants particularly describing the place to be searched and the persons or things to be seized. These are prohibited by the Fourth Amendment, while the Fifth Amendment forbids the use of things so seized as evidence against an accused person. These prohibitions do not extend to wire tapping by federal agents.   JJR.

unreconstructed. Pertaining to a Southern attitude of refusing to accept in full the constitutional amendments and Reconstruction acts of Congress after the Civil War.   s.

unwritten constitution. A constitution like that of Great Britain which, consisting largely of common law and custom, has never been comprehensively formulated as a single document; also the usages and conventions which supplement and often modify the provisions of a written constitution.   z.

unwritten law. 1. A name sometimes given to customary law or law contained in judicial decisions which has never been reduced to statutory form. 2. An understanding in certain parts of the country that a jury will not convict a person of a crime committed to avenge the seduction of a member of his immediate family.   s.

upper chamber. Usually the less numerous branch of a bicameral legislature.   s.

urgent deficiency bill. A bill providing additional appropriations when the regular appropriations are apparently inadequate to meet the needs of a department or service during an entire fiscal year.   s.

usage. Long-continued practice which results in customary action or procedure as distinguished from procedure formally defined in writing and having the force of law. In constitutional development usages are important in providing procedures within the legal framework which supplement and extend the words of the document for practical application.   CS-H.

use tax. An ad valorem tax on the use, consumption, or storage of tangible property, usually at the same rate as the sales tax, and levied for the purpose of preventing tax avoidance by the purchase of an article in another State.   S.

U.S.H.A. *See* United States Housing Authority.

usurpation. The forcible seizure of property or arbitrary assumption of a title or privilege rightfully belonging to another. JWF.

usury. The lending of money at exorbitant interest. Nearly all the States limit interest rates by statute and heavily penalize usury.   JWF.

Utah. The 45th State, admitted to the Union Jan. 4, 1896, from territory acquired by the Mexican cession of 1848. Capital, Salt Lake City; area, 84,990 sq. mi.; population (1940), 550,310; presidential electors, 4. The original constitution, which is still in effect, has been amended to provide for the statutory initiative and referendum. With minor exceptions, all adult citizens may vote. S.

utopia. An ideal commonwealth or nearly perfect society, so called from the title of a book by Sir Thomas More first published in 1516.   JWF.

V

vacancy. An office temporarily unfilled because of the death, resignation, disqualification, or removal of the incumbent and the failure to provide an immediate successor.   Z.

vagrancy. The condition of a person without a fixed habitation or reputable means of self-support.   Z.

validating act. A curative statute (*q.v.*)   S.

validity. The quality of legal sanction or authority.   Z.

valuation. The process of appraisal used for determining rates, "fair" profits, taxes, assessments, or money indemnity due property owners as a result of destruction, or alienation by eminent domain. Criteria used in the valuation process include current market value, replacement cost, original actual cost, prudent investment, and capitalized earnings or earning power. Although American practice purports to fix utility rates so as to insure a "reasonable rate on the fair value" of the property concerned, most economists argue that value is the product of earnings from rates charged, and hence cannot logically be used as the point of departure in determining fair rates.   CHS.

vassal state. A state, such as Manchukuo, apparently independent but actually subject to the overlordship of a more powerful state.   JWF,

Venezuela Boundary dispute. A controversy of long standing between Great Britain and Venezuela over the western boundary of British Guiana. In 1895 President Cleveland served notice that the United States would determine the true boundary line, whereupon Great Britain agreed to arbitration. The award gave her most of the disputed territory.   s.

venire. An ancient writ, venire facias, summoning jurymen. z.

venue. The locality, normally the county, in which a criminal trial or legal action is held or from which the jury is chosen.   z.

verdict. The decision of the jury in the trial of either civil or criminal cases.   JWF.

Vermont. The 14th State, admitted to the Union Mar. 4, 1791, from a district, claims to which had been relinquished by both New Hampshire and New York. Capital, Montpelier; area, 9,564 sq. mi.; population (1940), 359,231; presidential electors, 3. With minor exceptions all adult citizens may vote.   s.

Versailles, Treaty of. The treaty, signed at Versailles on June 28, 1919, between Germany and the Allied and Associated powers, following World War I. By its terms Germany was shorn of her overseas possessions and lost Alsace-Lorraine to France, parts of her eastern territory to the newly formed states of Poland and Czechoslovakia, Eupen and Malmédy to Belgium, and northern Schleswig to Denmark. She was compelled to pay reparations, to limit her army and navy to a small force, and to agree to the demilitarization of much of the Rhineland. Part I of the treaty contained the Covenant of the League of Nations. The treaty was never ratified by the United States.   s.

Veterans Administration. An independent agency authorized by Congress in 1930 to consolidate all administrative units dealing with veterans' affairs. Under its head, known as the Administrator of Veterans' Affairs, the agency administers all laws for relief or benefit, including pensions, death benefits, retirement pay, and institutional care of veterans or their dependents.   z.

veteran's preference. Preferential treatment accorded under United States civil service laws to honorably discharged members of the armed services. They are exempted from the usual requirements of age and physical fitness and are entitled to have five points (ten points, if they are physically disabled) added to the rating they have earned. Widows of disabled veterans and wives of veterans incapacitated for employment are also entitled to an addition of ten points.   s.

veto. The return, to the legislative house in which it originated, of a bill unsigned and with objections in writing by a chief executive whose signature is necessary to complete the enactment of a law. The Constitution of the United States requires that before becoming a law, every bill or resolution must be submitted to the President for his signature. If he does not sign and return it within ten days (Sundays excepted) while Congress is in session, it becomes a law without his signature; but if Congress stands adjourned at the end of the ten-day period, the bill is lost (pocket veto). Congress may override the President's veto by repassing a bill by a two-thirds vote in each house on roll call. All the States except North Carolina grant a veto power to the governor. In 39 States the governor may veto items of appropriation bills, in some of them he may reduce items, and in two States he may veto sections of nonfinancial bills. The number of votes required to override a gubernatorial veto ranges from a majority to two thirds of all members elected to a legislature.   s.

Veto Mayor. A nickname of Grover Cleveland.   s.

vice. In place of; when prefaced to the title of an office it usually identifies a deputy or substitute for the holder of the office, capable, under certain circumstances, of exercising some or all of the powers and duties of the office.   z.

vice consul. A consular officer ranking below a consul but above a consular agent.   s.

Vice President. The officer who succeeds to the presidency in case of the death, removal, resignation, or inability of the President. He is elected on separate ballot by majority vote of the electoral colleges; but if no candidate has a majority the Senate, a quorum of two thirds being present, elects from the two candidates having the highest electoral vote. The Vice President presides over the Senate except when the President is being tried on an impeachment; but he has no vote and little or no influence on its proceedings unless the Senate is equally divided. By invitation of the President, the Vice President sometimes sits in the cabinet.   s.

victory tax. A national income tax of 5 (later 3) per cent, payable at source, levied during World War II, in addition to regularly authorized income taxes, upon all income in excess of a minimum declared exempt by law.   z.

vigilance committee. A group of citizens formed in a frontier community for the maintenance of law and order by summary proceedings.   s.

village. A settlement of limited territory and population, larger than a hamlet but not comparable to a town or city, which may, or may not, be incorporated.   z.

Villa's raid. An attack on Columbus, New Mex., by Pancho Villa, a Mexican bandit leader, Mar. 9, 1916, which resulted in the dispatch of an American army into Mexico to arrest Villa and his followers.   s.

Virginia. One of the original States and the tenth to ratify the Constitution of the United States, June 25, 1788. A convention adopted an ordinance of secession Apr. 17, 1861, and the State was readmitted June 26, 1870. Capital, Richmond; area, 39,899 sq. mi.; population (1940), 2,677,773; presidential electors, 11. The present constitution, adopted in 1902, imposes literacy and poll tax requirements for voting.   s.

Virginia Dynasty. Three Virginians, Thomas Jefferson, James Madison, and James Monroe, who successively served as President, 1801-1825.   s.

Virginia plan. A plan of union, largely the work of James Madison, which was submitted to the Convention of 1787 by Virginia's governor, Edmund Randolph. It provided for the popular election of the lower house of Congress, which would choose the upper house, and for executive and judicial departments chosen by Congress.   s.

Virginia Resolutions. Resolutions drafted by James Madison and adopted by the legislature of Virginia in December, 1798, which declared that the Constitution was a compact among the States and that the States should interpose when the general government attempted to exercise powers not granted in plain terms. Other States were invited to concur in declaring the Alien and Sedition acts unconstitutional. The resolutions were more temperate than the Kentucky Resolutions (*q.v.*)   s.

Virgin Islands. A group of three small islands, St. Thomas, St. Croix, and St. John, lying east of Puerto Rico, which was purchased from Denmark Jan. 17, 1917, for $25,000,000. The legislature, consisting of the popularly elected councils of the three islands sitting together, may enact measures only by a two-thirds vote, and legislation is subject to congressional disallowance. The governor and the judiciary are appointed by the President and Senate.   s.

Virginius, The. A vessel owned by Cuban insurgents and unlawfully registered in the United States which was captured on the high seas by a Spanish warship Oct. 31, 1873, and taken to Santiago de Cuba, where the authorities executed 53 of her crew and passengers, including some American citizens, as pirates. Spain later surrendered the vessel, released the remaining prisoners, and paid an indemnity.   s.

visa. A stamped or written endorsement entered upon the passport of a national of one state by proper officials of another to indicate that they have examined his papers and permit him to enter their state or continue traveling through it.   jwf.

visit and search. The right of belligerent warships to halt and board neutral vessels to determine if they are carrying contraband, running a blockade, or rendering some unneutral service.   jwf.

vital statistics. Data concerning births, marriages, sickness, deaths, and population mobility collected by State and local governments.   jmcc.

viva-voce voting. Voting by word of mouth. The presiding officer of an assembly determines the result from the volume of sound after each side has been called in turn.   s.

vocational education. Training for skilled and useful occupations. Beginning in 1917, grants-in-aid have been made to the States for such training under the supervision of the Federal Board for Vocational Education.   s.

Volstead Act. An act of Congress Oct. 28, 1919, which provided for the enforcement of the 18th Amendment under stringent penalties and defined intoxicating liquors as those containing more than one half of one per cent of alcohol by volume.   s.

voluntary association. A group of individuals not comprising a legal entity and hence not subject to suit.   s.

vote of thanks. A formal resolution of an assembly expressing gratitude for services rendered to the assembly or to the public.   z.

voter. Any person legally qualified to cast a ballot or express a formal choice at a public election or referendum.   z.

voting machine. A mechanical substitute for the paper ballot which has on its face a lever above the name of each candidate or referendum proposal. The voter expresses his preference among

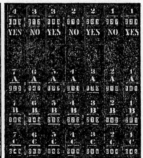

Voting machine — Front view showing levers   Total votes shown when machine is unlocked

candidates or proposals by pulling down levers and leaving them down. As he opens a curtain preparatory to leaving the booth containing the machine, the levers spring back into place and the machine automatically registers and counts the vote. When the polls are closed election officials, by unlocking the machine, may read the total vote for each candidate at a glance.   s.

W

WAC. The popular name of the Women's Army Corps or of one of its members, derived from the initial letters of the Corps. z.

Wage and Hour Division. A division of the Department of Labor whose primary purpose is to secure enforcement of the wage and hour provisions of the Fair Labor Standards Act of 1938.   z.

waiver. The relinquishment by a party of some legal privilege, usually in exchange for another, in a judicial or other cause. Persons possessing diplomatic immunity from civil suit may in some cases waive the privilege by becoming a plaintiff in court, thus risking the defendant's counterclaim.   JWF.

Wake Island. A small American possession west of Hawaii with a military post and a station for trans-Pacific planes. It was occupied by Japanese forces early in World War II.   JWF.

Walker Tariff. The tariff law of July 30, 1846, drafted by Secretary of the Treasury Robert J. Walker, and based on the principles of free trade and heavy taxation of luxuries.   s.

war. Hostile operations conducted by one state against another whether or not such operations have been preceded by a formal declaration of war; also an armed conflict between organized rebels and the *de jure* government of a state if the *de jure* government expressly or impliedly recognizes that the rebels have a belligerent status or if other states accord such a status to them. The outbreak of hostilities brings about a severance of diplomatic relations between the contending states and automatically abrogates such mutual treaty engagements as have governed their political and commercial relations or any other such engagements not deemed to have established a permanent condition of affairs at the time they were entered into. Nationals of one belligerent who are in the territory of the other receive the status of enemy aliens; and the respective belligerents may confiscate public enemy property discovered within their own territory and sequester or impose restrictions upon the private property of enemy nationals. Multilateral international conventions and international usage prescribe that warfare should be conducted according to certain rules. These relate to the use that may be made of certain weapons, to the status of the noncombatant civilian population, to the exemption of undefended localities from attack, and to the treatment of private property within the zone of combat or in the zone occupied by the enemy. They also govern the use of flags of truce, armistices, and capitulations; the right to quarter on the part of enemy forces which surrender; the treatment and exchange of prisoners of war; the duties and immunities of medical and hospital services; and the rights and duties of belligerents toward neutral states and the lives and property of their nationals. It is a principle of the traditional rules of war that belligerents ought not to direct hostile acts against the enemy's civilian population but rather against the enemy's public forces or strongholds. But contemporary methods of warfare make this distinction increasingly meaningless. Total blockade, expanded conceptions of contraband, bombing from the air, shelling from long-range guns, and the mobility of mechanized armament, inevitably jeopardize civilian lives and welfare. Moreover, contemporary belligerents are resorting to a complete mobilization of national life for war purposes. Labor is conscripted, civilians are inducted into a variety of semimilitary or defense agencies, and the entire national economy is geared to the needs of a community at war. Under such circumstances, it is difficult to distinguish between the practical military value of hostile acts against soldiers or fortifications on the one hand and against civilians and so-called undefended areas on the other. Bombing or other hostile operations against any part of the enemy's civilian population or any portion of enemy territory become logically defensible as having military value; and even the breaking of enemy civilian morale becomes a military objective to be achieved by any means whatsoever. Thus is being born the conception of "total war" — a conception in which the entire national life of a belligerent is placed on a war footing; entire populations are pitted, in virtually a physical sense, against each other; and hostile acts are directed indiscriminately against enemy civilian life or property and the enemy's public forces or its military weapons and installations. Such a conception will undoubtedly throw many of the previously accepted rules or usages of war upon the scrap heap.   z.

war cabinet. An inner cabinet consisting of a small number of important officials which makes major decisions concerning governmental policy in wartime.   s.

ward. A municipal territorial subdivision for the election of one or more members of the council and for convenience in the administration of certain public works and services.   z.

War Democrat. A Democrat who supported the military policy of the national government during the Civil War.   s.

War, Department of. One of the ten principal administrative departments of the United States government, created Aug. 7, 1789. Its divisions, branches, and services exercise general supervision over the nation's military forces and all matters relating to military defense or strategy; over the construction of public works, such as the Panama Canal and river, harbor, and flood-control improvements; and over the issuance of permits for the building of dams, piers, bridges, or other projects which may affect navigation. Before 1939, the Department had charge of civil governments in certain dependencies.   z.

ward heeler. A local political hanger-on; a professional politician in the entourage of a district leader or local political boss. z.

Ware plan. A system of preferential voting (*q.v.*), also used in proportional representation, under which the weakest candidates are eliminated in order, and the votes cast for them are counted for other candidates as directed by the voter in the second and later choices marked on the ballot.   s.

War Food Administration. A wartime agency established March 26, 1943, and given its present title a month later under which have been consolidated many existing agencies of the Department of Agriculture including the Commodity Credit Corporation, the Extension Service and the Food Distribution Administration. It has general charge of budgeting the nation's military, foreign and civilian food requirements. To meet these requirements, it may allocate resources for agricultural production, advise the War Production Board as to materials and supplies needed for farm production, establish food priorities, and advise the Office of Price Administration as to civilian rationing.   z.

war guilt. The responsibility for having begun a war without sufficient cause. A statement to the effect that Germany was so responsible for World War I was incorporated in the Treaty of Versailles.   z.

war hawk. An advocate of war; a jingo. The term is especially applied to a group of young congressmen elected in 1810 who wanted war with Great Britain or Spain in order to seize Canada or Florida, though it had also been applied to those who favored going to war with France in 1798.   s.

war horse. A party orator or leader who has participated effectively in a great number of election campaigns.   s.

War Labor Board. *See* National War Labor Board.

War Manpower Commission. A wartime agency of nine officials, with the Federal Security Administrator serving as chairman, established by executive order in the Office for Emergency Management, Apr. 18, 1942, to secure maximum utilization of manpower for the war period. It co-ordinates labor market data collected by national agencies; establishes civilian and military manpower requirements; formulates basic policies for recruiting, training and placing workers in industry, agriculture, and civilian governmental services; and recommends legislation when this is necessary to effectuate its policies. All national government agencies having to do with the utilization and allocation of manpower, including the Selective Service System in its classification of manpower for essential civilian purposes, must conform with the regulations of the Commission.   z.

War Mobilization Director. *See* Office of War Mobilization.

War of 1812. A war between the United States and Great Britain resulting chiefly from American resentment at British commercial restrictions, impressment of seamen, and alleged encouragement of Indians in the Northwest. It was declared by Congress, June 18, 1812, and was officially closed by the Treaty of Ghent, signed Dec. 24, 1814. The news of the treaty did not arrive in time to prevent the battle of New Orleans, Jan. 8, 1815.   s.

war powers. Such powers as are constitutionally committed to the executive and legislative branches to wage war against other states, to raise, organize, equip, and command the necessary public armed forces and to apply such regulations affecting personal liberty and the national economy as the exigencies of actual war or threat of war may require. The war powers, when fully applied as a result of a wartime emergency, are broader in scope and less affected by constitutional limitations than any other powers of government.   z.

War Production Board. A wartime agency of the national government, consisting of a chairman and eight other government officials, created within the Office for Emergency Management by executive order of the President Jan. 16, 1942. The Board controls national production and the procurement of supplies for war purposes. The chairman determines the policies and procedures of all national establishments in purchasing or procuring supplies, establishes priorities in the procurement of goods and services throughout the national economy, and issues directives for plant conversion and expansion to facilitate production for war purposes. The Office of Production Management, established Jan. 7, 1941, has been merged with this agency.   z.

war profits tax. A tax the burden of which is intended to fall directly upon profits of private enterprise attributable to war contracts or to the abnormal wartime demand, particularly from the government, for goods and services.   z.

warrant. A written order issued by a magistrate or court directing an officer to make an arrest or conduct searches or seizures. Constitutional restrictions prevent the issuance of a warrant except for good cause, duly certified, and the warrant must describe the place to be searched or the person or property to be seized.   z.

war risk insurance. Insurance offered by the national government to private persons against wartime loss of vessels and property on the high seas, death or injury while in the armed forces, etc.   s.

War Shipping Administration. A wartime agency created by executive order Feb. 7, 1942. It exercises powers and duties formerly assigned to the United States Maritime Commission (*q.v.*) relating to the purchase, charter, requisition, and operation of merchant vessels, including the powers to assign commission-controlled ships to agents for operation, insure cargo and personnel against loss, fix rates and determine the type of cargo to be carried, and recruit, train, and assign merchant seamen and officers.   z.

war to end wars. A catch phrase frequently heard during World War I.   s.

Washington. The 42nd State, formerly a part of the Oregon Country, admitted to the Union Nov. 11, 1889. Capital, Olympia; area, 69,127 sq. mi.; population (1940), 1,736,191; presidential electors, 8. The original constitution, as amended, provides for the initiative, referendum, and recall, and for a literacy test for the suffrage. s.

Washington, City of. The capital of the United States; a populous urban area whose boundaries coincide with those of the District of Columbia (*q.v.*) It lost its identity as a municipal corporation in 1871. s.

Washington, Treaty of. A treaty between the United States and Great Britain signed at Washington May 8, 1871, which provided for the settlement of the *Alabama* claims (*q.v.*) and a dispute over the San Juan Islands (*see* Northwest boundary) by arbitration, and allowed Americans certain privileges in the North Atlantic fisheries on payment by the United States of an amount to be determined by a joint commission (*see* Halifax Fishery Commission). s.

Washington's Farewell Address. A statement of President Washington, published Sept. 17, 1796, in which he renounced a third term and warned the people against the evil effects of political parties and entanglements in foreign affairs. s.

watch dog of the treasury. A nickname given to a Senator or Representative who distinguishes himself by close scrutiny of items in appropriation bills. s.

watcher. The representative of a party present at a polling place on election day to insure fair conduct on the part of election officials. z.

watchful waiting. President Wilson's characterization of his policy toward the Huerta government of Mexico, Dec. 2, 1913. s.

water power. *See* Federal Power Commission.

water supply. The collection and purification of an adequate supply of water and its distribution among the inhabitants of a municipality or other jurisdiction, a service originally, and to some extent still, rendered by a public utility company but nowadays generally performed by the city or other area of local government under municipal ownership and operation. z.

WAVES. An abbreviation of "Women Appointed for Voluntary Emergency Service," the popular name for the Women's Reserve, United States Naval Reserve, created during World War II. z.

waving the bloody shirt. *See* Bloody shirt.

Ways and Means Committee. A standing committee of the House of Representatives first created in 1795 to supervise all financial legislation, but which since 1865 has confined its attention mainly to the preparation and consideration of tariff and internal revenue bills. s.

weak-mayor plan. A name given to the system of municipal government almost universally in vogue in America during the 19th century. The mayor lacked effective power over administration because officials were chosen by the council, or by popular vote, or, if appointive, were subject to confirmation by the council; his powers of removal and direction were limited by law or the council; the council initiated the budget, awarded contracts, and granted franchises; and the mayor possessed no veto power.   z.

Weather Bureau. An agency of the national government concerned with weather forecasting and providing meteorological data. First organized in 1870 and long a part of the Department of Agriculture it has, since 1940, been under the jurisdiction of the Department of Commerce.   z.

Webb-Kenyon Act. An act of Congress Mar. 1, 1913, which divested intoxicating liquors of their interstate character when shipped into dry territory for use in violation of State laws.   CHS.

Webb-Pomerene Act. An act of Congress Apr. 10, 1918, which exempted associations solely engaged in export trade from the United States from the restrictions of the antitrust laws.   CHS.

welfare. 1. Individual or social good. 2. Pertaining to legislative or other acts calculated to further individual or social good.   CHS.

Well-Born, The. A derisive nickname applied to the Federalists by their opponents because John Adams and others had expressed aristocratic sentiments.   S.

Western Reserve. The northeastern area of the State of Ohio reserved by Connecticut for her own settlers when she ceded her rights to western lands to the United States. Connecticut gave up her title to the district in 1801.   z.

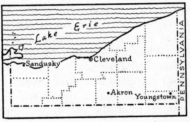

Western Reserve

West Florida. A strip of territory along the Gulf of Mexico east of the Mississippi which was partly colonized by France and ceded to Great Britain in 1763. The latter country erected it into a separate colony with boundaries extending eastward to the Chattahoochee and Apalachicola rivers and northward to the parallel through the mouth of the Yazoo River (32° 28'). By the Treaty of 1783, Great Britain ceded both the Floridas to Spain and at the same time agreed that the southern boundary of the United States should be at the 31st parallel. Spain retained the post at Natchez and refused to relinquish her claim to the region as far north as the parallel of 32° 28' until the signing of Pinckney's Treaty (*q.v.*) in 1795. When Spain in 1800 retroceded to France all of her former colony of Louisiana and when the United States purchased it in 1803, the ownership of West Florida was again in dispute. In 1810 the United States formally asserted its title to the district between the Mississippi and the Pearl rivers; and in 1813 occupied the district between the Pearl and the Perdido rivers. *See* map, page 330.   S.

West Point.   The site of the United States Military Academy
(*q.v.*)   JWF.

West Virginia.   The 35th
State, formerly a part of Virginia, admitted to the Union
June 20, 1863, with the consent of the legislature of the
Restored [Union] Government
of Virginia. Capital, Charles-
ton; area, 24,282 sq. mi; population (1940), 1,901,974;
presidential electors, 8. The
present constitution was adopted in 1872. With minor exceptions, all adult citizens may
vote.   s.

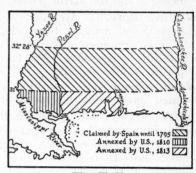

West Florida

wet.   An advocate of the manufacture and sale of intoxicating
liquors; opposed to a "dry."   s.

Whig party.   1. In England after 1680 the name regularly used
for the party which supported the primacy of Parliament and which
was largely responsible for the "Glorious Revolution" of 1688, the
constitutional settlement which followed it, and the maintenance
of the Protestant succession. The name continued until well into
the 19th century when the term Liberal gradually supplanted it.
2. An American party founded in 1834 by a combination of National Republicans, Antimasons and various personal followings.
It was dominated in the North by manufacturing, commercial, and
financial interests, and in the South by the large slaveholding class.
It advocated protective tariffs, the recharter of the Bank of the
United States, and internal improvements. It won the presidential
elections of 1840 and 1848, in both cases with candidates who were
military heroes and inexperienced in politics. The Whigs' attempt
to settle the slavery issue by the Compromise of 1850 alienated
members in both North and South. After being soundly beaten in
1852 the party disintegrated.   s.

whip.   A member of a legislative body, designated by the caucus of his party, whose duties are to remind members of his party
to be present when important votes are to be taken; to arrange pairs
for members unavoidably absent; to conciliate members who are
dissatisfied with the party program; and to keep his party leaders
informed as to the attitude of members toward public questions. s.

Whisky Insurrection.   Violent resistance in western Pennsylvania in 1794 to the collection of excise taxes on whisky imposed
by the federal excise law of 1791. A force of 15,000 militia, ordered
into the region by President Washington, overawed the rioters. s.

Whisky Ring. A combination of government officials and distillers in St. Louis which, it was disclosed in 1875, had defrauded the United States of $1,000,000 annually in internal revenue taxes. The scandal forced several close friends of President Grant out of office.   s.

whispering campaign. The circulation by word of mouth of false or scandalous statements concerning a candidate or party. s.

White House. The official residence of the President of the United States in Washington, D.C.; hence the presidential office. s.

White House Office. The staff of personal aides of the President which includes three presidential secretaries who handle presidential relations with other branches of the government and with the public, and three presidential administrative assistants who perform such duties as the President may direct.   z.

White League. A secret organization in Louisiana during the Reconstruction period which excluded Negroes from the polls by violence.   s.

white man's burden. The alleged duty of members of the Caucasian race to spread their civilization to backward peoples. According to Kipling and other apologists for imperialism, this humanitarian responsibility, and not economic exploitation, was the prime motive for penetration into undeveloped regions. JWF.

White Phosphorus Match Act. An act of Congress, 1912, which levied a tax of two cents per hundred upon poisonous phosphorus matches, thereby effectively preventing their manufacture. z.

white primary. The name given to the primary elections held in several Southern States from which Negroes are excluded by party rule. The recognized basis of the white primary is that the party is a voluntary organization competent to determine its own membership through its own authority. *See* Texas Primary cases.   CS-H.

White Slave Act. An act of Congress June 25, 1910, which forbade aiding, causing, or inducing the transportation in interstate commerce of any woman or girl for immoral purposes.   s.

whitewash. The report of a legislative or other investigating committee which, from friendly or partisan motives, exonerates a public official from grave charges of corruption.   s.

Whitley Council. A factory council representing labor and management in a particular British industry or an equivalent body in various departments of the British civil service representing public employees and the government, so called because their creation was recommended by a special parliamentary commission headed by Speaker John Whitley.   JWF.

who's who ballot. A ballot on which is printed a brief biographical statement after the name of each candidate.   s.

wildcat bank. A bank in the period before the Civil War with inadequate resources to redeem its circulating notes.   s.

Wilmot Proviso. An amendment proposed by Representative David Wilmot of Pennsylvania to a bill appropriating funds to enable the President to make peace with Mexico, 1846, which would have prohibited slavery in any territory acquired from Mexico. It passed the House and was narrowly defeated in the Senate.   s.

Wilson-Gorman Tariff. The tariff law of Aug. 27, 1894, which disappointed the advocates of reduction of high tariff duties.   s.

wirepulling. The unethical conduct of individuals who secretly, or in ways not readily discerned by the general public, exert personal influence or some other form of pressure upon public officials.   z.

wire tapping. Clandestine "listening-in" to telephonic conversations and other communications by wire. Although the Supreme Court has held that the constitutional prohibition of unreasonable searches and seizures does not extend to wire tapping, an act of Congress interdicting such activity has been upheld and applied to federal officers.   z.

Wisconsin. The 29th State, formerly part of the Northwest Territory, admitted to the Union May 29, 1848. Capital, Madison; area, 56,066 sq. mi.; population (1940), 3,137,587; presidential electors, 12. The original constitution is still in effect. Provision is made for the recall. With minor exceptions, all adult citizens may vote.   s.

Wisconsin Rate case. A case, *Wisconsin* v. *Chicago, B. and Q. Ry. Co.,* 257 U.S. 563 (1922), in which the Supreme Court extended the doctrine first elaborated in the Shreveport Rate case (*q.v.*) that there is no invasion of a State's power over intrastate commerce if the Interstate Commerce Commission requires equalization of intrastate rates with interstate rates in order to overcome existing discrimination to shippers and make national control over interstate commerce effective.   z.

witness. 1. An individual who gives evidence under oath in a court or other body as to what he knows about a pending case. 2. An individual called upon to be present at a transaction in order that he may subsequently be able to testify that it took place.   z.

Wizard of Kinderhook. A nickname of Martin Van Buren. s.

Wolverine State. A nickname of Michigan.   s.

woman suffrage. The right of women to participate in public elections. It was advocated in both the United States and Great Britain as early as 1850, and the successful struggle to secure it lasted in both countries for almost three quarters of a century. After having made steady gains in the States, particularly those of the West, suffrage equality was guaranteed in the United States by the adoption of the 19th Amendment (*q.v.*) In Great Britain suffrage was granted to women over 30 in 1918 and to women between 21 and 30 in 1928. z.

workhouse. 1. An institution in an American county where those convicted of less grave offenses are confined and put to useful labor. 2. In Great Britain, a public shelter for transient vagrants or indigent inhabitants who are able to work. JWF.

working class. Individuals dependent upon the income from wage labor for a livelihood. Except in Marxian theory the term is usually restricted to manual laborers and their families who may be considered a distinct social class because of the relative meagerness and uncertainty of their income and the resulting low living standard. *See* Proletariat. JMCC.

Workingmen's party. An organization in New York about 1830 which later became identified with the Locofocos (*q.v.*) s.

workmen's compensation. A system of social insurance financed by payroll taxes whereby workers employed in certain industries receive a money payment either as a lump sum or as regular monthly income in consequence of financial loss resulting from incapacity for normal employment due to industrial accident or occupational disease. JMCC.

work relief. Employment furnished persons by a government or private social agency primarily because of their economic need. The object is to alleviate distress and, by increasing purchasing power, to stimulate recovery in periods of economic depression. The national government first engaged in direct work relief in 1933. CHS.

Works Projects Administration. A national agency which in 1939 succeeded the Works Progress Administration created in 1935 to substitute direct payment of wages by the national government for subventions to States and local governments. The national government approved work projects and set wage scales, and local governments administered the projects and provided necessary equipment and materials. Its activities were terminated in June, 1943. JMCC.

World Court. A popular term for the Permanent Court of International Justice established at The Hague in 1920. Its eleven judges and four deputy judges were elected by concurrent balloting in the Assembly and Council of the League of Nations. The court's jurisdiction extended to justiciable controversies between states such as questions involving the interpretation of a treaty and obligations of a state under its treaties or international law. For the court to have jurisdiction, the consent of the parties to a controversy was required either before or after the controversy arose. JWF.

World Economic Conference. 1. An international conference which met in Geneva in 1927 to study means of regulating inter-

national commerce by international agreement.   **2.** An international
conference in which the United States participated which met in
London in 1933 to seek an end to the economic depression, especially by international stabilization of currencies.   JWF.

World War I.   A global conflict, Aug. 1, 1914 — Nov. 11, 1918,
in which the Central powers, Germany and Austria-Hungary (later
joined by Turkey and Bulgaria), were pitted against the Allied
and Associated Powers, an aggregation which ultimately included
nearly all the other states of the world. Because of Germany's
practically unrestricted submarine warfare the United States declared war against her Apr. 6, 1917, and against Austria-Hungary
Dec. 7, 1917. German or Austrian armies overran Belgium, Serbia,
and Roumania, penetrated deeply into France and Italy, and forced
Russia to accept the harsh terms of the Treaty of Brest-Litovsk,
Mar. 3, 1918. But by the autumn of 1918 the weight of Allied
manpower and material on several fronts forced Germany to sue
for an armistice which was granted Nov. 11. The Versailles Treaty
(*q.v.*) was signed June 28, 1919, but was not ratified by the United
States Senate. The United States remained at war with Germany
until July 2, 1921, when Congress passed a joint resolution declaring the war at an end, but reserving American rights. Subsequently
Germany and the United States signed the Treaty of Berlin Aug.
25, 1921.   S.

World War II.   The global struggle between the Axis powers
— Germany, Italy, Japan and certain satellite nations — and the
loose coalition of United Nations consisting of Great Britain, the
British dominions, the United States, France, Soviet Russia, China,
and most of the remaining states of the world, which began with
Germany's invasion of Poland in September, 1939, and joint declarations of war on Germany by Great Britain and France as guar-
antors of Poland's integrity. Italy entered the war June 10, 1940,
and Russia on June 22, 1941. The surprise Japanese attack on
Pearl Harbor, Dec. 7, 1941, brought the United States into the
war, ranged Japan actively on the side of the Axis and had the
effect of merging her war with China, which began with the seizure
of Manchuria in September, 1931, with the global struggle. Japan
and Soviet Russia, however, remained nominally at peace with
each other. In the earlier phases of the war, Germany conquered
Poland, Norway, Holland, Belgium, and France; penetrated deeply
into Soviet Russia; and with her ally, Italy, seriously threatened
Egypt. Japan conquered the Philippines, the Dutch East Indies,
Singapore, and Burma, maintained her extensive conquests in
China, and seriously threatened India and Australia. The tide
began to turn in favor of the United Nations towards the end of
1942 and the campaigns of 1943 made it clear that victory would
eventually be theirs.   Z.

W.P.A.   *See* Works Projects Administration.

W.P.B. *See* War Production Board.

writ. A formal written order issuing from a court or tribunal having judicial authority commanding an individual or individuals identified in the order to do or abstain from doing some specified act. z.

writing in. Voting for a candidate whose name has not been printed on the official ballot. s.

writ of assistance. A general search warrant, not specifying the place to be searched or describing the goods sought, which was issued prior to the American Revolution to authorize customs officers to seize smuggled goods. The constitutionality of British statutes authorizing this writ was widely debated in colonial courts. JJR.

writ of certiorari. *See* Certiorari.

writ of error. An order issued by an appellate court to a lower court of record usually requiring the latter to send up the entire record of a proceeding after judgment in order that the appellate court may examine into errors allegedly committed by the lower tribunal and either affirm or reverse the latter's decision and judgment. It is chiefly by this means that exceptions taken by counsel to the court's rulings in an original proceeding may be reviewed by a competent higher tribunal. z.

writ of execution. Process issuing from a court in a civil action authorizing the sheriff or other competent officer to carry out the court's decision in favor of the successful party. z.

writ of prohibition. An order issued by a superior court to a court of inferior grade demanding that it refrain from exercising jurisdiction over some specific suit then pending before it. z.

writ of quo warranto. *See* Quo warranto.

written constitution. That part of the fundamental law of a jurisdiction which sets forth in formal terms the general organization of the government in its major organs and departments and defines the extent of their powers. The written constitution, as distinguished from interpretations of its clauses by official bodies, especially the judiciary, and from customs and conventions which are regarded as fundamental, is made and can be changed only by the constituent power (*q.v.*) JJR.

Wyoming. The 44th State, admitted July 10, 1890, from territory carved out of the Louisiana Purchase, the Mexican cession of 1848 and the Oregon Country. Capital, Cheyenne; area, 97,914 sq. mi.; population (1940), 250,742; presidential electors, 3. The original constitution is still in effect. Suffrage is limited by a literacy test. s.

X

XYZ Papers. Documents sent to Congress by President John Adams in 1798 disclosing demands by agents of the French government for bribes and a loan to France as a price for making a commercial treaty with the United States. The letters X, Y, and Z were substituted for the names of the French agents.   s.

Y

Yankee. Originally a native of New England; during the Civil War, any Northerner; and often applied by foreigners, especially during the World Wars, to any American.   s.

Yap. A small mid-Pacific island, important as a cable crossing, which at the close of World War I was offered to the United States, but was later assigned to Japan.   s.

Yazoo Land Fraud. The grant, by the legislature of Georgia in 1795, of 35,000,000 acres of land in the Yazoo Valley to several companies for a consideration of $500,000. With one exception every member of the legislature was a stockholder in at least one of the companies. The next legislature, 1796, repealed the grant, but it was upheld by the Supreme Court of the United States in the case of *Fletcher* v. *Peck*, 6 Cr. 87 (1810), under the obligation-of-contracts clause of the Constitution.   s.

yeas and nays. A method of voting in a deliberative body or legislature which requires calling the roll of the members and recording the affirmative or negative vote of each. The Constitution of the United States requires that the yeas and nays shall be entered upon the Journal when either house of Congress acts upon a measure vetoed by the President, and on any question when one fifth of the members so demand.   z.

yellow dog contract. A contract between an employer and an employee in which the latter agrees not to join a labor union. By the Norris-LaGuardia Act of 1932, such contracts were made unenforceable in national courts.   chs.

yellow peril. The alleged danger to the world supremacy of the Caucasian race discerned by some writers and race theorists in the rising political power and the vast numbers of the Japanese, Chinese, and Mongol peoples.   z.

yield. The net proceeds of a tax after expenses of collection and administration have been subtracted from the gross returns. z.

Young Hickory. A nickname of James K. Polk.   s.

Young plan. A revision of the Dawes plan of reparations payments by Germany to certain Allied states of World War I, prepared by a commission of experts headed by an American, Owen

D. Young, and signed at Paris June 7, 1929, under which the amount of reparations was fixed at approximately 25 billion dollars to be paid over a period of 59 years, and Germany was freed from foreign financial supervision. z.

Z

Zimmerman Note. A note from the German government to its minister in Mexico, Jan. 19, 1917, proposing an alliance with Mexico and aid in reconquering "lost territory" in New Mexico, Texas, and Arizona if war occurred between the United States and Germany. s.

Zionism. The movement for the establishment in Palestine of a national home for the Jewish people. JWF.

Zollverein. A customs union among sovereign states, particularly the several customs unions among the German states beginning in 1818. JWF.

zoning. Regulation by statute or local ordinance of the use and occupancy of land in metropolitan areas. A zoning regulation usually subdivides the physical area of a city into specific zones or districts and determines whether the land in each district, and the buildings constructed upon it, shall be devoted primarily or exclusively to mercantile, industrial, or residential uses, or to some combination of these uses. The zoning regulations may supply numerous specifications affecting the design and construction of buildings in each district. The Supreme Court of the United States has upheld zoning ordinances as a legitimate exercise of the State's police power. z.

INDEX GUIDE TO THE CONSTITUTION

Amendments

     I. Freedom of religion, speech, press, and assembly; right of petition.

    II. Right to keep and bear arms.

   III. Limitations in quartering soldiers.

   IV. Protection from unreasonable searches and seizures.

    V. Due process in criminal cases.
Limitation on right of eminent domain.

   VI. Right to speedy trial by jury, and other guarantees.

  VII. Trial by jury in suits at law.

 VIII. Excessive bail or unusual punishments forbidden.

   IX. Retention of certain rights by the people.

    X. Undelegated powers belong to the States or to the people.

   XI. Exemption of States from suit by individuals.

  XII. New method of electing President.

 XIII. Abolition of slavery.

 XIV. Definition of citizenship.
Guarantees of due process and equal protection against State action.
Apportionment of Representatives in Congress.
Validity of public debt.

  XV. Extension of suffrage to colored persons.

 XVI. Tax on incomes "from whatever source derived."

 XVII. Popular election of Senators.

XVIII. Prohibition of intoxicating liquors.

 XIX. Extension of suffrage to women.

  XX. Abolition of "lame duck" session of Congress.
Change in presidential and congressional terms.

 XXI. Repeal of 18th Amendment.

CONSTITUTION OF THE UNITED STATES *

Adopted September 17, 1787
Effective March 4, 1789

WE the people of the United States, in order to form a more perfect union, establish justice, insure domestic tranquillity, provide for the common defense, promote the general welfare, and secure the blessings of liberty to ourselves and our posterity, do ordain and establish this Constitution for the United States of America.

ARTICLE I

SECTION 1. All legislative powers herein granted shall be vested in a Congress of the United States, which shall consist of a Senate and House of Representatives.

SECTION 2. 1. The House of Representatives shall be composed of members chosen every second year by the people of the several States, and the electors in each State shall have the qualifications requisite for electors of the most numerous branch of the State legislature.

2. No person shall be a Representative who shall not have attained to the age of twenty-five years, and been seven years a citizen of the United States, and who shall not, when elected, be an inhabitant of that State in which he shall be chosen.

3. Representatives and direct taxes[1] shall be apportioned among the several States which may be included within this Union, according to their respective numbers, which shall be determined by adding to the whole number of free persons, including those bound to service for a term of years, and excluding Indians not taxed, three fifths of all other persons.[2] The actual enumeration shall be made within three years after the first meeting of the Congress of the United States, and within every subsequent term of ten years, in such manner as they shall by law direct. The number of representatives shall not exceed one for every thirty thousand, but each State shall have at least one representative; and until such enumeration shall be made, the State of New Hampshire shall be entitled to choose three, Massachusetts eight, Rhode Island and Providence Planta-

---

* Spelling, punctuation, and capitalization have been modernized.
1 See the 16th Amendment.
2 See the 14th Amendment.

341

tions one, Connecticut five, New York six, New Jersey four, Pennsylvania eight, Delaware one, Maryland six, Virginia ten, North Carolina five, South Carolina five, and Georgia three.

4. When vacancies happen in the representation from any State, the executive authority thereof shall issue writs of election to fill such vacancies.

5. The House of Representatives shall choose their speaker and other officers, and shall have the sole power of impeachment.

Section 3. 1. The Senate of the United States shall be composed of two Senators from each State, chosen by the legislature thereof,[1] for six years; and each Senator shall have one vote.

2. Immediately after they shall be assembled in consequence of the first election, they shall be divided as equally as may be into three classes. The seats of the Senators of the first class shall be vacated at the expiration of the second year, of the second class at the expiration of the fourth year, and of the third class at the expiration of the sixth year, so that one third may be chosen every second year; and if vacancies happen by resignation, or otherwise, during the recess of the legislature of any State, the executive thereof may make temporary appointments until the next meeting of the legislature, which shall then fill such vacancies.[1]

3. No person shall be a Senator who shall not have attained to the age of thirty years, and been nine years a citizen of the United States, and who shall not, when elected, be an inhabitant of that State for which he shall be chosen.

4. The Vice President of the United States shall be President of the Senate, but shall have no vote, unless they be equally divided.

5. The Senate shall choose their other officers, and also a president pro tempore, in the absence of the Vice President, or when he shall exercise the office of President of the United States.

6. The Senate shall have the sole power to try all impeachments. When sitting for that purpose, they shall be on oath or affirmation. When the President of the United States is tried, the Chief Justice shall preside; and no person shall be convicted without the concurrence of two thirds of the members present.

7. Judgment in cases of impeachment shall not extend further than to removal from office, and disqualification to hold and enjoy any office of honor, trust, or profit under the United States; but the party convicted shall nevertheless be liable and subject to indictment, trial, judgment, and punishment, according to law.

---

1 See the 17th Amendment.

SECTION 4. 1. The times, places, and manner of holding elections for Senators and Representatives shall be prescribed in each State by the legislature thereof; but the Congress may at any time by law make or alter such regulations, except as to the places of choosing Senators.

2. The Congress shall assemble at least once in every year, and such meeting shall be on the first Monday in December, unless they shall by law appoint a different day.

SECTION 5. 1. Each House shall be the judge of the elections, returns, and qualifications of its own members, and a majority of each shall constitute a quorum to do business; but a smaller number may adjourn from day to day, and may be authorized to compel the attendance of absent members, in such manner, and under such penalties as each House may provide.

2. Each House may determine the rules of its proceedings, punish its members for disorderly behavior, and, with the concurrence of two thirds, expel a member.

3. Each House shall keep a journal of its proceedings, and from time to time publish the same, excepting such parts as may in their judgment require secrecy; and the yeas and nays of the members of either House on any question shall, at the desire of one fifth of those present, be entered on the journal.

4. Neither House, during the session of Congress, shall, without the consent of the other, adjourn for more than three days, nor to any other place than that in which the two Houses shall be sitting.

SECTION 6. 1. The Senators and Representatives shall receive a compensation for their services, to be ascertained by law, and paid out of the Treasury of the United States. They shall in all cases, except treason, felony, and breach of the peace, be privileged from arrest during their attendance at the session of their respective Houses, and in going to and returning from the same; and for any speech or debate in either House, they shall not be questioned in any other place.

2. No Senator or Representative shall, during the time for which he was elected, be appointed to any civil office under the authority of the United States, which shall have been created, or the emoluments whereof shall have been increased during such time; and no person holding any office under the United States shall be a member of either House during his continuance in office.

SECTION 7. 1. All bills for raising revenue shall originate in the House of Representatives; but the Senate may propose or concur with amendments as on other bills.

2. Every bill which shall have passed the House of Representatives and the Senate shall, before it become a law, be presented to the President of the United States; if he approve he shall sign it, but if not he shall return it, with his objections, to that House in which it shall have originated, who shall enter the objections at large on their journal, and proceed to reconsider it. If after such reconsideration two thirds of that House shall agree to pass the bill, it shall be sent, together with the objections, to the other House, by which it shall likewise be reconsidered, and if approved by two thirds of that House, it shall become a law. But in all such cases the votes of both Houses shall be determined by yeas and nays, and the names of the persons voting for and against the bill shall be entered on the journal of each House respectively. If any bill shall not be returned by the President within ten days (Sundays excepted) after it shall have been presented to him, the same shall be a law, in like manner as if he had signed it, unless the Congress by their adjournment prevent its return, in which case it shall not be a law.

3. Every order, resolution, or vote to which the concurrence of the Senate and House of Representatives may be necessary (except on a question of adjournment) shall be presented to the President of the United States; and before the same shall take effect, shall be approved by him, or being disapproved by him, shall be repassed by two thirds of the Senate and House of Representatives, according to the rules and limitations prescribed in the case of a bill.

SECTION 8. The Congress shall have power:

1. To lay and collect taxes, duties, imposts, and excises, to pay the debts and provide for the common defense and general welfare of the United States; but all duties, imposts, and excises shall be uniform throughout the United States;

2. To borrow money on the credit of the United States;

3. To regulate commerce with foreign nations, and among the several States, and with the Indian tribes;

4. To establish an uniform rule of naturalization, and uniform laws on the subject of bankruptcies throughout the United States;

5. To coin money, regulate the value thereof, and of foreign coin, and fix the standard of weights and measures;

6. To provide for the punishment of counterfeiting the securities and current coin of the United States;

7. To establish post offices and post roads;

8. To promote the progress of science and useful arts, by securing for limited times to authors and inventors the exclusive right to their respective writings and discoveries;

9. To constitute tribunals inferior to the Supreme Court;

10. To define and punish piracies and felonies committed on the high seas, and offenses against the law of nations;

11. To declare war, grant letters of marque and reprisal, and make rules concerning captures on land and water;

12. To raise and support armies, but no appropriation of money to that use shall be for a longer term than two years;

13. To provide and maintain a navy;

14. To make rules for the government and regulation of the land and naval forces;

15. To provide for calling forth the militia to execute the laws of the Union, suppress insurrections, and repel invasions;

16. To provide for organizing, arming, and disciplining the militia, and for governing such part of them as may be employed in the service of the United States, reserving to the States respectively, the appointment of the officers, and the authority of training the militia according to the discipline prescribed by Congress;

17. To exercise exclusive legislation in all cases whatsoever, over such district (not exceeding ten miles square) as may, by cession of particular States, and the acceptance of Congress, become the seat of the government of the United States, and to exercise like authority over all places purchased by the consent of the legislature of the State in which the same shall be, for the erection of forts, magazines, arsenals, dockyards, and other needful buildings; and

18. To make all laws which shall be necessary and proper for carrying into execution the foregoing powers, and all other powers vested by this Constitution in the government of the United States, or in any department or officer thereof.

SECTION 9. 1. The migration or importation of such persons as any of the States now existing shall think proper to admit, shall not be prohibited by the Congress prior to the year one thousand eight hundred and eight, but a tax or duty may be imposed on such importation, not exceeding ten dollars for each person.

2. The privilege of the writ of habeas corpus shall not be suspended, unless when in cases of rebellion or invasion the public safety may require it.

3. No bill of attainder or ex post facto law shall be passed.

4. No capitation, or other direct, tax shall be laid, unless in

proportion to the census or enumeration hereinbefore directed to be taken.[1]

5.   No tax or duty shall be laid on articles exported from any State.

6.   No preference shall be given by any regulation of commerce or revenue to the ports of one State over those of another; nor shall vessels bound to, or from, one State be obliged to enter, clear, or pay duties in another.

7.   No money shall be drawn from the Treasury, but in consequence of appropriations made by law; and a regular statement and account of the receipts and expenditures of all public money shall be published from time to time.

8.   No title of nobility shall be granted by the United States; and no person holding any office of profit or trust under them shall, without the consent of the Congress, accept of any present, emolument, office, or title, of any kind whatever, from any king, prince, or foreign state.

SECTION 10.   1.   No State shall enter into any treaty, alliance, or confederation; grant letters of marque and reprisal; coin money; emit bills of credit; make anything but gold and silver coin a tender in payment of debts; pass any bill of attainder, ex post facto law, or law impairing the obligation of contracts; or grant any title of nobility.

2.   No State shall, without the consent of the Congress, lay any imposts or duties on imports or exports, except what may be absolutely necessary for executing its inspection laws; and the net produce of all duties and imposts, laid by any State on imports or exports, shall be for the use of the Treasury of the United States; and all such laws shall be subject to the revision and control of the Congress.

3.   No State shall, without the consent of Congress, lay any duty of tonnage, keep troops or ships of war in time of peace, enter into any agreement or compact with another State, or with a foreign power, or engage in war, unless actually invaded, or in such imminent danger as will not admit of delay.

ARTICLE II

SECTION 1.   1.   The executive power shall be vested in a President of the United States of America. He shall hold his office during the term of four years, and, together with the Vice President, chosen for the same term, be elected, as follows:

---

1 See the 16th Amendment.

2.   Each State shall appoint, in such manner as the legislature thereof may direct, a number of electors, equal to the whole number of Senators and Representatives to which the State may be entitled in the Congress; but no Senator or Representative, or person holding an office of trust or profit under the United States, shall be appointed an elector.

3.   The electors shall meet in their respective States, and vote by ballot for two persons, of whom one at least shall not be an inhabitant of the same State with themselves. And they shall make a list of all the persons voted for, and of the number of votes for each; which list they shall sign and certify, and transmit sealed to the seat of the government of the United States, directed to the President of the Senate. The President of the Senate shall, in the presence of the Senate and House of Representatives, open all the certificates, and the votes shall then be counted. The person having the greatest number of votes shall be the President, if such number be a majority of the whole number of electors appointed; and if there be more than one who have such majority, and have an equal number of votes, then the House of Representatives shall immediately choose by ballot one of them for President; and if no person have a majority, then from the five highest on the list the said House shall in like manner choose the President. But in choosing the President, the votes shall be taken by States, the representation from each State having one vote; a quorum for this purpose shall consist of a member or members from two thirds of the States, and a majority of all the States shall be necessary to a choice. In every case, after the choice of the President, the person having the greatest number of votes of the electors shall be the Vice President. But if there should remain two or more who have equal votes, the Senate shall choose from them by ballot the Vice President.[1]

4.   The Congress may determine the time of choosing the electors, and the day on which they shall give their votes; which day shall be the same throughout the United States.

5.   No person except a natural born citizen, or a citizen of the United States at the time of the adoption of this Constitution, shall be eligible to the office of President; neither shall any person be eligible to that office who shall not have attained to the age of thirty-five years, and been fourteen years a resident within the United States.

6.   In case of the removal of the President from office, or of his death, resignation, or inability to discharge the powers and duties of the said office, the same shall devolve on the Vice President, and the Congress may by law provide for the case of removal, death,

---

1 Superseded by the 12th Amendment.

resignation, or inability, both of the President and Vice President, declaring what officer shall then act as President, and such officer shall act accordingly, until the disability be removed, or a President shall be elected.

7. The President shall, at stated times, receive for his services a compensation, which shall neither be increased nor diminished during the period for which he shall have been elected, and he shall not receive within that period any other emolument from the United States, or any of them.

8. Before he enter on the execution of his office, he shall take the following oath or affirmation:—"I do solemnly swear (or affirm) that I will faithfully execute the office of President of the United States, and will to the best of my ability, preserve, protect, and defend the Constitution of the United States."

Section 2. 1. The President shall be commander in chief of the army and navy of the United States, and of the militia of the several States, when called into the actual service of the United States; he may require the opinion, in writing, of the principal officer in each of the executive departments, upon any subject relating to the duties of their respective offices, and he shall have power to grant reprieves and pardons for offenses against the United States, except in cases of impeachment.

2. He shall have power, by and with the advice and consent of the Senate, to make treaties, provided two thirds of the Senators present concur; and he shall nominate, and by and with the advice and consent of the Senate, shall appoint ambassadors, other public ministers and consuls, judges of the Supreme Court, and all other officers of the United States, whose appointments are not herein otherwise provided for, and which shall be established by law; but the Congress may by law vest the appointment of such inferior officers as they think proper, in the President alone, in the courts of law, or in the heads of departments.

3. The President shall have power to fill up all vacancies that may happen during the recess of the Senate, by granting commissions which shall expire at the end of their next session.

Section 3. He shall from time to time give to the Congress information of the state of the Union, and recommend to their consideration such measures as he shall judge necessary and expedient; he may, on extraordinary occasions, convene both Houses, or either of them, and in case of disagreement between them with respect to the time of adjournment, he may adjourn them to such time as he shall think proper; he shall receive ambassadors and other public ministers; he shall take care that the laws be faithfully executed, and shall commission all the officers of the United States.

SECTION 4. The President, Vice President, and all civil officers of the United States, shall be removed from office on impeachment for, and conviction of, treason, bribery, or other high crimes and misdemeanors.

ARTICLE III

SECTION 1. The judicial power of the United States shall be vested in one Supreme Court, and in such inferior courts as the Congress may from time to time ordain and establish. The judges, both of the Supreme and inferior courts, shall hold their offices during good behavior, and shall, at stated times, receive for their services a compensation, which shall not be diminished during their continuance in office.

SECTION 2. 1. The judicial power shall extend to all cases, in law and equity, arising under this Constitution, the laws of the United States, and treaties made, or which shall be made, under their authority; to all cases affecting ambassadors, other public ministers, and consuls; to all cases of admiralty and maritime jurisdiction; to controversies to which the United States shall be a party; to controversies between two or more States; between a State and citizens of another State;[1] between citizens of different States; between citizens of the same State claiming lands under grants of different States, and between a State, or the citizens thereof, and foreign states, citizens, or subjects.

2. In all cases affecting ambassadors, other public ministers, and consuls, and those in which a State shall be party, the Supreme Court shall have original jurisdiction. In all the other cases before mentioned, the Supreme Court shall have appellate jurisdiction, both as to law and fact, with such exceptions, and under such regulations as the Congress shall make.

3. The trial of all crimes, except in cases of impeachment, shall be by jury; and such trial shall be held in the State where the said crimes shall have been committed; but when not committed within any State, the trial shall be at such place or places as the Congress may by law have directed.

SECTION 3. 1. Treason against the United States shall consist only in levying war against them, or in adhering to their enemies, giving them aid and comfort. No person shall be convicted of treason unless on the testimony of two witnesses to the same overt act, or on confession in open court.

2. The Congress shall have power to declare the punishment of treason, but no attainder of treason shall work corruption of blood, or forfeiture except during the life of the person attainted.

---

1 See the 11th Amendment.

ARTICLE IV

SECTION 1. Full faith and credit shall be given in each State to the public acts, records, and judicial proceedings of every other State. And the Congress may by general laws prescribe the manner in which such acts, records, and proceedings shall be proved, and the effect thereof.

SECTION 2. 1. The citizens of each State shall be entitled to all privileges and immunities of citizens in the several States.[1]

2. A person charged in any State with treason, felony, or other crime, who shall flee from justice, and be found in another State, shall on demand of the executive authority of the State from which he fled, be delivered up to be removed to the State having jurisdiction of the crime.

3. No person held to service or labor in one State, under the laws thereof, escaping into another, shall, in consequence of any law or regulation therein, be discharged from such service or labor, but shall be delivered up on claim of the party to whom such service or labor may be due.[2]

SECTION 3. 1. New States may be admitted by the Congress into this Union; but no new State shall be formed or erected within the jurisdiction of any other State; nor any State be formed by the junction of two or more States, or parts of States, without the consent of the legislatures of the States concerned as well as of the Congress.

2. The Congress shall have power to dispose of and make all needful rules and regulations respecting the territory or other property belonging to the United States; and nothing in this Constitution shall be so construed as to prejudice any claims of the United States, or of any particular State.

SECTION 4. The United States shall guarantee to every State in this Union a republican form of government, and shall protect each of them against invasion; and on application of the legislature, or of the executive (when the legislature cannot be convened) against domestic violence.

ARTICLE V

The Congress, whenever two thirds of both Houses shall deem it necessary, shall propose amendments to this Constitution, or, on the application of the legislatures of two thirds of the several States, shall call a convention for proposing amendments, which, in either

---

1 See the 14th Amendment, Sec. 1.
2 See the 13th Amendment.

case, shall be valid to all intents and purposes, as part of this Constitution, when ratified by the legislatures of three fourths of the several States, or by conventions in three fourths thereof, as the one or the other mode of ratification may be proposed by the Congress; provided that no amendment which may be made prior to the year one thousand eight hundred and eight shall in any manner affect the first and fourth clauses in the ninth section of the first article; and that no State, without its consent, shall be deprived of its equal suffrage in the Senate.

ARTICLE VI

1. All debts contracted and engagements entered into, before the adoption of this Constitution, shall be as valid against the United States under this Constitution as under the Confederation.[1]

2. This Constitution, and the laws of the United States which shall be made in pursuance thereof; and all treaties made, or which shall be made, under the authority of the United States, shall be the supreme law of the land; and the judges in every State shall be bound thereby, anything in the Constitution or laws of any State to the contrary notwithstanding.

3. The Senators and Representatives before mentioned, and the members of the several State legislatures, and all executive and judicial officers, both of the United States and of the several States, shall be bound by oath or affirmation to support this Constitution; but no religious test shall ever be required as a qualification to any office or public trust under the United States.

ARTICLE VII

The ratification of the conventions of nine States shall be sufficient for the establishment of this Constitution between the States so ratifying the same.

Done in Convention by the unanimous consent of the States present the seventeenth day of September in the year of our Lord one thousand seven hundred and eighty-seven, and of the independence of the United States of America the twelfth. In witness whereof we have hereunto subscribed our names.

[Names omitted]

---

1 See the 14th Amendment, Sec. 4.

AMENDMENTS

First Ten Amendments passed by Congress Sept. 25, 1789.
Ratified by three fourths of the States December 15, 1791.

Articles in addition to, and amendment of, the Constitution of the United States of America, proposed by Congress, and ratified by the legislatures of the several States, pursuant to the fifth article of the original Constitution.

ARTICLE I

Congress shall make no law respecting an establishment of religion, or prohibiting the free exercise thereof; or abridging the freedom of speech, or of the press; or the right of the people peaceably to assemble, and to petition the government for a redress of grievances.

ARTICLE II

A well regulated militia, being necessary to the security of a free State, the right of the people to keep and bear arms shall not be infringed.

ARTICLE III

No soldier shall, in time of peace, be quartered in any house without the consent of the owner, nor in time of war, but in a manner to be prescribed by law.

ARTICLE IV

The right of the people to be secure in their persons, houses, papers, and effects, against unreasonable searches and seizures, shall not be violated, and no warrants shall issue, but upon probable cause, supported by oath or affirmation, and particularly describing the place to be searched, and the persons or things to be seized.

ARTICLE V

No person shall be held to answer for a capital, or otherwise infamous crime, unless on a presentment or indictment of a grand jury, except in cases arising in the land or naval forces, or in the militia, when in actual service in time of war or public danger; nor shall any person be subject for the same offense to be twice put in jeopardy of life or limb; nor shall be compelled in any criminal case to be a witness against himself, nor be deprived of life, liberty, or property, without due process of law; nor shall private property be taken for public use without just compensation.

ARTICLE VI

In all criminal prosecutions, the accused shall enjoy the right to a speedy and public trial, by an impartial jury of the State and district wherein the crime shall have been committed, which district shall have been previously ascertained by law, and to be informed of the nature and cause of the accusation; to be confronted with the witnesses against him; to have compulsory process for obtaining witnesses in his favor, and to have the assistance of counsel for his defense.

ARTICLE VII

In suits at common law, where the value in controversy shall exceed twenty dollars, the right of trial by jury shall be preserved, and no fact tried by a jury shall be otherwise re-examined in any court of the United States, than according to the rules of the common law.

ARTICLE VIII

Excessive bail shall not be required, nor excessive fines imposed, nor cruel and unusual punishments inflicted.

ARTICLE IX

The enumeration in the Constitution of certain rights shall not be construed to deny or disparage others retained by the people.

ARTICLE X

The powers not delegated to the United States by the Constitution, nor prohibited by it to the States, are reserved to the States respectively, or to the people.

ARTICLE XI

Passed by Congress March 5, 1794. Ratified January 8, 1798.

The judicial power of the United States shall not be construed to extend to any suit in law or equity, commenced or prosecuted against one of the United States, by citizens of another State, or by citizens or subjects of any foreign state.

ARTICLE XII

Passed by Congress December 12, 1803. Ratified September 25, 1804.

The electors shall meet in their respective States, and vote by ballot for President and Vice President, one of whom, at least, shall not be an inhabitant of the same State with themselves; they shall name in their ballots the person voted for as President, and in distinct ballots the person voted for as Vice President, and they shall make distinct lists of all persons voted for as President, and of all persons voted for as Vice President, and of the number of votes for each, which lists they shall sign and certify, and transmit sealed to the seat of the government of the United States, directed to the President of the Senate; the President of the Senate shall, in the presence of the Senate and House of Representatives, open all the certificates and the votes shall then be counted; the person having the greatest number of votes for President shall be the President, if such number be a majority of the whole number of electors appointed; and if no person have such majority, then from the persons having the highest numbers not exceeding three on the list of those voted for as President, the House of Representatives shall choose immediately, by ballot, the President. But in choosing the President, the votes shall be taken by States, the representation from each State having one vote; a quorum for this purpose shall consist of a member or members from two thirds of the States, and a majority of all the States shall be necessary to a choice. And if the House of Representatives shall not choose a President whenever the right of choice shall devolve upon them, before the fourth day of March next following, then the Vice President shall act as President, as in the case of the death or other constitutional disability of the President. The person having the greatest number of votes as Vice President shall be the Vice President, if such number be a majority of the whole number of electors appointed, and if no person have a majority, then from the two highest numbers on the list, the Senate shall choose the Vice President; a quorum for the purpose shall consist of two thirds of the whole number of Senators, and a majority of the whole number shall be necessary to a choice. But no person constitutionally ineligible to the office of President shall be eligible to that of Vice President of the United States.

ARTICLE XIII

Passed by Congress February 1, 1865. Ratified December 18, 1865.

Section 1. Neither slavery nor involuntary servitude, except as a punishment for crime whereof the party shall have been duly convicted, shall exist within the United States, or any place subject to their jurisdiction.

Section 2. Congress shall have power to enforce this article by appropriate legislation.

ARTICLE XIV

Passed by Congress June 16, 1866. Ratified July 28, 1868.

Section 1. All persons born or naturalized in the United States, and subject to the jurisdiction thereof, are citizens of the United States and of the State wherein they reside. No State shall make or enforce any law which shall abridge the privileges or immunities of citizens of the United States; nor shall any State deprive any person of life, liberty, or property, without due process of law; nor deny to any person within its jurisdiction the equal protection of the laws.

SECTION 2.   Representatives shall be apportioned among the several States according to their respective numbers, counting the whole number of persons in each State, excluding Indians not taxed. But when the right to vote at any election for the choice of electors for President and Vice President of the United States, Representatives in Congress, the executive and judicial officers of a State, or the members of the legislature thereof, is denied to any of the male inhabitants of such State, being twenty-one years of age, and citizens of the United States, or in any way abridged, except for participation in rebellion, or other crime, the basis of representation therein shall be reduced in the proportion which the number of such male citizens shall bear to the whole number of male citizens twenty-one years of age in such State.

SECTION 3.   No person shall be a Senator or Representative in Congress, or elector of President and Vice President, or hold any office, civil or military, under the United States, or under any State, who, having previously taken an oath, as a member of Congress, or as an officer of the United States, or as a member of any State legislature, or as an executive or judicial officer of any State, to support the Constitution of the United States, shall have engaged in insurrection or rebellion against the same, or given aid or comfort to the enemies thereof. But Congress may, by a vote of two thirds of each House, remove such disability.

SECTION 4.   The validity of the public debt of the United States, authorized by law, including debts incurred for payment of pensions and bounties for services in suppressing insurrection or rebellion, shall not be questioned. But neither the United States nor any State shall assume or pay any debt or obligation incurred in aid of insurrection or rebellion against the United States, or any claim for the loss or emancipation of any slave; but all such debts, obligations, and claims shall be held illegal and void.

SECTION 5.   The Congress shall have power to enforce, by appropriate legislation, the provisions of this article.

ARTICLE XV
Passed by Congress February 27, 1869.   Ratified March 30, 1870.

SECTION 1.   The right of citizens of the United States to vote shall not be denied or abridged by the United States or by any State on account of race, color, or previous condition of servitude.

SECTION 2.   The Congress shall have power to enforce this article by appropriate legislation.

ARTICLE XVI
Passed by Congress July 12, 1909.   Ratified February 25, 1913.

The Congress shall have power to lay and collect taxes on incomes, from whatever source derived, without apportionment among the several States, and without regard to any census or enumeration.

ARTICLE XVII

Passed by Congress May 16, 1912. Ratified May 31, 1913.

The Senate of the United States shall be composed of two Senators from each State, elected by the people thereof, for six years; and each Senator shall have one vote. The electors in each State shall have the qualifications requisite for electors of the most numerous branch of the State legislatures.

When vacancies happen in the representation of any State in the Senate, the executive authority of such State shall issue writs of election to fill such vacancies: *Provided,* That the legislature of any State may empower the executive thereof to make temporary appointments until the people fill the vacancies by election as the legislature may direct.

This amendment shall not be so construed as to affect the election or term of any Senator chosen before it becomes valid as part of the Constitution.

ARTICLE XVIII

Passed by Congress December 17, 1917. Ratified January 29, 1919.

SECTION 1. After one year from the ratification of this article, the manufacture, sale, or transportation of intoxicating liquors within, the importation thereof into, or the exportation thereof from the United States and all territory subject to the jurisdiction thereof for beverage purposes is hereby prohibited.

SECTION 2. The Congress and the several States shall have concurrent power to enforce this article by appropriate legislation.

SECTION 3. This article shall be inoperative unless it shall have been ratified as an amendment to the Constitution by the legislatures of the several States, as provided in the Constitution, within seven years from the date of the submission hereof to the States by the Congress.

ARTICLE XIX

Passed by Congress June 5, 1919. Ratified August 26, 1920.

The right of citizens of the United States to vote shall not be denied or abridged by the United States or by any State on account of sex.

Congress shall have power to enforce this article by appropriate legislation.

ARTICLE XX

Passed by Congress March 3, 1932. Ratified February 6, 1933.

SECTION 1. The terms of the President and Vice President shall end at noon on the 20th day of January, and the terms of Senators and Representatives at noon on the 3d day of January, of the years in which such terms would have ended if this article had not been ratified; and the terms of their successors shall then begin.

Section 2.   The Congress shall assemble at least once in every year, and such meeting shall begin at noon on the 3d day of January, unless they shall by law appoint a different day.

Section 3.   If, at the time fixed for the beginning of the term of the President, the President-elect shall have died, the Vice President-elect shall become President. If a President shall not have been chosen before the time fixed for the beginning of his term, or if the President-elect shall have failed to qualify, then the Vice President-elect shall act as President until a President shall have qualified; and the Congress may by law provide for the case wherein neither a President-elect nor a Vice President-elect shall have qualified, declaring who shall then act as President, or the manner in which one who is to act shall be selected, and such person shall act accordingly until a President or Vice President shall have qualified.

Section 4.   The Congress may by law provide for the case of the death of any of the persons from whom the House of Representatives may choose a President whenever the right of choice shall have devolved upon them, and for the case of the death of any of the persons from whom the Senate may choose a Vice President whenever the right of choice shall have devolved upon them.

Section 5.   Sections 1 and 2 shall take effect on the 15th day of October following the ratification of this article.

Section 6.   This article shall be inoperative unless it shall have been ratified as an amendment to the Constitution by the legislatures of three fourths of the several States within seven years from the date of its submission.

ARTICLE XXI
Passed by Congress February 20, 1933. Ratified December 5, 1933.

Section 1.   The eighteenth article of amendment to the Constitution of the United States is hereby repealed.

Section 2.   The transportation or importation into any State, Territory, or possession of the United States for delivery or use therein of intoxicating liquors in violation of the laws thereof, is hereby prohibited.

Section 3.   This article shall be inoperative unless it shall have been ratified as an amendment to the Constitution by conventions in the several States, as provided in the Constitution, within seven years from the date of the submission hereof to the States by the Congress.

PRESIDENTS OF THE UNITED STATES

No.	Name	Native State	Party	Term
1	GEORGE WASHINGTON (1732-1799)	Va.	Federalist	1789-1797
2	JOHN ADAMS (1735-1826)	Mass.	Federalist	1797-1801
3	THOMAS JEFFERSON (1743-1826)	Va.	Rep.-Dem.	1801-1809
4	JAMES MADISON (1751-1836)	Va.	Rep.-Dem.	1809-1817
5	JAMES MONROE (1758-1831)	Va.	Rep.-Dem.	1817-1825
6	JOHN QUINCY ADAMS (1767-1848)	Mass.	Rep.-Dem.	1825-1829
7	ANDREW JACKSON (1767-1845)	S. C.	Democrat	1829-1837
8	MARTIN VAN BUREN (1782-1862)	N. Y.	Democrat	1837-1841
9	WILLIAM HENRY HARRISON (1773-1841)	Va.	Whig	1841
10	JOHN TYLER (1790-1862)	Va.	Democrat	1841-1845
11	JAMES KNOX POLK (1795-1849)	N. C.	Democrat	1845-1849
12	ZACHARY TAYLOR (1784-1850)	Va.	Whig	1849-1850
13	MILLARD FILLMORE (1800-1874)	N. Y.	Whig	1850-1853
14	FRANKLIN PIERCE (1804-1869)	N. Hamp.	Democrat	1853-1857
15	JAMES BUCHANAN (1791-1868)	Pa.	Democrat	1857-1861
16	ABRAHAM LINCOLN (1809-1865)	Ky.	Republican	1861-1865
17	ANDREW JOHNSON (1808-1875)	N. C.	Republican	1865-1869
18	ULYSSES S. GRANT (1822-1885)	Ohio	Republican	1869-1877
19	RUTHERFORD B. HAYES (1822-1893)	Ohio	Republican	1877-1881
20	JAMES A. GARFIELD (1831-1881)	Ohio	Republican	1881
21	CHESTER A. ARTHUR (1830-1886)	Vt.	Republican	1881-1885
22	GROVER CLEVELAND (1837-1908)	N. J.	Democrat	1885-1889
23	BENJAMIN HARRISON (1833-1901)	Ohio	Republican	1889-1893
24	GROVER CLEVELAND (1837-1908)	N. J.	Democrat	1893-1897
25	WILLIAM MCKINLEY (1843-1901)	Ohio	Republican	1897-1901
26	THEODORE ROOSEVELT (1858-1919)	N. Y.	Republican	1901-1909
27	WILLIAM H. TAFT (1857-1930)	Ohio	Republican	1909-1913
28	WOODROW WILSON (1856-1924)	Va.	Democrat	1913-1921
29	WARREN G. HARDING (1865-1923)	Ohio	Republican	1921-1923
30	CALVIN COOLIDGE (1872-1933)	Vt.	Republican	1923-1929
31	HERBERT C. HOOVER (1874-)	Iowa	Republican	1929-1933
32	FRANKLIN D. ROOSEVELT (1882-)	N. Y.	Democrat	1933-